AF526639

Library and Information Studies in Cyber Age

Essays in Honour of Professor J.L. Sardana

Professor J. L. Sardana

Library and Information Studies in Cyber Age

Essays in Honour of Professor J.L. Sardana

Edited by
S. M. Dhawan

Worldwide Circulation through Authorspress Global Network
First Published 2004
by Authorspress

E-35/103, Jawahar Park
Laxmi Nagar, Delhi-110 092

e-mail: authorspress@yahoo.com

Typeset in NewCenturySchlbk by Chitra Computers

Library and Information Studies in Cyber Age
ISBN 81-7273-176-0

Printed in India at Tarun Offset, Delhi.

Foreword

I have great pleasure in writing this foreword to the volume entitled *'Library and Information Studies in Cyber Age'*, being brought out in honour of Prof J.L. Sardana. I learn that Professor Sardana has many academic and professional achievements during his career spanning over a period of 42 years. He has served with great distinction as a professor in Library and Information Science and has been the librarian of some of India's most prestigious institutions like the IIT, Kanpur and the IIM, Lucknow. I also learn that he is the second Indian to have been elected as Vice President of the International Federation for Information and Documentation (FID), The Hague, a body that is more than a hundred years old.

Libraries today are not mere repositories of books. They are a multiple source of information and knowledge. Their management is of vital importance. The Ministry of Human Resource Development and the University Grants Commission are seized of this aspect and have, therefore, sought to help the process of speedy computerisation of library house keeping functions and services. With the object of making optimal use of rich collections available in different types of libraries under the Ministry of Culture, the Government is currently working out a plan for the proper utilization of their collections through appropriate networking operations.

The present volume, I understand, generally includes essays written by eminent library and information scientists in the areas of teaching and research that are of great interest to Professor Sardana. Some of the important themes dealt with in the volume include: library and information science, education and research; resource sharing, networking and accessing information; library and information systems and services; Internet resources and Web access.

All the areas dealt with in the themes mentioned above have great relevance in today's context when we are deeply involved in the preservation and dissemination of our culture and civilization and knowledge management in the cyber age. The cyber technologies constitute an important input for all areas referred to above. The IT Task Force has laid great emphasis on human resource development, content creation and development. I am glad that all these areas that are of great significance have been included in the present festschrift volume. I am sure our libraries and information centres will greatly benefit from the essays contained in this volume.

Prof. Vasant Gadre
(Member University Grants Commission)

Festschrift/Editorial Committee

Festschrift Committee

Dr. R.N. Sharma
Director, Drain-Jordan Library, West Virginia State College West Virginia, USA.

Dr. R.C. Sharma
Former and Dean of Faculty of Arts Professor, Department of Linguistics, University of Delhi, Delhi,110007.

Prof. A.C. Tikekar
Former University Librarian and Head of Department of Library and Information Science, Mumbai University, Mumbai, 400032.

Dr. G.C. Bansal
Former Professor, and Head of Department of Library and Information Science, Punjab University, Chandigarh, 160014.

Prof. S. P. Narang
Former Professor and Head of Department of Library and Information Science, Punjabi University, Patiala, 147001.

Sh. P.C. Shah
Former Head, ATIRA, Ahmedabad.

Dr. M. Sankara Reddy
University Librarian, P.S. Telugu University, Hyderabad, 500004.

Dr. (Mrs) Neela Jagannathan
Former University Librarian, Indira Gandhi National Open University, Maidan Gari, New Delhi, 110068.

Dr. (Mrs) Alka Buragohain
Former Professor and Head, Department of Library and Information Science, Guwahati University, Guwahati, 781014.

Prof. M. Bavakutty
Professor and Head Department of Library and Information Science, University of Calicut, Calicut (Kerala).

Prof. (Ms) K. Navlani
Former Professor and Head, Department of Library and Information Science, Punjabi University, Patiala,147001.

Prof. M. P. Satija
Department of Library and Information Science, Guru Nanak Dev University, Amritsar,143003.

Prof. V.K. Nanda
Formerly, Officiating University Librarian, Jamia Millia Islamia, New Delhi, 110025.

Dr. Roshan Raina
Professor of Communication, Indian Institute of Management, Prabandh Nagar, Lucknow

Dr. B. M. Gupta
Scientist F, NISTADS, New Delhi,110012.

Prof. Prem Singh
University Librarian, Chaudhary Charan Singh Agricultural University, Hisar, 125004 (Haryana).

Dr. Harish Chandra
Librarian, Indian Institute of Technology, Chennai, 600036.

D.N. Gupta
Former Head, Education and Training Division and Scientist F, National Institute of Science Communication and Information Resources, New Delhi,110067.

Dr. O.P. Gupta
Library and Information Officer, University Grants Commission, New Delhi,110002.

Dr. S. Majumdar
Director, Central Secretariat Library, New Delhi,110001.

Dr. S.C. Jindal
Dy Librarian Incharge, Central Science Library, University of Delhi, Delhi,110007.

Dr. P.R. Goswami
Director, National Social Science Documentation Centre, New Delhi,110002.

Dr. D.L. Sachdeva
Former Librarian, Motilal Nehru College, University of Delhi, New Delhi.

Dr. Krishan Gopal
Deputy Librarian, Jawaharlal Nehru University, New Delhi,110067.

S. Deshmukh
Dy Manager, Library Services, C-DOT, Pusa Road, New Delhi.

Dr. R.K. Bhatt
Lecturer, Department of Library and Information Science, University of Delhi, Delhi,110007.

Dr. Narender Kumar
Librarian, Sukhdev College of Business Studies, University of Delhi, Delhi.

Dr. S.M. Dhawan
Scientist F and Head Library and Information Services, National Physical Laboratory, New Delhi,110012.

Editorial Committee

Dr. R. N. Sharma
Director, Drain-Jordan Library, West Virginia State College, West Virginia, USA.

Dr. M. Sankara Reddy
University Librarian, P.S. Telugu University, Hyderabad.

Dr. P.R. Goswami
Director, National Social Science Documentation Centre, New Delhi,110002.

Dr. S. Majumdar
Director, Central Secretariat Library, New Delhi,110001.

Dr. S. M. Dhawan *Convener & Editor*
Scientist F and Head Library and Information Services, National Physical Laboratory, New Delhi, 110012.

[illegible] Committee

Dr. [illegible]
[illegible] National [illegible] Science [illegible], New Delhi 110012

Dr. [illegible]
[illegible] Medical College, [illegible], New Delhi

Dr. [illegible]
[illegible] Librarian, [illegible], New Delhi 110067

Dr. [illegible]
Dy. [illegible] Services (IFLA), [illegible] Rome [illegible]

Dr. R.K. [illegible]
[illegible], Department of Library and Information Science, University of Delhi, Delhi 110007

Dr. [illegible]
[illegible] College of Business Studies, University of Delhi, Delhi

Dr. S.K. [illegible]
[illegible] National Physical Laboratory, New Delhi 110012

Editorial Committee

Dr. P.K. [illegible]
Director, [illegible] Library, [illegible] State [illegible], USA

Dr. [illegible]
University Librarian, P.S. Telugu University, Hyderabad

Dr. [illegible]
Director, National [illegible], [illegible], New Delhi

Dr. [illegible]
[illegible] National [illegible] Library, [illegible] New Delhi 1100[illegible]

Dr. [illegible]
[illegible] and [illegible], National Physical Laboratory, New Delhi 110012

Preface

This Festschrift is in honour of Prof. J. L. Sardana, the legendary figure of the library profession, well known for his high scholarship and intellect, his outstanding contributions to the knowledge pool, and his leadership roles in shaping the profession. His personality symbolises conviction, courage, integrity, and inspiration laced with simplicity politeness, maturity and worldly wisdom. During his 42-year-long professional career he has been a librarian, teacher, and leader. He has remained in the forefront of the profession for a long time, established his credibility in the field, earned the goodwill of the members of library fraternity, and left many imprints on every dimension of librarianship.

As Professor and former Head of the Department of Library and Information Science, University of Delhi, he has been friend, philosopher and guide to his students. He has left behind several deep and unforgettable reminiscences which the students he taught still continue to treasure and cherish most. His teaching and research methods were par excellence. He is well known for his communication and analytical skills. Many students feel privileged and honoured to have had the opportunity to work under his guidance for the M.Phil. and Ph.D. degrees. It is a great honour to Professor Sardana that many of his students have come to occupy positions of leadership and authority in the library and information centres in the government departments, academic and research institutions.

Professor Sardana had also served as Librarian in elite institutions such as University Grants Commission, Delhi; Indian Institute of Management, Lucknow; Indian Institute of Advanced Study, Shimla, and Indian Institute of Technology, Kanpur. As a model practising Librarian he had been a strong motivating force to his fellow colleagues.

Within the library fraternity he is fondly remembered for his excellent contributions to the profession as the President of the Indian Library Association, 1998-2000. He came to provide the leadership to the profession as the President ILA at a time when the Association was passing through its most critical phase. He gave it the much-needed momentum by catalysing its activities, and reviving thereby the members' trust and confidence in this apex national body of professionals in library and information science. He had been the Vice President (1998-2001) of the FID, The Hague (The Netherlands). He was the second Indian to have been elected to this international body.

He has travelled abroad as an authority on the subject, especially in East European countries. He has been to Hungary as a resource person. He had served on several academic and decision-making committees in various institutions, universities and governmental bodies. He had been member, Research Council, of the erstwhile institution INSDOC; member, IX Five Year Plan Working Group for the development and modernisation of libraries and information centres; and Chairman, National Organising Committee, 49th FID Conference and Congress hosted by INSDOC, 1998. Currently, he is member of the Bureau of Indian Standards, New Delhi, member of Review Committee the Delhi Public Library, Chairman of Central Secretariat Library Review Committee, and member of various committees of the Government of India.

The contributions for the festschrift document brought out in honour of Professor Sardana were invited from leading professionals in the field and on such select topics as were of immediate interest to Professor Sardana. These contributions are 49 in number and have been grouped under eight sections as follows:

i) Eulogy and Tributes
ii) Library and Information Science Education, Training and Research
iii) Information Systems, Techniques and Services
iv) Library Resource Development, Sharing and Access
v) Networking, Internet, Cyber Age and Libraries
vi) Electronic Publishing
vii) Librarianship, Management and Status
viii) Scientometrics, Use and User Studies

EULOGY AND TRIBUTES

This section comprises two contributions, one from D.K. Mukherjee, Librarian of Indian Institute of Advanced Study, Shimla, and the other from Dr M. Sankara Reddy of P.S. Telugu University, Hyderabad. Both of them unfold their reminiscences of their interactions with Professor Sardana. They pay rich and glowing tributes to him in their own inimitable styles, chronicling his contributions to the profession, to the knowledge pool in library and information science, and recalling his leadership roles in shaping the profession

LIBRARY AND INFORMATION SCIENCE EDUCATION, TRAINING AND RESEARCH

The section includes contributions by Prof G. C. Bansal formerly in Punjab University, Chandigarh, Prof. A.A.N. Raju from Osmania Univerity, Hyderabad, Prof. P. Soma Raju from Andhra Pradesh University, Visakhapatnam, Prof. Bavakutty, University of Calicut, and Dr R.K. Bhatt from the University of Delhi and their respective co-authors.

Prof. A.A.N. Raju, Prof. Soma Raju and Prof. Bavakutty in their respective contributions have raised the issue that training in IT in library and information science is being neglected in the university education, as well as in research institutions despite the strong evidence that IT has a big role to play in shaping the quality of library and information services in the country. The gap needs to be filled up and the onus in this regard lies on the teaching community in library and information science, on the UGC, the research agencies in the country, and also on the professional bodies. Dr Bhatt has brought out the fact that evaluating distance education mode of LIS education is a vexing issue, and in this regard he has highlighted the problems and suggested some solutions. Even as we do recognise that there are several shortcomings in LIS education system in India, yet the paper by Prof. Bansal and Hassan Kiani on LIS education system in Iran does allude to the fact that comparatively the Indian model of LIS education is by far better than that of Iran.

INFORMATION SYSTEMS, TECHNIQUES AND SERVICES

This section includes contributions by Prof. M.P. Satija from Guru Nanak Dev University, Amritsar, Ms Masumeh Bagheri from Punjab University, Chandigarh, Mr J. Dominic from Karunya Institute of Technology, Coimbatore, M.K. Jain from International Library and Information Consultancy Centre, Delhi, Professor K. Navalani formerly in Punjabi University Patiala, Dr S.R. Gunjal from Lingayat Central Research Library, and Dr O.P. Gupta from University Grants Commission, New Delhi.

Prof. Satija has reviewed the 21st edition of Dewey Decimal Classification in print form and the Dewey Decimal Classification edition on CD-ROM (DfW). He has highlighted important changes in the classification schedules made in this edition, and also the important features of the DfW and of its user interface, and explained how such features make the task of document classification easier and simpler. Ms Bagheri and Professor G.C. Bansal have described the indexing and abstracting services brought out by various institutions in Iran and also brought home the point about how frustrating it is for anyone to bring out such services without the aid of computing tools. Mr Dominic has traced recent trends in information retrieval system, and in this context discussed the parameters for evaluating such systems. Sh M.K. Jain, based on his long experience in managing Planning Commission library, has described guidelines for providing effective reference service in government departmental libraries. Prof Navalani and P.C. Sehgal have profiled the Indira Gandhi Memorial Library in Hyderabad University, highlighting its achievements in resource building and library computerisation and LAN-based Intranet library and information services. Dr S.R. Gunjal has profiled the Central Library on Lingayatism of which he is the librarian, and his efforts in making it as a world class information centre on the Lingayat religion. Dr O.P. Gupta has brought out the need to reshape the present library and information systems for optimum utilisation of their resources, and explained the role information technology can play in this regard.

LIBRARY RESOURCE DEVELOPMENT, SHARING AND ACCESS

This section includes contributions by Dr (Mrs.) Neela Jagannathan, from IGNOU, Delhi, Dr Narender Kumar from Sukhdev College of Business Studies, University of Delhi, Dr B. Ramesh Babu from University of Madras, Satyanarayana from BHEL, Hyderabad, Dr P.R. Goswami from National Social Science Documentation Centre, New Delhi and Dr M. Sankara Reddy from P.S. Telugu University, Hyderabad.

Dr Neela Jaganathan has outlined guidelines for evolving a useful acquisition policy for resource development in university libraries. Dr Narender Kumar has examined the status of collections in all the Indian Institute of Management libraries to underline the need for pooling and sharing resources in the distributed information environment. Dr B Ramesh Babu and Satyanarayana in their respective papers have illustrated the models for resource sharing, information exchange and document delivery. Dr Goswami has brought out that access to government documents in India is very poor and has provided suggestions to improve access to such a valuable resource in the country. Dr Sankara Reddy and his co-author L.S. Ramaiah have brought out that there is a need for developing information services for distance learners in the country and have provided suggestions in this regard.

NETWORKING, INTERNET, CYBER AGE AND LIBRARIES

This section includes contributions by Dr A. Lakshmana Moorthy from DRDL, Hyderabad, Dr (Mrs.) Amrit Pal from DLIS, Guru Nanak Dev University, Amritsar, Dr Venkata Ramana from University of Hyderabad, Dr (Mrs.) Sarita Jain from Lady Irwin College, University of Delhi, Ms Shoba D. Kulkarni from Indian Institute of Technology, Mumbai, late Dr (Ms.) Kamlesh Vinayak formerly in Hansraj College, University of Delhi, and K. Veeranjaneyulu from College of Fishery Science, ANGR Agricultural University, Muthukur, and Khalid K. Faruqi from Jamia Hamdard University, New Delhi.

Dr Lakshman Moorthy and his coauthor Prof. Karisiddappa have highlighted the current trends in e-commerce, citing several examples of sources of commercial information on the Internet only to conclude that cyber commerce has come to stay. Internet has indeed been recognised as a vast pool of information, and it is in this context Dr (Mrs.) Amrit Pal has discussed library information resources on the Internet. It is realised the world over that libraries in general own limited resources in their collections, and as such their scope for meeting information needs of users is limited. In this context Dr Venkata Ramana and Vartha Rajan have highlighted the importance of library networking and explained how it can be gainfully applied to improve user satisfaction. The different papers by Dr (Mrs.) Sarita Jain, Ms Kulkarni, late Dr (Ms) Vinayak, and K. Veeranjaneyulu have addressed different aspects of library automation in the college and university libraries. Faruqi highlighted the benefits of library automation. They have shared their experiences in library automation and library networking and have outlined strategies for transforming the traditional library into electronic and digital library.

ELECTRONIC PUBLISHING

This section contains papers by Dr D. Kaushik from Environment and Explosive Safety, DRDO, Delhi, Dr S.C.Jindal from Central Science Library, University of Delhi, and Ms Nishat Fatima from DLIS, Aligarh Muslim University. They all herald the advent of electronic publishing and explain how multimedia features in electronic publishing have given a new dimension to electronic documents on CD-ROM and on Internet. Dr Kaushik and Ms Relan have described guidelines for evaluating electronic journals. Dr Jindal has discussed the economics of consortium access to journals on Internet and by studying the pricing model of Elsevier Science he has concluded that multi-site access to electronic journals on consortium subscription basis is more economical than single site access on individual subscription basis. Ms Nishat Fatima has discussed the important features of multimedia publishing and their applications in libraries.

LIBRARIANSHIP, MANAGEMENT AND STATUS

This section contains papers by Dr R.N. Sharma of Drain-Jordan Library, USA, Prof. V. K. Nanda formerly in Jamia Milia Islamia, Dr Krishan Gopal from Jawaharlal Nehru University, New Delhi, Dr Brij Mohan Khanna from NGRI, Hyderabad, Dr S.D. Vyas from Banasthali Vidyapith, Rajasthan, Dr H.R. Chopra from Panjab University, Chandigarh, Dr S. Majumdar from Central Secretariat Library, New Delhi, Mr P.C. Shah formerly in ATIRA, Ahmedabad, Ms Prabhjot Kaur, Dr P.R. Goswami from National Social Science Documentation Centre, New Delhi,

Dr M. Sankara Reddy from P.S. Telugu University, Hyderabad, and Dr. S.M. Dhawan from National Physical Laboratory, New Delhi.

Dr Sharma has chronicled the contributions the Asian Americans have made by using American Library Association platform, in improving the status of library collection and services in the third world countries. Prof. Nanda has discussed important factors coming in the way of the management of university libraries, and in their emerging as effective instruments of research and teaching in the university system. Dr Krishan Gopal has discussed the TQM principles and their applications to library and information centres in improving their quality of services. Libraries not only deal with books but they also deal with raw scientific and technical data generated by scientific and research institutions. Dr Khanna has highlighted this point and also chronicled his experience on the management of quantitative data in his library. Dr Vyas has discussed the emerging trends in knowledge management. Dr Chopra has discussed the performance evaluation of staff working in libraries, and suggested various techniques which could be used for the purpose. Dr Majumdar has discussed the book pricing by publishers, the element of arbitrariness in this practice and explained how this practice has resulted in high prices of books, and how high profit margins are affecting good collection development activity in libraries, especially in developing countries. Shah and Dr Sewa Singh have discussed the current trends and practices in information marketing by libraries and information centres. Dr Goswami has discussed the identity and status of librarians in the university system and brought out arguments in favour of their parity with the teachers in matters of pay scale, career advancement, and retirement benefits and age and of superannuation. Dr Sankara Reddy has made futuristic projections on libraries in the 21st century in the light of ongoing developments in information technology. In the library profession there is a great concern about the future role of library and information professionals in the context of ongoing developments in electronic publishing and Internet resources. Dr Dhawan has addressed this issue to identify the roles that libraries and librarians would be playing in the near future in the emerging electronic library environment.

SCIENTOMETRICS, USE AND USER STUDIES

This section includes essays on use studies as well as on scientometric studies. This includes contributions from Dr P. Padhi, and Dr B.M. Gupta both from National Institute for Science Development Studies, New Delhi, L.S. Ramaiah, formerly Librarian CIEFL, Hyderabad, Dr (Mrs.) Paramjeet Kaur Walia of DLIS, Delhi University, Delhi, Prof. B.S. Maheshwarappa from Gulbarga University, and Dr D. Chandarn from S. V. University, Tirupati.

Dr. P. Padhi of Utkal University and Dr. Garg of NISTADS, Delhi, in their paper have discussed the development of different quantitative and qualitative techniques for analysing library activities, library output, and publications output. They have also outlined the contributions made by India in the field of scientometrics and informetrics. Dr Gupta from NISTADS, New Delhi, has mapped collaborative research in theoretical population genetics by analysing the bibliographic records covering the period 1881-1980. L.S. Ramaiah and M. Ramchnader have mapped research in Telugu literature and language by analysing research dissertations, and have reported the declining trend in research in the subject. Dr Walia in her paper has studied the use of government documents in economics in four university libraries. Prof B.S. Maheshwarappa from Gulbarga University has studied the use of information sources in social sciences in Gulbarga University. Dr Chandarn has mapped efforts in library science research by analysing the dissertations submitted in the subject to the S.V. University, Tirupati.

S.M. Dhawan

Acknowledgements

At the outset I would like to place on record my gratitude to Prof. Vasant Gadre, Member University Grants Commission, for having agreed to write foreword for this document brought out in honour of Prof. J. L. Sardana, former Professor and Head of Department of Library and Information Science, University of Delhi. This work is an outcome of relentless efforts put in by all the members of the Editorial Committee including Dr. R.N. Sharma, Director, Drain-Jordan Library, West Virginia State College, West Virginia, USA; Dr M. Sankara Reddy, University Librarian, P.S. Telugu University; Hyderabad; Dr P. R. Goswami, Director, National Social Science Documentation, New Centre, Delhi; Dr S. Majumdar, Director, Central Secretariat Library, New Delhi; and myself. But for their unflinching support and cooperation this work would not have been possible. They had provided valuable inputs in finalising the contents and in giving shape to this document. I thank them for their support and cooperation. I would also like to deeply acknowledge with thanks the role played by members of the Festschrift Committee in conceptualising the project. They provided valuable inputs in deciding the topics for the festschrift volume and in short listing contributors. I am indeed very much indebted to all the authors of papers who had gladly accepted our invitation to write the papers and for sending them in record time. Index to this volume has been compiled by Dr Narender Kumar. I am grateful to him for his valuable contribution in this regard. Sudarshan Kcherry of

Authorspress, New Delhi, deserves special appreciation for having taken up the publication of this work. Working with him was indeed a special and enjoying experience. I would like to place on record my sincere thanks for his total cooperation and in bringing out this document.

S.M. Dhawan

Our Contributors

Ms. Kalyani Accanoor is Assistant Librarian at Central Library, Indian Institute of Technology, Powai, Mumbai 400 076. She holds MA and MLISc degrees. She has contributed many research papers in various journals and conferences. She was the recipient of best paper award from Indian Library Association in 1999. Email: aknur@indus.library.iitb.ernet.in

Dr (Ms) Amrit Pal is Reader in Department of Library and Information Science, Guru Nanak Dev University, Amritsar. She is Ph.D in Library and Information Science. She has won gold medals in her career and published many research papers in national and international journals.

Dr. B. Ramesh Babu is Professor, Department of Library and Information Science, University of Madras, Chennai 600 005. He holds Ph.D degree in Library and Information Science. He has contributed several Research papers in National and International Journals and attended several conferences.

Ms. Masumeh Bagheri is Lecturer in Department of Library and Information Science, University of Tehran, Iran. She pursued her doctoral programme at Panjab University, Chandigarh.

Dr G.C. Bansal was formerly Professor and Head of Department of Library and Information Science, Panjab University, Chandigarh. Prior to this, he has been Reader in Department of Library Science at Kurukshetra University.

He is MA from Kurukshetra University, MLibSc from University of Delhi. and Ph.D. from Panjab University. He has published several papers in the national and international journals. He has also served on several academic and professional committees in the country.

Dr M. Bavakutty is Professor & Head Department of Library and Information Science, University of Calicut, Kerala. Prior to this he was deputy Librarian-in-Charge of the University Library. He holds B.Sc., MA, MLISc, and Ph.D. degrees. He has been on the editorial boards of several journals, and has authored 4 books and contributed about 100 papers in journals.

Dr. R.K. Bhatt is Lecturer in senior grade in the Department of Library and Information Science, University of Delhi since 1998. Prior to this he had served for seven years as Assistant Librarian in Central Library, IIT Delhi. He is MA (History) from University of Rajasthan, MLISc from University of Delhi and Ph.D. from Agra University. He has published many research papers in national and international journals. He is managing editor of *Libraries, Information, and Knowledge: An International Journal.*

Dr. D. Chandran is Associate Professor in Department of Library and Information Science, S V University, Tirupati since 1985. Prior to this he had served as Assistant Librarian in State Central Library, Andhra Pradesh. He holds MA (Commerce), MLISc. and Ph.D. degrees. He has contributed several research papers in national and international journals. Email: chandrand2001@yahoo.co.in

Dr. Hans Raj Chopra is Professor and Head in the Department of Library and Information Science at Panjab University, Chandigarh. He holds M.A (Political Science) and Ph.D. degrees. He has been in teaching profession since 1979. Prior to his, he had served in Panjab University Library during 1969-1979. He is recipient of Panjab University Medal, India Book House award and Punjab Govt. award. He had won international fellowships: IFLA/NIJHOFF award (1980), UNISIST/FID award (1983), Commonwealth Academic Staff Fellowship (1987-88), and UGC Exchange Fellowship to visit Hungary in 1994. He has visited several countries including USA, UK, Netherlands, Belgium, Germany, Italy, Denmark, Austria, Hungary, etc. He has been guiding Ph.D. scholars. He is well known for his contributions in journals of national and international repute. He has also authored/edited six books

Dr S. M. Dhawan is Scientist F at National Physical Laboratory, New Delhi. He is MSc (Physics) from Sardar Patel University, Vallabh Vidyanagar; MLIS from State University of New York, Buffalo, USA; and Ph.D. from University of Delhi. His areas of interest are library management, IT in library operations, and scientometrics. He has published many papers in national and international journals. He has been on the editorial board of the *ILA Bulletin, and Annals of Library Science and Documentation.* He had edited ILA conference volume—Quest for Quality. He has been the resource person at several training programmes. He has conducted research projects in scientometrics funded by NISSAT, New Delhi. He is responsible for developing NPL website, in-house library management system, specialised databases, and web-based electronic library services on Intranet. Currently, he is member of CSIR task forces for the Planning Commission projects on CSIR Consortium for e-journals access, and National Science Digital Library.

Dr. Dewendra K. Singh is Assistant Librarian at Central Library Banasthali Vidyapith, Rajasthan. He holds Ph.D. degree from Banaras Hindu University. He has contributed research papers in national and international journals. His area of interest is IT applications in library operations. E-mail: dksingh9@hotmail.com

Sh. J. Dominic is Assistant Librarian at Karunya Institute of Technology, Coimbatore. He holds MLibSc degree from Annamalai University. He has published more than 12

papers in Indian journals and in conference proceedings. He also teaches for MLISc, BLISc, CLISc courses run by Annamalai University under the contact programme.

Ms Nishat Fatima is Lecturer in Department of Library and Information Science, Aligarh Muslim University, Aligarh. She holds MLibSc degree from AMU, and M.Phil degree from Delhi University. She has contributed many research papers in various journals and in conference proceedings.

Dr K. C. Garg is Scientist E-II at National Institute of Science Technology and Development Studies, New Delhi. He holds M.Lib.Sc. and Ph.D. degrees. He has published several papers especially in the field of scientometrics, in national and international journals.

Dr P.R. Goswami is Director, National Social Science Documentation Centre (NASSDOC), New Delhi. Prior to this, he was Librarian at Faculty of Management Studies, University of Delhi, Delhi. He is MA (History) from Ranchi University, MLibSc and Ph.D. from University of Delhi. He has served as General Secretary, Indian Library Association during 2000-2002. He has contributed research papers in national and international journals.

Dr S.R. Gunjal was formerly Professor of Library and Information Science, and Librarian, Gulbarga University, Gulbarga. Currently, he is Director Central Research Library of Lingayat Studies Naganur Shri Rudravimath, Shivabasava Nagar, Belgaum.

Dr Om Prakash Gupta is Library & Information Officer in the University Grants Commission, New Delhi. Earlier he was Assistant Librarian in the UGC (1974-1980) and College Librarian (1971-1973). He holds MA, MLibSc and Ph.D degrees. He has served on several national committees, and was General Secretary of the ILA (1998-2000). He has authored six books, and contributed several articles in national journals and conferences.

Dr. B.M. Gupta is Scientist F in National Institute of Science Technology and Development Studies, New Delhi. He holds

MLibSc and Ph.D. degrees. He has authored several books and contributed many articles especially in the field of scientometrics in national and international journals. He has served on several committees. Email: bmgupta1@yahoo.com

Smt. Bhagyashree Havanur is a graduate in science and post-graduate in library and information science from Karnatak University, Dharwad.

Dr (Mrs.) Neela Jagannathan is former University Librarian and Information Officer of Indira Gandhi National Open University (IGNOU), New Delhi. Prior to this she was in B R Ambedkar Open University, Hyderabad. She holds MA, MLISc and Ph.D. degree from University of Bombay. Her areas of interest are information facilities for distance mode learning. She has produced number of educational study materials for distance learners. She has edited many publications on distance learning. She has contributed extensively in national and international journals She has visited several countries abroad under Distance Learning Programme.

Sh. M.K. Jain is Director, International Library and Information Consultancy Centre, Delhi. Prior to this, he was Director, Planning Commission Library during 1972-1986. He has been member of several professional committees. He has authored seven books in library and information science and contributed many research papers in national and international journals.

Dr (Mrs) Sarita Jain is Librarian in Lady Irwin College, University of Delhi. She holds MA, MLISc, and Ph.D. degrees from University of Delhi. She has contributed in many national and international journals.

Dr S.C. Jindal is Deputy Librarian in Central Science Library, University of Delhi. He holds MSc (Chemistry) degree from Rajasthan University and MLISc and Ph.D. degrees from University of Delhi. He has been counselling IGNOU and

Open School students in library science for the past many years. He has contributed many research papers and book reviews in various journals.

Prof. C.R. Karisiddappa is Head of Department of Library & Information Science, Karnatak University, Dharwad. He is MA from Karnataka Univeristy, MLibSc from Banarus Hindu University, and Ph.D. from Gulbarga University. He has been guide to Ph.D. scholars. He has been on the editorial board of many journals in library and information science. He was member of the UGC Subject Expert panel in library and information science He has authored several research papers in national and international journals. He is recipient of Granthalaya Ratna award from State Youth Librarians Association, Bangalore. He was President of Indian Library Association during 2002-2004.

Dr D.K. Kaushik is Scientist F at Centre for Environment and Explosive Safety, (DRDO) Delhi. Prior to this he has been in Defence Science Documentation Centre, Delhi and Defence Metallurgical Research Laboratory, Hyderabad. He holds M.Sc. (Physics) and Ph.D (Library Science) degrees. He has contributed many research papers in journals and conference proceedings.

Dr. Khalid K. Faruqi is presently working as University Librarian of HMS Central Library (University Library) of Hamdard University since 2003.

Dr Brij Mohan Khanna is Scientist E-II, National Geophysical Research Institute, Hyderabad.

Sh. Hassan Kiani is Lecturer in Department of Library and Information Science, Az-zahra Univeristy, Tehran, Iran

Dr Krishan Gopal is Deputy Librarian at Jawaharlal Nehru University, New Delhi. He has officiated as Librarian at JNU. He has published several books and written many research papers in national and international journals and also in conference proceedings.

Ms. Shoba D Kulkarni is Senior Professional Assistant in Central Library, Indian Institute of Technology, Mumbai. Email: osdk@indus.library.iitb.ernet.in

Prof. B.S. Maheshwarappa is Professor and Chairman, Department of Post Graduate studies & Research in Library & Information Science, Gulbarga University, Gulbarga. Earlier, he was Reader in the Department (1988-1995) and Lecturer in Mysore University (1981-1988). He holds M.Sc., M.Phil and Ph.D degrees. His areas of interest are informetrics, user studies, information technology, academic, special and public libraries. He has guide to Ph.D. scholars. He has edited one book and contributed more than 90 research papers in national and international journals.

Dr S. Majumdar is Director, Central Secretariat Library, Department of Culture, Government of India, New Delhi since 2002. Earlier he was Deputy Librarian (Professor Grade) in Indian Institute of Public Administration, New Delhi. He had also served in Jawaharlal Nehru University Library, New Delhi. He is MA (Sociology) from Lucknow University, MLISc and Ph.D. from University of Delhi. He has contributed many research papers in national and international journals. Email: sm1949@rediffmail.com

Dr. A Lakshmana Moorthy is Scientist F at Defence Research and Development Laboratory, Hyderabad. Earlier he was with Defence Scientific Information & Documentation, Centre, Delhi (1987 - 2002), DRDO, Hyderabad (1984 - 1987) and ISRO (1979 - 1984). He is M.Sc (Physics) from Sri Venkateswara University, Tiruparti, ADISc from DRTC, Bangalore and Ph.D. from Karnatak Univeristy, Dharwad. He has edited more than 15 books, conference proceedings, and monographs. He was editor of *Defence Science Journal, DESIDOC Bulletin of Information Technology, AGLIS Journal, and ILA Newsletter*. He has contributed in many national and international journals and conferences.

Muhammed Salih T.K. is Library Professional, CHMK Library, University of Calicut, Kerala. He has been associated with the automation process at CHMK Library. Currently he is working in the Computer Section of the University of Calicut. He is doing part-time research on computerisation of libraries. He has published several papers on this subject.

Mr D.K. Mukherjee is Librarian in Indian Institute of Advanced Study, Shimla. Prior to this he was Asstt Librarian at IIAS. He has contributed many papers in national and international journals.

V. K. Nanda was Officiating Librarian in Dr Zakir Hussain (Univ) Library, Jamia Millia Islamia, New Delhi. He has also worked in Brooklyn Public Library, USA; Library of Congress, USA; Institute of Applied Manpower, Delhi in various capacities. He is MALS from Rosary College, USA. He has been teaching in Department of Library and Information Science, Jamia Millia Islamia, New Delhi as part time faculty member. He has been counselling IGNOU library science students also. He has contributed several research papers in national and international journals.

Dr Narender Kumar is Librarian at Shaheed Sukhdev College of Business Studies, University of Delhi. He is M.Com, MLISc, and Ph.D from University of Delhi and holds a PGDCA diploma also. His areas of interest are library management, library system development, and IT applications. He has developed a library management software package. He was Secretary Indian Library Association and Managing Editor, *ILA Bulletin* during 1998-2000. He has been contributing papers in journals and conference proceedings. He is managing editor of *Libraries, Information, and Knowledge: An International Journal.* E-mail: cbsdu@nde.vsnl.net.in

Prof. (Ms.) K Navalani was Professor and Head of Department of Library and Information Science and Dean, Faculty of Arts and Social Sciences, Punjabi University, Patiala. She was a member of the UGC Expert Panel on Library and Information Science. She has authored and edited several books and has contributed several research papers in national and international journals. She is the recipient of UNESCO-IFLA-FID fellowship in 1981 and Fulbright Fellowship in 1988.

Sh. P. J. Nirmala is Assistant Librarian at Karunya Institute of Technology, Coimbatore.

Ms. Rekha S. Oltikar is serving as Senior Professional Assistant, Central Library, Indian Institute of Technology, Powai, Mumbai. E-mail: orso@indus.library.iitb.ernet.in

Dr. P. Padhi is Reader in the Department of Library and Information Science, Utkal University, Bhubaneswar, Orissa.

Smt. Prabhjot Kaur is Librarian, Government College, Bholath (Kapurthala).

Prof. A.A.N. Raju is UGC Emeritus Fellow at the Department of Library and Information Science, Osmania University, Hyderabad. He is MA from Osmania University, MLibSc from Banaras Hindu University, Ph.D from Osmania University. He retired as Dean, Faculty of Social Sciences from Osmania University in 1998. He has published more than 75 research papers in national and international journals, and edited several books. His areas of interest are library classification, library movement and information systems. He was closely associated as an editor and course writer with BLISc/MLISc programmes of IGNOU and Dr Bhim Rao Ambedkar Open University, Hyderabad. He had organised and directed a number of professional conferences, seminars and workshops. He is life member of several professional bodies which include ILA, IASLIC, IATLIS, ALSD, APLA, ISKO and ASRC. He had served as Vice President ILA (1986--87), IASLIC (1988-89 and 1992-93), President ASLD (1989-91) and IATLIS (1996-98). He is recipient of IATLIS-Motiwale Best Teacher Award for 1995.

Dr P. Soma Raju was Professor and Head Department of Library and Information Science, Andhra University, Visakhapatnam. He is Ph.D. in library and information science. During his extensive career in teaching spanning over 40 years he has been guide for research work for doctoral programme, and contributed many papers in national and international journals.

Sh L. S. Ramaiah was Librarian, Ramesh Mohan Library, Central Institute of English Foreign Languages, Hyderabad, a deemed university. He was a member of the research committee of the RRLF and of the UGC LIS panel. He has published and edited 25 books and bibliographies, and contributed over 100 papers in national and international journals in library and information science. He has experience of serving for 25 years as Librarian. He is the recipient of Prof. Parvathaeni Gangadhara Rao Award, Best Librarian Award from IASLIC, and many other awards. He has travelled several countries including UK, USA, Cuba, and Yemen.

M. Ramchander is officer on Special Duty, Department of Distance Education, P.S. Telugu University. He is M.Com and MLISc form Osmania University. He has been in the profession for over 7 years and published papers in Journals and conference proceedings.

Prof. M. Sankara Reddy is University Librarian in P.S. Telugu University, Hyderabad. He is MA and MLISc from Osmania University and Ph.D from Gulbarga University. He was awarded gold medal for his thesis. He has been in the profession for the last 33 years. He has authored several books and contributed papers in national and international journals. He is member of several professional organisations which include ALSD, IASLIC, IATT, ILA, IATLIS, IAFH & AFLA. Earlier he has been Sr Vice-President of the ILA (1998-2002) Email: dr.msreddy@eudoramail.com

Ms. Sonia Relan is Scientist E in Defence Science Documentation Center, Delhi. She has contributed many research papers in journals and conference proceedings.

Prem Chand Sehgal is involved in research in library and information science.

Dr Mohinder Pratap Satija is Professor, Department of Library and Information Science, Guru Nanak Dev University, Amritsar. In three decades of professional experience, he has authored more than a dozen books and published about 100 papers in Indian and foreign library science journals. In some of his works he has collaborated with international experts. He has visited Germany, Finland, England, Nepal, the Netherlands, and Belgium in connection with professional work. He is associated with many journals such as *Information Management Report* (Bowker-Sour, UK), *Library Times International* (USA), *Knowledge Organisation* (USA/Germany), *Lucknow Librarian* and *Ranganathan Research Bulletin*. He is the Indian coordinator of the International Society for Knowledge Organisation (ISKO) (The Netherlands). Dr Satija is a life member of many library and information science associations and has delivered lectures in many universities. He served as a visiting fellow for three months in Masstricht McLuhan Institute of University of Masstricht in summer of 1999.

Sh V.V.V. Satyanarayana is Manager, Bharat Heavy Electricals Limited, Corporate Research and Development, Hyderabad. He obtained his post-graduate in Library and Information Science from Osmania University, and graduation from Andhra University. He has been in the profession for the past 35 years having worked in libraries of the then Regional Research Laboratory, Hyderabad; Indian Institute of Technology Madras and Indian Institute of Science, Bangalore. He is presently in charge of the Technical Information Centre BHEL CORP R&D, Hyderabad. He has to his credit a number of research papers published in journals and conference proceedings. He has published a book 'UDC: a practical primer'.

Dr Sewa Singh is Professor, Department of Library and Information Science, Guru Nanak Dev University, Amritsar. He is Ph.D. in Library and Information Science. He has authored several books and contributed many research papers in national and international journals.

P.C. Shah was formerly Head of National Information System in Textile (NICTAS) under the umbrella of Ahmedabad Textile Industry's Research Association, Ahmedabad. He spearheaded the development of NICTAS as a leading information centre in textile in the country and had run it on self sustainable basis.

Dr R.N. Sharma is Director of the Drain-Jordan Library, West Virginia State College, Institute, West Virginia, United States of America. He is an active professional and has published/edited ten books, and written over 300 articles, interviews, reports, editorials and book reviews. A frequent speaker at conferences, Dr Sharma is the editor of *Library Times International*. He has won many awards, grants, and honours. He has chaired and served on many committees of ALA, Association of College & Research Libraries (ACRL). He was President of the Asian/Pacific American Librarians Association (APALA) for 1993-94. He is listed in over twenty biographical dictionaries including *Who's Who in the World, Outstanding People of the 20th Century, Who is Who in American Education, Dictionary of International Biography, and Who's Who Among Asian Americans.* Dr Sharma held B.A. (Honours), and M.A. degrees in History from the University of Delhi, Master's in Library Science from North Texas State University, and Ph.D. in Library and Information Science from the State University of New York, Buffalo, USA.

Dr T.G. Tadasad is Lecturer in the Department of Post Graduate Studies in Library and Information Science, Gulbarga University. He is MLISc and Ph.D from Karnatak University, Dharwad. He has been in the teaching profession for the last 6 years. He has contributed many research papers in national and international journals and conferences.

Dr V. Venkata Ramana is Deputy Librarian in University of Hyderabad. He holds B.SC, MA, MLISc and Ph.D. degrees from different universities. He has over 28 years of professional experience. He authored 5 books and contributed several research papers in national and international journals.

N. Vartha Rajan is Assistant Librarian in University of Hyderabad since 1993. He holds MA and MLISc degrees. He has written many papers.

K. Veeranjaneyulu is Assistant Librarian in College of Fishery Science, ANGR Agricultural University, Muthukur, Andhra Pradesh.

Dr (Ms.) Kamlesh Vinayak (late) has served as Librarian, Hans Raj College, University of Delhi. Earlier she served in Institute of Home Economics, University of Delhi and Satyawati Co-educational College (Evening), University of Delhi. She holds MA, M Lib Inf Sc., and Ph.D. degrees from University of Delhi. She was awarded Best College Librarian Award by Delhi State Publishers and Booksellers Association in 1998. She has contributed many papers in national journals.

Dr S.D.Vyas is Librarian, Central Library, Banasthali Vidyapith, Rajasthan. E-mail: sdvyas15@hotmail.com

Dr (Ms) Paramjit Kaur Walia is Lecturer in Library and Information Science, University of Delhi. Earlier she was the Chairperson of Department of Library and Information Science, Panjab University, Chandigarh. She had also served in different capacities in academic and special libraries. She holds MA, MLISc, MPhil and Ph.D. degrees from University of Delhi. She had authored many research papers in national and international journals and also in conference proceedings.

Contents

PART V

Networking, Internet, Cyber Age and Libraries

PART VI
Electronic Publishing

PART VII
Libarianship, Management and Status

PART VIII
Scientometrics and Use Studies

Part I

Eulogy and Tributes

1

A Trip to Nostalgia : Remembering Professor J.L. Sardana

D.K. Mukherjee

> "Memories are like books; a few live in our hearts through our life, and the rest, like the bills we pay, are read and then forgotten".
>
> — *Gerald Bendall, Mrs. Jones' Bonnet*

It has been three decades since I took up my first job as a temporary Librarian in the British Council's Textbook Section at South Extension, New Delhi, on daily wages, on 16 January 1970. It is going to be three decades since I joined the Indian Institute of Advanced Study, the institution that I am presently serving as the Librarian. I had also two stints; the first as Documentation Officer on deputation in the Research and Policy Division, Ministry of Home Affairs, New Delhi, during 1983/84, and again as Assistant Librarian in the newly established Assam University, Silchar (1994-96). Needless to say, I have traversed a long way. When I delve deep into my mind's eye and look for those who were responsible for shaping my professional career, I discern with gratitude many of my benefactors; my teachers, friends, seniors and a good number of intellectuals of world repute with whom I had the opportunity of having close contact during the long span of past 30 years. Their memories are like books, not only like best-sellers but like classics which one would always like to read, re-read and retain forever as priceless treasures. I have preserved the memory of Professor J.L. Sardana like one of such classics.

Professor Sardana happened to be my first boss and predecessor at the Institute. I would offend him if I comment upon his professional calibre and scholarship. It was he who initiated me into the profession, trained and groomed me enough for building up a successful career in library service. His achievements as a teacher, a prolific writer and as an activist of various professional bodies are well known and recognised, both nationally and internationally, even by his adversaries. The present write-up is aimed at remembering with fondness a couple of episodes that brought me closer to him during my formative years and helped me lay the foundation stone of my professional pursuits.

When I review in retrospect to narrate the episodes, I am reminded of my student days at the Tutorial Building, University of Delhi, where the Department of Library Science was located. Way back in 1968, I was pursuing my studies there for obtaining the Bachelor's degree in Library Science. The Faculty consisted of a team of brilliant outstanding teachers wedded to the profession; hard taskmasters performing the role of friends, philosophers and guides of the students. Led by Professor P.B. Mangla, then Head of the Department, the team included big names like Professor B.S. Kesavan, Professor George S. Bonn, Shri D.S. Agrawal, Shri Krishan Kumar, Mrs. V.K. Sundaram and Shri Kamaleshwar Nath Gupta. I was lucky to have a nice batch of classmates including girls; smart, intelligent, studious and mature enough to help each other in studies.

The method of teaching was different from the method followed by other universities conducting similar courses. The teachers wanted the students to come to class only after studying the relevant documents on the topic of their lectures so that a fruitful discussion could take place between them and the students for better comprehension of the topics. As such the teachers would painstakingly prepare long lists of references and distribute the mimeographed copies to each and every student beforehand. Defaulters were badly pulled up. The students were given regular assignments on the topics decided upon during lectures which had to be submitted within the scheduled timeframe. The submission of such assignments was essential as these were accounted for in the final examinations. Besides, it was also mandatory for the students to appear for the terminal examinations. At times, the students found it extremely difficult to cope up with the pressure of work.

There used to be a heavy rush of students scrambling for books in both the departmental and the central library after the classes were over. However, in spite of all the pressures, there used to prevail a good rapport between the teachers and the taught; marked at times by occasional witty and humorous remarks during the lectures which were enjoyed by all. Each and every student talked to the teachers with respect and the teachers in turn showered their affection and never hesitated to extend their help and guidance if sought even outside the classroom.

One of the greatest qualities of the teachers was their deep concern for the future pursuits of the students. I still remember as to how we were advised to adopt the principle of wait and watch and not to make haste to take up jobs below the scale of Rs. 250-400 for the commencement of our careers. There used to be a lot of interpersonal communication and heart to heart discussions. It was during one of such discussions that I first heard the name of Professor Sardana and came to know about him as a bright and outstanding product of our Alma Mater who, in a very short span of time, had been able to carve a niche for himself in the professional circle through his participation in various academic, administrative and organisational activities. Many of my classmates longed to meet and talk to him in order to seek his help and guidance for building up their future professional career as he was known to be a helpful person, but only a few could actually make it. I happened to be the one who could not meet him during the entire duration of the course due to the excessive pressure of studies. I got the first opportunity of meeting him at a very late stage, after successfully completing my examinations. It was a chance encounter that took place because of Professor Mangla.

As a regular practice, after the completion of final examinations, the department used to maintain a select list containing names and addresses of fresh library science graduates for the purpose of nominating them as internees to the libraries and institutions on request. My name also figured in the list. It was in January 1970, long after I left the department, when I received a message from Professor Mangla advising me to meet the Librarian of the University Grants Commission at the earliest for trying my luck to get a job in the British Council's Textbook Section on a contract basis. I had been passing through a very lean phase of my personal life at that time, struggling hard like many of my classmates to find out a suitable job at any cost. In spite of good performances at the interviews, success was at large. The regular failures in my efforts made me depressed, diffident and dejected. I had even started thinking of giving up my hopes for making a career in library service and try my luck elsewhere. Professor Mangla's message, therefore, turned out to be a boon in disguise as it provided me not only an opportunity to try my luck again but also to meet and talk to Professor Sardana who then happened to be the Librarian of the University Grants Commission. I lost no time in rushing to the University Grants Commission.

My first meeting with Professor Sardana is unforgettable. The moment I entered his room wishing him good afternoon, I was enthralled by his reception. He did not behave at all like many of the big bosses who then mattered in the profession, ridden with ego, reluctant to spare time to talk to strugglers and job seekers, eager to dispose them of at the earliest after exchanging pleasantries. Instead, he welcomed me with a broad smile, letting me feel as if he knew me for a very long time and had been my close confidante. He first offered me a glass of water, then a nice hot cup of tea and made me completely feel at home before engaging himself with the main conversation. For strugglers, such a nice treatment used to matter a lot. I found him to be a very soft spoken person, sophisticated, compassionate and eager to help the needy with lots of words of encouragement. He informed me about the nature of the job that I was supposed to undertake at the British Council and also generated enough confidence in me by telling that for a student like me who was the product of his own Alma Mater, it would not be difficult at all to attend to the job which, in fact, turned out be very simple, viz., ascertaining bibliographical data of English textbooks prescribed in various Indian universities. He then asked me to go to the South Extension branch of the British Council for a brief interview with Mr. Vincent Foreshaw, then heading the Council's Textbook Section. However, before sending me off, he ensured and satisfied himself that I had a thorough knowledge of the various printed publishers' catalogues including the *British Books in Print*. He also advised me not to get nervous during the interview as Mr. Foreshaw happened to be British. As the daily wages were to be bargained during the interview only, he advised me to ask for a reasonable amount in the event of my selection; an amount not less than what I deserved.

My interview with Mr. Foreshaw was successful and I was offered the job on daily wages @ Rs. 15/- per day. Relieved and happy, I reported back to Professor Sardana to deliver him the good news. Professor Sardana seemed relieved to know that I got the job but at the same time did not seem to be very happy to know about the wages agreed upon by me. He told me that I should have demanded more as the British Council observed five days a week and I wouldn't be paid wages for holidays. His comments depicted one great human quality, a deep concern for the welfare of a fellow human being, for a person like me who till then happened to be a stranger to him. He obviously did not want me to be exploited just because I was badly in need of an employment. I, however, informed him that it was more important for me to keep myself engaged rather than think over the wages. I did not mind even if I was offered less so long as it helped in getting me a break. And thus my first meeting with Professor Sardana ended with getting the first break of my professional career. Before I departed, he wished me good luck and advised me to keep in touch with him for my future pursuits.

I commenced my service in the British Council on 16 January 1970. The job was of purely temporary nature. On the very first day of my joining, my immediate superior, Mr. Z.A. Ansari, who happened to be a nice and friendly person advised me as an insider to keep on trying for other suitable jobs as there was very little chance for me to continue in the British Council after the job assigned to me was over. Accordingly, I kept on submitting applications for the posts advertised in the newspapers. The office hours of the British Council used to be from 9.00 am to 5.00 pm and commuting between residence and office also consumed a lot of time. I was able to perform my duties to the satisfaction of my superiors in the office but remained too occupied to establish further contact with Professor Sardana during the following four months.

In May 1970, I received a call for interview for the post of Professional Assistant lying vacant in the Indian Institute of Advanced Study, Shimla. At the interview, a pleasant surprise awaited me. When I was called in I was surprised to see Professor Sardana sitting in the room as a Member of the Selection Committee beside Professor Nihar Ranjan Ray, the then Director of the Institute, and Professor J.S. Sharma, then Librarian, Punjab University, Chandigarh. The presence of Professor Sardana instilled new hope and confidence in me. I was able to perform fairly well at the interview. Before allowing me to leave, Professor Sardana did not hesitate to tell the members of the Selection Committee that he already knew me. He asked me to meet him after the interview was over. When I met him after the interview, he first enquired as to why I did not contact him before coming for the interview and whether I knew that he had since joined the Institute as Librarian on deputation from the University Grants Commission. In fact, I really did not know about his joining the Institute as Librarian. Nor did I make any effort to seek his help before appearing for the interview, simply because the idea did not come to my mind. I informed him about the same. He was not annoyed but there was an air of complaint in his voice for not keeping any contact with him when he carried on the conversation. However, he was curious to know about my work in the British Council, enquired about my future plans after leaving the British Council. I informed him that I was still trying to find an alternative job but was not able to find a suitable one so far. Throughout our conversation, no reference was made to the results of the interview. I took enough care to desist from enquiring about the results directly from him. He on his own, however, did not forget to advise me to contact him in case I faced any problem. I came back to Delhi the next day.

I was not sure as to whether I would receive any further communication from the Institute about the result of my interview. More than one and a half months had elapsed since I appeared before the Selection Committee. There was no communication from the Institute. I was about to presume that I was not selected when I received an unexpected phone-call in my office from my classmate and close friend, Shri R.C. Dutta, then serving as Librarian in the Evening College, Shimla (now Librarian, Himachal Pradesh University). Dutta has been sincerely trying for me for getting me appointed as a Professional Assistant in the newly established Himachal Pradesh University Library. Over the phone, he gave me two good news. First, that a letter appointing me to the post of Professional Assistant had been despatched by the Himachal Pradesh University and second, I had also got selected to the post of Professional Assistant in the Indian Institute of Advanced Study, Shimla, and the appointment letter was on the way. He advised me to opt for the Institute as it provided the facility of official accommodation and had Professor Sardana as the Librarian. My own opinion also happened to be the same. On receipt of the appointment letter, I left the British Council on 3 August 1970 and headed for Shimla to take up my new assignment at the Indian Institute of Advanced Study. That heralded the second phase of my professional career which provided me an opportunity to work under the direct supervision of Professor Sardana.

I joined the Institute on 10 August 1970. It had been then only five years since it came into existence but it had already earned the reputation of being one of the prestigious research institutes in the country where senior scholars of world repute were engaged in exploring the new horizons of knowledge in the areas of Social Sciences and the Humanities. Big names like those of Professor S. Radhakrishnan, the Philosopher-President and Founder of the Institute, Professor Nihar Ranjan Ray, the famous Art Historian, and Founder-Director, Dr. C.D. Deshmukh, Professor M.C. Chagla and the names of scores of other outstanding scholars and individuals were associated with it.

The basic infrastructure of the library was built up by a team of dedicated professionals, led by one of the stalwarts of the profession, Professor B.S. Kesavan, who was subsequently succeeded by librarians like Dr. Prabhu Narayan Gour, translator and editor of the Hindi edition of Dewy Decimal Classification and Shri N.B. Marathe, a well known Sanskrit scholar coming from the National Library, Kolkata. They developed the library by acquiring the private collections of great scholars like Professor R.C. Majumdar, Professor Abdul Majid Khan and Professor Hem Chandra Ray Chowdhury and others. Professor Sardana had inherited their legacy and had already engaged himself with the task of furthering the activities of the library for catering to the requirements of its distinguished clientele. Professor V.K. Gokak, a well-known Kannada writer, scholar of Indian-English literature, philosopher and winner of Sahitya Academy Award, Member of the UGC, had already joined as the second Director of the Institute by then. Briefly, the academic atmosphere prevalent at the time of my joining inspired me greatly to put in my optimum possible efforts in carrying out my duties and responsibilities under the guidance and supervision of Professor Sardana.

My first assignment was to deal with all the jobs pertaining to the periodicals section which was considered by many as a chaotic section. The technical knowledge that I had acquired during the training did help but not in all the cases. I had to face a large number of unforeseen problems while dealing with official files. I was still a novice, raw and inexperienced, yet to learn the intricacies of official rules and procedures, the various official norms that are required to be observed before putting up the cases to the higher authorities. I was totally ignorant of the basics of official noting and drafting. It was Professor Sardana who gave me the first lessons in this respect and I owe my gratitude exclusively to him. As my immediate superior and first boss, Professor Sardana handled me with great care, love and compassion, always eager to teach whatever I did not know. The keen interest shown by him facilitated me to handle not only the jobs relating to the periodical section but also the jobs pertaining to the various other sections of the library. He also made me competent enough to perform the jobs that came under purview at the supervisory level. He never got irritated with my failures, nor did he ever use any harsh words for my errors and lapses but always encouraged me to learn more to promote my career. There existed a deep personal touch in our relations. He never forgot to call me everyday to enquire about not only my official problems but also my personal ones and rendered every possible help in solving them. He had been very popular not only with his subordinates but also with the entire staff of the Institute.

It was our ill luck that Professor Sardana decided to join back the University Grants Commission after completing the term of his deputation in 1972 but the training imparted by him in a short span of less than two years enabled me to successfully compete for the post of Junior Librarian (Group II cadre) that fell vacant at the Institute. Shortly after his departure, I was appointed to the post through open selection in November 1972. Subsequently, I worked with many of his successors, some of whom happened to be intellectuals. Due to the conviction, confidence and work culture inculcated in me by Professor Sardana, I was able to serve them to their utmost satisfaction and, in due course, was able to scale to the top of the professional ladder. I got a few opportunities to meet Professor Sardana after he left the Institute but whenever we met, the meeting was always cordial and full of encouragement in my professional endeavours.

In the library profession, one excels either as a good working librarian or as a good academician and teacher. In professor Sardana, there has been a rare combination of both the qualities. Added to these, he held top portfolios in various professional associations and contributed constructively towards the cause of the library profession. It is true that with his superannuation he has reached the twilight of his career, but I am sure the twilight would lead not to darkness but to light, and Professor Sardana with his vast knowledge, scholarship and experience would continue to bless the younger generation with his help, guidance and active participation in professional activities.

I wish him a long, healthy, prosperous and active life.

2

One Man: J.L. Sardana—a Pen Portrait

M. Sankara Reddy

Professor J.L. Sardana is widely acclaimed as 'Librarian par excellence' and verily regarded as a living legend. He contributed for the all-round growth of the library movement and in the process had brought many a laurel to our profession. I am glad to be writing about a luminary who had, as the President of the Indian Library Association (ILA), left behind a legacy for others, to emulate with pride. He endeavoured to pave the way for better governance in the profession, which doubtlessly has its motto as, "Knowledge is power in an Information Society".

Professor Sardana was born on 9 July 1934 in West Pakistan. He had his early education at Sukkur Sridh (now in Pakistan) and Delhi. Having had a good scholastic career, he joined B.Sc. (Hons.) course in physics in 1952 in India's premier educational institution—the Delhi University—and successfully passed in the year 1955. He did P.G. Diploma in library science from Delhi University in 1957. Later, he completed M.A. in economics from Meerut University and still later he pursued M.L.I.Sc. from Delhi University.

Initiating a glorious career that was to last for long, Professor Sardana entered the fraternity of library professionals way back in 1957 and there was no looking back thereafter. From that time onwards he had held many high positions in the profession. He worked as Librarian for about two decades, having served such institutions of repute as the University Grants Commission (UGC), New Delhi, Indian Institute of Advanced Studies (IIAS), Shimla, Indian Institute of Technology (IIT), Kanpur, Indian Institute of Management, Lucknow, etc.

Professor Sardana's passion for learning which seemingly had become more intense with the passage of time, motivated him to join as a teacher in library science in the University of Delhi that was his 'Alma Mater'. His stint at the university, starting from 1976, afforded him opportunities to teach various subjects in library science at graduate and postgraduate levels as also to guide research. Such teaching pursuits provided him the opportunities to keep learning day in and day out, accumulating more and more knowledge . A large number of students have earned M.Phil. and Ph.D. degrees under his supervision. Thus, eventually, the professor blossomed as an authority on the subject and in the years that followed he came to be acknowledged as an authority of repute in the professional circles in India and abroad.

Known to his students and the library professionals as an eloquent speaker and an orator with conviction, Professor Sardana had for long been accredited as 'the brave new teacher'. He introduced umpteen novel methods of imparting knowledge to the learners in his own inimitable style. He always believed in the sagacity of paying individual attention to the students by faithfully following the approach of "teacher-centred teaching" that was earlier set in motion by the father of India's library science, Dr. S.R. Ranganathan. This approach seemed to have paid off in the long run as had been evident from the promising career in librarianship that a major chunk of his students had come to enjoy, as they had earned a name for themselves. And, as history has it, the 'born teacher' in Professor Sardana had became known to one and all as a 'teacher par excellence'—a fact that our fraternity will continue to recall with pride forever.

The professor had been teaching library science for almost a quarter of a century. His specialisation has been in subjects such as academic library systems, information systems and services, statistical methods and research methodology. Even while working as a teacher, he did not lose interest in library movement in the country. He has been taking an active part in professional activities too. This paved the way for him to go to administration.

After having achieved the recognition as an academician of repute, Professor Sardana proved his mettle as an able administrator when he officiated as the Registrar of Indian Institute of Advanced Studies. At the UGC, he made lasting contributions in the areas of editing, printing and sale of UGC publications nationwide. His association with the UGC, which he served for nearly two decades, gave him an insight into the problems of managing men and material resources. In later years this experience came in handy in introducing reforms when he was presiding over the national body. Professor Sardana has had the distinction of serving on innumerable committees of various universities as also of the UGC and the Planning Commission as a member and in various other capacities. In the ultimate analysis, he always left his indelible mark by making commendable contribution in all the tasks that he was associated with. He has been the member of the IXth Five-Year Plan Working Group on libraries, and was Chairman of the sub-groups.

Professor Sardana possesses consummate skills in editorial work, a fact that was amply driven home when he edited the *Journal of Library and Information Science*, brought out by the University of Delhi, and *Annals of Library Science and Documentation*, brought out by the erstwhile INSDOC, New Delhi.

Professor Sardana was drawn into international arena in the year 1992, when he was voted to the office of Organising Secretary of the Indo-American (USA) Conference on LIS education held in New Delhi. Later, in 1998, he served as

Chairman of the National Organising Committee of the FID international meet. The professor participated in several international events, travelling extensively from time to time, presenting his viewpoints on various subjects, drawing vastly from his rich experience in the field as a professional, as an academician, as an administrator and as a member of several policy-making bodies in the country. The professor also holds the office of Vice-President of FID, the first Indian to hold this office after Dr. S.R. Ranganathan.

Professor Sardana has been associated for long with professional bodies like the ILA as its General Secretary during 1983-85 and subsequently as its President during 1998-2000. He has also served as a member of the Raja Ram Mohan Roy Library Foundation, Kolkata. He was honoured by the ILA for his outstanding contributions for the overall development of libraries and LIS profession. One unforgettable yet most valuable contribution that he made was that soon after he took over as President of ILA in 1998 he lost no time in getting all pending/backlog work/publications, annual reports, *ILA Bulletin, ILA Newsletter*, etc., cleared fast, having the accounts set in order, pending bills cleared, arranging for the publication of bulletin, newsletters, pre-conference volumes on schedule and undertaking all organisational activities for the smooth running of the national body, not to speak of taking expeditious steps for the conduct of elections to the new body of ILA on time. Laudable among his actions was infusing impeccable financial discipline, which has now become virtually a legacy in ILA. He took initiative in organising workshops, seminars, conferences, panel discussions, conferences and training programmes that attracted national attention bringing to the forefront the past glory of the ILA.

The most notable among Professor Sardana's latest contribution was the institution of the 'National Award' to be given away annually by the ILA to a library professional of 75 years or above in recognition of his/her lifetime contributions for the promotion and advancement of the LIS profession—an honour that is going to provide a satisfying finality to the already ageing soul. Yet another award, introduced by the ILA during the professor's tenure as President, was meant for the young professionals for their outstanding contribution and performance in the field of LIS. Prof. Sardana has always held the view that decentralisation of ILA activities percolating down to the state level would enhance its character as an all-India body and, therefore, he endeavoured all along to translate this idea into action. Furthermore, he was also responsible for the revival of 'Good Office Committee' and through it spearheaded efforts for restoring the code of ethics and standardising the terms and conditions for supply of books/journals. He served as Chairman of the Committee that comprised representatives of the Government of India libraries, Federation of Publishers and Book Trade, etc.

Displaying his remarkable negotiation skills, Professor Sardana liaised painstakingly with the 5th Pay Commission for attaining parity of pay scales of library professionals working in colleges and universities with the teachers.

A renowned writer, Prof. Sardana had rendered distinguished services by authorising/editing more than 10 books, and by contributing about 35 papers to research journals. What could be more satisfying that some of his books are prescribed as textbooks in some of the LIS schools/colleges of Indian universities.

An embodiment of simplicity, discipline, intellectual honesty and deep scholarship, Professor Sardana endeared himself to the students, academics, professionals and administrators alike.

As has been aptly put by someone, the world of books is the most remarkable creation of man. Nothing else that he builds ever lasts. Monuments fall, nations perish, civilisations phase out, new races take over others, but in the world of books the volumes that have seen all these events happening again and again live on still as young and as fresh as they were the day they were written—still reeling out the acts of the men centuries dead. I embolden myself to go on record by saying that the revered Sardana will remain for long like the book itself-keep reminding us and the posterity, of the rich values he imbibed in our profession—a profession that he made nobler than the noblest, thanks to the contributions that he made. He is like an unwritten book that will continue to remind us always of the ways we need to conduct in the profession in the times to come.

PART II

Library and Information Science Education, Training and Research

3

LIS Research in India : Trends and Developments

A.A.N. Raju

INTRODUCTION

Libraries and information centres play a vital role in the socio-economic development of the nation. The R&D activities in science and technology and in other fields of human endeavour have contributed to a phenomenal growth in the universe of subjects, resulting in information explosion and inter-disciplinary approach to research during the past seven decades. These developments have generated new demands on the services offered by libraries and information centres.

The rapid strides our country has made in different spheres of national endeavour since independence, and the efforts being made to sustain this progress and attain new heights have added new dimensions to the services rendered by libraries and information centres. In order to meet the new challenges and find proper and suitable solutions and to investigate new areas, research has become one of the most important and essential aspects of library and information science. *The Webster's Third New International Dictionary* defines research as 'studious inquiry of examination; specifically and usually critical and exhaustive investigation or experimentation, having for its aim the discovery of new facts and their correct interpretation, the revision of accepted conclusions, theories or laws'.[1] Research is essential to examine the existing situations and problems and find new solutions. It is a means to the advancement of any subject/discipline, Library and Information Science (LIS) being no exception.

GENESIS OF LIS RESEARCH IN INDIA

The genesis and development of LIS research in India may be traced back to 1924 when Dr. S. R. Ranganathan appeared on the scene. His seminal contributions to various facets of librarianship enriched the discipline and elevated its status from arts to a discipline in science. He was primarily responsible for introducing university level courses in LIS in our country He started undergraduate level courses in LIS for the first time at the University of Madras in 1931. Later in 1937 this course was upgraded to Postgraduate Diploma in LIS. After India attained independence, many universities in the country slowly started introducing LIS courses.

At present there are nearly 100 universities in the country having LIS departments offering BLISc/MLISc courses, and about 50 universities offering MPhil/PhD programmes. The credit of introducing a doctoral programme in LIS for the first time in the country goes to Dr. S.R. Ranganathan. He introduced the programme in 1950 at the University of Delhi. Dr. D.B. Krishna Rao was the first scholar to obtain the PhD degree in LIS from the University of Delhi in 1957 under the guidance of Dr. S.R. Ranganathan. The topic for his research was 'Facet Analysis and Depth Classification of Agriculture'.

For nearly two decades no other university in the country seems to have either introduced a PhD programme or conferred a PhD degree. It was Panjab University, Chandigarh, which turned out the second PhD scholar in India in LIS in 1977.[2] At present about 50 university LIS departments in the country are offering MPhil/PhD Programmes. The exact number of scholars registered for these programmes in the various LIS departments is not readily available. Unfortunately, this is also the case with regard to the number of candidates who have actually obtained MPhil/PhD degrees from different universities in India since 1950.

LIS RESEARCH OUTPUT

It has been estimated by Kumar that between 1950 and 1997 a total of 293 research scholars were awarded doctorates out of which 264 belonged to LIS and the rest 29 to disciplines other than LIS.[3] The maximum number of doctorates were awarded in 1992, the birth centenary year of Dr. S.R. Ranganathan. Varalakshmi[4] estimated that during 1950 to April 1993, Indian universities awarded 186 PhD degrees out of which 180 were submitted in English language and the rest six were in Hindi. Raju has estimated the LIS research output during 1993 to 1997.[5] According to him 87 candidates have obtained PhD degrees during this period : 17 in 1993, 19 in 1994, 23 in 1995, 13 in 1996, and 15 in 1997.

LIS RESEARCH OUTPUT : 1993-1999

To provide uptodate information an attempt has been made to look into the state of LIS research carried out in Indian universities for PhD programme during the past seven years : from 1993 to 1999. The primary source for this exercise is *University News*.[6] All the universities, including deemed universities and institutions of higher learning, send communications about award of research degrees to the qualified candidates, to AIU for publication in the *University News*.

Number of Candidates who obtained Doctoral Degrees

On the basis of the data gathered from *University News* we find that a total of 156 candidates obtained PhD degrees during the past seven years, i.e., between 1993 and 1999. The years-wise break-up is: 17 in 1993, 18 in 1994, 23 in 1995, 13 in 1996, 26 in 1997, 16 in 1998, and 43 in 1999. The annexure indicates the broad topics under which candidates submitted their doctoral theses and also the year-wise break-up. Among several areas of research, 'User studies' occupies the pride of place as a favourite subject area for research. Twenty-five scholars have obtained doctoral degrees on different aspects of user studies. This is followed by 22 theses on information centres/services/ systems/networks, 21 on university libraries, 19 on management and 16 on biobliometrics/citation analysis.

Analysis of Doctoral Theses

The annexure lists the broad topics on which doctoral dissertations were accepted by the Indian universities. It provides year-wise break-up of degrees awarded under each topic. The focus of research under "user studies" includes: attitudes, information seeking behaviour of university teachers, botanists, social scientists, economists, fisheries scientists, women teachers and medical and paramedical professionals. The sub-topics under "university/libraries" include: planning, development, evaluation of services, finance, new educational policy, personnel, organisational structure, collection development, and development of university libraries in Andhra Pradesh, Madhya Pradesh and Punjab. The specific areas under "bibliometrics"include: assessment of agriculture literature output, use pattern of literature in economics and bio-sciences, analysis of literature in social sciences, horticulture literature, analysis of science journals, nuclear science productivity, and analysis of doctoral dissertations. The focus of research under "information storage and retrieval systems" includes: rural information systems, nutrition, health sciences and laser technology. The sub-areas under "management" include: development, services, and impact on the community and public library system in Orissa. The other broad areas under which research work has been carried out include: cataloguing, computerisation, community information, indexing, information management, library legalisation, library history, library profession, library associations, marketing of information, national libraries, reference tools and sources, school libraries, and special libraries.

OBSERVATIONS

During the seven-year period, the largest number (45) of PhD degrees was awarded in 1999. With the exception of computerisation (three scholars) and marketing of information (two scholars), the successful candidates (151) carried out their research work in traditional areas of LIS as listed in the Annexure. The main reason for this trend might be that research can be successfully pursued by selecting easy and amenable topics under traditional areas of LIS. The other reasons might be: (a) non-availability of expertise in the LIS departments to guide the scholars on newly emerging areas such as computer application in LIS and information technology; (b) lack of confidence and enthusiasm on the part of research scholars to select topics under information and communication technologies and computer applications; and (c) lack of infrastructure facilities, resources, and computerised LICs which can be used as laboratories for pursing research. It is hoped that in the coming years, information and communication technology scenario in the LICs will improve, and library schools in the country might provide the necessary impetus to research in the newly emerging areas.

CONCLUSION

In the preceding paras, an attempt has been made to present the state of LIS research in the country during the past seven years based on the data gathered from *University News*.

Research in LIS is slowly but steadily progressing right from 1970s to reach new heights. Thanks to LIS departments in the universities, many young and enthusiastic research scholars and practising young librarians are coming forward to utilise the research fellowships offered by the UGC and pursue research for obtaining doctoral degrees. In addition to UGC, national agencies like ICSSR, ICMR, ICAR, DST, CSIR, ICHR, ICCR and other funding agencies should come forward in a big way to offer scholarships/fellowships/travel grants to accelerate LIS research in the country. The LIS departments in the country should be strengthened with required and qualified faculty to guide the scholars, and with infrastructure facilities like computer laboratories, online search, and e-mail facilities. It is hoped in the twenty-first century and in the context of emerging information society, LIS research in the country will attain new heights.

REFERENCES

1. *Webster's Third New International Dictionary*, Vol. 2, London: Bell, 1964, 1930.
2. Raju, A.A.N., Library and information science research in India In *Academic Libraries: Role in the National Development*, ed. Dorothy Isaac, and others, T.T. Publications, Madras, 1993, p. 16.
3. Kumar, P.S.G., Doctoral studies in library and information science in India: A study, *DESIDOC Bull of Inf. Tech.* 1988, 18, 1, 5-9.
4. Varalakshmi, R.S.R., Library and information science research in India: Subject perspectives. *Library Science*, 1994, 31, 2, 91-109.
5. Raju, A.A.N., A Look into LIS research in India during the past seven years In *Fifty years of library and information science education in India,* ed. A.A.N. Raju and others, Hyderabad, Suchithritha Graphics, 1997, p. 191
6. "Theses of the month", *University News*, 1993-1999, 31-37.

ANNEXURE

Break up of Doctoral Theses in LIS by Subject: 1993-1999

Broad Areas of Research	*1993*	*1994*	*1995*	*1996*	*1997*	*1998*	*1999*	*Total*
Bibliometrics/citation analysis	–	2	2	2	6	–	4	16
Library catalogue	1	2	–	–	–	–	1	4
Computerisation	1	–	1	–	1	–	–	3
Community information	–	–	1	–	–	1	1	3
Indexing	1	–	1	–	–	–	–	2
Inf.centres/services/systems/ networks	–	1	2	3	3	4	9	22
Inf. management	1	–	–	–	–	–	–	1
Inf. storage and retrieval	2	2	3	–	1	–	–	8
Inf. technology	–	–	–	–	–	–	1	1
Library classification	–	–	–	–	–	–	2	2
Library legislation	–	–	–	–	1	–	–	1
Library history	–	1	–	–	–	–	–	1
Lib. profession/association	1	–	1	–	–	–	–	2

(Contd...)

(Contd...)

Broad Areas of Research	*1993*	*1994*	*1995*	*1996*	*1997*	*1998*	*1999*	*Total*
LIS education	–	–	–	–	–	2	–	2
Management	–	–	2	3	5	2	7	19
Marketing of information	–	1	–	–	–	–	1	2
Nartional libraries	–	–	1	–	–	–	1	2
Public libraries	1	2	1	1	2	–	2	5
Ref. tools sources	1	1	–	–	1	–	2	5
School libraries	–	–	–	–	1	–	–	1
Special libraries	2	–	–	1	–	–	2	5
University libraries	3	3	4	–	1	1	9	21
User studies education	3	3	4	3	4	6	23	25
Total	17	18	23	13	26	16	43	156

4

Restructuring Library and Information Science Curriculum

M. Bavakutty and *Muhammed Salih T.K.*

INTRODUCTION

We are passing through an era of change. Library and information science is not an exception to this phenomenon. Various information sources reveal that library and information science education facilities in our country are better compared to those of other developing countries. Dr. S. R. Ranganathan, the father of library science in India, had significantly contributed a lot to spread the library science education in the country. At present most of the universities in the country are imparting education and training in library and information science. But the curriculum followed in many of these universities is not able to meet the present-day manpower needs of libraries and information centres in the country. Library and information centres are one of the prime facilities where computer and related technologies are widely used for their functioning. Nowadays libraries are highly dependent on computers for gathering, storing, processing and retrieving information. Thus the library and information science professionals, capable of meeting the present day challenges of the profession, are in great demand.

FACILITIES FOR LEARNING IT APPLICATIONS IN LIBRARIES

In recent years many of the universities in the country have revised the syllabus of BLISc and MLISc courses to introduce computer applications in libraries and information centres. The Associateship courses run by INSDOC and DRTC give much importance to computer application in libraries. A two-year course conducted by Indian Institute of Science, Bangalore, is also much useful in learning application of computers in libraries. Some of the universities in the country have even started special diploma courses in the IT applications in libraries. Besides, short-term courses are also conducted by many organisations like DRTC, INSDOC, etc., to train professionals in the application of information technology. The UGC through its 'INFLIBNET' programme is conducting practical training in the application of computers both at their headquarters at Ahmedabad and on-site training at university libraries on request. Many of the refresher courses conducted by Academic Staff Colleges for working librarians and teachers of library and information science also concentrate on computer applications in libraries. The professional associations and organisations are also conducting short-term programmes in this subject. Despite such widescale efforts there exists a shortage of professionals who can take up the challenge and implement automation in libraries with confidence. Given this state of affairs we need to understand shortfalls in the IT trained manpower in the country.

CHANGING ROLE OF LIBRARY PROFESSIONALS

The importance and potential of computer and related technologies has not yet been fully understood by many of the professionals. At least, for some people it is a magic box that can do anything and everything that may be logical or illogical, while some others have yet not understood that a computer is of great help to make work speedier and accurate. So to make professionals aware about the potential and limitations of computer there is need for a well-designed curriculum of computer application and its uses in libraries. Different aspects of computers like the internal working of computer, programming languages and operating systems, programming logic, etc., need to be understood by library professionals.

The role performed by librarians in olden days was mere preservation of documents and other reading materials. Later, when provision of information became more popular, librarians were expected to expose this stored knowledge to the users. Different techniques like classification and cataloguing of documents were applied to bring these to the notice of users. Frequent users of libraries generally became familiar with the techniques used in libraries. But in these days of changing information scenario the concept of information gathering is also changing and users are no more bothered about the type of documents or of their arrangement in libraries. What they are interested in is information only, irrespective of its physical form or appearance. Traditional ways of finding information from books and journals are being replaced by searching information from remote computers through internet or other storage media like CD-ROMs, DVDs. To prepare the professionals to work in such an environment we need to change the traditional curriculum being followed in our universities and other educational institutions and we have to tailor it to meet the challenges of present days.

INTERNET AND ITS USES IN LIBRARIES

Internet facilities in libraries help to gather information from anywhere in the world without any geographical barrier. Present-day libraries have started using internet for information gathering and libraries in the coming days will definitely depend more and more on internet for satisfying the information needs of their users. Internet and e-mail facilities increase the communication between libraries and with other organisations. Inter-library loan facilities and other areas of library cooperations can be further improved by the internet facilities. This tendency necessitates the library professionals to learn about networking, internet and various internet connectivity options, etc. Moreover, by hosting the web pages of their own libraries on the internet, library professionals can extend the area of their operations. To exploit the facilities of internet, library professionals themselves need to know more about internet and they need to instruct the library members in the use of internet.

SUGGESTIONS

The following are some suggestions to improve awareness of IT among library and information science students:

a) As computer and communication technologies would be extensively made use of by library and information profession, the curriculum of library and information science should be suitably modified.

b) Computer laboratory facilities in each library and information science department should be provided. The facilities should consist of maximum hardware and software needed in teaching IT to library and information science students.

c) The teachers of library and information science should be given rigorous training in teaching applications of computer and communication technologies in libraries and information centres. Specially designed and practical oriented programmes should be made compulsory for teachers. As and when required, services of resource persons from computer science departments should be sought by library and information science departments.

d) The manpower needs of science and technology libraries are different from that of other libraries. Therefore, adequate special training programs for those working in such libraries should be organised.

e) There is a need for a change in the method of teaching also. The traditional method of devoting more time for classroom teaching should be replaced by a balanced method of classroom teaching, library hours and practical work. Considerable time should be set apart for training the students in computer laboratories to learn various aspects of information storage, processing and retrieval. Students should be given assignments in various aspects of IT.

f) The UGC must provide special grants for setting up advanced computer laboratories, to library and information science departments in various universities.

CONCLUSION

Though some of the institutions in the country are providing excellent training programmes in IT applications, yet there is a greater need of professionals who can work confidently in automated libraries in the country. This situation has come to prevail even as almost all institutions imparting training in library and information science have introduced applications of IT as part of their curricula. It shows that the present curriculum and teaching methods followed in many of the institutions are not capable of meeting the actual requirements of libraries and information centres. The syllabi of the library and information science courses of many of the departments do contain theoretical aspects of IT but there is still lack of practical training. Hence, there is need for a complete overhauling of the already revised curriculum and importance should be given to practical applications of IT in laboratories. No doubt this alone will not help the professionals to keep up with the fast changing technology, therefore, library and information science organisations and associations should conduct continuing education programmes. The teachers of library and information science should realise the fact that they cannot do justice to the students and ultimately to the profession unless they acquire knowledge in information technology and in particular in its practical use in libraries and information centres. The above discussion on IT does not mean that the whole library and information science education needs to be made IT-biased, rather it should be a blend of both conventional concepts of library science and application of information technology. If we do not come to learn the latest trends in technology we will definitely become outdated and will be replaced by professionals from engineering and computer science.

5

Growth and Development of LIS Education in Iran

G.C. Bansal and *Hassan Kiani*

INTRODUCTION

Historically, Iran (Persia) is an ancient country. It has a little more than 2,500 years of civilisation, more than 1,400 years of Islamic culture, and a rich background in education, literature and arts. This Asian country, covering an area of 1,648,000 sq km, is the 16th largest country of the world and has a population of about 60,000,000 which includes 99.5 per cent Muslims.[1]

Until 1979, Iran was a constitutional monarchy headed by "Shah". A prolonged struggle for a popular government culminating in 1978, resulted in the downfall of the Shah, and victory for the Islamic revolution. In February 1979, centuries-old monarchy was replaced by a popular Islamic government.

Ever since then, Iran has had many reforms and developments in different areas including education and higher education. During the last 18 years, a number of schools, colleges, universities and other educational institutions have increased enormously. The number of students at various levels and that of teachers has also risen accordingly. With advances in education, establishment of libraries and consequential need for library education were the natural outcome.

LIBRARY SCIENCE EDUCATION

A peep into the annals of history of Iran would show that it has had rich and well organised libraries even in the distant past. Some of its libraries are famous for their rich collections, especially that of manuscripts relating to religion, medicine, philosophy and arts. But somehow, Iran had no facilities for formal training and education in librarianship on modern lines till 1966. Its libraries, therefore, continued to be organised and administered, by educated people without any formal education in librarianship, according to local needs and procedures for a long time. During the second half of this century, the role of libraries in educational, scientific, industrial and cultural development has been recognised. As such, concerted efforts to reorganise libraries, library systems and library services on modern lines, have been made by the government.

In fact, training for librarianship in Iran preceded the Second World War.

Historically, the growth and development of library and information science education in Iran can be divided into three phases :

i) 1939-1965 : Short term courses and informal library science education;

ii) 1966-1978 : Formal science library education up to the Islamic revolution; and

iii) 1979 to (1997) : Growth and development of library science education after the Islamic revolution.

Short-term Courses and Informal Library Science Education 1939-65

Mohammad Reza Shah, the last King of Pahlavi dynasty, ruled Iran from 1941 to 1978. During this period, under the policy of his government, a number of new universities, colleges, schools and other institutions were established.

When Shah took over the reigns of government in 1941, Iran had only one university, that is, Tehran University, Tehran, established in 1934. In 1962-63, there were seven universities and four institutions of higher education.[2] By 1965 the number of universities and other institutions of higher education grew further. All these institutions required library facilities. Hence, new libraries came into being. The government also established a number of special and public libraries during this period. The development of libraries created the need for trained library staff. Actually, there was no evidence of the existence of even a single trained librarian in Iran till Mohsen Saba who studied librarianship in France, returned home in 1936.[3]

The first training course in librarianship was introduced at the National Library in 1939 just before World War II. After the War, during 1946 to 1965, the academic libraries felt the need for trained library staff. As such, some American and Unesco library experts were invited by the government to give in-service training and to establish short-term courses in librarianship in Iran.[4] These experts, with the help of Iranian educationists who had returned home after receiving education in librarianship abroad, introduced concepts of library science and professional librarianship in the Iranian system of higher education.

Librarians were sponsored to attend these short-term courses, by the Teachers' Training College, Tehran; the Ministry of Education; the University of Tehran; and Ministry of Culture and Arts. About 50 librarians benefited and they returned to their respective libraries after training. However, until the early 1960's, librarianship as a profession was unknown in Iran. Even the idea of setting up a graduate library school was considered unrealistic.[5]

Formal Library Science Education up to the Islamic Revolution 1939-65

After about three decades of activity in short-term courses, a regular degree, 'Master of Library Science', was introduced in 1966 by the oldest university of Iran, i.e., the Tehran University, Tehran. The year 1966, besides being a milestone in the growth and development of library science education in Iran, is also important, because Iranian Library Association (ILA) was also founded during this year.

The planners, organisers, and teachers of the first formal course, i.e., MLS, were two Americans : Alice Lohrer and Margaret Hopkins. These library scientists, being capable architects and teachers associated with the first course in library science, had to face many problems in terms of the shortage of teachers, teaching materials, other infrastructural facilities and that of the language.

Somehow, though the first graduate programme was introduced in 1966, yet informal programmes in librarianship did not stop. These were continued by the government organisations like : Ministry of Education, Ministry of Culture and Arts; Tehran Book Processing Center (TEBROC); Institute for the Intellectual Development of Children and Young Adults; Iranian Library Association and by some universities.

The University of Tabriz, Tabriz (in the north-west of Iran), was the first university to have introduced BLS degree in 1968. This is a post-high school programme of four years duration. Prof. P.B. Mangla of the University of Delhi, Delhi (India), was invited by the Tabriz University to establish this course. The university introduced MLS programme after two years, in 1970. Hence, Tabriz was the second university in the country to introduce MLS programme and the first to start BLS degree. MLS programme was discontinued in 1973, after training only seven librarians.

Following the University of Tabriz, Iran-Zamin College, Tehran established a post-diploma course (2 years duration) in library science in the year 1969. After four years, i.e., in 1973-74, the course was replaced by a regular BLS degree. Hence, Iran-Zamin College, Tehran, was the second institution in Iran to introduce BLS course after Tabriz University.

Between 1969 and 1978, three universities followed the universities of Tehran and Tabriz in introducing MLS course. These were : Pahlavi University, Shiraz (1974), Jundi Shapur University, Ahwaz (1977), and Farah Pahlavi University, Tehran (1978).

An important fact that needs mention is that academic staff for the establishment and development of library schools in Iran came from USA, India and Pakistan. A distinct feature of Iranian library science education is the development of medical librarianship as a specialised branch. Even in the absence of a regular training course in the field of medical librarianship, health science libraries were managed reasonably well in Iran for a long time.

This is evident from a report by the World Health Organisation (WHO), "in 1975, Iran's support to health science libraries was better than that of many other countries in Middle East, except Saudi Arabia".[6] However, this does not mean that the need for well qualified professional manpower to manage the medical libraries in Iran was not felt. In fact, in the 1970s the need for well trained and qualified medical librarians was realised fully, and to provide for this need, the Imperial Medical Centre, Tehran, introduced the MLS course in the field of medical librarianship in 1978. It was of two years duration. Therefore, at the end of the Shah's regime (1978) in Iran there were six library schools which offered library science education at two levels : BLS, of four years duration after high school diploma; and MLS, two years duration after a bachelor's degree. In addition to these, one specialised MLS course, exclusively devoted to medical librarianship, also existed.

At this time, Farah Pahlavi University, Tehran had the lowest number of teachers, i.e., four only. It should be noted that out of seven library schools, four were established between 1974 and 1978. As such, they had not been able to produce many professional librarians before the Iranian revolution.

Therefore, the number of librarians that had been produced by all the schools of library science put together, was not at all enough to meet the increasing demand for such manpower at that time.

Growth of Library Science Education after the Islamic Revolution 1979-1997

After the Islamic revolution, a popular government was established in Iran in February 1979. This marked the beginning of a new era in all spheres of life. In the field of education also, a reformatory revolution was brought about by the new government. The concerned authorities in the government tried to reorganise library science education to the best of their ability under the given conditions. But most government officials apparently saw little need for the modern information services in the public education, research and ministry sectors.[7] Under pressure of these circumstances, the University of Az-zahra, Tehran, discontinued MLS programme in 1978-79. In 1980, all institutions of higher education, including universities, were closed for a period of about three years. During this period, all courses, rules, procedures and total functioning of these institutions were reviewed with a view to reorganise them to serve the society in the changed conditions. The obvious effort was to bring all these institutions under the umbrella of Islamic culture and religious rules. Names of a large number of institutions were changed, some curricula were restructured to make reforms in education. Teachers, students and employees were suggested to adhere to Islamic dress and behaviour, as far as possible.

After suspense of three years, in 1983, library science education restarted and a new Associate Diploma programme was introduced. During this period, a large number of foreign teachers had left the country and some faculty members, especially old and conservative, were allowed to retire. These reforms were popularly known as "Cultural Revolution" and were done by a new established educational body named "Committee of Cultural Revolution" (founded in 1980). During this period the government also decided to establish new universities, colleges, other institutions of higher education and to strengthen the existing ones.

Post-revolution period in Iran was a period of high expectations, strong desires, rapid all around development, paucity of funds and, therefore, an era of great stress and strain. All these factors influenced the field of library science education also. After the exit of foreign teachers, faculty was available in lesser strength. More institutions wanted to introduce library science education. Funds, reading materials, space, and all other infrastructural facilities required were scarce. Evidently, there was enhanced and varied demand, and resources were squeezed.

Later, the 'Committee of Cultural Revolution' had permitted library schools to introduce a new course named "Associate Diploma" in 1983.[8] It was of two years duration after high school. This diploma was supposed to replace the old BLS course run by universities so far. Such schools that had switched over to "Associate Diploma" from BLS course had a difficult time in absorbing these sweeping changes. On the other hand, students who passed this diploma had unfavourable reaction to the substitution of BLS by Associate Diploma, because it caused hindrance in their further studies. The minimum qualification for admission to MLS was BLS. This was abolished and after passing Associate Diploma students could not join MLS and enjoy the benefit of it. The teachers of library science who had been teaching BLS students earlier, shared the feelings and difficulties of the students of Associate Diploma and were not happy to teach at the diploma level. The situation continued till 1989, whereafter these library schools were permitted to revert to BLS course.

However, four new universities which did not have library schools earlier, established LIS schools between 1994 and 1995. On account of non-availability of qualified faculty to teach at higher levels, the schools introduced Associate Diploma.

As a whole, during the last 18 years (1979-1997) the number of departments of library science schools has increased from seven in 1978 to 23 in 1997. But, unfortunately, a majority of the pre-revolution weaknesses and limitations such as limited funds, paucity of qualified faculty, inadequacy of latest reading materials (especially in Persian language), and dearth of other physical facilities continued. The position as of today has been given in Table 1.

From the foregoing narration, it is clear that today there are 23 higher education centres in Iran, conducting the LIS programmes. Of these, 22 are supported by government funds. Only one university, namely, Islamic Azad University, Tehran, is a private university, because it does not depend on government funds. Seven offer Associate Diploma, whereas only one university has facilities for the three courses, i.e., BLS, MLS and PhD degrees. Five universities offer both BLS and MLS courses only. One university has facilities for MLS course only. Nine universities have facilities for BLS programme only.

As far as selection of students, admission requirements and procedures, duration of courses, curriculum, course contents and methods of examination and evaluation are concerned, a uniform pattern is followed by all the 22 government-supported universities. However, various universities are allowed to follow different methods of teaching and practical training. They also differ with regard to other infrastructure and other facilities available with them. The Library Science Committee, an organ of the High Council of Educational Planning in Humanities, is responsible for overseeing the maintenance of uniformity in these universities with regard to the aspects mentioned above. The committee consists of professionals and some officials of the Council. The Council is a part of the Ministry of Culture and Higher Education.

LEVELS, ADMISSION, DURATION, AND OBJECTIVES

There are four levels of education in library science in Iranian

Table1: List of LIS Schools in Iran

S. No.	University	City	Year of establishment of LIS Deptt.	Year of establishment of Courses/Programmes			
				Ass. Di.	BLS	MLS	Ph.D
1.	Tehran University	Tehran	1966	1983-89*	1974-78	1966	—
			1989-				
2.	Tabriz University	Tabriz	1968	1983-89*	1968-80	1970-73*	—
		1989-					
3.	Shiraz University	Shiraz	1974	1983-89*	1987-	1974	—
4.	Shaheed Chamran University	Ahwaz	1978	1983-89*	1989-	1977-79	—
			1966-				
5.	Medical Sc. University of Iran	Tehran	1978	—	1991	1978	—
6.	Az-zahra University	Tehran	1978	1983-89*	1990-	1978-79*	—
7.	Ferdowsi University	Mashhad	1985	1985-89*	1992-	1997-	—
8.	Isfahan University	Isfahan	1986	1986-89*	1994-	—	—
9.	Islamic Azad University	Tehran	1987	—	1987-	1990-	1992
10.	Tarbiat-e-Moddares Univ.	Tehran	1988	—	—	1988	—
11.	Allameh Tabatabai Univ.	Tehran	1990	—	1990-	—	—
12.	Shahed University	Tehran	1990	—	1990-	—	—

(Contd...)

(Contd...)

S. No.	University	City	Year of establishment of LIS Deptt.	Year of establishment of Courses/Programmes			
				Ass. Di.	BLS	MLS	Ph.D
13.	Higher Education Library Science (National Library)	Tehran	1991	—	1991	—	—
14.	Shaheed Bahonar Medical Science University	Kerman	1992	—	1992	—	—
15.	Isfahan Medical Science University	Isfahan	1993	—	1992	—	—
16.	Birjand University	Birjand	1994	1994	—	—	—
17.	Yazd University	Yazd	1994	1994-	—	—	—
18.	Tabriz Medical Sciecne University	Tabriz	1995	—	1995	—	—
19.	Tarbiat-e-Moallem University	Tehran	1995	1995-	—	—	—
20.	Khalij Fars University	Booshehr	1995	1995	—	—	—
21.	Shaheed Bahonar Univ.	Kerman	1997	1997	—	—	—
22.	Bool Ali Sina University	Hamadn	1997	1997	—	—	—
23.	Razi University	Kermanshah	1997	1997	—	—	—
		Total		7	15	7	1

* = Discontinued

universities. There are : Associates Diploma (Ass. Dip.), Bachelor of Library Science (BLS), Master of Library Science (MLS) and PhD.

A candidate desirous of joining Associate Diploma must have passed high school diploma. Students are admitted to the BLS course from two concurrent streams, consisting of candidates who have qualified Associate Diploma in Library Science (two years duration), and fresh candidates who have passed high school diploma only. Candidates in the first steam spend two years to complete BLS course, while candidates from the second stream spend four years to get the same degree. Candidates from both the streams are treated on par and become graduates in library science.

It would be very relevant to state here that in Iran, to earn a Bachelor's Degree in Science, Arts, Humanities or Commerce, a candidate has to spend four years after high school diploma. Candidates who qualify for BLS also spend four years after high school diploma. As such, these graduates in library science are treated on par with graduates in Arts, Science, Humanities, Commerce, etc., for all academic and employment purposes.

The minimum qualifications for admission to MLS course is Bachelor of Arts or Humanities or Science or Commerce or Library Science. Candidates from all these streams are treated alike. Such candidates who have passed BLS do not get any concession or preference either for admission or in the completion of MLS course in any manner.

For admission to Associate Diploma candidates are considered on the basis of their performance in the National Entrance Test only, irrespective of their performance at the high school diploma level. Similarly for admission to BLS course, candidates are considered on the basis of their performance in the National Entrance Test only and no advantage is allowed for their performance at the high school diploma or Associate Diploma level.

However, two separate National Entrance Tests are conducted for admission to BLS course: one for the candidates holding high school diploma only, and the other for the candidates holding Associate Diploma (LIS). Each school has reserved separate number of seats for candidates from each of the two streams. Candidates are admitted on the basis of relative merit in the respective streams for the seats reserved for them.

For admission to the MLS course, only such candidates are allowed to sit in the National Entrance Test who have scored at least 3 points in scale of 4 points at the BLS or Bachelor level in any subject. Since two separate National Entrance Test are held for admission to BLS courses, the course prescribed for these tests vary. The course for the candidates holding high school diploma only does not include topics of library science whereas, course for the candidates holding Ass. Dip. (LIS), includes topics of library science as well.

The course prescribed for National Entrance Test for admission to MLS is uniform for the candidates holding BA; BSc or BCom or BLS degree. In the entrance test, for admission to BLS or MLS, besides topics in library science, candidates are tested for proficiency in English language, general knowledge, reasoning, logic, etc. The summary of the admission requirements and duration for all of the LIS programmes is tabulated as Appendix 1.

Efforts to Establish Doctoral Programme at Government Universities

In January 1990, the Faculty of Education in the University of Tehran, which sponsors the Library Department, agreed to a proposal for the establishment of a doctoral course, and requested the library science department to draw up an appropriate educational programme. The department prepared a programme accordingly. Later, the doctoral programme was approved by the Educational Deputy of the university. In 1993, it was sent to the Ministry of Culture and Higher Education for Accreditation by the 'Committee of Librarianship'. The committee pointed out that the establishment of doctoral course in librarianship would run into major problems on account of the lack of qualified academic staff to teach the programme, as well as non-availability of textbooks and computer facilities.[9] Thus the proposal was rejected in 1994, by the High Council Educational Planning. Secondly, the course needed at least two full-time associate professors which the Department of Library Science did not have at that time.[10]

Currently, the University of Tehran has qualified teaching staff, including two full time associate professors, and fresh efforts are being made to organise the doctoral course in librarianship at this university. The Shiraz University, Shiraz, and University of Ferdowsi, Mashhad, also have the necessary facilities now. These universities are also in the process of seeking accreditation for this course.

TEACHING STAFF

The authors have recently conducted a survey of the library science schools in Iran by circulating a questionnaire. It has been discovered that about 80 per cent of library science schools in Iran have full time faculty and heads, whereas the remaining, 20 per cent are functioning with part-time faculty only. Most of these departments have been established after 1994.

The total number of teachers in library science in Iran, in all the universities, is about 110. Of these about 85 per cent are full-time teachers. The faculty in Iran is divided into four cadres, viz., lecturer, assistant professor, associate professor and professor. A majority of the teachers in Iran (about 73.5%) are lecturers, 15 per cent are assistant professors, 6.5 per cent are associate professors. There is only one professor (Dr. M.H. Dayyani) in this field at Ferdowsi University, Mashhad (1%) whereas, about 4 per cent are librarians.

Tehran, the capital of Iran, has the largest number of departments in the country. There are as many as nine departments in this city alone. Hence, about 51 per cent of the total number of teachers in this field are stationed in Tehran.

The concentration of schools and teachers of library science in Tehran has created an imbalance in the country in this field. As a result, qualified and experienced teachers are not readily available outside Tehran. Consequently, education in this field in general and short term training programmes in particular have been suffering in the other parts of the country. Schools outside Tehran are scattered all over the country, but the number of qualified teachers and other facilities are not much and as good as are available in Tehran.

Evidently, satisfactory facilities for research, leading to PhD degree are, not available in Iran. However, about 18 per cent of the teachers have managed to earn research degrees from abroad especially USA, UK and Australia. Recently, i.e., during the last three years, some of the teachers, holding MLS degree, have been allowed to continue their education leading to PhD degree. A number of such teachers have gone to India for the purpose, most of them under the cultural exchange programme. These facts have been presented in Table 2.

Table 2 : LIS Teachers in Iran

Country-wide	*Total No.*	*%*	*Status*										*Education*			
			Lecturer	*%*	*Asstt. Prof.*	*%*	*Assoc. Prof.*	*%*	*Prof.*	*%*	*Librarian*	*%*	*MIS*	*%*	*PhD*	*%*
Tehran	54	51	41	38.6	8	7.5	5	4.7	–		–	–	43	41	11	10
Others	52	49	37	34.9	8	7.5	2	1.8	1	1	4	4	41	39	11	10
Total	106	100	78	73.5	16	15	7	6.5	1	1	4	4	84	80	22	20

Pay Scale for the LIS Teaching Staff

In Iran, the pay scales for any profession depend on various factors such as geographical location (e.g., climatic conditions;

social services, and the distance from the capital). Generally, the pay scale for the LIS teachers working in the provinces far away from Tehran (provinces) is comparatively higher than the pay scale of teachers in Tehran

According to the service years in universities, the approximate minimum and maximum pay scales for LIS teachers in Tehran have been tabulated in Table 3.

Table 3: LIS Teachers' Pay Scale in Tehran (The Capital)

Status	*Minimum per month Iranian currency (Toman)**	*US$*	*Maximum per month Iranian currency (Toman)**	*US$*
Lecturer	65,000	371	1,10,000	629
Assistant Professor	85,000	486	1,40,000	800
Associate Professor	95,000	543	1,60,000	914
Professor	1,20,000	686	1,85,000	1057

* The official banking rates fixed at Tomans 175 per US$

CURRICULUM

The current curriculum for LIS programmes conducted by the Iranian universities is largely based on recommendations of the specialised Committee of Librarianship, which was approved by the High Council of Educational Planning (HCEP), in 1995.

The curriculum approved by the HCEP is based on a national scheme. The core LIS papers which are in vogue for all of the LIS departments in Iran have been listed for Ass. Dip., BLS, MLS, and PhD courses separately in Appendix 2

CONCLUSION AND SUGGESTIONS

From the description given above, a few characteristics emerge predominantly. The system of education in Iran is uniform at the national level inasmuch as admission requirements, methods of admission, duration of courses, syllabi, methods of teaching and evaluation are concerned. In other countries, generally, each university is independent on deciding these matters, especially the syllabi and methods of evaluation. But in Iran everything is decided at the national level by the government, and universities are bound to follow these decisions. This a special characteristic.

To ensure uniformity is the duty of the 'Special Committee of Librarianship'. Education in librarianship is not very old and has received better attention after the Islamic Revolution. Most of the students who join library science courses come from the humanities stream (arts, human sciences, economics, etc.) There is scarcity of qualified teachers (PhD holders) and the existing facilities for research are not satisfactory (plans, budgets, motivation). Resources (books, journals, audio-visuals, etc.) are meagre in many ways.

To improve the existing conditions, systematic, planned and phased efforts are necessary. Schools of library science should be allowed more freedom with regard to developing their own syllabi and in the choice of methods of admission, teaching and evaluation. To achieve better results with limited resources, specified number of institutions, duly identified, should be asked to specialise in certain areas of library science or various types of services.

More schools should be established in other parts of the country. Efforts should be made to attract students from other streams like science, commerce, etc., by providing improved service conditions to the professionals. More facilities for research and continuing education should be made available to the teachers. Better conditions of service should be considered for attracting teachers to work in other parts of the country.

REFERENCES

1. Statistical Centre of Iran. Salnameh Amari Keshwar, 1375-76, *Iran Statistical Year Book,* 1996-97, Tehran, 1998, p.35.
2. Country education profiles, *Iran : A comparative study*, Canberra, Australian Government Publishing Services, 1992.
3. Saidi, Farkhondeh, Education for librarianship in Iran : Some factors affecting its development (Ph.D Thesis). Ohio : Case Western Reserve University, 1977.
4. Hayati, Zouhayr, An examination of aspects of the history of librarianship and library education in Iran (Ph.D Thesis). Sydney : University of New South Wales, 1998.
5. Garvey, M.V., *Library Journal Iranian Libraries*, 1953, 9;775.
6. Harvey, John F. Iran. In Jackson, Miles, *International handbook of contemporary developments in librarianship.* : Green Wood Press, Westport, 1981.
7. Harvey, John F., Iranian Information Education. *Journal of Education for Library and Information Science,* 1989, 3; 194.
8. Hayati, Zouhayr..., 1966: p.347.
9. *Ibid.*, p. 308.
10. *Ibid.*, p. 310.

APPENDIX 1

Summary of Admission Requirements and Durations

S. No	*LIS Programme*	*Objectives*	*Minimum Duration*	*Requirements to Complete the Course*	*Placement*
1.	Associate Diploma (Ass. Dip.)	To prepare technicians (para-professional librarians) for small libraries	2 Academic years (4 semesters) after high school	Passing 70 credit hours with at least 50% marks	Small public and school libraries, etc.
2.	Bachelor of Library Science (BLS)	To prepare professionals for large academic, public or special libraries	4 Academic years (8 semesters) for freshers, after high school 2 academic years for Ass. Dip. holders in Lib. Sc.	Passing 134-136 credit hours with at least 50% marks	Large academic, public and special libraries
3.	Master of Library Science (MLS)	To prepare professionals to hold the highest position in all types of libs. & in lib. science education	2 Academic years (4 semesters) for graduates in Arts, Sciences, Commerce or Lib. Sc.	Passing 32-34 credit hours with at least 50% marks and a compulsory dissertation	Middle and top managers and professors
4.	Ph.D	To produce academic staff for library school, for education and research	3 Academic years (6 semesters) after MLS	Passing of 26 credit hours, with at least 50% marks, thesis, and viva-voce test.	Teaching in LIS education, research

APPENDIX 2

LIS Curriculum of Different Programmes

1. Associate Diploma in Library Science (ASS. DIP.)

An introduction to libraries and librarianship; cataloguing and classification (part I & II); reference materials (part I and II); collection building; public services for children's and young adults' libraries; library materials and services for newly literate adults; audio visual materials; typewriting; and internship.

2. Bachelor in Library Science (BLS)

Acquisition; cataloguing and classification; reference materials; library building and equipment; audio-visual materials; and services for newly literate adults; materials and services for children and young adults; typewriting; internship; introduction to libraries and librarianship; library management; report writing; kinds of libraries; archives materials; databases, computers and programming; printing and publishing industry.

3. Master in Library Science (MLS)

Foundation of library science; general management; research methods; cataloguing and classification, collection building, reference materials; library management; information technology and retrieval systems; periodicals; internship; and dissertation (compulsory).

4. PhD in Library Science

Research method; research seminar; comparative literature for children; communications; comparative librarianship; bibliographic control system; manuscripts; information science system, classification systems; books and periodicals publishing; progressed statistics for librarianship; introductory course in computers; and thesis (compulsory).

6

Evaluation of LIS Education through Distance Education Mode

R.K. Bhatt and *Narender Kumar*

INTRODUCTION

Higher education in India after independence has expanded enormously. About 44,27,000 students were studying in universities and colleges during 1990-91[1] in about 147 universities and 7,126 colleges. In 1997-98 the number of universities in India swelled to 229.[2] It is estimated that there are over 250 universities and over 9,000 colleges in the country at present.

In spite of such a tremendous growth in the number of higher education institutions in the country the state of higher education in the country is still not healthy as access to higher education in the country is restricted only to 6 per cent of the people in the age group of 18 to 23,[3] and India being a developing country it cannot afford to restrict the access to higher education to such a low percentage of the people in the country. The vexing issue is that if greater access is to be provided, how can this be done? Of course, the answer lies in distance education system which has proved to be a powerful instrument to achieve laudable result.

Today, distance education has found a strong foothold on the educational scene in India and can boast of a fairly strong distance education system in the world. About 14 per cent of the students enrolled in higher education are studying through distance mode.[4] The distance education system is emerging as an important mode of education for all those who, for a variety of reasons, cannot go through the conventional system of education. Even for those who want to go to the conventional system of education, but cannot find a place in the system, distance education is of great help.

Distance education has certainly played a key role in extending the traditional as well as professional education not only in India but also in several other countries of the world like. As far as India is concerned, around 69 universities have already started to offer various professional courses under the distance or correspondence system of education. Some of the courses being conducted by various universities/institutions through distance education system are: Public Relations and Advertising, Journalism, Education, Management, Office Organisation & Procedures, Tourism and Hotel Management, Computer Applications, Language Teaching, Automobile Engineering, Rural Development, Food and Nutrition, etc. Perhaps, drawing motivation from such like efforts and the need to fill the increasing demands of library and information centres for qualified librarians and information specialists, the experts in the field in the country initiated library and information science education through the distance education mode. As a result there are 25 institutions which are conducting LIS courses at different levels in the country. These have been given in the Annexure.

OBJECTIVES OF LIS EDUCATION THROUGH DISTANCE TEACHING

a) To meet the increasing demand of qualified workforce;

b) To make available educational facilities to the rural and remote areas;

c) To provide an opportunity to the working library and information personnel to acquire formal qualifications;

d) To improve professional competence among working non-professional library staff;
e) To make the library and information science teaching and learning process more cost-effective;
f) To provide an opportunity to the people who desire to learn and earn simultaneously;
g) To provide an opportunity to those who could not find entry in formal stream due to various factors; and
h) To provide an opportunity for career development to the working librarians and information personnel.

EXISTING PROBLEMS

There are a number of problems which come in the way of imparting professional education through distance learning and education. Some of them are:

a) Contact classes are conducted at far-off places which create considerable hardship to those attending such contact programmes;
b) Library facilities which are a prerequisite for such a programme are quite inadequate;
c) Duration of contact programme is insufficient to cover the contents of the courses by the resource persons or counsellors invited to perform the job;
d) The medium of instruction of the courses is usually English which many a times creates problems of comprehension for the students;
e) Professional courses need more emphasis on practical training without which they fail to develop adequate skills needed for shouldering the professional responsibilities and duties assigned to them by their organisations;
f) Delayed delivery of study materials and response sheets;

g) There are problems of coordination between the university offering the course and the centres acting as the coordinating centres to the course. Also there is lack of coordination among various universities offering such like programmes; and

h) Study tours which provide lot of exposure to the students studying in LIS courses through regular stream, are not available in LIS courses imparted through distance education programmes.

NEED FOR EVALUATION BENCHMARKS

It is evident from the list of universities/institutions offering library and information science education in India that the country has made an impressive progress in imparting LIS education through distance education programmes. But the question now is how to make it effective and efficient. Therefore, assessing the impact of training programmes of LIS through distance education is necessary to:

a) Examine the fitness for the purpose;
b) Determine the value for money;
c) Get feedback to improve the programmes; and
d) Ensure quality of the system.

Some of the benchmarks suggested for evaluation of the training programme are:

1. The goals and sub-goals of the training programmes. For this we may use the following checklist:.
   a) Are the goals clear and specific ?
   b) Are they relevant ?
   c) Are they attainable ?
2. The background materials or the study materials. For this we may use the following checklist :

a) Are the materials relevant ?
b) Are the materials sufficient ?
c) Do they generate any self-learning activities ?
d) Do they generate intellectual curiosity ?

3. The target group. The following checklist is suggested
   a) Is the programme a felt-need of the participants?
   b) Is the programme integrated with the career development of participants?
   c) Are the participants sufficiently motivated to learn?
4. Methods of training. For this we may use the following checklist:
   a) Are the methods appropriate for participatory learning/ experience-sharing?
   b) Are the methods appropriate for achieving the goals of the programme?
   c) Are multimedia support materials used in the programmes?
   d) How far are the distance mode and face-to-face mode integrated?
   e) To what extent are new technologies used?
   f) How far is the design of the programme linked to its objectives?
   g) How far is the content related to the goals?
   h) Are the trainers competent?
   i) How far are the administrative arrangements made for training appropriate?
   j) To what extent are the conditions conducive to learning?
   k) What are the opportunities for associational learning?
5. Feedback on training programmes. For this we may use the following checklist:
   a) What are the responses of participants to the programmes?

b) What are the perceptions of the heads of the institutions about the impact of training on the trainees working in their institutions?
c) What are the impressions of resource persons?
d) What is the assessment of organisers about the programme?

The above check points will certainly help the LIS programme organisers of distance education to have a critical assessment and appreciation of the process of training in LIS and in learning how to maintain the quality of education through this mode. In addition to the above checklist, we need to take several measures to make full use of this mode of education. Some of them are:

a) There should be no compromise on the quality of the materials produced by distance education institutions. Many times many universities offering LIS education through distance education are found to be producing substandard reading materials. This is extremely dangerous because the students who depend on it would be the biggest sufferers. However, there are a few universities which are alert and careful in preparing a very high standard course material. Among them IGNOU certainly deserves the words of appreciation. Similarly, the television programmes broadcast by this university also help the students both from conventional as well as distance education systems;
b) Timely delivery of study material should be ensured so that students before they come to attend contact programmes at their respective centres have an opportunity to go through the contents of the courses being taught to them;
c) Both teachers of library and information science as well as practising librarians should be involved for counselling;
d) Existing frequency and duration of personal contact programmes should be increased;

e) Modern trends and traits of library and information science should be incorporated in the prescribed syllabi; and

f) The conventional as well as the distance education systems need to be brought together and the country has to take an integrated view of the total system of education.

CONCLUSION

The New Education Policy (NEP) emphasizes that people living in remote and rural areas who are not able to have formal qualifications due to various unavoidable reasons should be provided an opportunity to learn and earn formal qualifications through distance education facilities. Library and information science education is not an exception to this. However, the quality of distance education should be one of major and central concerns of the system. The staff competencies have to be built to ensure the effectiveness of the system.[5] We must also ensure adequate organisational and social environment for the success of distance education system in the country including the LIS education failing which the sound base of such a system cannot be established and the sole objective of the open learning and open education will be defeated.

REFERENCES

1. *Economic Intelligence Science. Basic Statistics. India,* August 1994, Table 2.4 and 2.6
2. Ibid.
3. Reddy, G.Ram, Distance Education in India. *University News*, 1995, 33, 12, 15.
4. Ibid.
5. Jennifer O' Rourke, *Roles and competencies in distance education*, The Commonwealth of Learning, Vancouver, Canada, 1993.

ANNEXURE

Institutions Conducting LIS Education through Distance Education in India

i) Directorate of Distance Education, Alagappa University, Karaikudi-623003.

ii) Directorate of Distance Education, Annamalai University, Annamalainagar-608002.

iii) School of Correspondence Courses and Distance Education, Awadhesh Pratap Singh University, Rewa-486003.

(Institute of Open and Distance Learning), Barkatullah Vishwavidalaya, Bhopal-462026.

(Centre for Distance Education), Bharathidasan University, Tiruchirapalli-620024.

iv) School of Distance Education, Calicut University, P.O. Calicut-673635.

v) Dr. Babasaheb Ambedkar Open University, Govt. Bungalow No. 9, Dafnala, Sahni Marg, Ahmedabad-380003.

vi) Dr. B.R. Ambedkar Open University, Road No. 26, Jubilee Hills, Hyderabad-500033.

vii) Institute of Distance Education, Guru Ghasidas University, Bilaspur-110068.

viii) Centre for Distance Education, University of Hyderabad, Central University PO, Hyderabad-500046 (AP).

ix) Indira Gandhi National Open University, Maidan Garhi, New Delhi-110068.

x) Department of Library Science, Shri Onkarmal Somani College of Commerce, Jai Narayan Vyas University, Jodhpur-342003.

xi) School of Distance Learning and Continuing Education, Kakatiya University, Warangal-306009.

xii) Department of Distance Education, University of Kashmir, Waseem Bagh Campus, Srinagar, 190006.

xiii) Kota Open University, Rawat Bhata Road, Akhelgarh, Kota, 324010.

xiv) Department of Distance Education, Kurukshetra University, Kurukshetra-132119.

xv) Institute of Correspondence Education, University of Madras Chepauk, Madras-600005.

xvi) Directorate of Distance Education, Madurai Kamraj University, University Buildings, Palkalainagar, Madurai-625021.

xvii) Institute of Distance Learning and Continuing Education, Mahatma Gandhi Gramodya, Vishwavidayalaya, Chitrakoot, Distt. Satna-485331.

xviii) Directorate of Distance Education, Maharishi Dayanand University Rohtak (Haryana)-124001.

xix) Nalanda Open University, Campus office 9, Adarsh Colony, Kidwai Puri, Patna-800001.

xx) Directorate of Distance Education, Patna University, Patna-800005.

xxi) Department of Correspondence Courses, Punjabi University, Patiala-147002.

xxii) Directorate of Distance Education, Sri Venkateswara University, Tirupati-175002.

xxiii) Yashwantrao Chavan Maharashtra Open University, Onyangangotri, Near Gangapur Dam, Nashik-422005.

7

Need for IT Skills for Library Professionals

P. Soma Raju

INTRODUCTION

Library being a service organisation has the obligation to give information service and support, on demand as well as in anticipation. In order to meet these obligations the library has to undertake tasks in library operations such as selection, analysis, consolidation, and storage of documentary resources, and retrieving from this resource the required information. Given the profound processing power they possess, computers are more amendable to performing these tasks. Computer handling is indeed much better than handling them manually. Over and above, information technology has added another dimension to information processing and retrieval. It permits access to library resources at a distance, overcoming thereby the barriers of time and distance.

Thus the modern information technology has offered the library profession a unique tool for seeking universal access to information. The new tool enables us to interact with anybody, anywhere in the globe, seek access to any number of databases on the web, browse any piece of information, and download information from the web on a PC for use. It is like churning the ocean of knowledge to obtain relevant piece of information, much like the way we retrieve gems and jewels from the ocean bed. The impact of ongoing developments in the information technology has been far reaching. It has reduced the world to a global village. One can afford to have access to any piece of information from anywhere and at any time. Information scientists have before them a great opportunity to improve access. The challenge lies in harnessing and assimilating information technology for the purpose.

NEED FOR INFORMATION TECHNOLOGY SKILLS

Besides gaining professional knowledge in library and information science, the professional needs to acquire the knowledge and skills in information technology for library applications. They need IT knowledge both at practical and theoretical level. The purpose is to make the professionals competent and efficient in the management of information.

In particular, the need is to better equip them with IT tools so that they could handle their tasks such as follows more effectively:

a) Jobs related to library operations;
b) Optimisation of available resources;
c) Information services to users;
d) Access to information resources of other libraries;
e) Developing new and better strategies for information handling; and
f) Higher productivity in information management.

EDUCATION AND TRAINING IN INFORMATION TECHNOLOGY

It is the responsibility of library schools to prepare and produce competent manpower in information technology applications. The library schools all over the country should, therefore, include information technology in their course curriculum as one of the core subjects for education and training. The emphasis in IT education should be given on imparting theoretical knowledge, practical experience, hands-on training, etc. The students in the final year should do project work on any topic relating to IT application. This would enable them to gain practical experience in the IT applications. By the time a student comes out of the school after having done his postgraduation course he must become proficient in handling computer-oriented library tasks with confidence.

Imparting IT skills to library professionals can be done at three levels.

a) MLib Sc/PG Course;
b) Working Librarians; and
c) Teachers.

TRAINING WORKING LIBRARIANS AND TEACHERS

For working librarians, practical training in IT is of immense value and use. It enables them to handle their regular jobs in the library more effectively. This in turn is going to benefit the library.

Teaching the trainers, the teachers in the IT subjects, is equally important. This will have catalysing effect since it would help teachers in imparting education and training in IT to hundreds of students. Therefore, while planning training programme in the IT, preference should be accorded to teachers. It would be better if training programmes are planned exclusively for teachers in library schools in various universities.

The NISSAT has been providing financial support and assistance for IT training and education to several organisations such as DRTC, ILA, and IASLIC. In this regard, the efforts made by NISSAT are commendable. Although such training programmes have indeed been useful, yet they failed to focus on certain important areas of interest. The need of the hour is that the following areas be given immediate focus and attention in IT training and education:

a) Creation of databases;
b) Use of internet services;
c) Use of e-mail services;
d) Use of CD-ROM services;
e) Various aspects of networking systems;
f) Use of web-based information sources;
g) Creation of web-pages;
h) Use of databases of local, regional, national, and international;
i) Familiarity with different operational software and protocols; and
j) Familiarity with internet hosts.

CONCLUSION

The degree of IT applications in library and information science is IT skill dependent. The more the training and education in the IT skills, the greater the scope for IT-oriented library infrastructure.

Part III

Information Systems, Techniques and Services

8

Dewey-21 (1996) and the Current Trends

M.P. Satija

INTRODUCTION

The 21st edition of the *Dewey Decimal Classification Scheme* (DDC) was released in July 1996, for the first time, simultaneously, both in traditional print form in four volumes and in CD-ROM form. The latter one is known as *Dewey for Windows* (DfW). Availability of DDC-20 on CD-ROM facilitated and accelerated the publication of the new edition. By now the relationship of IT and DDC has crossed the teething trouble to enter a mature and fruitful era. As with the earlier edition, the editorial work for the DDC-21 was also done on the (Editorial support system) ESS, now a UNIX-based system.

As another innovation, members of the DCEPC now hold electronic meetings via the Dewey list serve on the internet. *DC&* in print form has been discontinued and, instead, is now available on the internet at http://www.oclc. org/fp. The Dewey Home page also includes the OCLC Forest Press Catalogue, Dewey News, and the 'hot' classification topics and internet addresses of online catalogues using Dewey. The text in four columns has been edited by a new editor Joan S. Mithcell, appointed Chief Editor in 1993. She is an expert in information technology.

DDC-21(1996)

Structure of the DDC-21

The DDC-21 has the following bibliographic details :

Dewey, Melvil *Dewey Decimal Classification and Relative Index* devised by Melvil Dewey. Ed. 21 edited by Joan S. Mitchell, Julianne Beall, Winton E. Matthews, Jr. and Gregory R. New. Albany, N.Y. Forest Press a Division of OCLC Online Computer Library Centre, Inc. 1996, 4 Vols. ISBN 0-910568-50-4.

Volume 1	:	Prefatory material, Editor's introduction, Glossary, Tables 1-7 and information on the changes in the new edition.
Volume 2	:	Schedules 000-599
Volume 3	:	Schedules 600-999
Volume 4	:	Relative index, Manual

The four volumes, spread over to 4,126 pages, have been divided into nine sections marked A/I.

User's Convenience

The DDC-21 furthers on all aspects, the line set by the previous 20th edition, with emphasis on user's convenience and modernisation. Entries are clear with copious notes. Editor's introduction is brief and simple with improved captions. Many brief manual like notes are also appended to entries in the schedules. Some new types of notes and theoretical concepts have also been introduced.

Changes in the Schedules

The changes in the DDC-21 are numerous and far reaching in the form of additions, expansions, relocations, deletions, and change of heading and newly added notes. The major new schedules are for :

a) 296 Judaism and 297 Islam

b) 350-354 Public administration

c) 368 Insurance

d) 370 Education

e) 560-570 Life sciences

Some select revisions have been made in 004-006 Data processing, 342-349 branches of laws, 355 military science, 362-363 social problems, 420-490 specific languages, 636 animal husbandry, 790 theatre, 810-890 literatures of specific languages, 940-990 general history of the modern world. As an important change in 370 Education, the schedules of 376 education of women and 377 schools of religions have been made subdivisions of 371 education, whereas distance education has been expanded.

Reduction of Bias

A commendable effort has been to reduce Christian bias in religion by shifting Christian religion from 200 to 220-289. Similarly, US bias has been reduced in wording and structure in 350-354 Public administration. It is a big step towards reduction of western and Christian bias and a commendable move towards internationalisation.

Changes in Tables

Changes in the tables are not less either. Regularisation of standard subdivisions has been carried on bit further. The foremost example is in 370 Education where irregular use of standard subdivision has been replaced by the regular use of TI-07. There has been a regularisation of the use of standard subdivisions at 370.7 and elsewhere in the schedules and related adjustments in T1-071. This brings uniformity and makes the notation mnemonic and faceted. But still more remains to be done, e.g., the inconsistency given below:

a) 340.1 Theories of laws
b) 342.02-09 other standard subdivisions of laws

The area table has many significant changes especially in the area table for 47 Russia, 499 Bulgaria. Area numbers for new nations and other geopolitical changes have been incorporated. There are minor changes in other tables.

Transparent Facet Structure

The completely revised schedules (the new edition also avoids the term phoenix schedule adopted in DDC-16/19) not only incorporate new subjects with details but also provide opportunity to rectify the order of classes and the facet structure to reflect modern thinking in the profession. In the DDC-21 the new schedules have transparent facet structure. It means the DDC is getting more and more faceted. For good or bad the DDC-21 abounds in options in facet formula for local emphasis. For example, in 560-590 life sciences the major taxonomic subdivisions have remained the same, but the order of facets has changed from entity-process to process-entity. Biochemistry from 574.19 has been raised to the status of a section at 572 with ample details and many facets. This is keeping in view the current status of the subject. In 350-354 public administration structure has been improved by reducing US bias. The facet order has been changed from jurisdiction-topic to topic-jurisdiction. There is also an option here to bring together all topics of public administration by area. There are many facet indicators used through many internal tables. Number building has been simplified. For example :

(Public) Administration of Justice in India

353.4 + 09 (T1) + 54 (T2) = 353.40954 (Option A, Vol. 2 p. 601)

or

351 + 54 (T2) + 0 (Facet indicator) + 34 (from 353.4) = 351.54034

It simply means that the topics of public administration can be collocated by country/place or by topic. In public administration the new numbers are not only shorter but also do away with dual provision of the DDC-20, e.g.:

Topic	*Ed 20*	*Ed 21*
Abuse of power	351.991	353.46
	352.002	
Decentralisation	351.0073	352.283
	352.00472	

Relative Index

Relative index now of 895 pages has been increased by 150 pages due to the addition of so many terms and headings. The index includes terms in the headings, and most terms in notes appended with entries in the schedules, and terms in all the seven tables arranged in word-by-word order. Notes in the manual have also been indexed which lead classifiers to relevant discussion. *See also* references have been employed to draw attention to the broader and related terms. It also indicates the place for the interdisciplinary works in the subject. As in DDC-20, *See* references for synonyms terms have not been used. Instead a term has been indexed under all equivalent terms. For example, birds and aves both have been indexed. Under aves *see also* reference leads to birds and all their related aspects.

In DDC-21, in accordance with other subject indexing tools such as *Sears List of Subject Headings*, and the *Library of*

Congress Subject Headings, uninvited, i.e., direct and natural form of phrasal headings have been used. Personal and geographic names have been indexed on AACR-2 specifications. For instance, entry is civil engineering, not engineering, civil; commercial art, not art, commercial. Some synthesised numbers have been restored in the index based on literary warrant. It incorporates more terms to make it more hospitable to non-US users.

Some concepts and terms implied and some terms obtainable through number building but having sufficient literary warrant have also been included in the index. Apart from physiogeographic names and features, countries and their provinces have also been included in the index. The US geographic details are up to the country level. Some historical events, personalities, kings, queens, eras, names of (literary/social/political) movements have also been included in the index. The index of DDC-21 has best of both the two previous indexes, i.e., it has simplicity of DDC-20 and exhaustiveness of DDC-19 indexes. It works smartly.

ABRIDGED DDC-13 (1997)

Abridged edition of DDC-21 has been published as Abridged DDC-13. It was first published in 1894 as an abridged edition with shorter numbers (normally up to two digits beyond the dot) which are easy to remember and can be easily written on the spine of the document for shelving. Besides it is less expensive. In brief it is efficient for a collection up to 20,000 books of a school or public library, and makes a handy tool for teaching DDC. It is also used to assign subject headings in children's libraries.

Abridged 13 comprising a total of 1,026 pages has the following major parts: Prefatory material (pp i-iii), Four tables (pp. 1-57), Schedules (pp. 59-651).

It is a true abridgement of the DDC-21 (1996) which has been printed from a database prepared at the Library of Congress by a computer-assisted Editorial Support System. Abridged 13 subcommittee of ALA Subject Analysis Committee, and (British) Library Association Dewey Decimal Committee have guided the preparation of this edition as they did in the case of DDC-21. Accordingly, it has all the new features of the unabridged DDC-21, namely, revised schedules of 350-354 public administration, 370 education, 570-590 life sciences and new numbers for the countries of the erstwhile Soviet Union among other major revisions. Many notes have been added to provide guidance in the use of standard subdivisions in case of multidisplinary topics. Terminology has been updated to reflect international and current usage; number building instructions have been made explicitly simple. Caption headings have been improved and made more informative. Notes appended to various entries have been simplified and made more comprehensive. Use of standard subdivisions has been regularised to a certain extent. It helps in better decision making. There is a long-term multi-edition plan to reduce Christian bias. The first step has been taken in this edition by shifting the comprehensive number for Christian religion to 230 from 200. In public administration and life sciences the citation order of facets has been reversed to reflect the shift in the current literature of these disciplines. The manual has been expanded, made more explicit and indexed; and there are more references to the manual in the schedules. In brief, the new abridged edition in a single volume provides the small libraries the updated features of the unabridged DDC-21 at a much lower price.

DEWEY FOR WINDOWS (DFW)

The electronic version of DCC-21, named Dewey for Windows (DfW), was released simultaneously with the traditional print version in 1996. It is a Microsoft window-based LAN compatible version of the Electronic Dewey with DDC-21 database. It provides a window interface which is different from the DOS version of DDC-20 (Electronic Dewey, 1993). Search engine in both the cases remains the same. Obviously it requires a microcomputer with windows version 3.10 or higher, a 486-based PC or higher with a minimum of 8 MB memory, colour monitor and CD-ROM drive. The DfW database began as a database in the Editorial Support System (ESS) at the Library of Congress. The ESS format is different from the MARC format, yet there are many similarities between the two. The tapes generated form ESS database are used to produce both the print and CD-ROM format as well as the abridged DDC. DfW is updated between editions by issuing a new CD which incorporates changes announced in DC&, now published only on the internet.

Unlike the print editions, the CD Dewey is not constrained by the physical size and space. The database includes all built numbers from the relative index of the print version and thousands more added to the electronic version. Each readymade number is accompanied by index terms and the nearest matching DDC schedule number with its verbal heading. It includes the segmentation (prime) marks used by the Library of Congress to show either the end of an abridged number or the beginning of a standard subdivision. A convenient work area displays and stores the parts of the Dewey number being built as one moves among the schedules and tables for instructions.

LC subject headings have been added to each class number by statistical matching. These headings provide additional terms for searching. It is an additional help for libraries using LCSH for subject headings, and a source of additional terms for other DfW users. There are some inbuilt readymade numbers. Keyword access is helpful for finding these already inbuilt numbers. Future edition may contain many more such bullet-in numbers. In DfW, movement upward and downward in the hierarchies is possible by highlighting and clicking. For interface it uses single function windows. If a number or term is dragged and dropped into a search window, the search for number or the term will begin. For full record display of a number, including caption notes, relative index entries and associated LCSH headings, the Dewey number is dragged and dropped. If the term is dragged and dropped into an index window set for the relative index the relevant part of the relative index will be displayed looking like that of the printed relative index.

The windows are arranged in a tiled fashion to facilitate dragging and dropping. These are standard as well as customisable views for the user to set. The standard views are:

a) search view-search window and DDC number window;
b) browse view-search window, DDC pages window and DDC number window;
c) scan view-index window, search window, and DDC number window; and
d) summary view-DDC summary window, search window, DDC pages window, and DDC number window.

It also provides facility to customise our own views to the windows to suit one's own approach. The standard views are described in the Dewey for windows reference card. As we use the print version of the DDC in different ways, i.e., either through the schedules or through the index, so are there different ways to use DfW. Mary Mortimer explains that in any view we can :

a) maximise any window to see a larger display;
b) choose display to see appropriate LCSH;
c) choose bibliographic record to see a sample record using the number selected;
d) choose LCSH to review the frequency of headings used with the number;

e) contents of a window may be printed by choosing print;
f) choose notes to make a permanent record of a DDC number and its specific use;
g) choose past to review the searches made during the current session; and
h) use help to understand a term or procedure.

It has an augmented index with natural language terms from other thesauri to provide enhanced access. Some of the important advantages of DfW over the traditional print version are :

a) keyword access to the entire print DDC-21;
b) additional terms for search;
c) hierarchic display;
d) standard and customised view; and
e) dragging and dropping of numbers and terms.

It also remains uptodate without any manual addition from the DC as a new version is issued annually. However, the basic principles and number building techniques are the same. Future electronic versions may provide some built-in expert system for automatic synthesis of numbers whenever required. Many surprising features may be in store in the near future including the one Dewey without notation.

Version 2.00 Features

This version issued in January 2000 has the following improvements:

a) Improved annotation feature is helpful to add as many as 16,000 notes to the schedules; can categorise in four different ways and assign a label and multiple keywords for fast and easy retrieval;

b) enhancement to the Dewey for windows database;

c) Changes as published in *Decimal Classification, Additions, Notes and Decisions*, Vol. 6, Nos. 1-3;

d) Updated area for France, and the Canadian territory of Nunavut and South Africa; and

e) An expanded index, including more than 500 built members and accompanying index terms added for popular topics in literature.

For example compare the entry in the indexes of print edition and the DfWs on computer sciences:

"Computer science" in DDC-21:

Computer science	004
	T1-028 5
	See Manual at 004-006; also at 004-006 vs v 621.39

"computer science" in Dewey for Windows:

The entries above, plus:

Computer science - dictionaries	004.03
Computer science - education	004.071
Computer science - examinations	004.076
Computer science - higher education	004.0711
Computer science - problems	004.076
Computer science - secondary education	004.0712
Computer science - vocational guidance	004.023

As another example Mitchell (2000, p. 85) cites that ecology of tundras indexed as "Tundras - ecology" in print edition has an additional entry as "Tundra ecology" in the DfW.

a) Automatic cuttering, with two options for constructing four-figure cutter numbers.

b) New instructions for use of standard period tables for affiliated literatures.

Any of the following search options can be availed :

a) Relative index words and phrases;
b) captions, words and phrases;
c) LCSH words and phrases;
d) Dewey number; and
e) Basic index of all the fields except LCSH.

FUTURE TRENDS

The next edition, i.e., DDC-22 is likely to be published in 2003. Joan Mitchell (2000, p.84) informs:

> We are investigating major updates in computer science and medicine, continued changes in religion, and other updates as needed. We are exploring ways of simplifying number building in literature, an area in which classifiers are often daunted by the complexity of the instructions. We are also considering the deletion of Table 7 (groups of persons) because most of the notation is already available in Table 1 and in the schedules 001-999.

As evinced by the two previous editions the DDC is moving towards internationalisation by gradually removing White, Anglo-Saxon and Protestant (WASP) bias. Though able to classify in complex situation it is getting simple to operate. Facet structure is becoming transparent with a capability to hold together many facets in a single class number.

Since the acquisition of the Forest Press by the OCLC Online Computer Library Center, Dublin, Ohio, many innovative efforts have been made to create many Dewey products, such as bookmarks, Dewey rap music, AV teaching kit, Guides to the full, abridged and electronic versions of the DDC, and Dewey posters and exclusive publication of three main summaries. OCLC has sponsored pioneering and successful research to study the use of classification in online databases. Most important of all, research is going on to find wider application of the DDC in all sorts of information management. Three summaries of the DDC are already being used to organise information on the internet. For example, a browser based on the DDC has been developed for NetFirst, an OCLC database of source accessible on the internet. Some of the questions currently addressed to the DDC are :

a) How can the classification be made more effective for classifiers?

b) How can a standard English language classification be built that also meets the needs of international users?

c) How to make DDC more effective in OPACs?

d) How can the classification be made more useful for the end users?

e) What can be done to make the Dewey Decimal Classification relevant in the future ?

The DDC is geared to become a powerful and reliable subject access system in the new century.

BIBLIOGRAPHY

Beall Juliane, *Dewey for Windows Guide*. Albany, N.Y., Forest Press/ OCLC, 1998. It is also included in the CD version 2.00 and in Help, and on the Dewey Website <www.gurl.org/ocle/fp>.

Chan Lois Mai and others, *Dewey Decimal Classification: A Practical Guide 2nd revised for DDC-21*. Albany, N.Y., The Forest Press/ OCLC., 1966, pp. 1-24.

Chan, Lois Mai, and Mitchell, Joan S., Eds., *Dewey Decimal Classification Edition 21 and International Perspectives*. Albany, N.Y., Forest Press/OCLC, 1997, pp. 3-42.

Comaromi, John P. and Satija, M.P., *Exercises in the 20th Edition of the Dewey Decimal Classification*. New Delhi : Sterling, 1990, pp. 127 p.

Mitchell, Joan S., "Dewey behind the scenes", *DC&5*, 5, 1994, April : 7-11.

Mitchell, Joan S., "The Dewey Decimal Classification in the twenty first century". In Marcella, Rita and Maltby, Arthur, eds : *The future of classification*. Aldershot, UK, Gopwer, 2000, p. 81-92.

Mortimer, Mary, *Learning Dewey Decimal Classification*, Ed. 21 Canberra, DocMatrix, 1998, pp.87-88

Satija, M.P. and Comaromi, John P., *Exercises in the 21st edition of the Dewey Decimal Classification*, New Delhi, Sterling, 1998.

Satija, M.P., "Abridged DDC-13 and its workbook" *J. Lib & Inf. Sc.* 1998, 232 : 170-173.

9

Indexing and Abstracting Services in Iran

Masumeh Bagheri and ***G.C. Bansal***

INTRODUCTION

In Iran, scientific indexing started in the 1960s. Although some publishers annexed back-of-the-book index to their publications, a few subject indexes were prepared by individuals or some institutions, prior to that also. In fact, the beginning of indexing and abstracting in Iran is contemporaneous with two important events :

i) Foundation of Master of Library Science (MLS) programme, and

ii) Establishment of Iranian Documentations Centre (IRANDOC).

MLS programme in Iran was for the first time introduced in 1966 by the University of Tehran.[1] One of the requirements of graduation was writing of dissertation. Students were acquainted with the concept of indexing during the course. Some of them were allotted dissertation in the field of indexing. As a result, a few dissertations were written on indexing, and some indexes were prepared in particular subjects or for certain periodicals. For example, indexes of articles were prepared for management, geography, political science, history, archeology, etc., and for periodicals, viz., *Negin, Payam-e-Unesco, Payk-e-Javanan*, etc.

IRANDOC was established in 1968.[2] It was supposed to serve as the national documentation center and to perform all such functions that were expected of such a center according to UNISIST recommendations. To achieve its objectives, IRANDOC underIndexing and Abstracting Services in Iran took the following activities:

a) Indexing of dissertations produced by Iranian graduates, and that of government documents.[3]

b) Introducing a quarterly abstracting service in 1969 for science and social science articles published in Iranian periodicals.[4] The first issue carried abstracts of 148 articles. Abstracts were bilingual—Persian and English. Due to the non-availability of sufficient number of experienced staff, the English version was discontinued. After three volumes, the service was split into two parts: (i) Science Abstract and (ii) Social Science Abstract, both appearing independently. The first part stopped publication in 1977 and the second in 1979.[5] Subsequently IRANDOC published several indexes and abstracts in various fields in the form of monographs. A few indexing and abstracting services were also undertaken. Some of them are alive even today.

c) Encouraging and assisting the establishment and development of new documentation centres by way of providing facilities for the training of personnel.

d) With a view to improving the knowledge of documentalists and sharing the experience of IRANDOC with other documentation centres in Iran, in 1972 a quarterly journal entitled *Nashriye-ye Fanni* (*IRANDOC Technical Journal*) was introduced. This title changed to *Ettela Resani* (*Journal of Information Services*) in 1993. It also published manuals and standards for indexing and abstracting of Persian literature and, translated versions of important literature in the field of documentation from other languages to Persian. This included major textbooks and periodical articles about indexing and abstracting services. Under this activity, publication of *Guidelines for the establishment and development of monolingual thesauri* in Persian, originally published in English language by the International Standards Organisation, is a significant example. The centre published two other important monographs, viz. : *An alphabetical list of descriptors accepted by the Iranian Documentation Center*, in 1977 and *NAMA*, a thesaurus, containing Persian descriptors related to the centre's fields of activities in 1996. Meanwhile, the existing thesauri, *Bibliography of Thesauri* was published in 1997.

DEVELOPMENT OF INDEXING SERVICES

The foundation of Asian Cultural Documentation Centre for Unesco in 1976 was another important step in the development of indexing services in Iran. The first regular indexing service for Persian periodicals was introduced by this Centre in 1976. It was entitled *Index of Cultural Articles in Iranian Periodicals* and was published quarterly between 1976 and 1978. The Center also published a number of retrospective bibliographies on a variety of subjects related to culture. Besides books, these bibliographies, included articles, dissertations, etc. It also published a few indexes in this field, too.[6] The Asian Cultural Documentation Centre played an important role in the development of the Persian thesuari. It translated two thesauri from English to Persian and published the same in the years 1978 and 1979.[7] These thesuari are *Information Science Thesaurus* by FID, and *Cultural Development Thesaurus* by Jean Viet, UNESCO. Moreover, several books about indexing were translated by the Centre into Persian, such as *Manual for Indexing of Documents and Expansion of Cultural Development Thesaurus in Asian Countries*. The Centre was replaced by the Islamic Revolution's Cultural Documentation Organisation (IRECDO) in 1982.

The Council of Coordination of Iranian Documentation Centres, was established in 1971. It consisted of 10 documentation/information centres belonging to : University of Tehran; Iran National Oil Company; Plan and Budget Organisation; the Standard Institution; Ministry of Financial Affairs; Ministry of Information; Technology Corporation; Iran Customs Office; Petrochemical Industries and IRANDOC. Soon it became the National Committee for FID and UNISIST.[8] IRANDOC was declared to be the secretariate of the council. With the technical and specialised assistance of USSR the Council organised a short-term course in documentation. It was conducted by USSR experts. About 20 Iranian documentalists underwent training in Tehran. As a part of this course, a visit to "VINITI" and other documentation centres in USSR was also arranged for the participants.

DEVELOPMENTS AFTER THE REVOLUTION

In the history of Iran, 'Islamic Revolution' is a great event. A revolt against the monarchy that started in the 1960s culminated in 1979, when the monarchy was replaced by the Islamic Republic. After the revolution the whole life in Iran underwent a change. No aspect of life escaped its impact. Technology, science, education, libraries and information services were no exception. Many cultural institutions, research centres, universities and information centres were founded, thereafter.

The most important documentation centre established after the revolution is the Islamic Revolution's Cultural Documentations Organisation (IRECDO). It was founded in 1982 as an affiliate of the Ministry of Cultural and Islamic Guidance.[9] It continued some of the activities of the erstwhile Asian Cultural Documentation Centre. These included the preparation of quarterly indexing service entitled *Index of Persian language articles in periodicals of the Islamic Republic of Iran*, since 1982. In 1991 the title of this service was changed to *Index of cultural articles in periodicals of the Islamic republic of Iran*. Subsequently, in 1992 its frequency was changed to monthly. It also published some other indexes. *Index of articles on the imposed war in the periodicals of the Islamic Republic of Iran*, which covers all Persian articles about Iran-Iraq war during 1980-1988 in five volumes, and *Subject Index Concerning Comprehensive discussion to be conducted in the Parliament*, from the first session of the Islamic Consultative Assembly (Majlis) todate, are the most important among them.

In 1996, IRECDO compiled a thesaurus under the title *ASFA*, which is an acronym for "Estelahname-ye-Farhengi-ye Iran" (Iran Cultural Thesaurus). *ASFA* contains descriptors in education; communication; sociology; economics; geography; psychology; and library and information science. The Centre also published some books about indexing and abstracting. *Abstracting and Indexing* by Jennifer E. Rowley was translated into Persian and published by the Centre in 1995.

OTHER DOCUMENTATION CENTRES

After the Islamic Revolution, many documents about the Pahlavi dynasty and the history of that period, especially pertaining to the relations between Iran (Mohammad Reza Phalavi) and United States of America and the behaviour of the Shah towards the democratic liberal activists were discovered. Therefore, some documentation centres were established for their retrieval, storage and dissemination. Some of these centres are : Islamic Revolution Documentation Centre, The Institution for Research and Cultural Studies of Bonyad-e-Janbazan va Mostaza fan,[10] etc.

Also some research centres were established for Islamic studies with emphasis on information services such as indexing and database management. Important among these are :

1. Islamic Sciences Research Centre, established in 1984.[11] The centre undertook the following activities for the preparation of:

a) Thesauri for Quranic studies, Islamic philosophy, Kalam (Islamic theology), and Fiqh (Islamic Law).

b) Several databases in Islamic subjects.

c) Several concordances for some of significant texts in Hadith such as Bahar ol-Anvar (Hadith is the Prophet's tradition narrated in a large number of volumes under various titles. *Bahar ol-anvar* is one such work and is available in 110 volumes).

d) Index to the Persian periodicals.

e) Index to the comprehensive works of Ayatollah Khamenei, and other religious scholars.

2. Centre for Computerised Research in Islamic Sciences

This centre was established in 1989.[12] It is responsible for the preparation of :

a) Concordances for more than 500 volumes pertaining to Quranic interpretation, Haditch, Islamic philosophy and other branches of Islamic studies.

b) Subject indexes for texts in Islamic : Law, history, philosophy, theology, Quranic interpretations, logic and Hadith.

c) Name indexes for books in 'Elm al-Rejal. (It is a kind of citation index for Islamic history and Hadith.)

d) Chronological indexes.

In addition to the above-mentioned centres which are exclusively devoted to documentation work and/or indexing services, some special libraries and information centres provide special indexing services, as a kind of information service to their respective clientele. In this area, libraries that merit mention belong to the Nuclear Energy Organisation; National Oil Company of Iran; Ministry of Foreign Affairs; Ministry of Agriculture; Ministry of Habitation; Ministry of Culture and Islamic Guidance; Plan and Budget Organisation, etc.[13] Some of the centres have published subject indexes, such as index of:

a) *Nutrition*, by Institute for Research in Nutrition and Food Industries.

b) *Woman*, by Cultural Research Bureau.

c) *Reviews of Iranian Movies*, by Iran Film Archive, and ;

d) *Agricultural Abstracts on Soil and Water*, by Documentation Centre of Agricultural Research Institution.

Also, some of these centres compiled lists of descriptors, thesauri to be used in their respective indexing systems, for example *Cultural, Communication and Information Thesaurus*, (extracted from UNESCO thesaurus by Jean Aitchison), published in 1996 by Cultural Research Bureau.

INDEXES AND ABSTRACTS FOR PERSIAN PERIODICALS

As F. Rahamipour has stated in her MLS dissertation "Survey of Persian Periodical's Indexes", published in Tehran during 1978-1994,[14] 1361 periodicals are published from Iran. 125 indexes and abstracts are available which cover some of these periodicals,[15] 17 periodicals carry their own index, as a part of the publication, or their cumulative indexes have been published separately.

Some of the current indexing services available in Iran are:

a) *Index to Persian Articles* (about Iran and Islam) by Iraj Afshar, 4 (Published occasionally since 1961-).

b) *Index of Cultural Articles in Periodicals of Islamic Republic of Iran*, Monthly, 1982.

c) *Index : Table of Contents of Scientific and Cultural Periodicals and uptodate Books*, Monthly, 1991-

d) *Education Information. Quarterly*, 1993-

ABSTRACTS

Most of abstracting services are published by IRANDOC, such as :

a) *Scientific and Technical Articles Abstracts*. Quarterly, 1993-
b) *Caspean Sea Abstracts*. Quarterly, 1993 -
c) *Research Projects in Iranian Universities and Research Centres*, Quarterly, 1993 -
d) *Dissertation Abstracts*. Quarterly, 1993 -

Moreover, several separate abstracts have been prepared by individuals for particular subjects, such as *Dissertation Abstracts of Linguistics : 1966-1993* by N.J. Someehsarai, published by National Library of Iran in 1994. Also some universities like Shras, Al-Zahra and Tarbiat-e-Modarres have compiled abstracts of their graduate dissertation.

CONCORDANCES

After the Islamic Revolution, more significance was attached to Islamic values, culture, ideology and ways of living. This brought about a profound cultural change in the country and Islamic lifestyle became the order of the day. In these circumstances increased interest in the religious literature among the people was natural. Hence, more and more people got interested in the study and understanding of Islamic ideology and religious literature. In fact, a strong national movement in this direction became evident. Consequently, the demand for tools to enable easy and fast use of scriptures and other literature pertaining to Islamic culture, philosophy, history, law, etc., became stronger. To meet this demand several concordances started appearing. The most important of these are for the *Holy Quran* and Quranic interpretations; the Prophet Mohammad's tradition and Nahjoi-balaqah (contains Imam Ali's speeches, correspondence, etc. Similarly, concordances for classics in Persian literature became more common. Some of the works for which concordances have been prepared and deserve mention are *Masnavi-ye Molavi* and *Divan-e Hafez. As darya be darya: Kashf ol-abyat-e Masnavi* by Mohammad Taqi Ja fari published by the Ministry of

Culture and Islamic Guidance in 1985, and *Vazhenama-ye Hafez* by Mahindokht Sadaquiyani, published by Farhang-e Mo`aser in 1989, respectively are their concordances.

COMPUTERISED DATABASES

In recent years information technology has brought about enormous changes in information services and information centres. With no exception, Iranian information centres are exploiting computer in many ways. Among them are several computerised databases that have been founded in Iran, especially in Tehran and Qom.[16] Some of them use natural language for retrieval of keywords or full texts, such as statistics database in Statistical Centre of Iran. Others use a thesaurus, as indexing language, for example, *Education Information Database* in IRANDOC.

A few computerised databases are produced in CD-ROM form also, such as *Sahifeh-ye Nur* which contain the collection of Imam Khomeini's speeches and statements, produced by IRECDO; and *Flora of Iran* produced by Markaz-e Ettela Resani-ye Vezarat-e Jahad-e sazandegi (Information Centre of Ministry of Construction).

EVALUATION

If we look around, nowadays a variety of indexing and abstracting services are available in a large number of subjects. Most of the countries depend on these services. These are available in the form of periodicals, CD-ROMs, online databases, etc. Since these services meet the needs of most of the readers, a large number of countries avoid the production of such services locally. However, these services have some problems also, for example, time lag in production and receipt, deficiency in the coverage of local products, meeting the local special requirements, etc. As such, in some cases, indexing and abstracting services are produced in Iran as well. Their number is limited as compared to the number of periodicals published.

The areas which have received special attention so far include economics and culture. Religion, as subject, dominates in such database services. In the field of religion, therefore, even some duplication of efforts has been pointed out. In any case, among Islamic countries, Iran could be considered as an active nation in this area. However, the areas of science, technology, arts, and government publications are still at a developing stage. And there is ample scope for improvement.

Moreover, currency and consistency are the other problems that are faced in indexing and abstracting services in Iran. Also a few existing current services are usually published with a considerable delay.

SUGGESTIONS

To meet the local needs and for quicker availability of such services more indexing and abstracting services in the field of science, technology and arts are needed. Some of the existing services make only one key word entry. In such cases improvement is required so that more access points are served.

Existing thesauri, in Persian in the fields of science, technology, social sciences and humanities need to be expanded.

a) Existing facilities for the training of documentalists in five library and information science schools which have provision for MLS programme, short-term courses (conducted by IRANDOC, National Library of Iran and schools of Management and Medical Science) are not sufficient to meet the growing needs of the country. Therefore, existing facilities need to be strengthened and advanced facilities need to be introduced.

b) Most of the available literature on the subject is either in English language or its translation in Persian. In some cases translations have been produced by people who have no or little practical experience in indexing and abstracting work. Hence, these do not serve the purpose effectively and efficiently. Hence, better literature in Persian language can go a long way in improving the situation.

c) Though Persian thesauri, indexing and abstracting practice, and research and the local literature in the field are at the initial stage of their development, yet it would be appropriate to review and evaluate the existing situation so that difficulties and limitations are identified and efforts made to give it a proper direction.

d) Some individuals have made contributions by producing indexes and abstracts in the form of monographs. Some of these that merit mention are:

   i) *Book Review Index*

   ii) *Iranian Movie Review*

   iii) *Bibliography of Iran*, which contains many articles about Iran in European languages published in foreign periodicals, by Mahyar Navabi who has produced six volumes so far in the fields of history, literature, art and religions of Iran. It would be better if such works are undertaken by the relevant institutions and are made available in the form of regular services.

It may be concluded by saying that regular services be kept uptodate and time lag should be minimised. Duplication in documentation work should be avoided through better coordination and control. Existing services should be improved by reviewing their structure, access points, language, coverage, frequency, etc., wherever possible.

REFERENCES

1. Azarang, Abd-Ol Hoseyn, *A brief report of information services in Iran*. Tehran : Plan and Budget Organisation, 1990.
2. Sinai, Ali, Research and services of IRANDOC, Librarianship, *The Bulletin of the Central Library and Documentation Center of Tehran University,* 1976, 6; 4-123.

3. Azadiyan, Anush; Etemadi, Parichehr and Javaher Kalam, Mohammad. A critical survey of IRANDOC's project for indexing of dissertation and government publication. In Proceedings of seminar on IRANDOC's problems and difficulties. Tehran, 1980, pp. 78-86.
4. Title of this abstract was : Chekide-ye Maqaleha-ye Majalleha-ye Iran dar Zamine-ye Olum va Olum-e Ejtemai (Science and Social Science Abstracts Bulletin).
5. Mosavat, Jalal-E-Din, Abstract and abstracting services in Iran. In: *Proceedings of seminar on IRANDOC's problems and difficulties*, Tehran, 1980, pp. 133-151.
6. Azarang, 'Abd-ol Hoseyn, op.cit.
7. The translated version of these thesauri were entitled "Estelahname-ye Elme-e Ettele Rassani" and "Estelahname-ye Tose e-ye Farhangi", respectively.
8. Azarang, abd-ol Hoseyn, op.cit.
9. *A brief introduction to the Islamic Revolution's Cultural Documentation Center (IRECDO)*, Tehran : IRECDO.
10. Bonyad-E-Janbazan Va Mostaz Afan which is popularly known as "Bonyad", is a foundation which established in Iran to look after the private property of the Shah.
11. *Introduction to Islamic Sciences Research Center*, Qom, ISRC.
12. *Introduction to center for computerised research in Islamic sciences*, Qom, CCRIS,
13. For a complete list of such libraries see : Taavoini, Shrin and Bijari, Bijan, *Directory of documentation centres, specialised and university libraries in Iran*, Tehran, IRANDOC, 1985.
14. This dissertation is submitted to the school of Management and Medical Information Science, Iran University of Medical Science and Health Care Services for the Master's degree in Medical Librarianship and Information Science in 1995.
15. These periodicals are : *Ayandeh, Adabestan, Ettela at-e Elmi, Bandar va Darya, Peyvand, Tadbir, Ta avon, Rasanesh, Zamineh, Zane-e Ruz, Seytun, San at-e Chap, San at-e Haml va Naqle, Film, Keyhan-e Farhangi,* and *Gardun.*
16. Qom is a city in Iran at a distance of 130 kilometres from Tehran. It has a high importance in religious studies because of numerous schools and research centres.

10

Evaluation of Information Retrieval System

J. Dominic and *P.J. Nirmala*

INTRODUCTION

The term "Information Retrieval" was coined in a paper by Mooers[1] and later popularised in the writings of Faithorne[2]. Sparck Jones[3] stated that the International Conference on Scientific Information, held in Washington in 1958,[4] marked the beginning of information retrieval which is in the present form. The following years saw seminal work by researchers such as Doyle[5] and Salton[6] who, in considering the automation of existing manual retrieval tasks and in comparing manual and automatic approaches to indexing, were led to develop new methods of retrieval. Further, as the growth of the specialised scientific literature in the fifties has stimulated the development of new forms of indexing language, this period also saw several tests of manual indexing languages, culminating in Cleverdon's second set of Cranfield Experiments.[7] It established the basic evaluation procedures that are still in use in the performance of information retrieval systems and techniques.

The large collection of papers by Saracevic[8] includes not only important items but clearly illustrates the intellectual ferment that really took off. It captures, in particular, the feeling that new theories about information and its communication were needed to match the new technological world. More extended reviews of the early development of information retrieval are presented by Stevens et al,[9] and by Salton.[6]

PERFORMANCE EVALUATION

It is evident that, given the fundamental intangibles of retrieval systems, it is difficult to get reliable and informative answers to the questions, indeed increasingly so, from the first to the last. The special problem is not just that it is hard to reach the normal evaluation destination, and predict future from past performance, the problem is that it is normally impossible to obtain all the ground data that are in principle required for a full-scale assessment of performance. This is because it is impossible, with any document file of nontrivial (and hence currently common) size, to determine whether each document in the file is relevant to any particular user need. It will therefore be not known what documents "ought" to be retrieved.

Furthermore, the case is that as every information need is unique to a particular person at a particular time, performance evaluation will naturally depend on a large population of users and their needs. Therefore, evaluation of retrieval system implies compromise in relation to the authenticity, bias, and completeness of relevance judgements. With extensive sampling not only is it possible to offset these compromises but it also offers scope to cover the natural variation in user population, needs, etc. Users needs, document files, and relevance judgements are the necessary prerequisites for evaluation (when frozen in limited form). User request, files, and preserved judgement sets constitute the type of evaluation data commonly referred to as test collection.

Many evaluations have been conducted without comprehensive and rigorous specifications. In practice, many unexamined assumptions are made, and default models of retrieval testing may not be well related to important retrieval realities. Many studies have applied the academic, laboratory approach, well illustrated by the long-standing smart work under Salton at Cornell, without asking whether this approach is appropriate to the individual evaluation situation. This particular approach—abstracting information retrieval systems from operational set-ups, considering only a limited set of environment variables, and using precision and recall computed from extensive evaluation data-defines—has become the default model of retrieval testing. It is therefore important to recognise its limitations and many other aspects of evaluation.

It is indeed necessary to understand that a methodology for evaluation ultimately evokes a theory of evaluation, grounded in an analysis of system objectives or functions and thus providing a sound justification for the choice of evaluation measures. This has to provide, for example, an appropriate way of relating basic measures like recall and precision to simple classes of documents (relevant and retrieved, relevant but not retrieved, etc.) with ranked output.

COLLECTION EVALUATION

The recent retrieval system testing has so far been conducted on too small a scale. This has been partly attributable to lack of clarity about what constitutes a statistically valid sample and, more importantly, to lack of knowledge about the raw numerical characteristics of large file retrieval systems. But small-scale testing has been mainly the consequence of the effort and cost of providing relevance judgements. When different approaches to retrieval are applied to the same collection, it is possible to pool their output and have the pooled data judged. It allows relative performance assessment of each approach. For a long time test collections were used in only one or more projects; there is a natural tendency to go on testing with the same material in order to maintain comparability with earlier work. During the seventies in particular, the need to check environment variables led to an increasing use of several collections for tests, but these were often arbitrarily different from each other and were typically still small. Even by 1990, while test collections had grown slowly since sixties, experiments were often conducted with collections of order 75 against 2000. The study described in Sparck Jones and Van Rijsbergen[10] had shown how complex and costly it is to provide a coherent set of collections. At the same time, it became increasingly evident that large test collections were needed not only to capture user variation, mentioned earlier, and to support claims for statistical significance in findings, but also to demonstrate that performance levels become static as document file sizes grow. This was important not only for scientific reasons but also for achieving credibility with commercial system operators.

Sarcevic et al, have given five general classes of evaluation of information retrieval:

1. *User* : Effects of the context of questions and constraints placed on questions;
2. *Question* : Structure and classification as assigned by different judges and the effect of various classes on retrieval;
3. *Searcher* : Effects of cognitive traits and frequency of online experience;
4. *Search* : Effects of different types of searches; overlap between searches for the same question in selection of search terms and items retrieval; efficiency and effectiveness of searches; and
5. *Items retrieved* : Magnitude of retrieval of relevant and non relevant items; effects of other variables on the chances that retrieved items were relevant.

USERS IN THE CONTEXT OF INFORMATION SEEKING

The context of a question is a governing force to describe a set of variables affecting all events in information seeking and retrieving. The context can be considered as to its external or environmental aspects, or internal or cognitive aspects. The following variables are involved in information seeking and retrieval.

Problem

A problem is defined as an unknown something about which solution is unknown to a potential user of an information system, something which causes difficulty in finding or working out a solution. We assume that information is necessary to solve problems, make decisions, or improve understanding. Such information can be obtained in many ways. One of them is to obtain or deduce it from the existing body of public knowledge, such as organised retrieval systems, expert systems, and the like.

In cognitive science a problem is said to exist when (a) it is at a given state (b) it is desired to be at another state, and (c) there is no clear way to get.[11]

Intent

An information seeker inevitably has some purpose in mind for the use of requested information. In the framework of information retrieval, the intent is defined as a planned or prospective use of information. In other words, the users have some preconceived ideas about:

a) the use of information in respect to the problem;
b) the amount of time and effort they are willing to spend in absorption of or deduction from the provided information;
c) the desirable characteristics of responses to the question, such as completeness, precision, reliability, timeliness, etc.;
d) the form characteristics of responses deemed most desirable, such as to the language, source, etc., and
e) the economic value they attach to responses.

The intent in information retrieval and the goal in problem solving are related but not identical. They are treated separately because the information seeking intent can be a very specific aspect of problem solving, exclusively devoted to the use of supplied information within a broader context of a goal in problem solving.

Internal Knowledge State

People ask questions because they do not know something or they want to confirm something, because they have an anomalous state of knowledge in respect to a problem. Internal knowledge refers to the degree of knowledge an information seeker has about the problem in hand and/or the question arising from the problem.

Internal knowledge involves many aspects related to cognitive structures and process: how knowledge is stored, organised, associated, retrieved, and changed in one's mind. A considerable amount of research in cognitive science is devoted to these questions.[12]

Public Knowledge Expectation

Public knowledge is recorded knowledge on a subject in the public domain. In the context of information retrieval it refers to the records or literature on the subject. People ask questions within the framework of public knowledge. This involves a number of aspects such as their perception of what is (or what is not) there, how is it organised, what can they expect to get, etc. Thus, a user's estimate of public knowledge defines his/her expectations, which in turn affects the evaluation.

STRUCTURE OF QUESTIONS

Questions are a whole class of linguistic expressions, uttered with the intention of inducing a response. In addition to grammar, there is also a logic and pragmatic context of questions. Questions can have a number of functions. Of interest here are those that have a role in problem solving. Within the context of information seeking, questions are defined as statements that are verbalised (written or oral) representations of a problem at hand: their function is to elicit a response.

Questions in information retrieval consist of three parts: a lead-in, a subject, and a query. The lead-in is not directly searchable. It may consist of phrases such as "I want information about..." However, at times lead-in may have implication for searching: for instance "what is ..." implies request for definition, "where is ..." implies request for location, or "when was ..." implies involvement of a time element. In such cases, lead-ins are important for recognising presuppositions in a question, i.e., implications not expressed.

The subject of the question is the central concept of the question. It is a concept around which all other aspects of the question revolve and relate. A question can have more than one subject.

The query is the specific aspect asked about the question. It is an attribute, characteristic, component, or part of the subject about which information is desired. There can be more than one query about a subject.

Classification of Questions

It is not uncommon to hear searchers describe given questions as : "complex", "specific", "very general", "difficult", "unsearchable", "unclear", and the like. In such cases searches are (possibly even unwillingly) applying certain general attributes to classify questions. While not generally accepted, classification of questions in information retrieval exists. It is of practical interest to specify certain attributes which could be used to classify or describe questions in information retrieval. These are : domain, clarity, specificity, complexity and presupposition.

1. *Domain :* Classifies a question in the appropriate general subject or topic area in which it falls. This can be done on the basis of a general subject classification.
2. *Clarity :* Classifies a question on the basis of degree of clarity in respect to (a) semantics (meaning of terms) and (b) syntax (relation and logic between terms).
3. *Specificity :* Classifies a question on the basis of degree of specificity of (a) query terms and (b) subject terms. Specificity ranges from very general or broad (e.g., as found in a thesaurus under BT-Broader terms) to very specific or narrow (e.g., as found in a thesaurus under NT-Narrower terms).
4. *Complexity :* Classifies a question on the basis of complexity for searching as related to number of search concepts involved. The search concepts are those that are used as search terms or will be translated into one or more search terms (i.e., a search concept can have more than one search term as its synonyms or near synonyms). The search concepts in both the query part and subject part of the question are added together.
5 *Presupposition :* Classifies a question on the basis of presence or absence of implied (not explicitly stated) concepts derived from sharing of common linguistic and world knowledge. Of interest are those implied concepts that could be used as search terms or search constraints. Most commonly presuppositions are expressed by phrases such as "what is...", "where is ...", etc., implying existence or verification, identity or definition, quality, relation, number, location, or time.

SEARCHERS

A large number of environmental (or external) and cognitive (or internal) factors, e.g., organisational setting, economic constraints, affect searcher's decisions and thus retrieval effectiveness and efficiency. While recognising the external factors, we have concentrated on a limited number of cognitive traits of searchers:

a) Language ability or the ability to make inductive inferences through word association, as measured by a standard test called remote associates test;
b) logical ability or the ability to make deductive inferences as measured by a standard test called symbolic reasoning test;
c) preferred style or mode of learning as measured by a standard test called learning style inventory; and
d) online experience as derived from a questionnaire given to searchers.

SEARCH

The elements and subprocesses in a search have been modelled and categorised in a number of ways. While it is difficult to make a clear separation, a common way is to make a distinction between :

a) *Question analysis :* Procedures that deal with decisions on semantic and pragmatic (contextual) aspects of a question in preparation of a search statement, including determination of appropriate information sources, and a possible interview with a user.
b) *Formulation of search strategy :* Procedures that deal with decisions on syntactic and logical aspects of the search statement, including incorporation of constraints, if any, and selection of tactics related to a desired level of effectiveness and efficiency.
c) *Searching :* Procedures used in the conduct of search, including the use of protocols and capabilities of given information systems and obtaining the responses.

Effectiveness Measures

Two sets of measures for evaluation of the effectiveness of a search have been used, based on the two most often used criteria:

1. *Relevance* : the degree of fit between the question and the retrieved item. The criteria of "aboutness" is used. Each abstract should be evaluated according to its degree of relevance to the question submitted for searching. The degree of relevance should be determined using the following three point scale :
    1. Relevant
    2. Partially Relevant
    3. Non-Relevant
2. *Recall and Precision :* These are measures based on the relevance judgement of users where :

    Precision = Probability that a retrieved item is relevant

    Recall = Probability that a relevant item in the file is retrieved

These probabilities are estimated as follows for a given search :

$$\text{Precision} = \frac{\text{No. of relevant items retrieved by the search}}{\text{Total No. of items retrieved by the search}}$$

$$\text{Recall} = \frac{\text{No. of relevant items retrieved by the search}}{\text{Total No. of relevant item in the union of items retrieved by all searchers for that question}}$$

Precision is easy to establish directly from the output of evaluated items for a search. Recall is not easy to establish, because it is never apparent how many items in a file are relevant to the question. Each question is searched by a number of searches and types of searches. A union of retrieved items from all searches for the question is as established (i.e., by merging all the outputs and eliminating duplicates) and sent to the user for evaluation. In this way the evaluated items from the union served as the benchmark of individual search recall. This presents a comparative rather than absolute measure of recall performance for any given search.

Utility Measures

These are measures based on users' expression of degree of satisfaction and value of the retrieved items as a whole. Recall and precision are universally used measures. Unfortunately, there are no such universally used utility measures.

Efficiency Measures

The following measures have been used for online searches describing search characteristics as to :

a) Number of commands used by a search
b) Number of command cycles used by a searcher
c) Number of search items used by a searcher searching a question
d) Preparation time used by a searcher in preparing a search for a question
e) Online connect time used by a searcher in searching a question
f) Total time used by a searcher (connect time plus preparation time).

ITEMS RETRIEVED

The output from a search may be called by a number of names: references, answers, documents, abstracts, displays, etc. We have selected a neutral label, "items retrieved", to designate the output for a search, that is, the individual records retrieved from a database in response to a question. While databases provide different format options for each item retrieved, there are other aspects:

a) Observing the distribution of items retrieved.

b) Analysing the chances or odds that an item retrieved will be relevant.

Measures for Items Retrieved

The measures of quantity :

a) Total number of items retrieved for a question is calculated in two ways : (i) as a sum for all searches for the question including duplicates retrieved by different searches, and (ii) as a union of all searches for the question counting the distinct numbers only by excluding or eliminating the duplicates.

b) Total number of items evaluated by a user for a question is again calculated in two ways. (The items evaluated for a number of questions are smaller than items retrieved.)

c) Total number of items judged by users as relevant, partially relevant and not relevant for a question, is again calculated in two ways.

FAILURE ANALYSIS

The failure analysis is the most important part of the entire evaluation programme. Take a hypothetical search for which a recall estimate of 7/10 and a precision figure of 15/40 has been determined. In this search there are three known recall failures and 25 precision failures for analysis.

Failure analysis involves a careful examination of the documents involved, how they were indexed, the request posed to the system, the search strategy used, and the complete assessment of forms of the requester. The major causes of each failure can be determined. When such a failure analysis for a large number of searches is conducted, a large body of data will be established. When analysed and interpreted, it will clearly indicate the principal problem areas in the system—the areas that require attention and modification.

The analysis will attribute the recall and precision failures encountered to the principal sub-systems (indexing, searching, index language, and user-system interface). It will identify the particular kind of failure occurring in each sub-system. The most important of the possible sources of failure are illustrated in the figure below. Whether or not a requester approaches the system in the first place is dependent upon his expectations regarding system coverage. Presumably he will not approach the system unless he feels that the collection is likely to contain the type of document he is seeking. Having decided to consult the system, he must make his needs known by means of a verbal request.[13]

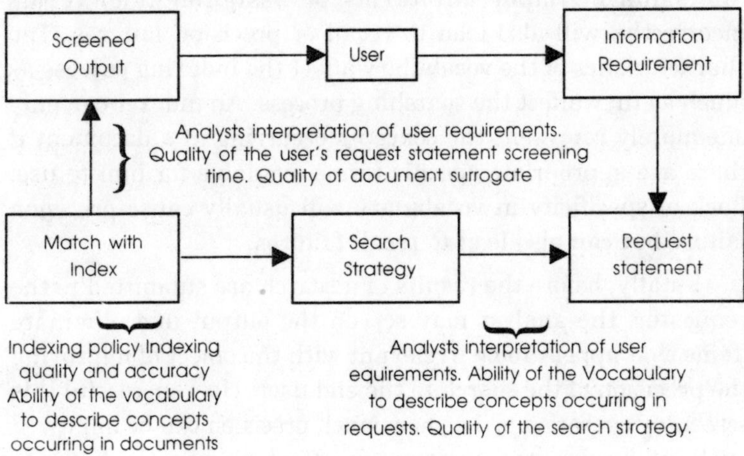

POSSIBLE SOURCES OF FAILURE

The quality of this request (i.e., the degree to which it actually matches his information requirement) is dependent upon:

1. His own ability to express himself.
2. His interpretation of system capabilities and limitations. There is a strong tendency for a user to ask for what he thinks the system can give him rather than to ask for what he is really looking for.
3. The degree of assistance given to the requester by the system. Such assistance can take various shapes : a carefully structured search request form, a formal "request interview" process, an interactive search procedure, or some type of user training programme.

The request having been made to the system, it must be translated into formal search strategy by a member of the information staff (a search analyst). When the search strategy is actually matched against the file of documents, surrogates (i.e., the search is conducted) further factors affecting performance come into play. One such important performance factor is that of indexing policy, particularly the policy regarding exhaustively of indexing. Inaccuracy of indexing (omission of important terms or assignment of terms incorrectly) will also lead to recall or precision failures. The characteristics of the vocabulary affect the indexing process as much as they affect the searching process. An indexer can only adequately represent the concepts occurring in a document if there are appropriate specific terms available for him to use. Lack of specificity in vocabulary will usually cause precision failure but can also lead to recall failures.

Finally, before the results of a search are submitted to the requester, the analyst may screen the output and eliminate items that appear to be irrelevant with the object of improving the precision of the search to the end user. How successful this screening operation is (i.e., how much precision can be improved without having too serious an effect on recall) depends primarily upon the accuracy of the analyst's interpretation of the requester's requirements. Secondly, the success of the screening will be affected by the quality of the document surrogates from which the analyst is working.

CONCLUSION

The importance of performance evaluation applied to information retrieval system is becoming widely recognised. Nevertheless, although a large body of evaluation literature exists, much of it is theoretical, speculative, or philosophical in nature. Only a very small number of papers pertain to evaluations of actual operating systems. Of the large national information systems only MEDLARS has exposed itself to a rigorous evaluation programme. It appears likely that funding agencies will become more insistent so that evaluation techniques be applied to information programmes to measure their performance from the viewpoints of both effectiveness and as a measure of justifying fund spent. Thorough evaluation tends to be expensive, and can only be justified if the evaluation programme is likely to lead to significant improvement in the performance of the system.

REFERENCES

1. Mooers, C.N., *Information Retrieval Viewed as Temporal Signalling.* Proceeding of the International Conference of Mathematicians, Cambridge, Massachusetts August 20-September 6, 1950. American Mathematic Society Providence, R.I. 1950, 572-573.
2. Faithorne R.A., *Towards Information Retrieval*, Butterworths, London, 1961.
3. Sparck, Jones, K., *Information Retrieval Experiment,* Butterworths, London, 1981.
4. Proceedings of the International Conference on Scientific Information 1959. National Academy of Sciences-National Research Council, Washington, DC. (2 Volumes).
5. Doyle, L.B., Semantic road maps for literature searchers. *Journal of the Association for Computing Machinery*, 1961, 8, 553-578.
6. Salton, G., *Automatic Information organisation and Retrieval.* McGraw-Hill, New York, 1968.

7. Cleverdon, C.W., The cranfield tests on index language devices, *ASLIB Proceedings,* 1967, 119, 173-192.
8. Saracevic T. et al., A study of information seeking and retrieving. I. Background and methodology. Karent sparck Jones, ed. *Readings in Information Retrieval,* 1987, 175-190.
9. Stevens et al., *Statistical Association Methods for Mechanised Documentation Symposium Proceedings.* National Bureau of Standards, Washington, DC: Miscellaneous Publication 269, 1965.
10. Saracevic, T., *Introduction to Information Science,* Bowker, New York, 1970.
11. Sparck Jones K. op.cit.
12. Meyer, R.E. op.cit.
13. Simon, H.A. op.cit.

11

Reference Service in Government Libraries

M.K. Jain

INTRODUCTION

The need for reference service led to the formation of Imperial Library at Calcutta in 1891. The Government of India, with its headquarters in Calcutta and its machinery devised on the pattern of the administrative structure in England, consisted of a few departments organised to deal with the problem of law and order, collection of revenue and regulating commerce, etc. Some statutes, reports, guide/reference books were collected by these departments to help and guide the officers and staff of these departments in their day-to-day working. As the number of these publications increased it became difficult to service them and the government felt the need of a regular library. Thus the library called Imperial Library came into being by pooling together the resources of the departmental collection of books and publications of these departments.

This library was primarily for the use of the Imperial Secretariat officials. Later on, the holdings of the Calcutta Public Library set up in 1835 were merged with it. In the words of Lord Curzon, "this library was intended to be a "Library of Reference". Thus began the genesis of the Government of India libraries. Seeing the utility, usefulness and better reference service more libraries were established. Before independence in 1947, the number of these libraries was about 35 only. After the independence their number started increasing considerably. As soon as new ministries/departments were established, the libraries were set up in each ministry/department simultaneously.

COLLECTION

The collections of the government libraries mostly comprise Official Gazettes, Reports, Budgets Papers, Acts, Parliamentary Debates, Census Report, Manuals, Serials, Monographs, Committee and Commission reports, Gazetteers and Civil Lists. These libraries also acquire published material like books, etc., in the areas of their specialisation. Most of the reference questions in these libraries are of long range type, requiring extensive searching. The officers of the government are not very much conversant with government publications. They depend on the library staff to cull out the information they want. *The Gazette of India* and *Census Reports* are important government publications.

Due to complexity of materials it is only the skill and the experience of library staff, which helps in searching out the information out of these publications. *The Gazette of India* is published in four parts, which are further sub-divided into various sections, sub-sections. Similarly, the *Census Reports* are also divided in many parts.

The government libraries have to acquire documents on government basic rules and regulations besides the *Manual on Office Procedure, Manual on Disciplinary Proceedings for the Government Servants*, Civil lists, etc., for the use of administrative staff dealing with the service matters of the official and staff working in department/ministry. The basic rules and regulations are compiled in one volume called *FR and SR (Fundamental Rules and Supplementary Rules)*, called the mother of all the basic rules. CCS (Conduct) Rules, General Provident Fund Rules, Central Civil Services Rules, General

Financial Rules, HRA and CCA Rules, CCS (CCA) Rules, Central Treasury Rules, Seniority and Promotion Rules, are some of the basic important Rules. The Central Civil Services Rules contain chapters on CCS (Conduct) rules. These rules are also published separately in a booklet form and kept uptodata of all the amendments published from time to time for reference by the administrative staff and put up on the files if required and necessary.

These rules and publications are frequently used and referred to in the library and various sections of the department/ministry. Their demand is much more and too frequent. These publications are loaned to the administrative staff on a long-term basis. A minimum good collection of reference books should be built up in a library irrespective of the type of the library whether it is government, academic, public or special library, depending upon the finances available. The reference collection of library should have the following kinds of reference books other than the general/subject books and government publications: dictionaries, encyclopedias, yearbooks, almanacs, handbooks, manuals, bibliographies, statistical sources, audiovisual sources, guidebooks, indexing and abstracting services publications.

The government libraries should acquire the following publications for their reference collection:

a) *National Accounts Statistics* (Central Statistical Organisation)
b) *Annual Survey of Industries* (Central Statistical Organisation)
c) *Economic Survey* (Ministry of Finance)
d) *Report on Currency and Finance* (Reserve Bank of India)
e) *RBI Bulletin* (Reserve Bank of India)

The above publications are very important and frequently consulted by the officers.

NEED FOR REFERENCE SERVICE

The purpose of reference service is to provide information to the users. Providing information, in view of the needs of the planners, administrators, advisors and many others at different levels in the government machinery, is a basic and imperative function of a government departmental library. The responsibility of providing information is that of the library and the onus of responsibilities is on the librarian and the library staff. The demand for information is much more and is of different kind in a government departmental library than in any other type of library, viz., public, academic and special. The libraries, first of all, started bringing out the 'List of New Additions' under classified headings for the use of their clientele. These lists were also mailed to other libraries, thus making users aware of the new acquired material. These lists helped libraries for inter-library loan transactions.

TYPES OF REFERENCE SERVICES

Soon the need was felt for providing bibliographical and documentation services and gradually following services were introduced in many libraries :

i) Current Awareness Service (CAS).
ii) Selective Dissemination of Information (SDI).
iii) Bibliographies.
iv) Indexing and Abstracting Service.
v) Digest Service.
vi) Current Contents Service.
vii) Article Alert Service.
viii) Press Clipping Service.

At present, 50 or more libraries are bringing out their regular publications on the above-mentioned services.

COMPUTER APPLICATION

Of late the application of computer is becoming popular. The National Information Centre (NIC) under the Planning Commission is helping and encouraging the ministries and departments in the introduction of computers.

The National Library, Kolkata, and the libraries of Ministries of Defence, External Affairs, Health and Family Welfare, Human Resource Development, Science and Technology, Parliamentary Affairs, Water Resources and Departments of Atomic Energy, Electronics and Space, are now using computers for various jobs in their libraries. The Planning Commission library, which introduced computers quite sometime back, is now under the process of being fully computerised. The Central Secretariat Library has also undertaken several programmes of computerising its stock and services. Important centres like the Bhabha Atomic Research Centre (Mumbai), Tata Institute of Research Centre (Mumbai), INSDOC (New Delhi), DESIDOC (Delhi), NASSDOC (New Delhi), are making use of computers in a big way. The Central Reference Library (Kolkata) has started bringing out a computerised Indian National Bibliography (INB). Application of computer in these libraries has improved their reference services in imparting quick and relevant information to their users.

ROLE OF NETWORKS IN REFERENCE SERVICE

There are some national and local library networks in India like INFLIBENT, NICNET, SIRNET, ERNET, DELENT, CALIBNET, MALIBNET, BONET, ADINET, MYLIBNET, etc. Many government libraries are connected with local networks. Most of the subscribers to DELNET (Delhi Library Network) are government libraries. A few libraries in Kolkata are connected to CALIBNET, similarly libraries in Mumbai are connected with BONET, in Chennai with MALIBNET, in

Mysore with MYLIBNET, in Ahmedabad with ADINET. The national network NICNET of NIC has expanded very much and it is providing INTERNET connections. Another national network, INFLIBNET, is mainly meant for university libraries.

The use of these networks has changed and improved the dissemination of information services to a great extent. Resource sharing, which is an important component of reference service, has become easy and convenient.

MINISTRY OF EXTERNAL AFFAIRS AND PLANNING COMMISSION LIBRARIES

Among the government libraries, the Ministry of External Affairs Library and the Planning Commission Library are in the forefront in the use of modern information technology. The Ministry of External Affairs Library is fully computerised and offers various services including Current Awareness, Reference, Bibliographic and Documentation using FAIRS (Foreign Affairs Information Retrieval System) database. Besides, the internet facility is also available. An important feature of this library is that FAIRS database is available to all its officers at the headquarters through computer network operating in the ministry and to personnel working in missions abroad through internet on NIC network. Efforts are on to post all its publications on website.

The Planning Commission Library is fully air-conditioned and computerised. A database of all important documents including Five-Year Plans, is being developed which will be made available to officers through computer network in the Planning Commission. The library will also get internet connection. In due course the library will undertake to prepare CD-ROM database of important publications.

REFERENCE STAFF

The Librarian in-charge should see that appropriate and right type of staff members are put on the job of providing service to the users. It is the reference service that builds the reputation of a library, and if a good and efficient service is provided, the usefulness of the library is recognised. Whatever be the size of the library, it will receive queries of one kind or another from the clientele, which must be answered promptly. Some questions can be answered immediately by simple consultation but in some cases, a search has to be made which takes time. In government libraries all sorts of queries are received not only pertaining to government publications but also on several topics. It is therefore essential that the following factors may be kept in mind:

i) Capable and skilled staff.
ii) Good collection of reference sources.
iii) Efficient arrangements and maintenance of the collection.

The staff employed in the reference section should be intelligent, trained in the use of reference books and reference methods and willing to help to readers. It may not be out of place to mention that the reference librarians should read the following books to enhance their knowledge and skills:

a) Foskett, D.J. - *Information Services in Libraries.*
b) Walfor, A.J. - *Guide to Reference Material sources.*
c) Katz, W.A. - *Introduction to Reference Work* (2 Vols).

EVALUATION OF REFERENCE SERVICE

There must be evaluation of reference service. How does the reference librarian evaluate the service he is giving (or not giving) to the users? Is that service bad, indifferent, good or excellent? The first query pre-supposes a methodology of measuring reference service. The second question is an ability to evaluate the data. Furthermore, before any evaluation measures can be employed, the librarian should have a clear concept of his objectives. In any evaluation of the reference process, certain considerations should first be made.

There should be a statement of purpose which includes goals and objectives not only of the reference process but of the library as a whole. There should be a statement defining the broad strategy which will be followed to reach the purpose, goals and objectives. There should be thorough analysis of what is going on at the present time in the reference process. There should be a plan, with due consideration to cost, personnel, over all library goals, etc., to make necessary changes from 'time present' to 'time future'. Finally, there should be periodic evaluation of the movement or movements towards 'time future'.

All this is to clarify and explain why the reference librarian does or does not do what. Harold Jenkins points out that "if we cannot say why we are doing what we think we want to do, we should then question the wisdom of doing it at all."

A valuable asset of evaluation, especially in government libraries, is to bring about a change from a rigid bureaucracy and thereby changing attitudes and basic positions, and opening up the possibility of self-examination, encouragement research and development activities as normal activities of librarians.

The following methods are generally employed to evaluate reference services:-

a) Interviews;
b) Direct Observations;
c) Questionnaires;
d) Case Studies;
e) Test questions; and
f) Inventory Procedure (level of services)

Each of these methods has limitations. The modern methodology calls for capturing quantitative data rather than just a summary of opinions or measurement of input data. If the evaluation has to be valid and reliable, it is imperative that the libraries measure the output. Neither are quantitative data of value unless they are measured against a specific standard or goal. For example, it takes no great skill to count the number of reference books in a collection, but quantitatively this means little unless one has a notion of what the optimum size of a reference collection should be in a certain type of library. The lack of such standards pose difficulty in evaluating the reference service. Meanwhile, of course the standards or lack of standards, need not prevent meaningful evaluation.

One of the favoured methods of evaluating the reference service is the library survey and report. The survey or study may be limited to a single library, be it at a informal level. All possible sources of data and means of analysis may be used in an attempt to see the library whole. The type of data and how that data are manipulated and compared are dependent upon the objectives of the survey, although in reference service the quantitative elements of such evaluation are normally limited to (1) the size of the collection; (2) the size of staff; (3) physical facilities, and (4) budget. Once the data are gathered, they are to be evaluated in terms of general standards, comparative data, and the heart of most such studies is the conclusions and the recommendations. These will be both quantitative and qualitative analysis. Also, in terms of the qualitative the survey should point to how service may be improved by doing this or that i,e. recommendations.

CONCLUSION

The departmental libraries of the Government of India play a crucial role in the socio-economic development of the country. These are providing access of every type of information needed by government officials and organisations in their day-to-day work. Reference service should be improved substantially through sharing of resources. Long-range questions may be answered with the use of computers and communication devices. Internet connections will go a long in handling reference queries efficiently and effectively, within less time and at comparatively low cost.

12

Indira Gandhi Memorial Library, Hyderabad University, Hyderabad

K. Navalani and ***Prem Chand Sehgal***

INTRODUCTION

The University of Hyderabad, a premier institution of post-graduate teaching and research in the country, was established by an Act of Parliament (Act No. 39 of 1974) on 2 October, 1974 as a central university, wholly financed by the University Grants Commission.

The "objects of the university" as envisaged in the Act are: "to disseminate and advance knowledge by providing instructional and research facilities in such branches of learning as it may deem fit and by the example of its corporate life, and in particular, to make special provisions for integrated courses in humanities and science in the educational programmes of the university and to take appropriate measures for promoting interdisciplinary studies and research in the university."[1]

The University's sprawling scenic, and serene campus spreads over a vast stretch of land measuring about 2,300 acres, 20 kms from the city of Hyderabad on the old Hyderabad-Mumbai road. Amidst the scenic environment of the campus, several buildings catering to the academic needs, support facilities and residential requirements of the campus community have been constructed over the years. The University also has a city campus. "The Golden Threshold' the residence of the Sarojini Naidu which was bequeathed to the university by her daughter, the late Padmaja Naidu. The jurisdiction of the University extends to whole of the state of Andhra Pradesh. No institution affiliated to any other university in the state shall be recognised by the university.

There are eight schools of study and 25 departments which impart instruction at postgraduate levels and conduct research; 2,018 students are on its roll and 933 researchers are registered for various degrees; 192 members are on its faculty; 1,960 employees including 59 administrative officers are serving the University.[2]

INDIRA GANDHI MEMORIAL LIBRARY

The library was started in 1974, soon after the University came into existence from its 'Golden Threshold' premises. Later the library for the science schools at the campus also came into being and the 'Golden Threshold' library catered to the needs of schools of humanities and social sciences. Two Assistant Librarians and Professor Incharge looked after these libraries.

Dr T.A. Murthy was appointed as its first University Librarian in 1987. The present Librarian, E. Rama Reddy, then seniormost Deputy Librarian, took over charge on February 13, 1990, when Dr. Murthy left. Later on (Feb. 1993) he became its librarian.

In the meantime, a new building for the library was completed and the library was named after Indira Gandhi, Dr. Shankar Dayal Sharma, the then Vice President of India, performed the inauguration ceremony in 1988.

The library remains open throughout the year except on the following holidays: Republic Day, Independence Day, Gandhi Jayanti, Holi, Dussehra and Diwali. It functions from 8.30 a.m to 10.00 p.m. on all working days including vacation and 10.00 a.m. to 5.00 p.m. on Sundays and other holidays.

During semester examinations, it is kept open till 12.00 midnight for four weeks.

Library Authority/Committee

Statute 24 of the University stipulates that there shall be a standing committee of the Academic Council called the library committee. It shall consist of the following :

a) Vice–Chancellor or Pro-Vice Chancellor
b) Deans of schools
c) Dean, Students Welfare
d) One person for each of the schools nominated by the Academic Council, but not necessarily member of the Council.
e) Two research scholars including M. Phil students and two postgraduates to be nominated by the Vice-Chancellor.
f) Librarian (Ex-office member and secretary).

It is empowered to frame rules, advise the librarian on regulating general library development, prepare budget estimates, allocation of funds, arrange for stock taking, prepare and submit annual report to the Academic Council.

Service

Library is for users, and service to them is the motto of every library. The library provides technical or input services such as selection, acquisition and accessioning of reading materials, processing, i.e., preparing items for use, their classification, cataloguing, indexing, care and repair of materials, maintenance and cleanliness, etc., of volume and building. The library maintains public catalogue, provides in-house borrowing and lending facilities, loan including inter-library loan, dissemination of information about new documents, references and reprographic services. It also provides current awareness, microfilming, documentation, bibliographic, book bank, database searching/retrieval, CD-ROM and online search services/facilities to its users.

Automation

With the acquisition of a computer PC-AT with 3 MB memory 80 MB hard disk at a cost of Rs. 1.45 lakhs for in-house operations in 1988-89, automation of the library was started. It received a special one-time grant under modernisation of libraries from the University Grants Commission and acquired a mini computer system, DECALPHA 2000, 4-multimedia systems, etc. It started retrospective conversion of records, the library card catalogue has been replaced with a computer Online Public Access Catalogue (OPAC). The OPAC allows search by author, title, subject, call number, keywords and Boolean search, etc.

The library database consists of all the books, back volumes of periodicals, current journals and theses dissertations. The library database can be accessed through tenet by outside users within and outside India. The library is in the process of creating a web page to make the database available over the internet. It has e-mail and internet facilities. Searches are made using internet on specific requests from the users. It is an active member of the INFLIBNET. The library has several CD-ROM and multimedia products and they are used in training the users in handling these products.

Finance

During the first five years of its establishment, the library received grants from the University and the University Grants Commission for its maintenance and development. The University apportioned on an average 12.5 per cent of its expenditure to the library while in the next five years (1981-82 to 1985-86) it decreased its allocation to 9.09 per cent. In the successive five years (1986-87 to 1990-91) and (1991-92 to

1995-96) it further came down to 5.91 per cent and 6.16 per cent, respectively. During the last four years (1996-97 to 1999-2000), it was all time low-5.65 per cent. In relative terms, as a share of the University budget, the library has been loser but in gross terms library expenditure has seen growth (Table 1). During the first five years of its life (1976-77 to 1980-81), the average expenditure per annum was Rs 24, 95, 623 while in the last four years (1996-97 to 1999-2000) of this study its average per annum expenditure was Rs 1,74,40,934, an increment of seven times. Barring the expenditure of the library during its birth year, which was too low, expenditure of the library has seen eightfold growth. The average expenditure per annum comes to Rs 87,14,635.

The average expenditure on salary during 24 years comes to Rs. 21,62,723. But quinquennial average tells a different story. During 1976-77 to 1980-81, it was Rs 1,60,840 and in the next five years, it rose by more than three times while in the successive five years it witnessed again almost three times growth. It nearly doubled during the next decade. The total increase was about 35 times. In terms of percentage of the total expenditure, the library spent only 2.58 per cent on emolument on its staff in 1977-78 while it incurred maximum expenditure, i.e., 40.81 per cent in 1995-96

Thus, the salary expenditure has been flattening with the growth of staff. Initially staff members were few, and salaries at entry points were low. With the growth of the library, more and more positions and senior posts were created. Promotion channels, increments in salaries and above all revision of grades and increments in D.A., etc., had enhanced this bill.

Quinquennial average of expenditure reveals that expenditure on collection building has been ever increasing. It rose by four times up to 1995-96. During the earlier period of its existence, the library had spent more as percentage of its budget (as high as 95.45% in the year 1977-78) for purchasing reading materials but in 1995-96 the percentage share fell to 51.68 per cent. Range of expenditure under this head comes to

Rs 18.7 lakh (1981-82) to Rs 141 lakh (1994-95), except in the birth year of the library, when it incurred expenditure of about Rs two and a half lakh on this. A cursory look at Table 1 depicts no consistency in grants under this head either by the University Grants Commission or by the University except for expenditure on periodicals.

The percentage of expenditure on binding and other operative costs over years has been very low from 0.33 per cent (1994-95) to 2.46 per cent (1982-84) except in the initial year of this study when it was 7.16 per cent. Studies of Preme Chand,[3] Devrajan,[4] Venkatraman,[5] Trishanjit Kaur[6] and others[7] also confirm that expenditure under these heads of university libraries was not much.

Collection Development

Collection is an intermediate input that supports other library programme such as reference/circulation and in-house use. University libraries supporting instruction work both at graduate and postgraduate levels must provide working collections for them. Research also requires a variety of material in the concerned subjects, hence the libraries should have comprehensive and indepth collection in special areas of research. So collection building is the responsibility of every university within the limits of the available funds.

The total collection of the library as on 31 March 1998 was 2,42,580 which includes 70,000 back volumes of periodicals, theses, other materials including volumes received through gifts and in exchange. Table 2 gives a picture of collection development efforts of the library. On an average, the library added 11,026 volumes out of which it purchased 9,618 volumes per year. Initially it received more donations from other sources. Hence, during the first five years of its life, the library added 15,485 volumes per year whereas in the successive five-year periods this average was almost half of this number, despite addition of back volumes of journals which kept this figure on higher side in later years.

Table 2: Growth of Collection

Year	*No. of Books Purchased*	*Total Collection*
1976-77	12,000	12,000
1977-78	21,000	33,000
1978-79	32,000	65,000
1979-80	5,300	70,340
1980-81	7,086	90,000
Total	77426	90,000
Q.A.	15485	18,000
1981-82	8,941	90,665
1982-83	7,060	100,393
1983-84	4,820	106,812
1984-85	11,052	119,736
1985-86	9,983	130,616
Total	41856	40,616
Q.A.	8371	8,123
1986-87	6,776	150,000
1987-88	14,967	175,000
1988-89	10,690	185,000
1989-90	9,817	189,000 *
1990-91	5,800	188,500 *
Total	48050	98,500
Q.A.	9610	19,700
1991-92	6,950	198,450
1992-93	8,600	210,000
1993-94	9,765	220,000
1994-95	8,650	229,750
1995-96	4,500	234,256
Total	38,456	144,256
Q. A.	76,91.2	28,851
1996-97	3,800	241,480
1997-98	2,000	242,580
Total	5,800	394,060
Q.A.	2,900	78,812
Average	9,618	11,026

QA = Quinquennial at Average

* there seems to be printing error in the Annual Report.

Journals

Starting with 150 journals in 1976-77, the library kept on subscribing to more and more journals every year, till the peak came in 1980-81, when it subscribed to 1,226 periodicals. After that, quinquennial average number of journals kept on declining even as the journal expenditure has been doubling every five years till 1990-91, and in the next five years it increased by Rs. 4.67 lakh only. In 1997-98, the number of journals subscribed to declined to 650 for which the library paid all-time high price.

Table 3

Growth of Periodicals Subscribed and Expenditure on them

Year *Price*	*Number*	*Expenditure*	*Quinquennial Average*		*Per*
		Rs	*Number*	*Expenditure*	*periodical*
1976-77	150	269,040			
1977-78	530	652,101			
1978-79	907	911,140	777	94,056	1,210.37
1979-80	1070	1,150,000			
1980-81	1226	1,720,001			
1981-82	1070	1,563,709			
1982-83	1027	1,588,453			
1983-84	1164	1,825,685	1,099	1,965,126	1,788.10
1984-85	1164	2,281,922			
1985-86	1070	2,566,060			
1986-87	1140	2,916,153			
1987-88	986	3,174,912			
1988-89	986	3,490,876	1,018	3,936,833	3,867.22
1989-90	1000	5,507,736			
1990-91	980	4,594,488			
1991-92	870	4,765,040			
1992-93	890	3,944,943			
1993-94	870	4,996,122	846	467,337	5,552.41
1994-95	900	7,864,607			
1996-96	700	1,915,708 *			
1996-97	700	7,210,000			
1997-98	650	10,630,000 BE			
1998-99		10,400,000 BE			

* There seems to be printing mistake in AR as Expenditure is Rs. 7,725,000.

(Table 3) Findings of research of some Indian scholars and institutions such as Saroj Bal,[8] Dr. Trishanjit Kaur,[9] Padma Hukmmi,[10] INFLIBNET,[11] and NISSAT[12] indicate the same trend.

Manpower

The staff of any organisation is the most important factor in its success or failure. In budget estimates of 1997-78, approved staff positions were 20 only whereas the revised budget estimates of the year indicate 35 members. At present, the staff positions are as under.

Librarian	1
Deputy Librarian	2
Assistant Librarian	4
Documentation Officer	1
Senior Professional Assistants	5
Professional Assistants	4
Junior Professional Assistants	15
Senior Library Assistants	3
Junior Library Assistants	6
Library Attendants	18
Book Binders	5
Other Office Staff	8
Total	72

The University has also laid down recruitment/professional policy for library staff.

CONCLUSION

Transformational leaders have to be excellent strategists, strong planners, synthesizers, charge agents and visionaries.[13]

The university has been fortunate to get such dynamic and foresighted leadership in Dr. Rama Reddy, the present University librarian. His vision, planning, hard work and dedication supported with funds have transformed this library to fully automated one. And the library has the distinction of being the first university library in India to computerise all its activities and also provide computer terminals (OPAC) to the users with network access across the campus-wide Local Area Network (LAN). The library has seen all-round growth. It has quickly integrated modern technology, developed human capital and elevated their technological skills and connected its clientele with knowledge electronically via internet.

Being a central university, the library gets grants from the University Grants Commission for its maintenance and development. Comparatively its financial position is much better than its sister state university libraries. Findings of this study indicate that during the first decade of its life, the library continued to get its share from the university as per norms (and sometimes even more) recommended by various committees and commissions. After that the library witnessed squeeze in finances. The growth rate in its expenditure continued to fall behind the growth in the University expenditure. There has been no consistency in the allocation of grants for readings material. Quinquennial growth of expenditure on salary was by 18 times, whereas on the reading material it was by four times during first two decades. A good chunk of the grant for collection development is eaten away by periodicals, as is the universal phenomenon in university libraries, yet the number of journals being subscribed has declined considerably.

The collection has expanded at a faster rate in the first decade of the library while it slackened thereafter. This library of repute could purchase only 2,000 books in 1997-98, book collection has fallen victim to high inflation in the cost of reading materials, increasing salary bill and perhaps to teaching faculty preference for subscription to specialised periodicals. How can such meagre inputs support instruction or learning and research in such academic institutions of excellence?

It is therefore suggested that the library should be given grants commensurate with inflation rate of the reading materials. Library friends and staff can also help raise the funds. The library can also market its services and products efficiently and earn some money to boost its resources.

There is a need to formulate policies and formula for allocation of funds to salaries, books periodicals, other materials and technology so as to make optimum use of resources to restore its eroded ability to purchase sufficient number of books for the benefit of its students and faculty.

REFERENCES

1. *Universities Handbook* AIV, 2000, New Delhi, p. 380.
2. University of Hyderabad : Prospectus —1992-2000, p.44.
3. Perm Chand, Financial management of university libraries in India, Ph.D. Thesis, Punjabi University, Patiala, 1998.
4. Devarajan, G., *Resource Allocation in University Libraries,* ESS ESS Publication, New Delhi, 1999.
5. Venkata Ramana, V., *Pattern and Development of University Libraries,* ESS ESS Publications, New Delhi, 1983.
6. Trishanjit Kaur. Development and growth of university libraries and their services in Punjab. Ph.D. Thesis, Punjabi University, Patiala.
7. Robinson, Barbara M. and Robinson, Sherman. Strategic planning and program budgeting for libraries. *Library Trends,* 1994, 42,3, p.438
8. Saroj Bala, University library finance : A case study of Punjab. Ph.D Thesis, Punjabi University, Patiala, 1996.
9. Trishanjit Kaur, *op cit.*
10. Hukmani, Padma, Acquisition of foreign periodicals in Indian universities : A system approach, Ph.D. Thesis, University of Rajasthan, Jaipur, 1990.

11. University Grants Commission (India) Inter Agency Working Group. *Development of an information and library network* : Report, 1989, UGC. New Delhi.
12. Laxman, Rao N. and Prefulla Chandra, Rationalisation of periodical subscriptions, *CLIS Observer*, 1993, 10-3-4.
13. Riggs, Doualb E., What's in store for academic libraries? Leadership and management issues. *Journal of Academic Librarianship*, 1999, 23, 1.

13

A Unique Library on Lingayatism

S.R. Gunjal

ANUBHAVA MANTA PA : A PARLIAMENT OF RELIGION

Sri Basaveswara has been a great reformer of India in the middle of the twelfth century at Kalyan, the capital of Chalukyan dynasty. King Bijjala of Kalachuri dynasty usurped the Chalukyan throne and ruled the kingdom from A.D.1157 to1167. Sri Basaveshwara was appointed as the Prime Minister and the Financial Secretary by King Bijjala.

During this period, Basaveswara established an institution by name 'Anubhava Mantapa' (the hall of spiritual experiences) through which he started his socio-religious movement in order to bring new life in the dying Hindu society, in which superstitions, blind beliefs, crooked practices, irrational religious pollution, etc., were rampart. Anubhava Mantapa could attract the attention of men and women, rich and poor, touchables and untouchables, etc. Those endowed with high spiritual qualities joined this movement. Under the able leadership and guidance of Basaveshwara, they assembled in Anubhava Mantapa to discuss their common problems and find out satisfactory solutions.

EMERGENCE OF VACHANA LITERATURE

As a result of their elaborate discourses on each problem, a lot of recorded material emerged that is popularly known as Vachana and Swaravachana literature. While going through these voluminous scriptures of Sharanas, we can very easily find the significant and revolutionary ideas brought by them into practice.

THEORY AND PRACTICE

Anubhava Mantapa proclaimed that God is one and He should be worshipped in the from of 'Istaling' which is to be carried on one's body till death. Every individual in the community had the right to enjoy the full liberty in social and religious matters. It eradicated the conception of rebirth or the theory of transmigration. It respected men and women equally against the Brahmanism wherein women were treated inferior to men. In other words, gentle sex was accorded the lowest position in the hierarchical system of Varnashrama in Hindu society. It raised the status of the downtrodden people who were constantly depressed and considered as sinful persons by birth. In the Anubhava Mantapa, on the contrary each member had to bring his/her knowledge into daily practice. Thought without action has no value. Action with the foundation stone of the Anubhava Mantapa says, "To know that one should not covet his neighbour's wife is knowledge, true, to translate that into action is knowledge complete; but to know it and act otherwise, behold, the same is ignorance Oh Lord Kudala Chenna Sangamadeva." The real test of a saint was not his outer appearance but his inner purity; not reason but action.

WORK IS DIVINE

If we examine the society before 'Basava', the fruits of labour were not enjoyed by the labourers but the high caste. People of minority were entitled to have the fruits as per the rules of Dharmashastra of Manu and Yajnavalkya. So the working class people of the society were kept in the utmost poverty without any right for earnings. Anubhava Mantapa strictly proclaimed that every man or woman in the society should do physical work without any exception. Whatever may be his/her status in the society, he/she should do job which yields material wealth for daily life. This compulsory work or job as called 'Kayaka'. Anubhava Mantapa made it a necessary rule that each one should earn his daily bread by his hard work and utilise it for his daily needs. At the same time some portion of earning should be given to others who were physically weak and disabled. Ultimately sincere, honest work, it declared, brings happiness and peace in one's life. 'Kayakave Kailasa' was its slogan. It preached love and dignity of labour.

SALVATION FOR ALL

In Hinduism there is no salvation for householders. He who desires to have the salvation has to renounce his family and become a recluse. But Anubhava Mantapa advocated and professed salvation not only for householders but each and every member of the society irrespective of status. Married persons were respected more and honoured for salvation.

ERADICATION OF UNTOUCHABILITY

Since time immemorial, Hinduism has been treating a major group of the society as untouchables or Abhindus/non-Hindus, denying them minimum human rights. Besides, they had been considered enemies of Hinduism and were treated as slaves. Anubhava Mantapa came forward for their rescue and it gave them education, taught them moral code of conduct and merged them in the Sharana community. It taught them to read and write Vachanas. This unprecedented revolution among untouchables can be seen for the first time in the religious history of India.

UNIVERSITY OF COMMON MAN

The Vachana literature produced in abundance by Sharanas through Anubhava Mantapa explicitly advocated the above-mentioned revolutionary reforms. Hence it may be called the University of the common man. The conception so far believed that education was meant only for select few, was changed and made free for all and they were admitted to it without any discrimination of caste, colour, sex and age. Thousands of ordinary people received free education and as a result, they became truth seekers, and spiritual leaders. In fact, they became the selfless servants of the new society. The literature produced by them contains the principles of socialistic pattern of society.

VACHANA BHANDARA

An adjacent building of Anubhava Mantapa was reserved for the main purpose of collecting, preserving and distributing palm-leaf manuscripts of Vachanas. They were arranged in a classified sequence. This was called 'Vachana Bhandara', a public library in the modern sense of the word. Shantarasa, a scholar and a mystic, was appointed as Librarian of the Vachana Bhandara and hence he was known as 'Vachana Bhandari Shantarasa'. He had composed a number of Vachanas of which only 64 are now available for reference. He was assisted by many scribes or copyists. Their main duty was to prepare a number of copies of the manuscripts of Vachanas for distribution among the learned and common folk as well. The copies were carried by them from place to place all over the country and spread the new message among the masses. The gospels contained in the Vachana literature attracted the people and they started studying them and imbided the principles in their daily life. As a result, their lifestyle was completely changed and they became the men of character.

BOOKS AND PERIODICALS

For intensive study of Vachana literature many of the disciples began to sing the contents in different forms of prosody. They are known as Dwipadi, Tripadi, Chowpadi, Satpadi, Ragale, Sangatya, Champu, Shatak, Dandak, Astaka and such other meters of prosody. Thousands of books have been written by hundreds of such mystic poets of Lingayat religion during the last 850 years in various languages such as Kannada, Telugu, Tamil, Marathi, Sanskrit, etc. Abundant literature has been produced in Kannada. It occupies nearly 50 per cent of the entire Kannada literature. This type of literature has been produced even in other languages but not on a large scale.

In the modern age, especially during a couple of hundred years back Lingayat literature has attracted the attention of many Western scholars and they have contributed significantly their share in English.

Similarly, many periodicals, with the main aim of propagating the principles of Lingayat religion, started publishing various articles by the end of the nineteenth century and 15 journals in Kannada, three in English and two in Marathi are being published with a frequency either as monthly or quarterly.

VIJAYA MAHANTESH LIBRARY AT SHIVAYOGA MANDIRA

It is estimated that about 6,000 books in Kannada and nearly 1,000 in other languages have been published from 1850 to this date. A sincere effort was made by Hangal Kumara Shivayogi, founder of the Shivayoga Mandira near Badami, and a rich religious library in the name of Sri Vijaya Mahantesh Granthlaya was established in 1909. Thousands of books and manuscripts on Lingayatism were collected and preserved in it. It has become an important reference library for the religious trainees at Shivayoga Mandira. The collection grew unabated until the death of Sri Kumara Shivayogi in 1930. Afterwards the collection decreased gradually and the residue today is of less value.

The reasons for its downfall may be enumerated as negligence and lack of personnel trained in library management. Now the services of this library are almost static.

CENTRAL RESEARCH LIBRARY OF LINGAYAT STUDIES

It is regretful that there is no such special library worth mentioning containing almost all published material on Lingayatism in India, particularly in Karnataka. Lingayat literature is gaining much popularity among the scholars and researchers nowadays. Such a type of library which could quench their thirst for knowledge in Lingayatism was a need. This scarcity was noticed by a young, energetic and well-educated pontiff, Sri Siddharama Swamiji of Naganur Rudraximath, Belgaum, and it was decided to establish a well equipped library of Lingayat literature for the sole purpose of providing the necessary books, articles and other authentic information to the researchers on Lingayatism. Providentially and fortunately he came in contact with Dr. S.R. Gunjal, retired Professor of Library and Information Science and Librarian of Gulbarga University. He persuaded him to be the Director of the proposed Lingayat Central Research Library to be established in the premises of his own Math. Accordingly, the Central Research Library of Lingayata Studies came into existence in July 1995.

ACHIEVEMENTS

During this short period, the library has made a tremendous progress. Its achievements are commendable.

a) The total collection of library exceeds 5,000 books. It includes the works of famous authors like Harihar,

Raghavanka, Bhima, Virupaksha Pandit, Chamaras, Shadaxara Deva, Sarvajna and others. The works of modern Kannada authors such as N.R. Karibasava Shastri, P.R. Karibasava Shastry, P.G. Halakatti Mallikarjun, B. Shivamurthy Shastry, M.R. Srinivas Murthy, R.R. Diwakar, Hardekar Manjappa, S.S. Basavanal, C.D. Uttangi, K. Ishwaran, R.C. Hiremath, M. Chidanandmurthy, H. Tipperudraswamy, L. Basavaraju, M.M. Kalburgi, B.R. Hireamth, Viranna Rajur, G.H. Hanneradumath, B. Puttaswamaiah, Siddayya Puranik, V. Shivananda, Sangamesh Savadattimath, etc. are also available in the library.

All works on and by Basaveswara, Chennabasaveswara, Prabhudeva, Siddarama and Akkamahadevi are maintained separately. Likewise books pertaining to Ekottara Shatasthala and Siddanta Sikhamani are kept as a special collection.

Felicitation and commemoration volumes offered to Lingayat pontiffs, political leaders, literary luminaries, are of special value in the library.

b) A scheme of classification has been developed to classify the whole collection of books under about 300 subject headings. It enables the researchers to choose all the relevant books and periodical articles on specific subjects of their interest within minutes. It saves the valuable time, energy and labour of the scholars. The scheme may be adopted by other libraries as a model to classify their collection of books on Lingayatism minutely.

c) Some useful classified indexes of books and periodical articles are prepared by the library staff. The library has obtained the back volumes of many important old journals. The indexes of articles appeared in felicitation volumes, *Basava path*, *Shivanubhava*, *Sharana*, *Prasad*, *Basava Journal*. Some of them are published in book form. In fact, such indexes are of indispensable value in research work.

d) Daily newspapers and monthly magazines such as *Deccan Herald, Indian Express, Times of India, Prajavani, Samyukta Karnataka, Kannada Prabha* are regularly scanned and cuttings containing relevant news-information on Lingayats, abbots, important personalities and events are taken out and maintained in the chronological order in the library. Many readers are visiting the library in search of such items of information.

e) The library maintains a rare collection of 200 bundles of written palm-leaf manuscripts which contain 587 works (books) by various authors. A descriptive catalogue of these manuscripts is compiled and published with the financial assistance of the Director General, National Archives, Government of India, Delhi 1998. A request has been made to the Director to grant a sum of Rs. 1,25,000 for the speedy development of the manuscript library in the coming years. The library is planning to conduct a survey in Belgaum district to collect manuscripts which are still lying in Lingayat maths.

f) Free food and accommodation shall be provided in the library for researchers coming from distant educational institutions and research organisations for reference and intensive study. There are many instances such as students from Japan, USA and England who visited the library and made use of the research material available in it. It is a matter of gratification that Kannada Viswavidyala at Hampi (Bellary district) has recognised the library as a research centre for its students. Similarly research students studying for MPhil and PhD in Karnatak and Gulbarga and other universities are benefited from this library.

FUTURE PLANS

The library intends to take up the following projects in the library on a priority basis in the near future.

i) An audio-visual section comprising documentary films, movies, cassettes, pertaining to Lingayat literature, culture and history to be set separately in the library.

ii) There is a plan to prepare an exhaustive concordance to the entire Vachana literature produced by Sharanas of twelfth century.

iii) A voluminous literature on Lingayatism was composed in Kannada language during the long period from the twelfth century to the twentieth century. The technical terms of Lingayatism have been profusely used by the poets and other authors in their works. Researchers sometime find it difficult to understand the implications of those terms. In order to assist them, we desire to compile a dictionary of technical terms of Lingayatism in course of time.

iv) Scholars are also in need of a comprehensive bibliography of books on Lingayat religion published in various languages. We are bringing out the bibliography as early as possible.

v) Valuable articles are being published in many current and back issues of periodicals. We are happy to prepare the indexes of articles which had appeared in periodicals like *Basava patha, Sharana, Basava Journal Prasada* and *Shivanubhava*. These are under print. Similarly classified indexes of articles of other important journals are to be compiled and we are striving for them.

vi) We have a proposal to open a museum of objects of interest on the social and cultural history of Lingayat religion and community.

VISITS OF EMINENT SCHOLARS AND PONTIFFS

Many distinguished literary persons visited our library during the last three years and expressed their satisfaction over a rich collection on Lingayat religion. Some of them are :

(1) Sri. Go.Ru. Chennabasappa, President of Akhil Bharata Sharana Sahitya Parisattu, Bangalore. (2) Dr. H.N. Karulasiddhaiah, retired Professor of social work, Bangalore University. (3) Sri. Chennaveer Kanavi, ex-President of Kannada Sahitya Sammelana, Dharwad, (4) Dr. K.M. Kalburgi, Vice-Chancellor of Kannada University, Hampi, (5) H.M. Nayak, Ex-Vice-Chancellor of Gulbarga University, (6) Sri Shantaras, Ex-President, Karnatak Sahitya Academi, Bangalore, (7) Dr. Niremallur Iswaran, Canada, (8) Dr. N. Chidanand Murthy, President, Kannda Shakti Kendra, Bangalore, (9) Dr. Guruling Hapse, Dharwad, (10) Dr. Basavraj Malashetty, Vijayanagar College, Hospet, (11) Dr. T.V. Venkatachal Shastri, Mysore, (12) Prof. B. Virupakshappa, Chief Editor Basava Journal, Bangalore, (13) Dr. Basavaraj Sadar, A.I.R. Dharwad, (14) Dr. V.V. Sirur Karnatak University, Dharwad, (15) Dr. Raghunath Bhatta, Karnatak University, (16) Dharwad, Sri. B.A. Sanadi, Mumbai.

Likewise, some abbots of Lingayat religion had been to our library to go through the books of great importance and they were very much pleased. They exclaimed that this was a unique library on Lingayatism. We are happy to mention some of the Swamijis: (1) Jagadguru Sri Sangana Basva Swamiji, Hospet, (2) Jagadguru Dr. Tontada Siddhalinga Swamiji, Gadag-Dambal, (3) Jagadguru Dr. Gangadhara Rajayogindra Swamiju, Hubli, (4) Jagadguru Sri Annadanishwara Swamiji Mundaragi, (5) Jagadguru Sri Shivamurthy Murugharajendra Swamiji, Chitradurga, (6) Jagadguru Sri Panchama Shivalingeswara Swamiji, Nidasosi, (7) Sri Siddheswara Swamiji, Bijapur, (8) Sri Kumara Swamiji, Hanagal, (9) Sri Shivakumara Swamiji, Pidarkundi.

Rani Satish, Bangalore, Vishwanath Reddy Mudnal, Nilgangayya Pujar and Bhimanna Khandre are some of the politicians among the visitors to our library. Brad Beaman from USA and Hagime Chiba from Japan, Tizana of Italy spent some days in the library and collected relevant information especially on Basaveswara during their stay.

It will suffice, if we quote here the opinion of an eminent scholar Sri. Siddheswara Swamiji, Jnana Yogeshrama, Bijapur, who visited the library on 15 October, 1996:

"The books are systematically arranged, and scientifically maintained. The brain and effort behind all this is Dr. S.R. Gunjal, a nationally recognised librarian. His four decades experience in the field will definitely help to make this library a unique reading centre and a rare place of spiritual knowledge, concerning Lingayat religion. His Holiness Sri Siddharama Swamiji who has blessed the centre in every way is a lover of learning. His committed mission is to spread the religious knowledge and awaken the people towards the higher values. This centre is his conception. I hope, it will grow into an ideal place of knowledge very shortly."

Indeed, his prophetic words have now become true.

14

Reshaping Library and Information Infrastructure to Integrate the Gains of Information Technology

O.P. Gupta

India's ancient civilisation had its progress in education at the highest level. We maintain that education is a liberating force and also an evolutionary force. It enables individuals to rise from mere materiality to superior planes of intellectual and spiritual consciousness. Whereas the foundation of modern western civilisation is on materials, ours is on spiritual use. The focus of modern civilisation is on investigating laws of matter, and employing human ingenuity in inventing or discovering means of production and weapons of destruction. Ours is chiefly into exploring spiritual laws, developing mental, physical and spiritual faculties. Education is a dialogue between the past, the present and the future, so that the coming generations receive the accumulated lesson of the heritage and carry it forward. In the words of Shri Aurobindo, the past is our foundation the present our material, the future our aim and submit. Each must have its due and natural place in a national system of education.

EDUCATION SYSTEM

Education helps us in better understanding of environment and international cooperation. To achieve the goals of education the country has constructed the largest education system consisting of institutions from primary to higher education. There are sub-systems based on specialised education such as engineering, management, medical services, computer application and information technology (IT), etc. The achievements made in these disciplines are continuously transmitted to the next generation for furthering the advancement. The present education system has created high order and men and women almost in all areas. They are always working on the problems like illiteracy, poverty, unity and scientific progress. This system has been influenced by our thinkers. Swamy Vivekananda said that we want that education by which character is formed, strength of mind is increased, the intellect is expanded and by which one can stand on one's own feet. Education is the manifesto of perfection already in men.

HIGHER EDUCATION FUNCTIONS

It is only after independence that the number of educational institutions in India has increased manifold. There are at present 214 universities and equivalent institutions, a large number of management institutions, engineering institutions and 9,703 colleges. Besides, there are specialised institutions for imparting education in science and technology, open learning facility in different disciplines and languages, etc., at different parts in the country. These are the means by which the best of achievement are transmitted down to the coming generation. In turn, the new generation will work to achieve objectives of higher education and provide the right kind of work ethos, professional expertise and leadership in all walks of life. Keeping this in mind, the functions for the modern world universities set up by the UGC are :

a) To seek and cultivate new knowledge, to engage vigorously and fearlessly in the pursuit of truth and to interpret old knowledge and belief in the light of new needs and discoveries;

b) To provide the right kind of leadership in all walks of life by helping the individuals to develop their potential;

c) To provide society with competent men and women trained in all professions who, as cultivated individuals, are inclined with a sense of social purpose;

d) To strive to promote equality and social justice and to reduce social and cultural difference through diffusion of education;

e) To foster in the teachers and students, and through them in the society generally, the attitudes and values, needed for developing the good life in individuals and society; and

f) To bring the universities closer to the community through extension of knowledge and its application for problems solving.

Higher education is of paramount importance for economic and social development. Institutions of higher education have the main responsibility for equipping individuals with the advanced knowledge and skills required for positions of responsibility in government, business and the professions. These institutions produce new knowledge through research and serve as cooperator for the transfer, adaptation and dissemination of knowledge generated elsewhere in the world. It also plays an important role by offering a forum for pluralistic debate.

INFORMATION INFRASTRUCTURE

Information generates knowledge power. Thus information has its own accepted value. The value of truth has been accepted by all throughout the world. As a result, at various levels at international, national, regional and local levels, information is collected, stored, processed and made available to those who use it. Specialised information centres have been created to pool information in identified disciplines. The work of these centres is carried out by specialists. There are schools to teach analysis and repackaging of information. The personnel engaged in these jobs have various nomenclatures such as librarian, documentation officer, library and information officer, analyst, programmer, computer scientist, information scientist and so on. Identification of information need and matching recorded documents, electronic data processing and communication system requires skills in the newer areas. As such information is the life support of all types of knowledge advancement. One needs techniques by which most relevant, accurate, complete, concise, timely, economic, reliable and efficient information can be made available. A good information infrastructure is required to feed academic community in particular and also to monitor the standards of education imparted at all levels. The UGC in its planning programmes had debated information technology application programmes and also formulated guidelines to provide funds to promote information management system.

UGC SUPPORT TO UNIVERSITY AND COLLEGE LIBRARIES

The UGC has funding provision to create library infrastructure. It monitors after every plan and allocates funds for five years keeping in view the fresh requirements. The UGC has also development programmes with financial assistance running between Rs. 3 lakh and Rs. 10 lakh based on student enrolment. This is to maintain proper standards, ensuring optimum utilisation of facilities and equalisation of facilities to the educationally backward areas. The major workforce is created by graduate courses. Therefore, a larger infrastructure as suitable to the education system with all the modern developments is an essential requirement. The courses taught therein should be restructured to include emerging inter-disciplinary areas.

The students should be asked to go for aptitude test before opting for any course of study. This will help in establishing relation between students and best chosen course suited to their interest and capability. Under D.1 (a) UGC guidelines there is provision for "Books and journals" including setting up of "Book Bank" and strengthening of the existing Book Banks in order to augment the facilities and improve reading habits among the students. There are recommendations that the procurement of books should be by a library committee constituted by the institution. Under equipment grant, there is a separate provision for fax, audio visual equipment and teaching aids, computer, generator, reprographic facilities, network and Internet connection. This apart, there is provision for library building and the commission has introduced a good number of vocational courses to create computer culture. In these courses, the papers to cover up subjects like computer fundamentals, introduction to IBM PC, operating system, business data processing, database management system, structure programmes, database management system, computer graphics, computer aided drafting, advanced topics in computer, etc., have been introduced.

But information management still has problem areas relating to issues like complexities in information flow, various records formats, speed difference in machine, changing communication devices, suitable techniques in evaluation of information, and so on.

INFORMATION SYSTEM

The information technology (IT) has great potentialities to facilitate persons engaged in knowledge advancement. Even then we do not know enough as yet how to take full advantage of IT or how to overpower some of its dangers. In spite of all, the number of users of information technology is increasing day by day, since it removes all barriers and takes us beyond the political and ideological boundaries. Globalisation is ushering a new information, and economic order. Probably, information management in future will dominate the economy. Computer applications will boost business. Thus, information technology will be most debated subject in this country. In spite of all that we need to be vigilant against market-oriented information systems as well as information systems which are not developed by government agencies. We should work on the strategies to create indigenous information system to foster all-around progress of the country. An awareness about information flow, its organisation, value, relevance and impact on progress should be created. Advancements are taking place very fast. As a result there is a greater need that human resources operating these fast improving technologies should be updated regularly. In this process again application of information has a tremendous role to play.

LIS HUMAN RESOURCE

IT application leads to more efficient, successful and accurate expeditious and effective full use of resources. For information management, trained and skilled personnel with all necessary infrastructure is an essential requirement. So far the quality of professionally trained personnel provided by the university departments, other agencies, professional bodies, associations, etc., has been the focus of transformation. Due to financial constraints the courses are either part-time, seasonal or vocational. Short-term courses are also offered to create workforce at different support channels. To keep the standards of the discipline, the courses in BLib Sc, BLI Sc BIT and MLib MLISc MIT, MICT, etc., should be examined in the light of advancements made and human resource required to operate information services at difference places and times. There should also be well defined national accreditation programme for this professional discipline.

At the national level the UGC has constituted subject panel in the library and information science to integrate advances in practice. The panel is supposed to suggest improvement measures in the field. It should be requested to provide revised syllabi on modern lines of development and which could be put into practice in Indian institutions. This is very much needed, as "Science and technology is growing rapidly, revolution in information technology is unfolding itself and the world is becoming smaller. International boundaries are toppling for knowledge workers in order that knowledge workers make their professional contributions in the emerging world order. The qualifications, skills and achievements must have recognition and acceptance in the global marketplace." The LIS professional's role is now to analyse the requisition or demand to locate information from various documents including those available outside the library. They have to be put in some sequential order of use. Therefore, one has to learn search techniques, search strategies, database formats, and search result files, etc., alongwith traditional repackaging methods.

An expression of one's information needs in the language known to each other and its translation in to mechanical process to achieve desired results is a another very important and basic task. To provide information in minimal time with accuracy there should be well thought information requirement format or expression test software. Standard requisition formats have been experienced in railway booking centres and the results are satisfactory. This will be helpful in keeping consistency. The resource sharing will be standardised. With networking culture online searches will increase. Their overwhelming use has invited interest of commercial people in creation of specialised databases. This computer interface is opening a large number of new jobs. Search specialists will work as intermediaries to the knowledge workers. The professionals will have to be more specialised. In near future users themself will be able to conduct the searches. There may be a period when a librarian will be able to provide expert system, computer programmes to facilitate through mechanical process. Such programmes may include outlining of the subject areas, selection of database to be searched, a number of references to be considered and special contributors if any and so on.

NEWER AREAS OF STUDY

In order to march with advancements and also to maintain the standards of education the libraries will have to develop search specialists to work as intermediary between machine search system and users. There is an immediate need to decide their skill, communication efficiencies, type of machine operations, software knowledge, network knowledge and knowledge of search and communication devices, strategies, knowledge of new management techniques and so on. With network use online searching has further widened. Now information user is supposed to know operation of connectivity, selection of terminals, understanding of cost involvement, changing policies, techniques used and selection of relevant database, downloading of required information, reorganisation of relevant information, and repackaging of the same for future use. These are all emerging areas and are inviting attention for inclusion in the syllabi of the information management courses.

Furthermore, the databases are created with different objectives such as commercial, public, specialised, general, etc. These are available for use to individuals, institutions, nation and international agencies. These can be categorised like, reference database, biblicgraphic database, source database, numeric database, full text database, abstract database, search service generated database, uplinking with other database and downloading process created database, and so on. These variety of databases are used by many different types of searchers for example general users, specialist users, commercial users, professional users, etc. Thus these newer areas of study should take place in LIS courses.

INFORMATION RETRIEVAL SYSTEM

Information retrieval has very close relation with human mind. In fact, every human mind is a powerful retrieval system. But this system has his own principles to work. Machine readable data in a retrieval system is designed and stored for use by a larger number of people. Therefore, the system is always designed on the principals that retrieval by all can be possible. The retrieval system should be designed in such a language and programme which can be understood by all without any difficulty. The retrieval/search may be priced, based on some formula considering devoted time, quality of collections, sophisticated equipment and engagement of qualitative human resource used for the purpose. The user should know for which period he will be charged. This knowledge will help in planning his computer use and use of communication links as well.

REVIEW OF LIS SERVICES

Many of the essential library services like current awareness service (CAS), select dissemination of information (SDI), indexing, abstracting, translation, subject bibliographies, library cooperation, and so on are disappearing due to lack of qualified staff and insufficient funds. In spite of all the technological developments in the IT, information flow is very slow. Proper communication generates learning ethos and it works to accelerate progress. Computer and IT application has the necessary potential to accelerate information flow. The present library and information services have been developed on the laws laid down by Dr. S.R. Ranganathan. His scientific approaches in LIS services are becoming less relevant in the context of information technology and communication advancements. It is, therefore, the period that we professionals review our strategies to integrate advances in IT into our traditional methods of designing services. A mixed approach to meeting traditional requirements by using traditional resources and advancements in scientific world will have to be followed.

NATIONAL ACADEMIC INFORMATION INFRASTRUCTURE

At university, college and similar other institutions we need a national information infrastructure which can also be used by other global agencies through network services This approach will enhance India's global competitiveness, awareness to healthcare, education, governmental management and electronic advancements. This will also open the doors to create new jobs in different areas. The libraries from the ages have been working as intermediary for dissemination of information and for advancement of knowledge. But information technology, computers, networkers and communication have widened access. One can use any library from any part of the globe provided it is digitised. The new developments have had very deep impact on human resource required to perform various jobs. The government and professional bodies are debating new areas of work to create awareness among the professionals and the society as well. The mankind is passing through a changing world order. It is being influenced by immense knowledge advancement. To welcome this change specialised information dissemination centres have to be set-up all around the country in the libraries of academic institutions. The syllabi of LIS education should include all advancements ushered by printing, publishing, electronic and communication revolutions. The necessary efforts for the creation of one-time infrastructure should also be monitored for regular updating with technical changes. In fact, timely planning and integration of control programmes has direct relation with the trouble-free information management.

Part IV

Library Resource Development, Sharing and Access

15

Developing Acquisition Policy for University Libraries in India

Neela Jagannathan

INTRODUCTION

Collection development is one of the most challenging tasks for university librarians since its very meaning has been enlarged with increasing specialisation in library management due to acquisition of multimedia resources and automation. Collection development and acquisition management are two sides of the same coin and are interdependent of each other. Collection development policy, selection policy and acquisition policy are by no means synonymous. They represent a hierarchy in which collection development, being a planning function, is placed at the highest level.

Selection is the second level of decision making and acquisition, the third level in the process of acquiring various types and forms of materials, implementing selection decisions and collection development policy.[1] The role of a library within a university is guided by the institutional philosophy. Thus the acquisition policy has to be developed to support the goals and objectives of the university keeping in view the primary users, namely, teachers, research scholars and students.

ACQUISITION POLICY : NEED AND PURPOSE

According to Pauline H. Anderson,[2] "Policies are a form of insurance." They are statements that guide decisions, suggest actions and provide structure for the governance of the library. Uniform application of policies is essential both for achieving desired results and providing equitable treatment for all. The acquisition policy is the detailed plan of procedure adopted by the university library for developing collection. It ensures consistency in the operations and continuity in the development of useful collection. A clearly articulated acquisition policy reduces the complexities of decision making, provides to operate efficiently, and assists in maintaining high standards of excellence.

In this era of sophisticated information technologies, university libraries develop resources in multimedia physical formats. The collections are developed both for print and non-print materials. They are :

Print Materials	*Non-print Materials*
i) Books & monographs	i) Graphic records
ii) Conference proceedings	ii) Photographic records
iii) Government reports, documents	iii) Sound records
iv) Reference books	iv) Audio-visual records
v) Periodicals and serials	v) Microforms
vi) Patents and standards	vi) Computer records
vii) Theses	vii) CD-ROMs, and
viii) Pamphlets	viii) Realia and three-dimensional records

The discussion in this paper is restricted to selection and acquisition of print resources. Moreover, acquisition policy discussed here is limited only to procurement of printed resources recommended for purchase and not to those books as are acquired through exchange, gift or by becoming institutional members to receive their publications as gratis, as each one of them needs formulation of a separate policy. Borrowing books on inter-library loan, especially out-of-print and other materials for fulfilling immediate demand of users can be a part of both acquisition as well as circulation policies. Consequently, it can be discussed under resource sharing policy.

The main purpose of the acquisition policy is to promote the acquisition of printed resources compatible with the objectives of the university as well as to meet the needs of the students, academic, administrative and technical staff of the university. In order to achieve this objective, "quality rather than quantity" should be the motto or goal of the acquisition policy of every university library as it ensures not only the maximum utilisation of the given resources but also improves the academic value of information provided to users.

PLANNED SELECTIONS : PROBLEMS & PRECAUTIONS

The acquisition policy can be effective only if it involves planned selection of resources and satisfies the needs of varied clientele of the library. In order to promote the sale of their publications, publishers and booksellers use varied strategies of marketing to outreach librarians and provide information of latest publications through printed and electronic means. The prominent strategies used are :

a) Publishing "Books in Print" of various countries, languages and physical formats of media resources;
b) Producing national and trade bibliographies;
c) Producing catalogues of publishers and booksellers either general or for publications in specific subjects and languages
d) Distributing pre-publication review jackets, new arrivals, brochures and pamphlets;
e) Publishing book reviews in journals and book trade periodicals;
f) Showing books to faculty members for approval and selection; and
g) Creating websites of publishers, booksellers, book trade and their associations.

Librarians help in selection of documents by compiling bibliographies on various topics/subjects by consulting various printed and electronic selection tools. They organise display of books and circulate book trade catalogues to facilitate selection of latest publications. Faculty members prepare lists of books by visiting other libraries, book fairs and exhibitions. They also refer to book reviews in journals and references at the end of articles/chapters. The selection of library materials in a university library is the joint responsibility of the academic faculty members and the library staff.

University librarians have to acquire publications considering the needs of all types of users and pertaining to all aspects covered in the selection policy. The publications, both books and serials, can be of:

a) General interest, namely, biographies, historical surveys, bibliographies and works of major authors, reports of institutions and so on;
b) Instructional needs for different subjects and disciplines, classics and collection of works by different well-known authors and critics, periodicals in various subjects, conference proceedings, etc.;
c) Reference value for enriching knowledge and seeking information such as encyclopaedias, dictionaries, yearbooks, directories, handbooks, manuals, guides, statistical reports, news summaries, etc.
d) Use for comprehensive and exhaustive research by faculty members, research scholars and students to pursue research in varies disciplines; and
e) Varied resources having chronological, geographical, and subject coverage, books of various levels, languages and varied range of physical formats of print and non-print media.

The selection process needs careful planning because there are number of factors which affect collection development. They are:

a) Increase in publishing actively due to information explosion;

b) Shrinking of infrastructural facilities including grants, space and staff;

c) Escalation in the cost of books due to rise in printing and production charges;

d) Frequent increase in conversion rates of foreign currencies due to devaluation of rupee in international market, etc.; and

e) Complexities of demand due to increase in multi-disciplinary publications.

Consequently, the responsibility of faculty members and library staff increases in manifolds to develop effective collections by judicious utilisation of grant. In this regard the selection committee should take precautions mentioned below :

a) Avoid duplication as far as possible;

b) Prefer to procure paperback editions instead of hardbound books;

c) Place standing orders for serials such as yearbooks, annuals, directories, etc., and procure expensive foreign publications every alternate year;

d) Give importance to latest publications and avoid selecting out-of-date books;

e) Take due precaution to get 50 per cent discount at least on 'remainder books';

f) Follow Good Offices Committee recommendations for getting benefits consistently and continuously; and

g) Demand for original invoice as price proof of foreign books rather than photocopies of pages from printed catalogues or book selection tools.

No library can be self-sufficient or can purchase all relevant and useful printed materials available in different subjects/ disciplines due to financial constraints. Hence, it is essential for libraries to :

a) Emphasise on resource sharing and enter into agreement for inter-library loan arrangement with leading libraries;

b) Be a member of library networks to get benefits of borrowing books on demand and out of print books from participating libraries; and

c) Download the relevant resources from Internet for users.

Resource sharing and networking facilitates the librarians to satisfy the needs of the users.

ACQUISITION POLICY: BASIC PRINCIPLES

In order to develop useful collection, the responsibility of library is to follow some basic principles of the acquisition policy. These are :

a) To provide resources, both books and journals - for enriching and supporting the curriculum, taking into consideration the varied interests of faculty and maturity levels of students;

b) To develop collection for stimulating growth in factual knowledge, literary appreciation, aesthetic values and ethical standards;

c) To anticipate and fulfil the information needs of the primary users by active and continuous liaison with the faculty members;

d) To allocate budget for the resources to different disciplines for meeting their instructional needs;

e) To procure resources and to provide support to faculties and research scholars in pursuing their research and scholarly work;

f) To evaluate the existing collection in each discipline and fill up the gaps if any by acquiring relevant resources; and

g) To maintain a current and easily accessible collection through judicious weeding out of obsolete and unused resources on a continual basis.

ACQUISITION CRITERIA

Librarians should follow some basic criteria/principles of acquisition to achieve concrete results in developing useful collection. The suggested criteria are :

a) Physical condition and durability considering the price and format;
b) Accuracy and authenticity of facts and content;
c) Reputation of the author for the subject concerned and the publisher in the book trade;
d) Relevance and significance of subject matter keeping in view the potential users of the library;
e) Timeliness and permanence of documents especially in fast developing disciplines;
f) Clarity of presentation and use of lucid style depending upon the levels of target groups;
g) Literary merit, accurate statistical inputs, artistic quality as well as reference, information and recreational value, and
h) Availability of the documents on the subject in the library and its importance to total collection.

Acquisition of each document need not fulfil all these criteria but the librarian should make sure that at least four or more criteria are met while selecting and acquiring books to ensure the optimum utilisation of resources added to the collection.

CONCLUSION

The process of developing and articulating policies is intellectually and professionally stimulating. The library policy cannot be static. The nature, content, scope and purpose are evolving constantly. All policy statements need to be reviewed, revised and updated frequently to respond to the changes. The procedure for review of acquisition policy presents an opportunity to the librarian to re-examine and alter the policy statements at regular intervals. The focus of the review should be the scope and depth of collection and its adequacy to support primary users and to achieve the motto or objective of acquisition of quality materials rather than aiming quantity.

REFERENCES

1. Gardner, Richard K., *Library Collections: Their Origins, Selection and Development*, New York, McGraw Hill, 1981.
2. Anderson, Pauline H., *Library Media Leadership in Academic Secondary Schools*, A Hamden, Connecticut; Library Professional Publications, 1985. pp. 16-56.
3. Bradley, Jana and Bradely, Larry, *Improving Written Communications in Libraries,* (Ch. 6 - Policies), Chicago, ALA, 1988, pp. 125-149.
4. Evans, G. Edward, *Developing Library Collection*, Littleton, Libraries Unlimited, 1979.
5. Gorman, G.E. and Miller, Ruth H., eds., *Collection Management for the 21st Century: A Handbook for Librarians,* Connecticut; Greenwood, 1997.
6. Hingwe, K.S., *Management of University Libraries in India : Principles and Practices Model Acquisition Policy Statement*, Calcutta, World Press, 1982. Appendix no. 3 - pp. 121-124.
7. Jagannathan, Neela, Collection development at Andhra Pradesh Open University Libraries. *Library Acquisitions: Practice and Theory,* 1988, 12, 4, 281-296.
8. Scammell. Alison, ed., *Handbook of Special Librarianship and Information Work*, Ed. 7, London, ASLIB, 1997.

16

Resource Sharing in Periodicals among Indian Institute of Management Libraries

Narender Kumar and *R.K. Bhatt*

INTRODUCTION

The need for technical and management education was strongly advocated and supported by the Government of India because of the rapid growth of industrial and commercial enterprises both in the private and public sector during the 1950s. A committee[1] under the chairmanship of Sir Ramaswamy Mudaliar, a distinguished industrialist, was appointed in 1960 to estimate the managerial manpower requirements for future expansion of industrial and commercial sectors and suggest necessary action plan. The committee proposed the setting up of special facilities for education and training, outside the universities with a view to provide autonomy, greater flexibility and for quickening the pace of management training and education in India.

In 1961, the Government of India, set up two Indian Institutes of Management, one at Ahmedabad and the other at Kolkata, with the objective of providing high-quality management education through teaching, training, research and consultancy and to make these institutions as the centres of excellence.

Due to the success achieved by the Institutes at Ahmedabad and Kolkata and the demand for more such institutes, the Government of India in 1972, setup the third Indian Institute of Management at Bangalore, and in 1984 the fourth one at Lucknow.

Looking at the demand for specialised managerial manpower after opening up the economy to foreign players, the Government of India has recently established two more Indian Institutes of Management, one at Indore (Madhya Pradesh) and other at Calicut (Kerala). Academic activities have started in these institutes from the session 1997-98.

GROWTH OF PERIODICALS

The amount of information generated every year is very vast. Under the present system of organisation, it is essential that it becomes a useful resource and retrieved efficiently, quickly and effectively. Various estimates about the growth of literature are available and according to Naisbitt[2] in his book *Megatrends* between 6,000 and 7,000 scientific articles are written every day and these double in every five years. Davinson[3] estimates that between 1and 1.5 lakh titles of periodicals have been published so far. *The Standard Periodicals Directory*[4] and *Ebsco's Serials Directory*[5] contain over 75,000 and 1,41,000 international periodicals respectively. *Ulrich's International Periodicals Directory*[6] (1998-99) lists a total of 1,57,200 periodicals as against 68,770 and 1,55,700 listed in its 1986-87 and 1997-98 editions respectively. A study of the number of periodicals in different editions of *Ulrich's International Periodicals Directory* gives an idea as to how fast periodicals in business and economics have been increasing (Table 1).

Table 1 : Growth of Periodicals in Business and Economics : (1984 - 1998)

Year	Ed	Total No of Periodicals	Growth over the preceding year	% of Growth	Cumulative %	Periodicals in Business	Growth over the preceding year	% of Growth	Cumulative % Growth
1984-85	23	67,650	Base	Base	Base	3,840	Base	Base	Base
1985-86	24	67,950	300	0.4	0.4	4,170	330	8.6	8.6
1986-87	25	68,770	820	1.2	1.6	4,260	90	2.2	10.9
1987-88	26	70,730	1,960	2.9	4.5	4,620	360	8.5	20.3
1988-89	27	1,08,590	37,860	53.5	60.5	10,620	6,000	129.9	176.6
1989-90	28	1,11,950	3,360	3.1	65.5	11,670	1,050	9.9	203.9
1990-91	29	1,16,900	4,950	4.4	72.8	12,390	720	6.2	222.6
1991-92	30	1,18,500	1,600	1.4	75.2	13,980	1,590	12.8	264.1
1992-93	31	1,26,000	7,500	6.3	86.2	15,510	1,530	10.9	303.9
1993-94	32	1,36,700	10,700	8.5	102.1	17,640	2,130	13.7	359.4
1994-95	33	1,47,000	10,300	7.5	117.3	19,980	2,340	13.3	420.3
1995-96	34	1,50,100	3,100	2.1	121.9	21,650	1,670	8.3	463.8
1996-97	35	1,52,800	2,700	1.8	125.9	23,460	1,810	8.4	511.0
1997-98	36	1,55,700	2,900	1.9	130.1	25,085	1,625	6.9	553.2
1998-99	37	1,57,200	1,500	1.0	132.4	26,340	1,255	5.0	585.9

Source: Various editions of *Ulrich's International Periodicals Directory.*

In *Ulrich's International Periodicals Directory* the subject management has been covered under business and economics. Table 1 reveals that the growth rate in periodicals in business and economics has escalated after 1988. In the year 1984, 3,840 titles were listed in *Ulrich's International Periodicals Directory*. In 1988 the number of titles went up to 10,620. Since 1988, there has been a yearly increase of 10 to 15 per cent in periodicals in business and economics rising to 26,340 in 1998.

Ward[7] described the publication trends in the general literature on management. In her study she examined management periodicals received during the second half of 1993 in the Institute of Management, Loughborough University of Technology, UK. In this study she identified areas on which most management literature was published. According to her the areas are: environmental scanning, organisational change, total quality management, performance measurement, staffing issues, women and culture issues, information technology, education and training, marketing and promotion, and corporate memory.

Holt and Schrank[8] estimated the long-term annual growth in articles in various disciplines which varies from 2.9 per cent (psychology) to 5.5 per cent (economics).

The rapid proliferation of periodicals, particularly in management, results in hyper specialisation, gives birth to new periodicals either by way of split or amalgamation and it further complicates the problem for the library.[9] Graham[10] has reported that in comparison to funds available, periodicals supply is more due to exceeding demand for publications. A study conducted in 1988 estimated a new title every day in the Western World.[11] Okerson[12] identified the reasons for growth in periodicals literature and concluded that it has been due to growth of university research and enhancement of the academic reward system.

DOCUMENT COLLECTION

Document collection in all IIMs is developed on the recommendations of students, research scholars, faculty members and Library Committee. The Librarian and library staff are responsible for reference and general collection. All IIM libraries follow acquisition policy which in fact is applicable to all types of reading materials.

The total collection has grown in all IIMs. The growth of library collection during last five years has been presented in Table 2.

The average annual growth of the collection in IIMs libraries is the highest, i.e., 7.0 per cent in IIML and lowest, i.e., 2.2 per cent in IIMA. The average annual growth of collection in IIMB has been 4.7 per cent, and 2.7 per cent in IIMC. IIML had highest growth rate because it was established in 1984 and was under the initial thrust of collection development. Data also revealed that IIMB gave considerable importance to the development of library collection and had superseded the IIMC collection 1994-95 even though it appeared on the scene 12 years after the inception of IIMC.

Table 2 : Document Collection in IIM Libraries 1993 - 1998

As on 31	*IIMA*		*IIMB*		*IIMC*		*IIML*	
March	*Total Collection*	*% of Growth*	*Total Collection*	*% of Growth*	*Total Collection*	*% of Growth*	*Total Collection*	*% of Growth*
1993	1,64,436	–	1,20,328	–	1,26,029	–	36,116	–
1994	1,68,471	2.4	1,24,733	3.7	1,28,895	2.3	38,652	7.2
1995	1,72,487	2.4	1,34,748	8.0	1,32,024	2.4	41,578	7.6
1996	1,76,762	2.5	1,41,537	5.0	1,35,129	2.3	44,186	6.3
1997	1,80,021	1.8	1,45,891	3.1	1,39,252	3.0	47,542	7.6
1998	1,83,856	2.1	1,51,083	3.5	1,44,507	3.7	50,529	6.3

CURRENT PERIODICAL SUBSCRIPTIONS IN IIM LIBRARIES

Current periodicals constitute the most important channel of information communication for research as well as for other academic activities. However, the escalating subscription rates, devaluation of rupee, and ever-increasing number of total periodicals published as also information scatter in these periodicals have made it difficult for the libraries to retain their current subscription list. In fact, the continuance of the same set of periodicals requires more than 30 per cent increase in the subscription budget every year. It is not possible due to financial constraints. Nevertheless, all IIMs have been increasing their subscription budget to some extent year after year with a view to have a good, representative, and balanced collection of periodicals as needed for teaching, training and research work. Table 3 provides comparative data of periodicals subscribed and amount spent by IIM libraries during 1988/89 to 1997/98.

The data in Table 3 reveals that the growth in the number of periodicals subscribed in IIMA, IIMB, and IIML has been marginal. In IIMG it has been rather negative. However, their expenditure has been steadily increasing. With costs going up, and knowledge overflowing, the trend of this kind is bound to persist. It is, therefore, important to find some way out to control the situation. The solution lies in resource sharing and in document delivery and networking.

The comparison of data reveals that IIMB has been subscribing the maximum number of periodicals during the last 10 years except during 1989-90 and 1991-92. IIMB subscribed 828 periodicals during 1988-89; IIMC, 739; IIMA, 562 and IIML, 409 titles. During 1989-90 IIMC topped the list subscribing 740 titles followed by IIMA with 630, IIMB with 539, and IIML with 425 titles. During 1996-97 all IIMs except IIML had subscribed 596 periodicals each but spent varying amounts. IIMA spent Rs.32.48 lakh, with an increase of 27.4 per cent over the

Table 3: Data on Periodicals Subscribed by IIM Libraries during 1988-89 to 1997-98 (Rs. in Lakhs)

Year	IIMA				IIMB				IIMC				IIML			
	No. of Titles	% increase in title	Amount	% increase in budget	No. of titles	% increase in titles	Amount	% increase in budget	No. of titles	% increase in titles	Amount	% increase in budget	No. of titles	% increase in titles	Amount	% increase in titles
1988-89	562		7.02		828		5.3		739		12.50		409		8.20	
1989-90	630	12.1	8.25	17.5	539	-34.9	6.96	30.6	740	0.1	13.00	4.0	425	3.9	10.31	25.7
1990-91	631	0.2	12.55	52.1	631	17.1	8.65	24.3	637	-13.9	15.00	15.4	427	0.5	13.09	27.0
1991-92	627	-0.6	13.75	9.6	582	-7.8	14.70	69.9	530	-16.8	18.02	20.1	435	1.9	18.53	41.6
1992-93	618	-1.4	20.30	47.6	666	14.4	19.50	32.6	545	2.8	18.42	2.3	429	-1.4	18.77	1.3
1993-94	577	-6.6	18.30	-9.8	600	-9.9	25.80	32.3	600	10.1	25.30	37.3	424	-1.2	23.20	23.6
1994-95	588	1.9	22.10	20.8	590	-1.7	27.00	4.6	476	-20.7	27.00	6.7	418	-1.4	25.00	7.8
1995-96	604	2.7	25.50	15.4	641	8.6	29.40	8.9	390	-18.1	32.50	20.4	437	4.5	27.00	8.0
1996-97	596	-1.3	32.48	27.4	596	-7.0	32.34	10.0	596	52.8	37.20	14.5	429	-1.8	30.89	14.4
1997-98	582	-2.3	39.26	20.9	866	45.3	58.40	80.6	528	-11.4	58.29	56.7	432	0.7	41.06	32.9

preceding year. IIMB spent Rs. 32.34 lakh, an increase of 10 per cent. IIMC spent Rs. 37.20 lakh, an increase of 14.5 per cent over the preceding year. During 1997-98, the number of periodicals subscribed in IIMB increased by 45.3 per cent because the library started subscribing ABI/INFORM (full text). It provides the full text of nearly 400 periodicals related to management and allied subjects.

During 1996-97 and 1997-98, all IIMs increased their subscription budget enormously even as the number of periodicals received declined. In the case of IIMB the trend was different.

The growth rate in the periodicals subscribed has been the highest in IIML. It was 5.6 per cent, followed by IIMB with 4.6 per cent and IIMA with 3.5 per cent. IIMC showed declining trend as its subscriptions came down by 28.5 per cent since 1988-89.

As of 1997-98, all IIMs, taken together, subscribed to 2,408 periodicals costing Rs. 197.02 lakh. These included 699 Indian periodicals, costing Rs.3.84 lakh, and 1,709 foreign periodicals, costing Rs.193.17 lakh. A comparative data of Indian and foreign periodicals and amount spent on them and extent of duplication among IIMs has been given in Table 4.

The data in Table 4 reveals the extent of duplication and the amount spent on duplication in periodicals. As against a total of 2,408 periodicals acquired by all IIM libraries during 1997-98, they received just 1,496 unique titles. This means that. 37.9 per cent of total periodicals were duplicates. Out of 912 duplicating titles, 277 (30.4%), costing Rs.1.75 lakh, were of Indian origin and 635 (69.6%), costing Rs. 73.56 lakh, of foreign origin. This means that 38.1 per cent subscription budget of IIM libraries was spent on duplicate subscriptions.

Further study of the periodicals subscribed by these libraries reveals that 134 periodicals, e.g., *International Journal of Production Research* (UK), *International Journal of Technology Management* (SZ), *Information and Management* (NE) etc., costing Rs.12.36 lakh, were commonly procured by all the four IIM libraries. Thė extent of duplication among any three or any two IIMs is shown in the Table 5.

Table 4: Data on Periodicals Subscribed by the IIM Libraries

(in Rs. in lakhs)

Library	*No of Titles*	*Amount Spent*	*Indian Titles*	*Amount Spent*	*Foreign Titles*	*Amount Spent*
IIMA	582	39.26	199	1.08	383	38.18
			34.2 %	2.7 %	65.8%	97.2%
IIMB	866	58.40	253	1.33	613	57.07
			29.3 %	2.3%	70.8%	97.7%
IIMC	528	58.29	112	0.73	416	57.56
			21.2%	1.2%	78.8%	98.7%
IIML	432	41.07	135	0.70	297	40.36
			31.3%	1.7%	68.7%	98.3%
Total	2,408	197.02	699	3.84	1,709	193.17
			29.0 %	1.9 %	71.0 %	98.1%
Total No of Unique Titles	1,496	21.70	422	2.09	1,074	119.61
			28.2 %	1.7 %	71.8%	98.3%
Duplication and % of total	912 37.9 %	75.32 38.2 %	277 39.6%	1.75 45.6%	635 37.1%	73.56 38.1%

Table 5: Duplication of Periodicals in IIM Libraries (1997-98)

Library				*No of Duplicate Titles*	*Total Cost in Lakh (Rs.)*
IIMA	IIMB	IIMC	IIML	134	12.36
IIMA	IIMB	IIMC		175	16.73
IIMA	IIMB	IIML		48	2.24
IIMA	IIMC	IIML		25	1.71
IIMB	IIMC	IIML		15	1.13
IIMA	IIMB			292	21.05
IIMA	IIMC			59	5.19
IIMA	IIML			29	1.59
IIMB	IIMC			62	4.53
IIMB	IIML			40	1.57
IIMC	IIML			41	7.51

In view of similarity in the nature, objectives, and functions of libraries of IIMs, one would not be surprised at the need for duplication and overlap in subscriptions. In view of the ever-increasing prices of current periodicals, devaluation of Indian currency, disproportionate increase in library budget, and high growth rate of literature, it is time to examine critically each and every expensive and commonly subscribed periodical, and work out mutually agreed upon ways of sharing such materials without, in any way, jeopardising the basic academic and research interests of any of the IIMs.

BOUND VOLUMES OF PERIODICALS IN IIM LIBRARIES

The periodical collection has been growing in all the libraries of IIM but a uniform pattern of growth has failed to emerge. A comparative data of growth of bound volumes of periodicals has been given in Table 6.

Data in Table 6 reveals that the annual growth rate has declined over time in all IIM libraries. In IIMA the growth rate of bound volumes of periodicals has been the highest, 15.6 per cent, in 1977-78 and lowest, 1.7 per cent, during 1996-97 and 1997-98. In 1976-77 the growth rate at IIMA was 15.3 per cent which came down to 11.7 per cent in 1986-87 and to 1.7 per cent in 1997-98. In 1997-98 the cumulative growth rate at IIMA has been 415.2 per cent, with an average annual growth rate of 7.8 per cent.

In IIMB the highest growth rate of bound periodicals was 50.6 per cent in 1978-79 and the minimum being 0.1 per cent in 1984-85. In IIMB the growth rate was 19.5 per cent in 1976-77 which declined to 8.7 per cent during 1986-97. Now it has come down to 5.2 per cent in 1997-98. Since 1976-77 the periodical collection of IIMB has increased by 903.5 per cent, with an annual average growth rate of 12.1 per cent.

In IIMC the maximum growth rate was 12.5 per cent in 1986-97, and the minimum was 1.3 per cent in 1993-94. In

Table 6: Growth of Bound Periodicals in IIM Libraries During 1976-1998.

As on 31	LIBRARY											
	IIMA			IIMB			IIMC			IIML		
March	No. of bound period	% Increase	Cummulative %	No. of bound periodicals	% Increase	Cummulative %	No. of bound periodicals	% Increase	Cummulative %	No. of bound periodicals	% Increase	Cummulative %
1976	6,794	Base	Base	–	–	–	12,053	Base	Base	–	–	–
1977	7,832	15.3	15.3	2,067	Base	Base	13,188	9.4	9.4	–	–	–
1978	9,056	15.6	33.3	2,470	19.5	19.5	13,540	2.7	12.3	–	–	–
1979	10,132	11.9	49.1	3,719	50.6	79.9	14,396	6.3	19.1	–	–	–
1980	11,365	12.2	67.0	4,635	24.6	124.2	14,701	2.1	22.0	–	–	–
1981	12,743	12.1	87.5	5,517	19.0	166.9	15,346	4.4	27.3	–	–	–
1982	13,974	9.7	105.7	6,257	13.4	202.7	16,522	7.7	37.0	–	–	–
1983	15,122	8.2	122.6	6,530	4.4	205.9	17,507	6.0	45.2	–	–	–
1984	16,762	10.8	146.6	7,590	16.2	267.2	17,935	2.4	48.8	–	–	–
1985	17,311	3.3	154.8	7,599	0.1	267.6	18,423	2.7	52.8	–	–	–
1986	19,374	11.9	185.2	8,449	11.2	308.7	19,001	3.1	57.6	–	–	–

(Contd...)

(Contd...)

As on 31	*IIMA*			*IIMB*			*IIMC*			*IIML*		
March	*No. of bound period*	*% Increase*	*Cummulative %*	*No. of bound periodicals*	*% Increase*	*Cummulative %*	*No. of bound periodicals*	*% Increase*	*Cummulative %*	*No. of bound periodicals*	*% Increase*	*Cummulative %*
1987	21,638	11.7	214.5	9,182	8.7	344.2	21,373	12.5	77.3	360	Base	–
1988	23,212	7.3	241.6	9,896	7.8	378.8	22,500	5.3	86.7	1,325	268.1	268.1
1989	25,523	10.0	275.7	10,460	5.7	406.0	23,741	5.5	96.9	1,821	37.4	405.8
1990	26,681	4.5	292.7	11,709	11.9	466.5	25,342	6.7	110.2	2,531	39.0	603.0
1991	27,961	4.8	311.5	12,282	4.9	494.2	27,083	6.9	124.1	3,073	21.4	753.6
1992	28,863	3.2	324.8	13,084	6.5	532.9	27,565	1.8	128.7	3,759	22.3	603.0
1993	30,000	3.9	341.6	13,628	4.2	559.3	28,597	3.7	137.3	4,631	23.2	944.2
1994	31,436	4.8	362.7	14,335	5.2	593.5	28,973	1.3	140.4	5,228	12.9	1186.4
1995	32,648	3.9	380.5	16,957	18.3	720.4	29,597	2.1	145.5	6,228	19.1	1630.0
1996	33,836	3.6	398.7	19,186	13.1	828.2	29,830	0.8	147.5	6,980	12.1	1838.9
1997	34,421	1.7	405.2	19,713	2.7	853.7	30,598	2.6	153.9	7,692	10.2	2036.7
1998	35,000	1.7	415.2	20,743	5.2	903.5	31,118	1.7	158.2	8,457	9.9	2249.2

1976-77 it was 9.4 per cent which declined to 3.1 per cent in 1986-87 and to 1.7 per cent in 1997-98. Since 1976-77 the periodical collection has increased by 158.2 per cent, with an annual average growth rate of 4.4 per cent.

In the case of IIML, which was established in 1984, the growth rate was relatively higher during initial years as in these formative years its collection was very small. The maximum growth rate of bound periodical was 268.1 per cent in 1987-88 and the minimum, 9.9 per cent, in 1997-98. Since 1976-77 the periodicals collection has grown by 2249 per cent with an annual average growth of 43.2 per cent.

In the total collection the cumulative growth was the highest at 2249 per cent in IIML, and the lowest, at 158.2 per cent in IIMC since 1976-77. The total collection was up by 415.2 per cent in IIMA and by 903.5 per cent in IIMB.

The highest average annual growth rate was 43.2 per cent in IIML, followed by IIMB with 12.1 per cent, IIMA with 7.8 per cent and IIMC with 4.4 per cent.

RESOURCE SHARING

Resource sharing has since long been heralded as an instrument of cooperation for harnessing library resources in the distributed information environment. Individually libraries are unable to acquire information material as much as they require on ownership basis. However, collectively these libraries do constitute a vast resource, good enough to fill the gap. Resource sharing provides the basic framework for pooling, sharing, and exploiting the vast but distributed resources.

Need for Resource Sharing among IIM Libraries

Literature explosion

Different studies have shown that there has been literature

explosion during the last two decades. According to an estimate the number of periodicals has increased from 62,000 in 1979-80 to 1,57,200 in 1998-99 and number of periodicals in business and economics has gone up from 4,260 to 26,340 during the same period. Thus periodicals literature in all disciplines has been increasing at an annual growth rate of 7.7 per cent. In contrast, annual growth rate of periodicals in the area of business and economics is 25.9 per cent. It has also been found that the annual growth rate of print periodicals has been declining due to emergence of periodicals in electronic format. In spite of this, the growth rate since 1995-96 is higher in business and economics (5.0% to 8.4%) than that of general periodicals (1.0% to 2.1). The doubling period, therefore, of periodicals in business and economics is shorter than that for periodicals in general.

Technological development

In view of the similarity in goals, objectives and activities of IIM libraries and the opportunities that information technology offer, library resource sharing through networking is the best solution to ensure better coverage and optimum utilisation of limited resources.

Increase in subscription rates

Though the average annual growth rate of subscription budget has been 97.1 per cent in IIMB, 43.9 per cent in IIMC, 43.8 per cent in IIMA, and 18.2 per cent in IIML during the last decade, yet decreasing trend has been found in growth of bound volumes of periodicals in all IIMs. The average annual growth rate was 30.1 per cent, 15.6 per cent and 6.6 per cent in IIMB, IIMA, and IIMC respectively during 1977/78-1987/88 which decreased to 10.9 per cent, 5.1 per cent, and 3.8 per cent during 1987/88-1997/98 in IIMB, IIMA, and IIMC respectively. In the case of IIML it was 53.8 per cent.

The growth in number of periodicals subscribed has been meagre: IIML (5.6%), IIMB (4.6%), and IIMA (3.5%) and even negative in IIMC (28.5%) though their expenditure has been steadily rising since 1988-89.

It has been found that IIMB has been subscribing a maximum number of periodicals during the last 10 years except in 1989-90 and 1991-92. It is a coincidence that during 1996-97 all IIMs except IIML had been subscribing 596 periodicals each but spending different amounts. The highest growth rate 5.6 per cent, in periodicals subscribed has been noted, in IIML followed by IIMB with 4.6 per cent, and IIMA with 3.5 per cent. IIMC has shown a decline by 28.5 per cent since 1988.

Duplicate subscription

It has been found that out of a total 2,408 periodicals procured by the libraries of IIMs in 1997-98, 1496 titles are unique. This means that 912 periodicals, 37.9 per cent of total periodicals, were subscribed in duplicate. Out of 912 such titles, 277 i.e. 30.4 per cent costing Rs.1.75 lakh were Indian and 635, i.e., 69.6 per cent costing Rs. 73.56 lakh were of foreign origin.

Moreover, 134 periodicals, costing Rs.12.36 lakh were being subscribed in common by all the four IIMs in 1997-98; 175 titles, costing Rs.16.73 lakh, were common among IIMA, IIMB, and IIMC. Among IIMA, IIMB and IIML 48 titles costing Rs.2.24 lakh were common, and among IIMA, IIMC and IIML 25 titles costing Rs.1.71 lakh. There were 15 titles, costing Rs.1.13 lakh common among IIMB, IIMC, and IIML.

It has been found that highest duplication was between IIMA and IIMB where 292 titles costing Rs.21.05 lakh were in common.

CONCLUSION

IIM libraries annually spend nearly Rs. 3.08 crore on acquisition of documents including periodicals. The subscription budget alone accounts for more than 64.0 per cent of library budget. It is in this context the need for resource sharing among the IIMs libraries becomes important.

The Indian periodicals constitute 29.3 per cent of the total periodicals subscribed by IIMB. Their number is 253 and it is the highest, costing Rs. 2.33 lakh, followed by IIMA with 199, i.e., 34.2 per cent of total titles, costing Rs.1.08 lakh, IIML with 135 Indian titles, costing Rs. 0.70 lakh, and IIMC with 112, i.e., 21.2 per cent of total titles, costing Rs. 0.73 lakh.

With improvements in internet connectivity and bandwidth of the internet, many publishers have moved to on-line publishing Online versions are economically cheaper to create and distribute. This avenue provides greater scope to share costs and get cheaper block subscription offers for access to the IIMs

In view of the ever increasing prices of the current periodicals, devaluation of Indian currency, disproportionate increase in library budgets, and enormous growth of literature, it is high time to examine critically each and every expensive and commonly procured periodical, and work out mutually agreed upon ways of sharing such materials without, in any way, jeopardising the basic academic and research interests of any of the IIMs. There has been enormous growth of periodicals literature and as such self-sufficiency is impossible to achieve even if given high budgetary allocations. It is in this context that application of IT and networking becomes essentials for resource sharing as well for the modernisation of libraries. Library effectiveness in the matter of service can be achieved faster through these techniques and by deploying competent and trained staff.

REFERENCES

1. Ministry of Education India, (*Chairman:* A Ramaswamy Mudaliar). *Committee on Managerial Personnel: A Report,* New Delhi, Ministry of Education, 1964.
2. Naisbitt J., *Megatrends : Ten New Direction Transforming our Lives*. MacDonald, London, 1984.

3. Davinson D., *Periodical Collection*. Rev ed. 1978, West view, Boulder, 1978.
4. *Standard Periodicals Directory*, Ed 18, Oxbridge Communication, New York, 1994.
5. *Ebsco Serials Directory,* Ebsco publishing, Birmingham, 1995.
6. Various Editions of *Ulrich's International Periodical Directory*, R.R. Bowker, New Jersey.
7. Ward Layzell, Review of the general literature on management, *IFLA Journal*, 1994, 20,4;449-458.
8. Holt C. C. and Schrank W. E., Growth of the professional literature in economics and other fields: Some implications. *American Documentation*. 1968, 19 18-27.
9. Holden Constance, Libraries stunned by journal price increase, *Science*, 1987, 236, 908-09.
10. Graham Gordon, Journal publishing : One publisher experience, *Library Acquisition: Practice and Theory,* 1989, 13, 103-07.
11. Mcewan P. J., Letter, *The Times,* October 17, Times; London, 1988.
12. Okerson A., Of making many books there is no end. In *Economic Services Inc. Report of the ARL Serials Price Project*, Association of Research Libraries; Washington, 1989.

17

Electronic Document Delivery System and Services

B. Ramesh Babu and *D. Chandran*

INTRODUCTION

Recent developments in the information technology have been influencing the library and information services. For example, CD-ROM technology has come to pave the way for electronic access to a wide variety of information sources. Internet and telecommunication networks have come to pave the way for Electronic Document Delivery Services (EDDS). Electronic media has given a new dimension to information sources.

CONCEPT OF ELECTRONIC DOCUMENT DELIVERY SERVICE

The EDDS is referred to as "one part of a multi-stage process". It provides the flexibility to access the required material across the world from a number of sources. It delivers on loan or supplies documents as physical objects. It provides access to information not held or immediately available in the library and information centre approached for the purpose. Document delivery can be viewed as :

a) Just-in-case (Journal holdings);
b) Just-in-time (Inter library loan); and
c) Just-when-you-like (Electronic document access).

It involves a dynamic interaction between three groups, namely:

1) Management including library and information professionals;
2) Information suppliers including even the publishers; and
3) End-users.

RATIONALE FOR EDDS IN LIBRARY AND INFORMATION CENTRES

A number of factors have influenced the demand for EDDS:

a) Increasing cost of journal subscriptions/escalating prices;
b) Static library budgets/decreasing budgets year after year;
c) Increasing demand from the clients;
d) Tremendous development in research activity;
e) Awareness about the DDS among the clients;
f) Cost-effective service; and
g) Impact of technology on information provision and handling.

SOME IMPORTANT ELECTRONIC DOCUMENT DELIVERY SYSTEMS

Ariadne/DDS

Ariadne/DDS is an integrated document delivery system developed at Tilburg University, which aims at providing fast document delivery to the users. It complied with the standards drafted and developed by the GEDE. This system was designed for image management and supports only journal article images. It has five modules, namely, request handling;

document production preparation; document handling; distribution handling; and messaging.

EI Reference Desk

The Engineering Information Inc. in the year 1990-91 developed it. It aims to provide one-stop workstation for the engineers. It offers search facility to search and retieve bibliographic information either from CD-ROMS or from online hosts. It has two delivery features such as Faxit for fax delivery and Ei View for network transmission. This system has got six facilities, namely, the Ei Page One CD-ROM database; the Compendex Plust CD-ROM database; Ei online; Ei order; Faxit and Ei view. In the recent years it has been refined and made available as a commercial service offering internet delivery.

IRIS

IRIS is an Irish-based system, which is being participated by the six libraries at Dublin since 1992. It was partly funded by the CEC Telematics Programme. It is concerned with the database searching and document ordering service. Currently it is being operated on a commercial basis. It is available to library users as well as business users in Ireland.

DALI

DALI stands for Document and Library Integration. It was funded by the CEC Telematics Programme. It is a joint collaboration by the libraries and system developers from Greece, Ireland and the United Kingdom. It is mainly concerned with the methods of document delivery including print and electronic delivery. It has incorporated the Z39.50 protocol in order make available to different communication systems and terminal types.

NAILDD

It stands for the North American Inter-library Loan and Document Delivery. It was started in the year 1993 by the Association of Research Libraries (ARL) through its Committee on Access to Information Resources. It aims to improve the efficiency of the document delivery to the end-users at a minimal cost.

FASTDOC

Like DALI and IRIS, the CEC Telematics funded this system in the year 1994. FASTDOC stands for the Fast Document Ordering and Document Delivery. The main participants are from Germany, Spain, and Greece. This system includes three ordering components via online host, remote PC, and in-house systems.

REDD

The Regional Document Delivery (REDD) is a joint project between Griffith University, Queensland University of Technology, and the University of Queensland Libraries in Australia. It provides Windows-based electronic document delivery system. It uses internet to scan the documents and send the same to the end users.

MAJOR COMMERCIAL ELECTRONIC DOCUMENT DELIVERY SERVICES

The commercial electronic DD services can be broadly divided into the following three categories, namely :

a) Collection-based services those;
b) Non-collection based services; and
c) Specialised collection-based services.

Collection-Based Services

The following services are identified as collection-based electronic document delivery services :

a) British Library Documentation Supply Centre (BLDSC);
b) The Canada Institute of Scientific and Technical Information (CISTI);
c) University Microfilms Inc. (UMI);
d) The Institute of Scientific Information (ISI); and
e) Knight-Rider Information/Uncover.

Non-Collection-based Services

The following are identified as the non-collection based services:

a) Online Computer Library Centre (formerly Ohio College Library Centre) OCLC;
b) Bath Information and Data Service (BIDS);
c) Infotrieve;
d) The Research Libraries Group (RLG);
e) Swets and Zeitlinger Subscription Agents; and
f) Silver-Platter Information.

Specialised Collection-based Services

The following are the important specialised collection-based services:

a) The Institute of Electrical and Electronic Engineers (IEEE)
b) Engineering Information Inc.;
c) The Welding Institute (TWI);
d) ADONIS;
e) Royal Society of Chemistry;

f) Disclosure Incorporation; and

g) BIOSIS.

TOOLS AND TECHNIQUES FOR MEASURING USER SATISFACTION WITH EDDS

Users of EDDS judge the service by its usefulness in meeting their information requirements. Different users need different types and levels of information. As such, often it becomes difficult to define information requirements.

Tools

The following factors may be considered in measuring the user satisfaction with EDDS:

a) Speed (quick delivery);
b) Timeliness (in time to be useful);
c) Urgency of need;
d) Accuracy (both by those placing the request and by the supplier);
e) Success (fill rate);
f) Cost;
g) Quality of materials received (like legibility and completeness);
h) Staff courtesy;
i) Staff knowledge;
j) Staff assistance;
k) Confidence in the service;
l) Consistency of the service;
m) Communication (provision of status reports, and so on);

The above factors represent both qualitative and quantitative measures.

Techniques

The following techniques can be used to determine the user satisfaction by evaluating performance on the above stated factors. They are :

a) Focus group interviews;
b) One-to-one customer interviews;
c) Survey instruments : either transaction-based or general, overall surveys; and
d) Effective complaint management.

Focus group interviews

These form an excellent technique to get direct feedback from the clients with regard to their satisfaction on the provision of DDS. They are simple to organise with minimum financial implications. These facilitate even qualitative data on the user feedback.

One-to-one customer interview

These are labour-intensive but at the same time they do provide a very valuable data. The useful aspect of this technique is that any member of the user community can provide relevant and useful data. This allows obtaining user feedback with regard to potential demand, pricing as well as time sensitivity.

Survey instruments

Survey instruments for measuring user satisfaction with DDS are of 'home grown' variety or in-house developed ones for a specific local population, or adaptations of existing user-based survey instruments from other fields more particularly from the field of marketing.

Complaint management

It is easier to identify user dissatisfaction rather than satisfaction. User complaints will pave the way for the service providers to rectify the loopholes and weaknesses. An effective complaint management programme will certainly rectify the identified drawbacks in a more satisfactory way.

STRATEGIES FOR EFFECTIVE EDDS

According to MacDougall, the following strategies and objectives are useful in developing a cost effective, efficient and seamless full text EDDS:

i) Globalisation is inevitable and global solutions will be necessary.

ii) There is an overwhelming need for both national government and institutions to incorporate document delivery as a central feature of any information strategy plan.

iii) There is a need to promote the requirement for national and international consortia across the whole range of document delivery matters that is, from communication infrastructure, content, services, licensing and so on.

iv) Any strategy must recognise the need to carry out mapping exercises so that the stakeholders are clear about their own priorities and those of the others.

v) Document delivery system must take due account of archive potential as well as current demand and of the need to negotiate on central databases and appropriate copyright arrangements.

vi) There will be a need to influence cost and content, of course in specific subjects.

vii) More sustained research into holistic economic models will be a major requirement

viii) There is a requirement to promote and apply consistent standards.

CONCLUSION

Academic and research libraries are facing a number of problems with regard to the collection management. Their limited budgets do not permit them to cope with the increasing information demands of the clients on ownership basis. In this context, the electronic document delivery is one of the effective means to meet the situation. The recent network developments at the national and international levels including the internet have paved the way for initiating electronic delivery services. Libraries will have to decide the strategies for the purpose. Certainly, partnership and collaboration could guarantee success in document delivery services in the twenty-first century.

BIBLIOGRAPHY

Etschmaier, G. and Bustion, M., Document delivery and collection development: An evolving relationship, *Serials Librarian*, 1997, 31, 3, 13-27.

MacDougall, A.F., The Prisoner's dilemma : The document delivery management game? In: *Document Delivery Beyond 2000*, edited by Anne Morris, Neil Jacobs and Eric Davies, London, Taylor Garham, 1997, p. 5-11.

Price, Sandra P., Morris, Anne and Daview, J. Eric, An overview of commercial electronic document delivery suppliers and services. *The Electronic Library*, 1996, 14, 6, 523-42.

Price, Sandra P., Morris, Anne and Davies, J. Eric, An overview of electronic document request and delivery research, *The Electronic Library,* 1996, 14, 6, 435-48.

Wettler, M.A., Evaluating document delivery services, *Database*, 1998, 21, 5,: 73-4.

18
Information Exchange and Resource Sharing—Electronic Way

V.V.V. Satyanarayana

INTRODUCTION

Developments in science and technology have been taking place at an enormous speed. Data that is being generated in science and technology is so vast and voluminous that it needs special storage devices for retrieval. Conventional print media had given place to microform, but later it was realised that even this media was hardly sufficient to cope with the ever increasing volume of data. In their search for new media, librarians/information scientists found the solution in computers and communication technologies.

INFORMATION STORAGE

Capturing data in a convenient media and accessing it in a user-friendly manner is the need of the hour. Traditional formats have undergone transformations: print, microforms, optical discs, and electronic media. In all these formats, the importance of transfer of information or exchange of information is paramount. Information is generated at one place, required at a second place, and utilised in a third different place. But the information has to flow to these places at a speed so that there is no visible loss of time and data. In such an environment the role of information technology is indisputable and computers are indispensable. Present day libraries and information centres cannot be imagined without computers.

Data on library holdings are being transformed into machine-readable format. A number of databases are also being created discipline wise. User friendly software is provided to access the databases. Users are turning themselves to use machine-readable databases. The library collections are being made available online for quick and immediate accesses. The access is provided first to the index or to the abstract of a complete text and then taken to the complete text itself.

RESOURCE SHARING

It is a well-established fact that no library is self-sufficient to cater to the needs of its own clientele. It has to invariably depend on other sources for acquiring the required information. Resource sharing is the need of the hour in many library and information centres. With the advent of networking and internet, resource sharing has become possible. It has been instrumental in removing barriers for information transfer and exchange. The distance between the geographical source of generation of data and the user end where the information is to be accessed has become immaterial. The gap between them is fast reducing. As a result we see a global village in so far as information exchange is concerned. Present technologies are not only permitting easy resource sharing but also help in communicating with co-professionals far and wide almost in an interactive mode.

ELECTRONIC METHODS

Developments in information technology and communication engineering have opened up new vistas in the information exchange and data transfer. Initially, the impact of these developments was seen in electronic mail or e-mail. While written matter can be transmitted through e-mail, the voice communication can take place through electronic chat between two sites. The scene is being expanded to electronic publishing and thus converting print media to electronic media. The advantages of electronic media are obvious. Global publishers have already realised the potential of electronic publishing and a number of documents are available on the net now for surfing. Though the process of electronic publishing started with microdocuments soon it has been extended to cover macrodocuments also. There are some limitations in making macrodocuments available electronically due to their dimensions. But these have not come in the way of major publishers to venture into electronic publishing.

BOOKS

Printed version of encyclopedias, dictionaries, handbooks, and directories were initially converted into CD-ROM discs by using optical technology. Each CD-ROM can store about 650MB of data and it can give fast response for searching which has prompted the publishers to make use of this media on a wider scale. As a result, *Encyclopedia Britannica*, McGraw-Hill *Encyclopedia of Science and Technology, Science Encyclopedias, Oxford English Dictionary, Harrap's dictionary, Metals Handbook, Thomas Directory of Manufacturers* in USA and Canada are some of the many reference books that are made in CD-ROM format. With the introduction of communication networks these reference books were also converted into electronic books. These books can be accessed through internet with the help of software provided by the publishers. The novelty aspect of these electronic books is the multimedia teachers that did not exist in the print formats. The search engine based searching capability is another feather in the cap of electronic book.

JOURNALS

Electronic journals are emerging much faster than their print counterparts. Electronic journals are offered on subscription. Many print journals are now being discontinued and are appearing only in electronic form. *Byte*, *Hitachi Review*, *British Medical Journal*, *EPRI Journal* and Elsevier, Wiley and McGraw-Hill journals are available in electronic format. These can be accessed online and can save a lot of costs through subscriptions to these journals. The vexed problem of missing issues, duplicate issues, issues lost in transit, prompt receipt of issues, etc., binding of journals, space for shelving, dusting and maintenance of bound volume racks, handling of bound volumes for photocopying simply disappear with journals in electronic format.

DATABASES

The database has been and will continue to be a potential tool for researchers in the pursuit of their knowledge. With the advents of new technologies, databases had undergone transformations. Their storage mediums were transformed from magnetic tapes to machine-readable files and to CD-ROM discs and then to web-based databases. Their search capabilities have also undergone changes enormously. Since it is not feasible to make full text databases of all the existing documents, the databases are created as bibliographic databases and full text databases. The period covered by the full text database is therefore much less than that covered by the bibliographic database. Hence, there are more numbers of bibliographic databases. The advantage with the databases is that they can be made web admissible without making any additional efforts. All they need is small web interface. In all the above developments an important and valuable aspect to mankind is preservation of the ecosystem. We are slowly going to paperless society. Correspondence by postal mail is virtually reduced. Photocopying of documents are comparatively less required. Voluminous books need not be printed by consuming paper. Transfer of information in print format can be completely avoided. Maintenance of paper files, dust allergies, disposal of wastepaper are some of the aspects not associated with the electronic format. Trees can be saved and environment can be preserved, and as such the entire ecosystem can be preserved in its natural form.

CONCLUSION

Digital information is the key to the evolution of information society. The publishing trade has realised the importance of electronic format. Libraries and information centres should acquire the necessary skills to create electronic journals. They must exchange information for resource sharing in an electronic way.

19

Public Access to Government Generated Information: A Critical Appraisal

P.R. Goswami

INTRODUCTION

The word 'information' is used more frequently than others in an organisation. Educated practitioners from all walks of life, e.g., a physicist, an engineer, a computer scientist, a sociologist or a health care professional all deal with information. From the viewpoint of a librarian, it is important to know how information is made available and what difficulties are faced by the users in the process of its utilisation.

In a large democracy like India, the ever increasing sphere of government activities has made the state the largest repository of data and information in the form of acts, laws, regulations, committee/commission reports, statistical serials on different socio-economic variables, etc. The purpose of this brief paper is to present an ambivalent view of the present state of affairs relating to provision of access to government information in India. This subject, i.e., access to information and knowledge has become a matter of concern all over the world. Unesco regularly publishes a *World Information Report*[1] which presents to non-specialists and particularly to decision makers and the public at large the wide reality of information provision as it exists throughout the world today and as it is being transformed by the technological, social and political developments of tomorrow. Similarly, the World Bank's report released in 1998-99 as *World Development Report*[2] had the theme 'Knowledge for Development'. It analysed the risks and opportunities that the global information revolution is creating for developing countries, and concludes that access to financial, technical, and medical knowledge is crucial to improving the health and living standards of the poor.

ACCESS TO PUBLISHED SOURCES

There are mainly two broad categories of government information. One is published data/records made available through various printed sources and lately also through electronic media; and the other one is unpublished administrative records and data contained in statistical returns/ questionnaires or schedules which remain confined to government offices.

In fact, the unique principle underlying information services is the provision of added value to information. The value is added by different groups of professionals. As regards published serials, statisticians working in government manipulate figures, construct tables, graphs and charts from raw figures or recorded information in order to make them meaningful.

Most of the ministries/departments feel that it is obligatory on their part to disseminate information on subjects which fall under the sphere of their activities. Apart from the annual report, which briefly enumerates the working of the organisation, the departments also publish annual compendium of information. A few examples are :

i) *Indian Labour Yearbook* (Labour Bureau, Ministry of Labour)
ii) *Indian Railway Yearbook* (Railway Board, Ministry of Railways)
iii) *Health Information in India* (Ministry of Health and Family Welfare)

iv) *Handbook of Industrial Statistics* (Ministry of Industry)

v) *Statistical System in India* (Department of Statistics, Ministry of Planning and Programme Implementation).

One stark feature of governments information dissemination activity is the absence of an agency which can coordinate the publication programme of the government. This often leads to duplication of efforts. A glaring example is the publication, *Handbook of Statistics on Indian Economy* (1998), by Reserve Bank of India. Many tables included in this compendium are mere reproduction of data contained in publications such as *Statistical Abstract* and *Economic Survey*. Moreover, the government does not pay much heed to the design of the structure and content of these publications. Most of these are published with a time-lag of two to three years. As a result, they are often rendered obsolete by the users.

A major component of government information is socio-economic statistics. The agencies like (i) Central Statistical Organisation (CSO), (ii) Registrar General and Census Commissioner of India (RGI), (iii) Director General of Commercial Intelligence and Statistics (DGCIS), (iv) Labour Bureau, etc., have been established exclusively for the purpose of collection, processing and dissemination of macro level data on different variables. A large number of serial and ad-hoc statistical reports are published by these agencies. Though India has a fairly developed statistical system, the users often question the reliability of data contained in them. An economist has commented.

"In economic analysis, one often comes across official data which appear doubtful or incorrect but generally no further exploration is made to pinpoint the inaccuracy for fear of running into dead end".[3]

The users of official statistics have raised certain questions regarding the availability, reliability and comprehensiveness of data. A few of these issues are stated as follows:

i) Recently launched education guarantee scheme in Madhya Pradesh has shown that enrolment figures in primary schools are overestimated. Official data regarding school enrolment is often misleading and give inflated figures. The Nobel Laureate, Prof Amartya Sen, has also endorsed this viewpoint.

ii) The National Sample Survey Organisation (NSSO) has so far avoided the collection of data on household income. The reasoning is that collection of income data is not reliable and when income data are collected, the quality of other data deteriorates. Thus income distribution data have had to be patched up, i.e., information on consumer expenditure (NSSO Survey Data) has had to be merged with other data.[4]

iii) An Index Number of Agricultural Growth is used for the overall assessment of growth in the sector. In Maharashtra, an error was made in constructing the index number some 25 years ago and the same has gone unnoticed. As having arrived at the weights, the compiling team did not care to compare new weights with the old.[5]

iv) At present, there is hardly any soil map of basic value depicting land capability, irritability or land suitability. Data about water resources are scrappy and mostly approximations based on empiricism. Most maps and information are restricted to the district or at the best block level. Micro level terrain variations are not reflected in such data.[6]

One can easily identify a few articles in economic and social science journals like *Economic and Political Weekly*, *Indian Journal of Economic*, *Margin*, etc., on reliability and quality of statistics. And on the contrary, quite a few data users have applauded the agencies like CSO, RGI, NSSO for releasing various analytical aggregate, special studies and so on. In fact, collection of national statistics is one of the pioneering achievements of India. The consistent execution and refinement of the Census of India has produced one of the richest demographic database. Similarly, NSSO has conducted scientifically designed household surveys during the last 40 years. It is unlikely that any other country has produced surveys of such higher standard.

In a bid to make official data accessible to the users (both published and unpublished), a National Policy on Dissemination of Statistical Data has been formulated and approved in 1998. The salient features of the policy include the following:[7]

a) The Department of Statistics will be the nodal agency for dissemination of official statistics;

b) Data which are sensitive in nature and supply of which can hamper the integrity and security of nation would not be supplied, and

c) Survey results data should be made available to the users after the expiry of three years from the completion of field work or after the reports based on survey data are released whichever is earlier; and

d) Validated data, though unpublished, including unit/household/establishment level data after deleting their identification particulars to maintain confidentiality, should also be made available to the national and international data users.

It is believed that the new policy would encourage many non-official users such as business analysts, researchers and foreign agencies who want to combine data from different sources for analytical purposes.

Apart from statistical data, there are other useful published records pertaining to regulations or regulatory agencies (e.g. import-export rules) or acts and notifications which are brought to the notice of public through the *Gazette of India*. Reference questions regarding the acts and notifications are difficult to understand. A key component in public access to government information is the ability of staff in providing accurate answers to reference questions received.

The *Gazette of India* is by far the most important document for persons in business, finance and industry as it contains governments' policy decisions in the form of circulars and notifications. Normally, there exists a gap between the date of notifications and its actual publications in the *Gazette of India*. In one of the judgements, the Supreme Court of India observed:[8]

"A Central Excise notification can be said to have been published when it is so issued to make it known as the public. It would be a proper publication if it is published in such a manner that persons can, if they are so interested, acquaint themselves with its contents. If publication is through a gazette, then mere printing of it in the gazette would not be enough. Unless the gazette containing the notification is made available to the public, the notification cannot be said to have been 1998, duly published."

While delivering the judgement in favour of a private limited company, the court took the meaning of the word 'publish' from the *Legal Glossary*. It says that the word publish connotes not only art of printing but also further action of making it available to the public. The court order and the condition under which the order was delivered reflects the callous attitude of government bodies towards information dissemination.

It is true that enormous quantity of data and information are collected and processed by the government and only a part of it is made available to the public. There are several reasons for such a state of affairs.

Firstly, there is the Official Secrets Act which is applied somewhat arbitrarily by the officials. Secondly, it is said that some of this type of 'veiled information' is obtained by government on the condition that its confidential nature will be maintained. Thirdly, personal data acquired for the purpose of doing a specific statutory duty should not be made available for other purposes. These rules have been embodied in the Collection of Statistics Act 1950; and finally, it is also argued that the primary task of official agencies is to carry out their statutory obligations and the dissemination of information collected in the course of these duties may be both a burden on the resources and deviation from their main activities.

The arguments made above in favour of withholding government data do not stand if one considers the role of the information in the national economy and open government. In a democratic society, all rights emanate from one's ability to access information. A common man must have ready access to government records to keep the state accountable.

ACCESS TO UNPUBLISHED RECORDS

The records of government agencies are mostly found in files, and the old files are generally kept in the record rooms. The Public Records Act 1983 makes it compulsory for the government agencies to regulate the management, administration and preservation of public records. The act says that every records creating agency shall nominate one of its officials as records officer to discharge its function which include:

a) review of all records and weeding out records of ephemeral value;
b) compilation of schedule of retention of public records in consultation with the National Archives of India;
c) periodical review for downgrading of classified public records; and
d) compilation of annual indices of public records, etc.

According to rules, records more than 30 years old kept in the National Archives are made available to the researchers. However, records pertaining to certain border states and Jammu and Kashmir are kept in abeyance for a much longer period. At present, records pertaining to these sensitive areas are open up to the year 1913 and in certain cases up to 1924 only.

In recent years, there has been renewed interest in local public records for writing history. Traditionally, history has been regarded from classical times onwards as an account of the doings of the great. However, in the second half of the twentieth century, the concept of 'history from below' entered the common parlance of historians. In India, a group of historians broadened the boundaries of their disciplines to open up new areas of researcher, and above all to explore the historical experiences of those men and women whose existence was hitherto ignored, Nobel Laureate Amartya Sen observes:[9]

"Here we run into one of the most exciting developments in historiography in India. There has been a significant shift of attention from the elite to the underdogs in the writing of colonial history focusing more on rural masses and exploited plebeians.... The move is entirely appropriate in its context and in understanding colonial history."

India has so far followed an archaic system of record management. The National Archives gets a sizeable number of records without any reference tool. It is often found that the finding aids produced by the archivists are difficult to use. They cling to outdated concepts inappropriate for modern researcher's approaches and needs.

FREEDOM OF INFORMATION

According to World Bank[10] there are four key dimensions of good governance; (i) public sector management; (ii) accountability; (iii) the legal framework for development and (iv) information and transparency. The documents of the OECD Development Assistance Committee draw upon the World Bank's definition of governance and proceed to link it with the participatory development, human rights and democratisation.[11] Needless to say, all these criteria of good governance can be applied in a condition which ensures free flow of information from the government to public.

India has so far followed the British style of administration. In Great Britain, the Official Secrets Act 1911 and 1989 are meant for defending national security by rendering inaccessible to the public certain categories of official information. In many of its policy documents, the Indian government recognises that access to information is an essential part of accountability of government. Moreover, the Constitution of India has included, 'freedom of speech and information' as a fundamental right. In certain cases, the Supreme Court of India has held that 'right to know' or 'right to information' emanates from fundamental right incorporated in Article 19(1)(a) of the Constitution. Another important provision has been made in Section 75 of the Indian Evidence Act, 1972. It binds every public officer having custody of a public document to give every person a copy of it on payment of the legal fee for it. However, the person seeking information must have the 'right to inspect'. All these positive aspects are not enough to ensure the free flow of information unless state's power to withhold information is curtailed. In short, the Official Secrets Act needs amendment, as it is violative of Article 19(1)(a) of the Constitution. The existing 'catch all' provisions of the act can make all kinds of official document and information for the use of officials only.

In many states of India, social workers and NGOs have started movements for free flow of information from government to public. The citizens should have the right to see the government files which particularly deal with development works and distribution of benefits. A few state governments have yielded under pressure and started deliberations on Freedom of Information Bill. Three states—Tamil Nadu, Goa and Madhya Pradesh —have so far passed the bill. The legislation made by the Madhya Pradesh government has been hailed as a bold step as it aims at bringing about transparency and accountability in administration by making government documents open to public scrutiny. Yet in most of these acts, there are provisions according to which the state can withhold certain categories of information from the public.

Moreover, as a part of programme to disseminate information on public amenities, the government has decided to set up citizen information centres under the aegis of the Department of Consumer Affairs and Public Distribution. The proposal has been made under the Action Plan for an Effective and Responsive Government. The centres will help people in securing various services and assist in getting replies to the complaints made by them. It has also been said that the government would set up public facilitation counters in all ministries and departments to ensure provision of all unclassified information on procedures and decisions of government.[12]

CONCLUDING REMARKS

The Indian government has a huge repository of data and information in the form of acts, notifications, rules, committee and commission reports and statistical publications. These are compiled and released in a dispersed manner. And a large number of agencies are involved in this venture. There is no uniform policy with regard to dissemination of information. To some extent, all powerful Indian bureaucracy is responsible for the present state of affairs. It has been said that lack of specialisation in civil service makes it mostly 'knowledge proof'. Civil servants are not inclined to use knowledge and expertise and they are somewhat insensitive to specialised information. Access to information does not figure in their priority.[13]

At present, there is a constant pressure from the social activists and NGOs to enact the Right to Information Bill. It is essential to create a conducive social environment in India in which such rights can be properly enforced. India has a complex divided and hierarchical society with a low level of social intelligence. The opportunity and competence to represent one's entitlements and rights is limited to only a few privileged. Under such conditions, it is doubtful whether 'Right to Information' Act/Bill is going to benefit the common man.

A National Information Policy is needed for India in order to ensure harmonious implementation and operation of information resources, services and systems. The major components of such a policy would be a set of all public laws, regulation and policies endorsed by the government that encourage, discourage or regulate the creation, use, storage and communication of information.

REFERENCES

1. UNESCO, *World Information Report, 1997-98,* Paris, p. 1.
2. World Bank. *World Development Report : Knowledge for Development, 1998-99.* Oxford University Press, 1998, p. iii.
3. Khare M. P., Assessing crops : Index number muddle, *Economic and Political Weekly*, 1982, 34, 29, 1999.
4. Bhalla Surjit S., and Vashishtha Prem, Income distribution in India: A re-examination, In Srinivasan T. N., and Bardhan Pranab K., Ed. *Rural Poverty in South Asia,* Delhi, Oxford University Press, 1988, p. 39
5. Khare M P., op.cit., p. 1982.
6. Sinha Subrata and Ghosh Arun, Literacy campaign, land literacy and watershed development, *Economic and Political Weekly*, 1997, 32, 6, 287-88.
7. Ministry of India, Planning and Programme Implementation, Department of Statistics, National policy of dissemination of statistical data, *Information Today and Tomorrow*, 1998, 17,3.
8. Notification should be made public, *PTI Economic Service*, 1998, 22, 11, 16-19.
9. Sen Amartya, Indian tradition and western imagination, *Deadalus*, 1997, 126, 2, 19.
10. World Bank, *Governance and Development*, Washington DC, 1992, p. 3.
11. Jayal Niraja Gopal, The governance agenda: Making democratic development indispensable. *Economic and Political Weekly*, 1997, 32, 8, 407.
12. Ministry of India, Personnel and Public Grievances, Department of Administrative Reports and Public Grievances, Action plan for an effective and responsive government. *Indian Journal of Public Administration*, 1998, 54, 3, 647-48.
13. Ghate Prabhu, Reforming the civil service : Meeting crucial need for expertise, *Economic and Political Weekly*, 1998, 33, 7, 359.

20

Distance Learners: Access to Library and Information Sources and Services in India

M. Sankara Reddy and *L.S.Ramaiah*

INTRODUCTION

India is the biggest democracy in the world with one billion people. Illiteracy and semi-literacy are the significant barriers to its socio-economic development. It is estimated that there will be about 200 million illiterates in India alone by the beginning of this century. So, the provision of facilities for education to all is a major challenge in our country. There are large sections of people in the country who are not fortunate to have access to education. They are:

a) Economically backward sections;

b) Large sections of SC and ST people;

c) Handicapped people; and

d) Women in the rural areas.

The above sections of people, for reasons well known like economic, social and traditional problems, do not join the formal centres of learning. Even if they join, they drop out soon and remain illiterate or lapse into illiteracy for the rest of their lives. For long they never had facilities to pursue education in their life. In the second half of the last century the open learning or distance education system has brought a silent revolution in the field of education. Now, in every country there are specific universities, or schools of correspondence education for the adult learners or dropped out learners or other categories of people who are self-employed or unemployed to pursue their education. Thus education is brought to the doorstep of the people. It is no longer expensive like the formal education.

DISTANCE EDUCATION

There are many nomenclatures to distance education. It is known as 'Open Learning', 'Open Education', 'Correspondence Education', 'External Study','Home Study', 'External Education', 'Private Study' and 'University Without Walls'. However the term 'Distance Education' has come to stay in India. M.G. Moore[1] defines it as "a learning system where the teaching behaviours are separate from the learning behaviours. The learner works alone or in a group guided by study material arranged by instructor, who together with the tutors, is in a location apart from the students, who however has the opportunity to communicate with a tutor/tutors with the aid of one or more media such as correspondence, telephone, television, and radio. Distance education may be confined to various forms of face-to-face meetings."

The characteristics that are essential for distance education are:

a) The separation of educators and learners;
b) The planning of a separate educational organisation;
c) The use of technical media; and
d) The organising of seminars or meetings between students and teachers for two-way communication.

Distance Education in India

The Distance education took roots in India as for back as 1980.

The first university for this kind of education was established in Andhra Pradesh in 1982 under the name of Andhra Pradesh Open University which later was renamed as Dr. B.R. Ambedkar Open University. The distance education idea caught like wildfire. Within a span of 20 years it became an important stream of education in India. The profile of the distance education is shown in Table 1.

Table 1 : Profile of Distance Education in India

S.No	*Name of the university*	*Year of establishment*	*Student enrolment*	*No. of programmers*	*No. of study centres*
1.	Indira Gandhi National Open University	1985	516,580	48	450
2.	Dr. B.R. Ambedkar Open University, Hyd	1982	318,650	21	130
3.	Kota Open University, Rajasthan	1987	8,793	21	36
4.	Nalanda Open University, Bihar	1987	641	9	4
5.	Yashwant Rao Chavan Maharastra Open University	1989	397,881	54	1,399
6.	Madhya Pradesh Bhoj Open University	1991	55,912	29	670
7.	Dr. Baba Saheb Ambedkar Open University	1994	24,700	9	70
8.	Karnataka State Open University	1996	27,231	23	218
9.	Netaji Subhas Open University	1997	434	3	36
10.	U.P. Rajashri Tandon Open University	1999	3,307	18	18
	Total		13,54,129	235	3,031

(Data supplied by G. Sujatha, Deputy Librarian, Dr. B.R. Ambedkar Open University, Hyderabad.)

The table profile does not provide complete picture of the distance education. There are many universities, which have established departments of 'Correspondence Courses', 'External Examinations' or 'Distance Education'. To mention a few belonging to this category are: Annamalai University, Madurai-Kamraj University, Andhra University, CIEFL, Osmania University, and University of Madras. Their number is large and it is increasing day by day. Distance education courses are covering many subjects in the humanities, the social sciences and the pure sciences too. Many new disciplines and inter disciplinary courses are also finding place in the distance education programmes. The demand for the distance education courses is growing all over the country.

Distance Learners: Who are They?

Distance learners are a blend of different sections of people. They are:

a) People who discontinued their education after the primary and secondary school due to poverty;
b) Students who were earlier dropouts after failing in the examinations;
c) Students who discontinued due to lack of motivation and aptitude but later find inspiration;
d) Tribal people who live in remote forests and hills and do not have access to universities;
e) Person working in government departments and private organizations and desire to improve their qualification for promotions;
f) Handicapped people who find it difficult to attend the formal educational institutions due to lack of facilities;
g) Housewives and other ladies who were denied education in the yester year due to social taboos;

h) Individuals who think education is a lifelong activity and desire to pursue study in new subjects for vision and enlightenment;

i) Job-oriented courses such as the Creative Writing, MCA, MBA, etc., which attract individual to take them up;

j) Students who are unable to get admission into the portals of the universities; and

k) Unemployed youth who desire to improve their qualification.

The distant learners are a mixed bag of people with different age groups, interests, qualifications, attitudes and aptitudes.

Difficulties of the Distant Learners

The distance learners have many disadvantages. Some of them are:

a) The distance learners are separated by long distances from their counsellors;

b) They have to depend largely on self-study;

c) They do not have the advantage of discussing or meeting regularly with their co-learners unlike the students in formal education system;

d) They have to depend mainly on the instructional materials provided to them;

e) The study centres of the open universities are not provided with proper facilities;

f) Their libraries are almost non-existent except for some old textbooks;

g) The public library system, which is supposed to come to the help of the self-learners, is hopelessly inadequate and obsolete. There are no libraries in most of the villages;

h) The academic libraries (college and university libraries), do not give access to distance learners;

i) They cannot discuss their difficulties in lessons immediately with their counsellors since classes take place only at the weekends;

j) Technical infrastructure such as audio lessons, video lessons, educational broadcastings, and video books, etc., has not developed to the extent required;

k) Open universities do not command dedicated channels to broadcast their lessons to the distant learners;

l) There are no internet facilities in the rural areas; and

m) Most of the open-university library collections are not computerised. Wherever computerisation has been achieved terminals are not within the reach of the students. They have to go all the way to the main libraries.

PRESENT POSITION OF LIS SOURCES AND SERVICES

Distance education implies self-study. Students have to read, refer and consult vast literature. Furthermore, most of the distance learners are aged, matured, motivated or serious people desirous of learning more than the regular students.

At present they get the following facilities:

a) Course material;

b) News bulletins published from time to time;

c) Access to inadequate study centre libraries without borrowing facilities;

d) Libraries of the concerned open universities; and

e) Some times the distance learners get books through postal service of open universities.

The library and information sources and services provided by almost all the open universities in India are inadequate. Though this mode of education has been functioning for the last 18 years, yet so far no survey has been conducted on the status of LIS services to the distant learners. It is worthwhile undertaking such a survey as it would also provide a perspective for future action in the matter.

University Libraries

Though open universities have brought educational facility to the doorstep of distance learners, the library and information facilities have yet to develop for the purpose. The headquarters of the open universities are generally located at distant places and difficult to reach. The universities may have established good libraries for students but they cannot physically reach them due to long distance. Besides, the library working hours are from 10 am to 6 pm whereas the distance learners who are workers or employees get time to come to libraries only after 6 pm. These libraries are closed on Sundays and holidays and as such remain underutilised.

Libraries of Study Centres

The study centers of the open universities are not properly developed. They do not have their own buildings. They are housed in buildings belonging to some schools or colleges. The accommodation at their disposal is inadequate.

The libraries in such study centres are utterly inadequate. Textbooks are few and kept in closed sequence. These libraries need to be equipped with books periodicals, audio video materials, and also with multiple copies of books as suggested in the course material. The reference tools should be adequate and uptodate. Books in Indian languages also should be acquired. The students should have facility of borrowing at least a book at a time against proper deposit.

They also need a well-qualified librarian along with supporting staff to render information, reference, and document delivery services. Extensive subsidised xeroxing facilities is also a requirement. The working hours of study centre libraries should be from 2 pm to 10 pm, and they should also be kept open on Sundays and holidays.

PUBLIC LIBRARY FACILITIES

The concept of distance education has been borrowed from the west. The Open University of UK is the model imitated in India. In an advanced country like UK, the distance learner depends heavily on a well-developed public library system. In the UK public library facilities are more than adequate. It is responding well and also improving the facilities as required.

In 1988 through the Department of Employment Training Agency, the government of UK funded an experimental service to provide free public access to open learning materials through a pilot project in North Wales. The success of this pilot scheme resulted in additional funds being granted to set up further 10 open learning projects during 1989 to 1990. In 1992 the government established Training and Enterprise Council (TEC's) and Local Enterprise Councils (LEC's) for spreading the provision of open learning materials nationally in partnership with the public libraries. Public libraries have been provided additional funds for this purpose.

In India too, governments should take the responsibility under the public library acts and gear up public library systems in the states. This is essential to help learners under distance education mode. Broadly speaking, government responsibility does not end with having established open universities or study centres. Just as it has sought to facilitate education at the doorstep of the people, for the same reason it has to bear responsibility to make available library and information facilities to distance learners. Improving public library system has to be made integral component of open learning system. Otherwise the distance learners will continue to remain isolated, like being in an island, and without access to globally-generated information. This might defeat the very purpose of open learning mode. People might get degrees but do they also get education?

INSTRUCTIONAL MATERIAL

The instruction material provided by distance education universities or institutions should be both in English and the mother tongue of distance learners. The initial education of the distance learner has been in their mother tongue. Hence, the instruction materials provided in English language may not be creating reading interest in them. Instruction material should be drafted in such a way that it creates interest and leads to further reading. The reading materials should be suitably supplemented with the audio lessons, video films, video books, etc. The learners should also get good books in their own mother tongue to understand the basic concepts in the subject of their study. Some students fail to do their assignments properly because of the language problem. They reproduce blindly for whatever they find in the instruction materials in completing their assignments.

DISCUSSIONS, MEETINGS AND SEMINARS

The open learners should get opportunities for regular discussions, meetings and seminars during their study period. This will enable them to know more information and about information sources. This will provide them a sense of participation and motivate them to sharpen their reading habits and study skills. There should be at least one meeting per month and one seminar every quarter.

DEDICATED BROADCASTING RADIO AND TV CHANNELS

The open universities should own their own broadcasting channels. They should prepare audio and video lessons and broadcast them according to a timetable. This will supplement the instructional materials provided to them. Further, through these channels, the doubts, questions, queries of the open learners received through correspondence should be cleared and answered. This will reduce to a great extent the physical distance barrier between the distance education institutions and the distance learners.

CONCLUSION

The following points must be considered as they are important in enriching the quality of distance education and distance learners:

a) Public libraries should be involved more and more in the open learning system. It benefits the libraries and the learners;
b) Information technology, which has brought a silent revolution in many sectors including education should be utilised in the cause of distance education;
c) There should be a dedicated satellite communication channel for use by the distance education universities, institutions and organisations;
d) Academic libraries should allow the distance learners to use their resources without restrictions;
e) There should be well developed and properly manned libraries at the study centres for the use of open learners;
f) Frequent meetings and seminars should be organized to improve students in their study. The libraries should be well stocked with books, periodicals and other non-book materials;
g) Reading materials should be supplemented with other media to create interest in the subject of study;

h) The study centre should create Local Technical Training Councils to provide proper advice and guidelines to the open learners;

i) The open universities should develop digital libraries, which can be used by their study centres on the internet. The digital database should contain among other information, the books mentioned in the course material and periodical articles; and

j) The availability of effective and efficient library and information facilities to distance learners alone cannot get them degrees, but at the best can enable them become literate and educated.

REFERENCES

1. Moore M.G.: *In a Theory of Independent Study.* Hague: Firm university, 1977.

BIBLIOGRAPHY

Alfred. John, Open learning and public libraries, In *EC Libraries Programme and Innovation in Public Workshop*, Luxembourg 11-12 November 1993 session papers, Luxembourg, Commission of the European Communication, Directorate General XIII, Telecommunications, Information Market and Exploitation of Research 1993.

Astbury, Raymond, The public library of the twenty-first century: The Key Information and learning counter in the community, In Ramaiah L.S. et al (eds.), *Public Library System, Services and Networks,* New Delhi, EASESS Publishers, 1996, pp. 15-33.

Baber, Anthony, L., *Look and learn : Library Association Adult Independent Learning Guidelines for Libraries and Learning Resource Centers,* London : Library Association. 1992.

Chandrashkhar Rao, V. and Sujatha G., Designing users education programmes for distance learners in Isaac, Dorothy et al (eds.),

Academic Libraries: Role in the National Development, Madras: T.R. Publications, 1993, pp. 295-301.

Manjulika. S and Venugopala Reddy V., *Distance Education: A Model for Developing Countries*, New Delhi: Vikas Publishing House, 1996.

Nigam, B.K. and Kaushik, Vijay Kumari, *Management and Evaluation of Distance Education,* New Delhi: Kanishka Publishers, 1996.

Raju A.A.N., 'Need for strengthening Library and information services to distance learners' (Memo).

Ramesh Babu. B., 'Measures to strengthen correspondence courses in library and information science In Issac Dorothy et al (eds.), *Academic Libraries: Role in the National Development*, Madras: T.R. Publications, 1993, pp. 267-277.

PART V

Networking, Internet, Cyber Age and Libraries

21

Cyber Commerce for Libraries

A. Lakshmana Moorthy and *C.R. Karisiddappa*

INTRODUCTION

Internet has brought in a new concept called electronic commerce (e-commerce), in marketing and business fields. It is, perhaps, one of the most impressive benefits of internet which made the institutions, industries, individual professionals having expertise in various fields and commercial organisations, contribute to the electronic information resources and thereby gain increased marketability of products, services and expertise. Variously known as e-commerce, e-biz, cyber commerce, online commerce, net commerce, etc., it is the latest phenomenon of internet. Individuals/professionals also can play a role in e-commerce by becoming consultants offering their expertise to customers for services/products over internet. E-commerce is redefining the way business is conducted by individuals, institutions and industries. It has provided new avenues for marketing, novel ways for advertising, and a large customer base. It has provided vendors and manufacturers increased visibility for products, and a variety of alternatives to customers.

Internet provides information including profiles of companies, institutions, industries, professional consultants, organisations and their activities, products, services, technologies, etc. The websites maintained by manufacturers, vendors, and financial institutions participating in e-commerce, and also of organisations supporting it like Commerce Net, Netscape, Microsoft, etc., will be more useful for those who would like to enter into the world of e-biz. E-mail distribution lists, manufacturer's and product directories, listservs, etc., are also available for product marketing. Realising its competitive edge/advantage, traditional commerce is fast becoming limited, the business companies have started looking for newer avenues to enhance profitability. They found that internet provides seamless access to customers, partners, suppliers, and distributors besides providing enormous opportunities to expand business beyond local and geographical boundaries. Thus, internet became a medium to achieve corporate competitiveness and profitability.

Internet allows selling of non-material goods directly while material goods can be delivered by conventional means. The former includes items like, software, downloading articles from e-journals and/or digital libraries, newspapers, magazines, etc. Ordering books and other goods by searching online book stores and shopping malls is an example where the items ordered are sent by post to the specified addresses. Internet facilitates e-commerce in three ways:[1]

a) It provides a very large customer base and reaches maximum number of countries,

b) The presence (creation) and maintenance of a site on internet is cheap, and results in reduced prices, makes business more competitive, facilitates instant updation, access and sales (i.e., it results in 'zero time lag' between advertising and sales), and

c) It caters to the customer's wide and varied interests, thus saving the time taken for travelling between different places (although physically seeing may help choose quality items).

E-commerce is influencing the structure of business dealings and supply chains. It is growing at a rate of more than 30 per cent, promoting business-to-business and business-to-customer/ consumer transactions manifold. This is mainly because web-based transactions offer low service costs. For example, sending a 40-page document from New York to Tokyo costs an average of US$ 26 through courier services, about US $ 30 by fax and a mere 10 cents via internet.[2] A host of electronic payment systems used over internet facilitate cheaper operational costs; about 5 cents per transaction for digital currency as against 45 cents per transaction for credit card payments, 75 cents for check payments and US$ 1 per transaction for paper currency payments.[3] In a typical Indian scenario, a typical internet online bank transaction costs 5 paise per transaction as against Rs 1.50 through a teller.[4] Internet is an inexpensive medium which allows widespread access to individuals, institutions and business industry without any discrimination. It provides the same facilities, opportunities and avenues to all, irrespective of any preference or favouritism to any product or firm. Thus, right from advertising and automobiles to software and value-added services, all thrive over cyberspace. Besides IT companies, non-infotech firms like those from automobile industry, drugs, groceries, books, etc., are all trading over the internet. See, for example, how e-commerce benefited some of the companies:

a) Yahoo! reported a revenue of US$ 86 million for the first quarter of 1999, nearly three times to the corresponding period in 1998; for 1998, it ranked US$ 203 million, a threefold increase over 1997.

b) Knight-Ridder New Media, an electronic publisher, has developed a web-based application for making financial operations more efficient, and attracting new subscribers and advertising revenue through innovative online publishing for all the company's newspapers.

c) The internet commerce of Cisco Systems, a major communications firm, in 1996 was US$ 100 million that rose to US$ 3.2 billion in 1997.

d) The worldwide e-business revenues of IBM in 1998 were US$ 27 billion, more than one-third of total revenues for the year.

e) Intel in its first month of operation on the net made sales of US$ 1 billion, an e-business record, and is gearing up for an online trade of US$ 3 trillion by 2003 end.

f) The website of Amazon.com was visited by 15,10,000 during the fourth quarter of 1997 and 22,60,000 in the first quarter of 1998; it achieved a book sales of US$ 610 millions in 1998, and a growth of 313 per cent over the sales for 1997.

g) Dell Computers encourages customers to design their own PCs online with daily sales running around US$ 10 million up from US$ 6 million daily during the December 1997 holiday period.

h) Auto-by-Tel, a web-based automotive marketplace, had auto sales worth US$ 1.8 billion (3,45,000 purchase requests) during 1996. By 1997, it rose to about US$ 6 billion (12,00,000 purchase requests).

i) The AIM Management Group, a mutual fund company, has developed an extranet to provide its customers with up-to-the-minute information, 24 hours a day accessible from anywhere. It is able to satisfy all customers and brokers with brochures, literature and financial information all the times.

j) The Hong Kong Telecom, the largest internet service provider in Hong Kong with an annual sales of US$ 32 billion (in 1997), developed and deployed an online application on internet to deliver higher levels of cost-effective service, 24 hours a day, seven days a week

k) Chrysler Corporation reportedly saved more than US$ 1 billion in cost of materials in 1997 merely by linking its suppliers through a web-based network and by the year 2000, the annual average savings estimated will amount to US$ 2 billion.

Although there are differences of opinion as to the revenues generated by global e-commerce, it is steadily growing. As per the NASSCOM report,[5] the value of global internet commerce in 1997 was US$ 9.61 billion; the projected values for the years 1998, 1999 and 2000 are US$ 13.06, 17.76 and 24.15 billion, respectively. Other reports published in the *Economic Times*[6] estimate that e-commerce would generate US$ 45.8 billion in 1998 and US$ 200 billion by the turn of the century. The IDC of USA estimated that transactions worth US$ 10 billion were executed over internet in 1997 (equal to a mere 0.05 per cent of the global commerce). It estimated the value of e-commerce for 1998, 2000, 2001, and 2010 to be US$ 45.8, 150, 220 and 1,000 billion, respectively.[7] The US Department of Commerce projected that e-commerce would reach US$ 310 billion in 1999 and by the year 2003 it would reach US$ 1.5 trillion.[8] As per the survey of CMP Research in December 1997, it was observed that nearly two-thirds of the US companies would be resorting to e-commerce by the year 1998. About 40 per cent of the US companies conducted business on internet in 1997 and another 23 per cent will be joining them by the year 1998.[9] This demonstrates the growing value and importance of e-commerce for global economy.

With more than 56.2 million computers attached to the internet spread over 190 countries, 1.6 million domain names, about 2.75 lakh internet protocol networks, 6.5 lakh websites, growing at the rate of 9-12 per cent every month, with a number of online shopping malls and over 100 million users, the internet can make a lot of difference in the business world. By the year 2000, about 36 million households from US alone, 20 million from the European Union and 12 million from India will be accessing the web.

The main characteristic of e-commerce is the anonymity it provides to the customers and vendors as well as to the transactions which take between them. Other characteristics include privacy, and integrity of messages sent, authenticity and non-repudiation of transactions taking place on the internet. This has given rise to initial hick-ups including insecurity, fraud, money laundering and impersonation. This situation in turn has led to the formulation of security protocols. In the case of online ordering and instant purchases, the payments have to be made either through deposit accounts or smart/credit cards or any of the electronic payment systems. A host of electronic payment systems like First Virtual Internet Payment System, E-cash, ICVERIFY, NetCash, Secure Internet Payment System, CyberCoin, MilliCent, Payword, PayNow, NetBill, etc., have been developed and are available for the customers to choose from.[10]

In electronic market place, search costs are heavily reduced, as all the information about an item/product is available at one place (when more than one location is involved, hyperlinks are provided). This reduces search time and related costs and also enables in locating suppliers matching the needs of the buyers. However, this is not true in all cases. As per a study, the average prices of second-hand cars sold through AUCNET, an electronic marketplace for used cars in Japan, were found to be much higher than that of traditional non-electronic markets. But the higher prices made many sellers list their cars on AUCNET, which in turn attracted more buyers as it offered better choices. It had also created risks of buying inferior quality vehicles as transactions are made without physical inspection.[11]

But all is not well with e-commerce. While it is growing steadily, many customers get dissatisfied, sometimes frustrated, with some sites. This is because of the 'out of stock' messages that are encountered by customers; it has been observed that 10 per cent of the orders could not be satisfied because of the non-availability of the advertised stocks. The consumers are annoyed for the failure to get feedback from the websites. A majority of the consumers felt that more information was needed on their purchases.

WEB ADVERTISING

Internet facilitates advertising, marketing and sales, thereby promoting e-commerce. Marketing through advertisements is one of the well established channels in business. Advertising over internet involves low premiums, assures easy access and has global appealing as against the conventional print media. Whereas the print media generally has a restricted domain, internet caters to all kinds of vendors and customers in almost all subject areas. Unlike, print media, there is no restriction on space; one can put up additional information. This avoids the follow-up material sent in the case of print media when a user wants to know more about a particular item advertised. Unlike the print media where it takes a longer time to know the popularity or otherwise of the product, it is immediately known to the vendor due to the instant feedback received from the customers. Whereas in the conventional commerce the advertiser goes to the consumer, in the internet commerce the latter goes to the former. Quite often, the interaction between the user and the website results in online ordering and receiving the products as well.

Advertising on the web (or Netvertising), i.e., hosting a home page on the web, is one of the best ways to make the world know about an institution, an organisation, a library or even an individual (say, a professional consultant). This would enable publicity about the various facilities, services and products offered to the users. It was estimated that there were 25 million home pages available on the Web in 1995 which was expected to reach 200 million by 1999.[12] The foreign web servers charge anywhere between a few thousands to a few lakhs of rupees (depending upon the size) for designing, developing and hosting a web page. In India NIC and VSNL from the public sector and also many private firms are providing this service at competitive rates. VSNL charges Rs 3 lakhs, Rs 6 lakhs, and Rs 12 lakhs for data transfer of up to 1 GB, 10 GB and 30 GB per month, respectively (with an additional Rs 3 lakhs towards general service charges in each case) for hosting a dedicated web server. As internet supports audio, video, animation and graphics, this area is gaining more and more attention. The web advertising and marketing are generally skewed towards educated, middle and high income groups. Many newspapers, newsletters, and ad agencies are advertising on the internet. The ad revenues for websites during April-June 1998 was US$ 422.7 million which is almost double when compared to the revenues for the same period in 1997. As per the Internet Advertising Bureau, the ad revenues have grown from US$ 267 million in 1996 to $ 906.5 million in 1997 and to $2 billion in 1998. During the first quarter of 1999, the ad revenues reached US$ 693 million, double the figure for the same period in 1998 (www.nua.ie/surveys/). The top three web advertising categories are computer-related goods, books and credit cards. As per a survey reported in *Computers Today* (16-30 September 1999, p. 35),[13] Amazon.com tops the list of companies with a "Net Presence" (a measure of internet visibility) rate of 57.6, closely followed by Barnesandnoble.com (56.1) and Microsoft (42).

As a result of the net advertising, the ISPs in Europe, especially in UK, are moving towards providing free internet access, without any limit on the hours of usage. Internet telephony and reduced-charge, limitless talk-time, and long distance telephony (with advertisements at the beginning and at every one-minute interval) are becoming the order of the day in the US. Some provide the new customers with cash incentives (up to US$ 100) on signing. All this is made possible because of the advertising revenues, which partially make up the revenue loss in these situations. The rapidly falling costs coupled with the availability of bandwidth due to the use of fibre optic systems, further helped such freebies possible.

E-COMMERCE AND LIBRARIES

The publishing industry is already exploiting internet by offering electronic/online journals, table of contents of journals, and catalogues of books and products over internet. Well-known bookstores around the world are offering their holdings over internet. It is possible to order a book from, say, Blackwell (www.blackwell.co.uk/bookshops), which maintains a database of over 150,000 active titles. Bookwire (www.bookwire.com) has links to 150 booksellers and over 200 publishers to select publications and for ordering. Many sites of publishers tell the user about the recently published books, include book reviews, and provide information on electronic books, rare book dealers, mailing lists, bestsellers in fiction, etc. Online services like AOL provide many forms of online content for attracting subscribers. These include a glimpse of title page, book reviews, contents and excerpts from books. Many well-known (and also obscure) books are available free of charge for downloading from Online Book Initiative, a Gopher site (world.std.com). A number of electronic reference sources and guides, and many e-magazines (e-zines), business publications and scholarly periodicals are available for subscription over the internet. These are increasing rapidly day by day and represent, perhaps, the largest single resource available to anyone at any given time.

Libraries with internet access can benefit from online book stores; they can acquire books and journals, reports and other information services from internet. Of particular importance to librarians is the Acqweb, a website intended for library acquisitions. A recent search (December 1999) of Yahoo! for online bookshops/bookstores gave a list of 454 websites covering various subject fields. Users can use these sites for online ordering of documents. The search also revealed 464 bookshops, 117 online book publishers, 2,709 book publishers (having a home page on the internet) in 11 categories. Many of these offer searching and ordering facilities. There were 1,123 sites for online ordering dealing with books, drugs and pharmaceuticals, computers, food, automobiles, art, tours and equipment.

Amazon.com is an online bookstore offering a wide range of books at prices that are lower than those at retail book stores. The selected book can be ordered through the online order form. Payment can be made through credit card or when the books are delivered. One can also view the contents of the book and some times read a part or whole of it. It is the most popular and number one destination for online book purchases over the internet. Its website was visited by 2,260,000 surfers for purchasing books during the first quarter of 1998, an increase from 1,510,000 customers during the fourth quarter in 1997. It reported US$ 16 million and $66 million in the first and fourth quarters of 1997, respectively thus achieving over 400 per cent growth during the year. The sales touched US$ 87.4 million during the first quarter of 1998 (Balasubramanian, 1998). It achieved a book sales of US$ 610 million in 1998, a growth of 313 per cent over the sales for 1997. In just three and a half year's. time Amazon.com became the third largest bookseller behind Barnes and Noble (US$ 2.7 billions in 1998) and Borders (US$ 2.3 billions). The music division of Amazon.com became the largest music seller in 1998 with US$ 33.1 million sales.

ELECTRONIC PAYMENT SYSTEMS

Electronic/digital payment, in brief, is a transaction process involving the customer, shopping mall (an intermediary representing various vendors/merchants), vendor, credit card bank and the customer's bank. In a simple process, it involves the customer, online vendor, vendor's bank and credit card bank. The mode of payment varies with different systems. One can choose to pay through a payment system sponsor (for instance, DigiCash) wherein the participants have to register with the system in some way. Another approach is payment through digital currency wherein the customer, having an account with a bank offering digital currency, can withdraw money and transact using digital wallets. Digital signatures and cryptographic techniques are used for safe and secure transactions. The procedure of different electronic payment systems has been extensively dealt in the literature (see for example, *Computers Today*,[13] June 1998; Freeman[14], 1996; Hamilton[15], 1997; Kambil[16], 1997 and Opplinger,[1] 1998).

Some of the important players involved in e-commerce include CommerceNet, CyberCash, DigiCash, First Virtual Holdings, IBM, MasterCard International, MicroSoft, Mondex International, NetCash/NetCheque, Netscape Communications, VeriSign, and Visa. There are a number of other firms involved as well. Also, to facilitate payments of very small amounts (of the order of a few cents) and to minimise overhead costs of using the other electronic payment systems, several micropayment systems came into existence. These include, CyberCoin from CyberCash, MilliCent from DEC, PayWord and MicroMint from Ron Rivest and Adi Shamir, and NetBill from Carnegie Mellon University.[17]

Electronic funds transfer (EFT) through electronic checking has been in usage since 1960s. This involves the customer, the vendor/merchant and the intermediary/financial institution. This resulted in improving speed of transaction, saving time, and reducing costs of paper handling. This has led to the development of digital cash ensuring anonymity of the customer and also made possible the usage of prepaid cards (like telephone cards) and later, electronic cash (e-cash).[19] In digital payment systems, to transact business, both the customers and vendors have to make some commitment to the payment system; some times they may have to open an account with the digital payment system, install software on their computers to operate and may have to enter into agreements. A detailed account of electronic payment systems has been dealt by the authors elsewhere.[18]

E-COMMERCE AND INDIA

As per the estimation of the Indian subsidiary of IDC, the value of e-commerce in India was about US$ 2.8 million (Rs 112 crore) in 1997 which is expected to reach US$ 160 million (Rs 7,000 crore) by the year 2001. During 1998-99, e-commerce worth 131 crore was carried out and by the year 2002, the e-commerce related business could touch US$ 1 billion (Rs 440 crore).[19] According to the Management Association for Information Technology, India at present has a PC base of 8,00,000 which is expected to reach two million by the year 2001 with an estimated 3,75,000 households which possess a PC. The per centages of PC owners and non-PC owners who access e-commerce are 26 and 15 respectively.

E-commerce is the new buzz word in the Indian business industry. Observing the successful exploitation of internet for promoting business across cyber space, many business firms in India are taking interest in e-commerce. A number of techno-commercial websites including those exclusively dealing with Indian scenario.[20] Indian software industry took the lead in establishing websites and home pages for marketing Indian software products and value-added services.

The publication industry is exploiting internet and e-commerce in a big way. In 1995 there were only 20 newspapers on the web; now there are over 4,000, of which 225 are Asian newspapers. Among the Asian papers, roughly one-fourth (60) are Indian. Many of the leading Indian newspapers including *The Hindu*, *Business Line*, *The Times of India*, *The Pioneer*, *The Economic Times*, *The Deccan Chronicle*, *The Deccan Herald*, *The Indian Express*, etc., are having internet editions. About 50 Indian computer and business magazines such as *Dataquest*, *PC Quest*, *Chip*, *Computers Today*, *Business India*, *India Today*, *Business Today*, *Voice* and *Data*, *Nayi Duniya* etc., are available over Internet.[21] A number of organisations/ institutions such as DRDO, NCSI, IISc, IITs, and many public sector institutions like SAIL, ECIL, ONGC, NIC, STPI, All India Radio, Doordarshan, Customs, etc are maintaining home pages on Internet. Some publication groups like The Hindu (first in the country to launch Internet edition in 1995), India Today, Deccan Herald, etc., are publishing internet editions of all their publications. The online Indian newspapers are attracting, besides Indian readers, many Non-Resident Indians (NRIs). *The Hindu Online* averages 50,000 page views daily; *The Hindustan Times* about 2,00,000 page views, *The India Today Online* gets 20,00,000 page views daily; *The Times of India* about 10,00,000 hits, and *The Indian Express* gets an average of 25,00,000 hits a day.[22] Rediff On The Net, one of the most popular Indian sites, started in early 1996 introduced chat, interactive cricket commentary, Real Audio hits, movie ticket booking, free home pages, online shopping, gift delivery etc. Over the years it now gets 70 million hits each month. The India-specific search engines like Khoj and 123 India link web pages are dealing with India. It is interesting to note that although 60 newspapers have internet editions, only 18 are in English, the rest are from vernacular languages.

Indian book publishers are also joining the race. We too have online books/CDs (www.indiabookshop.com; www.rediff.com) with UBS Publishers' Distributors website, the largest for Indian books covering 15,000 titles from 700 publishers to be launched shortly, online auction sites (www.webauction.com; www.bid.com; www.onsale.com; etc), job hunting (www.naukri.com), supermarket (www.cpmall.com), sites catering to travel, tourism, games, IT, and so on.[23] The Health Education for People, India's first free health library, offers doctors full text online access to 37 world renowned reference books and 48 of the world's best journals in the medical field, through internet, for only Rs 5,999. Malamall (www.malamall.com) is introducing e-card for safe, easy and convenient online shopping.

The computer-to-computer business transaction standard, EDI (Electronic Data Interchange), is gaining acceptance in India for both domestic and overseas transactions. Coupled with bar coding technology and Electronic Funds Transfer (EFT), EDI is capable of drastically reducing processing time manifold besides financial savings. It is most suitable in cargo handling systems where a number of players, viz., banks, customers, customs, cargo forwarders, transporters, and importing and exporting agents, are involved. With the active support of the EDI Council, Ministry of Commerce, Government of India, for adopting EDI technology by all departments in foreign trade, the scenario is fast changing. In India, the current usage of EDI (among the various internet services) is only 4 per cent and is expected to grow (NASSCOM, 1997, p. 111). VSNL is the first to start EDI services in the country in 1993 which installed an EDI system in Mumbai with access nodes at New Delhi, Calcutta and Chennai. EDI is being promoted to be adopted by all port trusts; Kochi Port Trust is the first to implement it. Apart from port trusts, the key players in EDI include BHEL, Electronic Research and Development Centre (ERDC, Kolkata), CMC, Customs and Director General of Foreign Trade (from public sector); and Tata-IBM, Satyam Infoway, Wipro Infosys, etc., (from the private sector). The Federation of Indian Export Organisations (FIEO) is encouraging its members for switching to e-commerce. EDI-based e-biz was expected to cross Rs 500 crore by the year 2000.

Internet banking has already been introduced in India for the first time a year back by the ICICI Bank, which, in collaboration with Infosys Technologies, developed a software 'Infinity-Internet Banking', a complete online banking solution, wherein internet can be used as a banking channel for retail and corporate consumers. With this, the ICICI Bank joined a select group of banks in the Asia Pacific region (about 150) which have banking sites on internet.[24] At present, a few companies in the country are offering web advertising services. The DSF Internet Services has exclusive advertising rights to two of the most popular Indian sites—the All India Radio and Doordarshan. The websites of IndiaWorld, Khel, Khoj, Dhan and NewsAsia of IndiaWorld Network, launched in August 1998 has generated Rs 5 lakh till November 1998.[13] Rediff On The Net is expecting to sell Rs 5.5 lakh worth of books, music titles and hotel reservations per day within next six months and Mumbai Mart is targeting Rs 5-10 lakh per month.[25]

CONCLUSION

The government is in the process of taking measures for the growth of internet and e-commerce in the country. A recent survey by NASSCOM puts the e-business during the fiscal year 1999-2000 at Rs 300 crore which was expected to reach Rs 10,000 crore by the end of 2002.[26] But there is no legal framework as yet to govern cyber commerce in the country. The e-commerce Act of Ministry of Commerce is pending with the government. The IT Action Plan of Government of India addressed critical national needs in the areas of e-commerce, internet access, information infrastructure and R&D in IT among others. It also envisages training citizens in the use of e-commerce, tele-banking, tele-documents transfer, and tele-library leading to IT-led economic development. The Plan also targets to achieve an annual export target of US$ 50 billion (Rs 2200 crore) of IT software and services in the coming 10 years (by 2008). To achieve this target, the Plan also targets improving the PC density from the present level of one PC to 500 people to one PC to 50 people with a universal access to internet and intranets. Important points favourable to e-commerce include:

a) Opening of internet access points by DOT and other authorised ISPs at all district HQrs by 26 January 2000.

b) Meeting data communication requirements for e-commerce and EDI by DOT.

c) Allowing (by RBI) purchase of and permitting advance payment for IT software and services over internet through International Credit Cards (ICC),

d) Giving maximum flexibility in organising marketing of software packages through internet,

e) Creating 'Mega Websites' on internet servers located in India.

The IT Panel has also urged the Reserve Bank of India to allow use of international credit cards for IT-related purchases (thus enhancing the e-commerce) and also for accessing latest technology as soon as it is available.

The Union Cabinet has recently approved the Information Technology Bill proposed by the Department of Electronics (DOE) to facilitate electronic communications and e-commerce, and to curb computer crimes. The Bill proposes amendments to the Indian Evidence Act (Section 2); and the RBI Act 1934. The salient features of the Bill include:

a) Expressing acceptance of contract by electronic means of communications (unless otherwise agreed),
b) Facilitating electronic recourse in trade and commerce.
c) Eliminating barriers to e-commerce resulting from uncertainties over writing and signature requirements.
d) Promoting the legal and business infrastructure development necessary to implement e-commerce.
e) Proposing a legal framework for authentication electronic record or communication through digital signature.
f) Appointing certification authorities for licensing, certifying and monitoring.

All these measures will result in a better e-commerce environment in the country that will be more beneficial to all the players including libraries.

ACKNOWLEDGEMENTS

The authors are thankful to Dr Mohinder Singh, Director, DESIDOC for providing facilities and for permission to present this paper. Thanks are also due to Smt K. Shailaja Reddy for her secretarial assistance.

REFERENCES

1. Opplinger, Rolf, Electronic commerce, In *Internet and Intranet Security*, Chapter 13. Boston, Artech House, 1998, p. 287-305.
2. Chasia, Henry, Internet-enabled commerce is rising opportunity for developing countries, Telematics India, 1998, February, 11, 5 p. 43.
3. ter Maat, Mike, The economics of e-cash, *IEEE Spectrum*, 1997, February 1997, 34, 2, pp. 68-73.
4. Balasubramanian, T.A. e-commerce: Is it working? *Computers Today*, 1998, June 1998, 14, 160, pp. 48-50.
5. NASSCOM, *The Software Industry in India : A strategic review 1997-98*, National Association of Software and Services Companies, Mumbai, 1997.
6. *The Economic Times*, 1998, 24 July, p. 11.
7. Brand Equity, *The Economic Times*, 12-18 June 1996, p. 4.
8. *The Hindu*, 5 September 1999, Weekly Edition 3, ix, xvi.
9. Punja, Manoj, Internet commerce—leveraging the Net for profit. *Dataquest*, 30 September 1998, 16, 18, 6-11 (Internet Commerce Supplement).
10. Loshin, Pete and Murphy, Paul, *Electronic Commerce: Online Ordering and Digital Money*. Ed. 2, Jaico, Mumbai, 1997, 326 p.
11. Lee, Ho Geun, Do electronic marketplaces lower the price of goods?. *Communications of the ACM*, January 1998, 41,1, p. 73-80.
12. Kaur, Kavitha, It's clicked, but will it hit? *Computers Today*, 16-30 November 14, 1998 167, p. 74-76.
13. *Computers Today*, 1998, 14, 160, p. 52; and 16-30 September 1999, 15, 187, p. 35.
14. Freeman, Eva, How to move e-cash around the Internet. *Datamation*, October 1996, pp. 58-60.
15. Hamilton, Scot, E-commerce for the 21st century, *IEEE Computer*, May 1997, 30, 5, pp. 44-47.
16. Kambil, Ajit, Doing business in the wired world, *IEEE Computer*, May 1997, 30, 5, pp. 56-61.

17. Panurach, Patiwat, Money in electronic commerce: DigitalCash, Electronic Funds Transfer and Ecash. *Communications of the ACM*, June 1996, 39, 6, pp. 45-50.

18. Lakshmana Moorthy, A. and Karisiddappa, C.R., Electronic commerce and networked libraries, In Kaul, H.K. Ed. NACLIN 98 ; *Library and Information Networking* : *Papers of the National Annual Convention on Library and Information Networking*, DELNET, New Delhi, 1998, pp. 210-226.

19. *The Times of India*, 11 June 1999, (Business Times), p. 17.

20. Sinha, Aparna and Tulasi, K., Techno-commercial information on the Internet, *Information Today and Tomorrow,* January-March 1998, 17,1, pp. 6-18.

21. Kogannurmath, M.M. and Angadi, Mallikarjun, Print media vs Internet media, In *CALIBER-99* : *Academic Libraries in Internet Era*. Papers presented in the Sixth National Convention for the Automation of Libraries in Education and Research, 18-20 February 1999, Nagpur, Ahmedabad, INFLIBNET Centre, 1999, pp. 134-140.

22. Cyber-update, Software for Internet banking, *Telematics India*, 11, 4, 1998, January p. 69.

23. *The Financial Express*, 8 September 1998, p. 11.

24. *The Hindustan Times,* 23 September, 1999, p.15.

25. India National Task Force on Information Technology & Software Development. Information Technology Action Plan. PMO, New Delhi, 1998. (http://www.nic.in)

26. *The Indian Express*, 5 November, 1999, 11.

22

Internet and Libraries

Amrit Pal

INTRODUCTION

Libraries the world over are witnessing a tremendous change in the ways information is accessed and distributed. A new information era is dawning. IT has come to centrestage of libraries. Applications of IT tools such as computers, online searching system CD-ROM systems and computer networks are growing more and more. Not only are these tools making libraries technologically stronger but also equipping them to cope with the increasing information overload. The internet is ushering up new means of sharing information. It is revolutionising the whole concept of the library access. The library paradigm is shifting from access on ownership basis to network connectivity and access to distributed information centres worldwide.

INTERNET

The internet is a worldwide communication system which links together a variety of computers with distinctive software and hardware. These computers communicate by translating messages into a mutually understandable language, referred to as communications protocol. The protocol used by internet is called TCP/IP. The origin of internet is traced to ARPANET, a military network established in the United States in the late sixties. Initially in 1969, it started with four computers and gradually grew in size with 213 computer connections by 1981. By 1996, it came to have an estimated 70 million users connected to it. It was expected that an estimated 100 million people will be connected to it by 1998.

The global interconnection of computers provides an ideal infrastructure for sharing resources. The internet allows users to transfer files between incompatible computers, send messages across the globe, and log into databases thousand of miles away. There is no central agency to control the internet. Each of its sub-networks are administered separately, and support tasks are accomplished by cooperative arrangements. In order to get hooked to the internet one must have a personal computer (PC), a modem (modulator and demodulator) with communication software and a telephone connection.

INTERNET AND LIBRARIES

The internet is a widely successful, rapidly-growing, global network built on a remarkably flexible communication technology. It offers a variety of services which are used to create, browse, access, search, view and communicate information on a diverse set of topics ranging from the results of scientific experiments to discussions of recreational activities. The sources of information available on the internet are electronic journals, pre-prints, technical reports, library catalogues, e-mail based information services, scientific data sets, patents, standards, directories, reference sources, content pages of journals, databases, online educational materials, Usenet news, etc. All these sources constitute a vast information resource. It can be utilised by the libraries in providing information to the users. It is high time that academic/research libraries should organise themselves and take advantage of the internet in realising their goals.

INTERNET SERVICES AND TOOLS

The services and tools to access information on the internet are:

E-mail

E-mail is the most used feature on the internet. It is used to send messages or programmes on computers linked to internet.

List Servers/Mailing Lists

A list/mail server is a discussion group created by someone to share ideas and knowledge on a subject. It is an excellent resource for distributing information to a group with shared interest.

Usenet/News Groups

Unlike list servers which disseminate information on a specific topic from one to many persons, newsgroup servers provide access to thousands of topic-based discussion group services that are open to everyone.

Telnet

Telnet enables internet users to log onto other internet computers to access online databases, electronic library catalogues and internet information services.

FTP

FTP facilitates transfer of files from one computer to another computer. It has become popular and the most widely used tool because a number of anonymous FTP servers are available for the purpose. An anonymous FTP server allows any user to download files or programmes.

Archie

Archie is a tool to assist the user to locate files accessible via FTP.

Gopher

Gopher is an internet search utility that offers easy access to online library guides, FTP sites and numerous internet information sources. It presents information in an hierarchical menu system.

Veronica

Veronica which stands for 'Very easy Roden-Oriented Netwide Index to Computerized Archives'. It permits a user to search Gopher menus by keywords to find relevant menus more quickly.

WAIS

Wais allows users to search text, sound or images from a single interface located anywhere on the network. It is suited for retrieving textual information. It provides a scored list of documents which are relevant to the query.

WWW

The world wide web of information is an advanced browsing service on the internet. It is similar to Gopher. However, instead of menu driven design, it uses hypertext links. This service is very useful. Within a few minutes, one can examine documents on myriads of topics located on a variety of computers at the internet sites around the world.

INTERNET BENEFITS FOR LIBRARIES

Bibliographic Verifications

Hundreds of research, academic, public and corporate libraries all over the world have made their catalogues available online. The internet offers a communication link to a multitude of library systems that have online public access catalogues (OPACs). Generally available free of cost, these are useful for finding books not available locally, to identify and select books for local acquisition, bibliographic data verification and to search holdings of periodicals and monographs. These can be accessed through telnet, Gopher and the world wide web.

Reference Resources

Many OPACs also have full text databases such as CIA World Fact Book on the Rutgers Library System. The libraries can use these databases to respond to queries from their patrons.

Means for Amplifying Resources

For academic/research libraries, the internet is the most indispensable means of amplifying their resources. The library world has tried several measures for optimum resource-sharing, but all of these have proved ineffective in document delivery. The internet can bring about real democratisation of intellectual resources by providing access to the world information.

Library without Walls

With internet connectivity, the boundaries of the library are expanded worldwide. The valuable information present in the library can be fed to home page and made available to users anywhere. The library can be a depository of local information/ resources to the worldwide community and at the same time provide its local users access to internet resources.

Assistance to Researchers

The internet can be a tool for accelerating the pace of research. A large number of technical reports which provide details of on-going or complete R & D projects and PhD theses are available on internet. These can be accessed free of cost. Besides technical reports, online information services of many universities providing web-based access to a variety of information are also available. These provide access to research literature, faculty and student directories, course details and research projects, library catalogues and other databases. The libraries can assist patrons doing research by demonstrating various databases, and by obtaining information from these databases on a regular basis. Moreover, there are hundreds of electronic discussion lists and conference proceedings available over the internet. They give direct access to scholars in disciplines they are interested in. Discussion lists give users an opportunity to ask or offer help. Video conferencing makes it possible for researchers to discuss latest developments.

LIBRARY SERVICES

Reference Services

The reference librarians can extend the scope of their reference services with the information available in FTP archives Gopher servers and list servers. This information is much more up-to-date than its printed counter parts.

Technical Services

The internet facilitates access to online catalogues. Cataloguers can benefit from such online catalogues in much the same way they benefit from using OCLC and RLIN systems.

Current Awareness Services

The tools available for current awareness on the internet are many. These include tables of contents of journals, discussion forums and Usenet news. Combining internet data with existing information resources, the libraries can generate most current awareness services despite limitations imposed by budget constraints. Besides, they can deliver information in a form compatible to the client's needs and requirements.

CONCLUSION

The internet environment can enable librarians and libraries to play innovative role in giving services to distant users. However, libraries in India have been slow in harnessing internet potential. Their internet usage has largely remained limited to e-mail and to tools like FTP, Telnet and the WWW. Very few libraries have so far been able to exploit WWW and set up websites. This may be due to a high cost of setting up a website and high telecommunication tariff. Internet facilities in libraries in India could expand faster provided internet infrastructure is made available and libraries are exempted from tariff. The UGC and other concerned agencies would do a remarkable work in this direction by providing financial support and facilities for setting up websites.

REFERENCES

1. Obenaus G., The Internet : An electronic treasure trove, *Aslib Proceedings*, 1995, 46, 4, p. 95.
2. Satyanarayana B., Internet: Its genesis, growth and benefits, In *Information Technology Applications in Academic Libraries* (Papers presented at the fourth National Convention for Automation of Libraries in Education and Research, Caliber-97, March 6-8, 1997, Patiala). Ed. A.L. Moorthy and P.B. Mangla, Information and Library Network Centre, Ahmedabad, 1997, p. 124.

3. Seng L.B., Using the Internet as a strategic business tool, *Aslib Proceedings*, 1996, 48, 2, p. 51.

Sources Consulted

1. Aptagiri D.V., Information superhighway : The Internet, *ILA Bulletin*, 1996, 31, 3-4, 80-83.
2. Berman Y., Discussion groups on the Internet as sources of information, *Aslib Proceedings,* 1996, 482, 31-36.
3. Buckle D., Strategic issues for libraries and librarians—a commercial perspective, *Aslib proceedings,* 1994, 46, 11/12, 259-62.
4. Comer D.E., The Internet book : *Everything you need to know about computer networking and how the Internet works,* 1994, Prentice Hall, New Jersy.
5. Furner-Hines J. and Willett P., The use of the world wide web in UK academic libraries, *Aslib proceedings*, 1995, 47, 1, 23-32.
6. Heslop B. and Angell D., *The instant Internet guide* : Hands on global networking, 1993, Addison Wesley, California.
7. Hoffman P.E., *The Internet instant reference,* 3rd ed. 1996, BPB Publications, New Delhi.
8. Jatana H.S., Welcome to the world of Internet, *The Tribune*, 1997, Jan. 16, p.14.
9. Moorthy A.L., and Mangla P.B., *Information Technology Applications in Academic Libraries* (Papers presented at the fourth National Convention for Automation of Libraries in Education and Research, Caliber-97, March 6-8, 1997, Patiala). Information and Library Network Centre, Ahmedabad.
10. Obsenaus G., The Internet : An electronic treasure trove, *Aslib Proceedings,* 1994, 46, 4, 95-100.
11. Rajashekar T.B., Science and technology information resources on the Internet, *Information Today and Tomorrow,* 1997, 16, 2, 5-12.
12. Seng L.B., Using the Internet as a strategic business tool, *Aslib proceedings*, 1995, 48, 2, 45-52.
13. Tewari R.K. and Gupta G.S., The wonders of Internet, *Employment News,* 1996, 21, 33. 1-2.
14. Weinstein L., Lifenet/Internet and the health science librarian, *Special Libraries.* 1996, 85, 1, 17-21.

23

Information Technology Strategy for High Quality Service and Greater User Satisfaction

V. Venkata Ramana and *N. Varatha Rajan*

INFORMATION AS A STRATEGIC RESOURCE

There has been a revolution in the way the organisations treat information and information systems. Today, leading libraries are using information and information system as tools for staying ahead of other resource stations. Several libraries and information centres have developed a special category of information systems called strategic information systems for this purpose. Strategic information systems change the goals, operations, products, services, or environmental relationships to help the library gain a competitive advantage. Even the traditional computerised record keeping is moving into a broad array of financial information services, including a monitoring service that allows a money manager to keep better tabs on their pension funds. Behavioural patterns often change with strategic information systems. Invariably, organisations need to change their internal operations to take advantage of the new information systems.

INCOGNITO

Information technology strategy is an integral part of any

library/institute just as a mouse is to a PC. Strategies are essential to any organisation to manoeuvre and ensure its needs to achieve the goals. The instances are many where even a minor lapse could cost millions. Many organisations across the globe are in a hurry in automating their day-to-day operations. Given the fast pace at which technologies are changing today, organisations need to adopt strategic planning for initiating simultaneous changes in their work culture, failing which there is a risk of huge investments in technology going astray. Thus information technology strategy has become an important measure for organising libraries and information centres. Marketing of information is becoming essential to any organisation as its maintenance costs have gone up steeply. Marketing of information demands strategic planning.

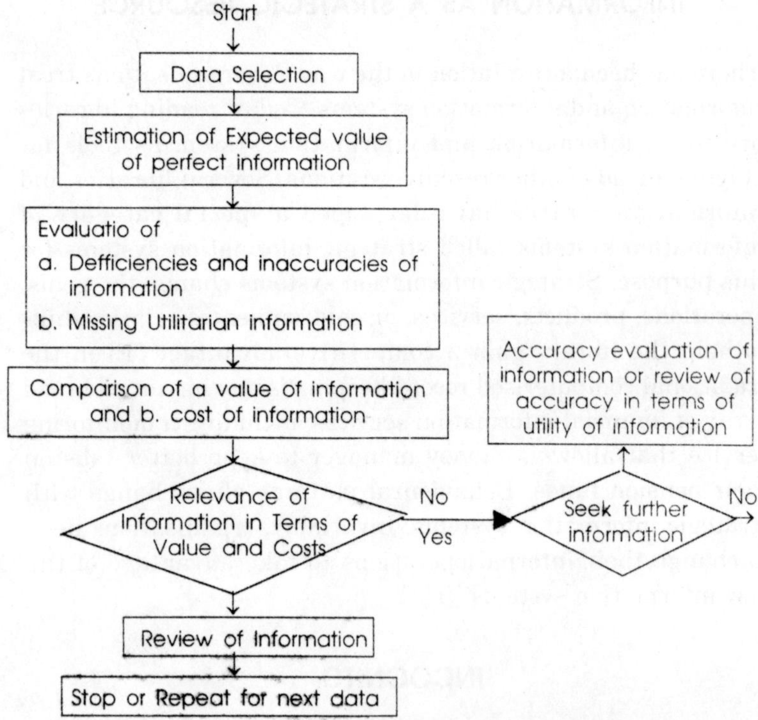

Evaluation of Information for Accuracy

A strategy is a design that integrates an organisation's major goals, policies and action sequences into a cohesive whole. Strategic planning in an organisation drives its resource allocations into a unique feasibility, based on relative internal strengths and weaknesses laying due emphasis on the anticipated changes in the external environment. An IT strategy emphasises broad directions that IT adopted in an organisation should pursue. The strategic planning lists the IT architecture necessary to achieve the strategy and the specific project necessary for implementing the architecture and IT opportunities.

THE VISION

Strategic planning lays out the vision, style, structure, staffing, and skills that are necessary for processing, and the tactics to move about. In addition, information technology strategy enumerates how it is expected to be used in the day-to-day survival and future planning.

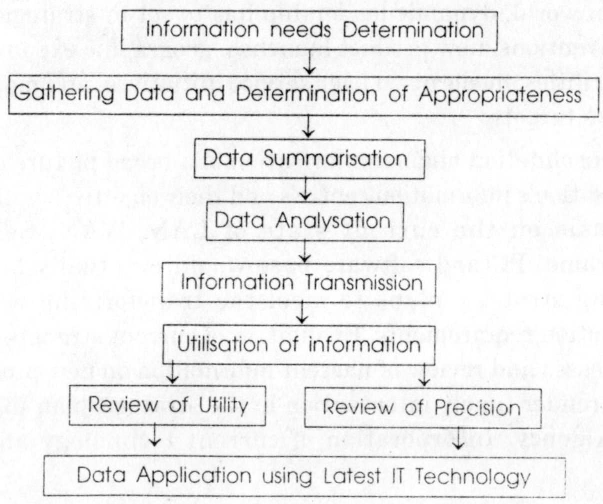

The business direction demands aligning the support to the enterprise's mission, goals and objectives. Any strategic plan considers the internal and external changes in the enterprise and the potential opportunities available. Strategy envisages the ways and means to use technology to gain competitive advantage, reduce costs and increase revenues, etc. Staff training in the technology would help the organisation in the long run in monitoring the pressures of global competition. The rapid pace of transformations in information technology demands that strategy be an ongoing process.

SETTING AND REVIEWING OF GOALS

The top executive leadership of an organisation should visualise the information centre goals and its basic business in relation to prosperity of the institution and its staff members. Any change in strategy may be necessitated by a change of guard at the top management levels in the organisation. The events, alliances and acquisitions are to be synchronised to the technology being adopted and demands of the day as well as the future at large. With the change in the attitude of information service centres to the marketing arenas of the modern world, dynamic leadership has to set in strategies for new inventions, new product launches, geographic expansions, new facilities, modernised user service initiatives, and modified revenue targets.

Consolidation and summarisation of a broad picture of the organisation's information centre's and their objectives with due emphasis on the current state of LAN, WAN, Server, Mainframe, PC and software base would eventually help in evolving strategic plans to meet the transforming world's information requirements. Evaluation of current strengths and weaknesses and review of nascent information on new products would render timely intervention in the strategic plan to meet any exigency. Incorporation of current technology and its standardisation would evolve the organisation's approach into the day's demand so as to meet the current level of information requirements. The library manager has to make a list of technology goals for the next one to three years. It would help in sorting the forthcoming information centre's/library's demand and in planning new initiatives of the organisation to extend the essential support for the ongoing research, and new products in the making, etc.

FINDINGS *VIS-A-VIS* PROJECTIONS

Developing a list of major technologies and the applications in the information world, and findings the previous year's trends in information seeking facilitates the projections for the forthcoming years. The proposed future projections should invariably have a realistic timeframe, for the acquisition and operation of the information system. This is important to support timely and appropriate provision of information to meet the challenges of the day.

BENEFITS OF INFORMATION TECHNOLOGY STRATEGY

Plenty of benefits may be envisaged through the means of IT strategy for libraries/information centres :

a) Establishment of appropriate momentum towards implementing the IT plan of the library/information centre.

b) Every user derivation of the benefit of IT for

c) Coordination and focus of IT efforts towards the goals and objectives of the library/information centres.

d) Success through the development of IT and its tactical application.

e) Enabling of a speedier disposal of business through IT strategy and its application on continuous basis to tap the vast potential of the information world.

f) Precision and appropriateness in information retrieval to help catalysing proper directions in research endeavours.

g) Periodical evaluation the IT and its application to match the growing demands of the organisation for information.

24

Retrospective Conversion: A Thematic Perspective

Shobha D. Kulkarni, Rekha S. Oltikar and
Kalyani Accanoor

INTRODUCTION

Retrospective Conversion (RECON) of a library collection is a major component of the automation process. It is time-consuming, labour intensive and expensive but necessary. Without conversion of bibliographic records the library automation is not effective in the real sense, and in particular for meaningful sharing of library resources with other libraries.

RECON is the process of converting manual bibliographic records to machine-readable files suitable for use with a computer-based library system. Such a conversion activity needs an appropriate standard to convert a record along with proper relationship to the entire automation project. Technological advances have facilitated fast access to information at various levels. Standardised records reduce the chances of error and increase the capabilities for remote access, searching and retrieval through network configuration. They offers several attractive advantages, viz;

i) The need for labour-intensive physical cataloguing is eliminated.

ii) Standardised records reduce the chances of errors or inconsistencies.

iii) Easy to locate current and accurate information and also transfer the same to remote places.

iv) Increase remote access capabilities for searching and retrieving through network.

v) These records can also generate spine labels, pocket labels and book cards to further reduce the time and labour costs.

However, one should not imagine automation as a means to reduce the work load, instead it should be viewed as a means to increase the efficiency, manage costs, improve library services, and to address shortcomings of existing manual systems. However, it will require tremendous planning and work.

Historical Background

LC originally initiated the RECON in the 1960s .The first pilot study was undertaken during 1965 to convert the English monographs. Presently OCLC has a wide role in promoting retrospective conversion. Services offered by OCLC are RETROCON, MICROCON, TAPECON, FULL MARC and online Retrospective conversion.

In India the automation of libraries is in progress. Some libraries have created the databases to support basic library functions but have given less importance to the standardisation. The national bodies like NISSAT, INFLIBNET and local networks like DELNET, CALIBNET have realised the problem and initiated brainstorming sessions for retrospective conversion projects.

PRE-PLANNING

RECON is a challenge even for a small library requiring

indepth implementation of management principles of POSCOB (Planning, Organisation, Staffing, Coordination, Budgeting).

Planning

It is necessary to make a decision as to whether the work will be undertaken as an in-house activity or any outside agency will be involved. If it is done in-house the availability of manpower with sufficient expertise and knowledge in computer programming and cataloguing rules is necessary. The arrangement of necessary hardware / software is to be made. The selection of software also depends upon the decision whether it is to be developed in-house or a readymade commercial package is to be purchased. A number of commercial packages are in the market and to know their performance, credibility and reputation is a must. The collection has to be examined to decide about complete or partial conversion. Similarly, the titles which are not in use may be weeded out before the actual project begins. So also the financial sources should be finalised. By considering the advantages / disadvantages of the existing system one can prioritise the functions for automation.

Organisation

The actual jobs involved in conversion project need to be drawn and a proper scheduling at each step has to be finalised. The finalisation of data capturing method and its implementation must also be completed. There are various ways to capture the data for conversion, viz, using main catalogue cards, shelf list cards, accession register, capturing data directly from the book or using datasheets for data collection, etc. Similarly the method for data validation should be finalised. Each source has its merits and demerits, but once the decision is taken, it should be planned out properly, viz, design of datasheets, decision about which part of the catalogue / shelf list is to be taken first, etc.

Staffing

The manpower has to be professionals with proper training in computers and cataloguing rules. It is also necessary to evaluate the impact of conversion activity on day-to-day work of the staff involved.

Co-ordinating

There should be proper coordination among the 5Ms, i.e., Men, Machines, Materials, Money and Methods for successful implementation. Any loophole in coordinating the actual procedure will lead to major chaos.

Budgeting

The entire project is to be budgeted. The budgeting process involves the cost of application software for both single / multi-user packages if a commercial package is to be procured, its delivery and installation costs, cost for training the manpower, cost of conversion services, etc. In addition to the initial costs, other expenses also have to be taken into account such as hardware / software maintenance, additional equipment, service contracts, staffing needs, etc.

For the RECON project of at IIT Mumbai the advantages and disadvantages of various conversion programmes and vendor services were studied and evaluated. This helped us to understand limitations in the existing packages which were addressed while developing an in-house RECON software. These are:

i) *Online shared cataloguing database*: In this the online databases can be searched to match the local holdings. The records can be edited and the library identifier such as the accession number or class number can be added. Such records are transferred to magnetic tapes and supplied to the various participating libraries.

ii) *Batch shared cataloguing database*: As the name suggests batch process entries are made on floppy diskettes and sent to the vendor. The entries are machine readable for matching.

iii) *Online local cataloguing database*: This contains a locally available database wherein the user library can search, edit, and add information.

iv) *Contracted service*: The cost of RECON varies from vendor to vendor and there is very little involvement of the library staff in the activity.

The first three options can be effective only when the parent organisation has a standard database, uptodate computer workstation with additional equipment necessary for networking facility, sufficient space and skilled manpower.

Whereas all the above options are feasible in developed countries it has its own problems in our conditions such as records can be cumbersome to convert, too expensive, and more dependancy on the vendors.

CONVERTING THE RECORDS

The procedure for transmitting records to and from the copy cataloguing service is quite easy. After validating the record sheets send them to the service in either hard copy or disc format (inexpensive software packages are available to record the identifying codes and to transmit these codes either via modem or mail / to services). Upon receipt the service matches each record against its own MARC database. Then records are downloaded to the disc or tape as specified along with any odd ones and shipped to the library for editing and processing.

Depending upon the software these will be either built in MARC interface or an optional MARC adapter available for capturing MARC fields and coordinating them with the fields set up in database structure.

PURPOSE

Thus with the above background and by considering its importance, the Indian Institute of Technology, Central Library, Mumbai, initiated the RECON project to facilitate efficient retrieval and exchange of bibliographic data. Initially the database was created to fulfil the basic library function, i.e., for the circulation section and has served the purpose well. But the database had certain shortcomings, such as data retrieval by keywords, conference / proceeding names was not possible. The users are used to retrieve the data by the basic approaches like author, title, etc., but the online catalogue users expect to find records with other approaches like keywords, series, free text, etc. The existing database, therefore, needed to be converted into a standard format to establish a meaningful communication at least among IITs as well as at the national and international level.

The RECON project was accomplished by the combined efforts of the library management and the staff. The active participation of all concerned is of utmost importance. In December 1993 the project got started as a pilot study . A separate RECON cell was created which included the project coordinator, a group of supervisors, data-sheet operators and data entry operators. The purpose was to find out the time and cost factors associated at different stages.

Methodology at I.I.T. Central Library, Mumbai

Among the various conversion options available to libraries, the IIT Central Library opted for in-house conversion. The main idea was to utilise the professional manpower available in the library. They are more familiar with the collection and also aware of the significant needs of the readers. It was also decided to utilise the LAN professionals who readily agreed to design the software for data entry and retrieval.

After careful planning and feasibility as to the location of the RECON Cell, the flow of the books in the cell and out, etc., the project got started on the following lines:

i) For the purpose of computerising circulation functions first data entry was started from shelf list cards and AACR II was followed for standardisation.

ii) Library of Congress Subject Headings (LCSH) was used for standardising subject headings. The highlights of the LCSH were explained to this group and instructions given for local modifications.

iii) A comprehensive data-sheet was designed to enter the various data elements. A lot of care was taken to ensure that it is indeed comprehensive with no lacuna in it.

iv) The programmers from the LAN group were explained the fields required for data entry. They were apprised about the data entry operations from data capturing, arranging, storing, reproducing to information dissemination keeping in view the library's needs.

v) The data-sheet operators (DSO) were identified. These were the professionals and non-professionals staff working from the library available for RECON work only after office hours. Other apartments were also explored as this type of jobs could be done by any educated employee from other departments of the Institute and campus residents such as educated housewives.

vi) A one-week crash training programme in AACR II and LCSH was conducted for these DSOs. The general guidelines for using AACR II were prepared and copies given for easy reference. The need for standardisation and data extraction techniques was stressed upon.

vii) Inventorying of the total collection was a major hurdle. This was a necessity to ascertain how many titles required special processing either by way of generating subject heading with LCSH or correcting the main access points in the catalogue. A special temporary help group was formed to identify such titles.

viii) The books would be brought to the cell where the data sheet for such books would be filled by the data sheet operators. These data sheets were further verified by the supervisors and the project leader and then sent for entering the data in the computer. After the data is entered a stamp RECON along with signature is affixed on the backside of the title page to mark the conversion of the particular book, thus avoiding duplication of work. At the same time this data on the computer would be checked by supervisors at regular intervals and before sending back the books for shelving. This would ensure that books need not be brought or referred for RECON.

The actual work of RECON project was initiated in March 1994 with the help of 24 data-sheet operators and two data entry operators. It was possible to convert 10,000 books till March 1995. During this study certain shortcomings were noticed such as books accumulated in the RECON cell deprived the readers from their usage.

As this programme was designed to support international standard formats the programmers had to work hard to create the database and to overcome any bugs in the programme. However, the major challenge was to achieve replacement of old entries with the new without affecting the day-to-day working of the library and to have a new database of the entire collection.

ISSUES OF CONCERN

Some steps of concern to the library were :

i) Periodical reviewing was necessary to make the catalogue perfect. For duplicate entries, odd or mismatched titles, subject heading/ added entries had to be altered or shortened. This was only possible by taking printout and correcting the same in the database.

ii) There were difficult records to handle such as multi-volumes, multi-copies, etc.

iii) Setting up of OPAC was the main goal of RECON. This system was easy to use and precise enough to retrieve documents even without complete bibliographic information, and could be searched by title, author, subject, free text and allowed various combinations in searches involving boolean operators.

CONCLUSION

The experience has shown that this type of a project requires a lot of efforts both intellectual and physical. It is a costly affair, time consuming and requires more labour force to complete the task. RECON is the best time for weeding out older editions and less used books. It also serves the purpose of collection development, knowing the strength and pitfalls in a particular subject area. Any wrongly classified book could be reclassified and sent to its rightful place. To make it successful, the library must effectively promote the system to the staff and end users.

The authors would like to take this opportunity to thank the authorities and all those concerned with this project.

BIBLIOGRAPHY

Boss, R.W., Retrospective conversion : investing in the future, *Wilson Library Bulletin*, 1984, 59, 173-178.

Boss, R.W., and Espo, H, Standard database design and retrospective conversion, *Library Journal*, 1987, 112, 54-58.

Clements, D.W.G., Conversion of the general catalogue of printed books to machine readable form, *Journal of Librarianship*, 1983, 15, 3, 206-213

De Gennaro, and Richard., Libraries and networks in transition: problems and prospects for the 1980's, *Library Journal*, 1981, 106, 1045-1049.

Drabenstott, Jou, Ed., Retrospective conversion : issues and perspectives, a forum, *Library High Tech*, 1986, 14, 105-120.

Epstein, Susan Baerg, Converting records for automation at the copy level, *Library Journal*, 1983, 108, 642–643.

Epstein, Susan Baerg, Converting bibliographic records for automation : some options, *Library Journal*, 1983, 108, 474-476.

Faust, Julia B., Microcomputers as on-line catalogue in special libraries, *Special Libraries*, 1986, 77,3, 133-139.

Inman, Ruth A., Are title II-c grant worth it !the effect of associated music library groups retrospective conversion project, *Library Resources and Technical Services*, 1995, 39,2, 167-176.

Riger, Robert E., Retrospective catalogue conversion in mid–sized law libraries: some practical guidelines for automation, *Special Libraries*, 1992, 83, 1, 10-15.

Special issue on Retrospective Conversion, *Cataloguing and Classification Quarterly*, 1992, 14, 3/4.

25

Working towards College Library Automation

Sarita Jain

INTRODUCTION

The word "automation", first used for automatic handling of motor parts, is today widely used as a "technology of automatic working in which the handling method, the process and design of purchased material are integrated to utilise in an economic justifiable and self-regulating chain of process." The mechanisation of libraries started from punched cards, used for circulation system in 1936, and by 1960 machines/computers were used for serial control and cataloguing by five newly established libraries in states of Ontario.

In 1963, two reports, first by King "Automation and Library of Congress" and the second "Planning Conference on Information Transfer", by INTREX (Information Transfer Experience), and the success of MARC shifted libraries from the offline system to online system. By 1980, with fast technological advancements, and reduction in computer size and cost and its improved capabilities, computers became common and were being widely used by libraries in United States and United Kingdom and the term "Library Automation" came in vogue. Today the term "Library Automation" refers to the processing of certain routine functions in the library with assistance of computers. Computers have widespread usage for automation of library activities viz. acquisition, cataloguing, circulation, serial control and information processing and retrieval by using a data and choosing a course of flow in a library environment.

In India, library automation was started in the late 1980s and early1990s by few special libraries. By 1992-93, few libraries became fully automated. Many were in the process of automation and started handling library routines (in parts or in full) by computers. Even today, for a college library, library automation remains a dream waiting for realisation.

In this paper, an attempt has been made to give guidelines, based on personal experience and queries received from professional colleagues for starting library automation in a college. The paper is not aspired to give specifics of automation. However, some generalisation is possible which could be used by the college libraries.

WHY AUTOMATION?

Why automation? It is a question to be asked to oneself. Is the automation for 'me too-ism,' i.e., everybody else has a computer so I should also have one, or for 'fascination towards technology' or the change of technology being forced by authorities? The most obvious reason for automation is to 'increase efficiency'. The initial impetus for the introduction to automation is when the standards of services do not match the standards the library wishes to achieve. At the most basic level, a computer can be regarded as a fast, accurate tool for library automation. Besides speed, accuracy, cost effectiveness, and long term advantages especially space saving, the ability of searching large volumes of data in a flexible manner by number of access points is one of the most illuring attributes of automation.Further, the demand for automated services particularly for information retrieval and online public access is becoming common even in small libraries. The origin of library network services at local, regional, national and international levels has also added the charm to library automation.

PLANNING LIBRARY AUTOMATION

Planning is a process to achieve long-term goals by means of analysis and evaluation of alternatives. The importance of planning in accomplishing a project successfully is undebatable. It points out the lacunae of a system even before carrying out actual tasks. College libraries are different in terms of their size, diversity of collections, operations, services and the way they are organised and linked with the objectives of their parent institutions. While planning automation one must take into account the specifics of a particular library, especially the size and diversity in its functioning.

The automation project can be a programme to run on a single PC to a full scale mini or mainframe system. It may be planned for one subsystem or for all the subsystems. For this the librarian must look in to the details before taking a final decision. However, few basic steps as listed below are necessary in planning.

Step one : Writing Plan Proposal

It is important to write a plan proposal and take the approval of senior management. For this, it is advisable to first discuss the project proposal with the authority informally. The aim should be to get the authority/principal/ management in favour of the proposal. The written outline of proposal must describe:

a) Objectives of library automation;

b) Need for automation;

c) Automation plan (for all functions of the library or for one system only);

d) Expected benefits;
e) Anticipated time scale;
f) Manpower and training needs;
g) Hardware, software needs; and
h) And cost involved.

If need be, a small committee could be formed comprising two or three faculty members, technical experts, one senior person from management and bursar or treasurer, to examine the proposal for recommendation.

The proposal should be brief and it should conclude with a request for authorisation to proceed and allocation of appropriate resources.

Step Two: Priortisation of Automation Activities

The librarian has to decide the sequence in which the library activities are likely to be computerised, and the manner in which these would be computerised whether independently one by one, or in an integrated manner. In the library, where user services are given more importance, librarian would like to start CAS (current awareness services) and SDI (Selective Dissemination of Information service) first along with database creation of holdings of the library. And if the aim is to have an effective management of periodicals it would be better to give first priority to serial control. And if the goal is to reduce the staff, those areas should be taken first which would effect manpower. If librarian decides to switch over to automation of circulation, the retroconversion of bibliographical data needs to be done before automation of circulation starts. Proper plans and line of action have to be decided before starting automation.

Step Three : Deciding Software

The decision on software for library automation should be done before the decision on hardware. The different possibilities for acquiring software are:

a) Writ own software,
b) Get one written in house, or
c) Buy a commercially produced package.

For most of the college libraries, the third option is better as one gets:

a) Tried and tested product;
b) All development work and support will be of third party ; and
c) Easily upgradable with technical development.

The library software packages available in the market are CDS/ISIS, LIBSYS, SANJAY, LIBRIS, TECHLIBPLUS, MAITRAYEE, SUCHIKA, LICON(UK), MINISIS(Canada) etc.

While choosing software one should keep in mind that a software package should have following features:

a) Integrated design to support library automation;
b) Supports all library functions
c) Supports database creation and information retrieval;
d) Modular design for phased implementation;
e) Compatible to Indian and international standards;
f) User friendly;
g) Export and import facility through standard format;
h) Available on multi-platforms
i) Single and multiuser and model.

Along with the library software the librarian needs to decide on its operating system also (depending upon single user and multi-user). The prevailing operating systems are DOS, NOVELL, UNIX , WINDOWS NT. The single user operating systems in use are DOS and WINDOWS. WINDOWS NT is more prevalent as multi-user operating system than UNIX.

For office routine work, MS Office 97 or Word Perfect, Wordstar, Lotus should be purchased. MS Office is good and has almost all provisions required for office work of college library.

Step Four : Deciding Hardware

The librarian needs to decide on hardware requirements in terms of microprocessors, RAM, monitor, keyboard, hard disc capacity, drives, input/output ports and so on. This all has to be decided on the basis of number of records to be handled and the number of databases to be created. For network connectivity to the other systems in the campus, LAN requirements should also be taken into consideration.

For complete automation of a library of size of 50,000 documents, the minimum requirements are : a powerful server up to the level of Pentium 4, two to three PCs for housekeeping operations, a printer, a UPS with at least 30 minutes to one hour backup, backup devices (DAT drive/Tape drive/Zip drive etc) and 4 to 8 terminals for OPAC (Open Public Access Catalogue). It needs to be supplemented by CD-ROM drive. All the devices need not be purchased at one go. Purchase of equipments has to be planned in accordance with the action plan of planned proposal.

The following criteria need to be kept in mind while choosing hardware:

a) System has to be expandable;
b) Network provision to add more terminals at a later stage;
c) Resource sharing on the network in the long run;
d) Robust, tried and tested and not likely to crash or break down.
e) Branded system be preferred;
f) Latest models of equipment;
g) Enough maintenance support and back-up support.

h) Purchase price, cost of maintenance, upgrading, repair, etc., are also essential factors for consideration.

However, all this has to be done very realistically in terms of what is available and what library can afford.

The list of vendors can be found from directories and their websites should be visited before final placement of orders. For deciding configuration of computers, the assistance can be sought from NISSAT, NIC or from any other professional experts. While purchasing provision should be kept for system reliability test.

Step Five : Cost Analysis

Cost analysis is to work out the cost of the project. The cost should be calculated to consider the financial implications over the expected life of plan-proposal. Secondly, it is advisable not to load the full cost into one year's financial calculations. It also helps to those providing funds in planning and allocation of budget for the project.

Hardware

An estimate needs to be made for the likely cost of hardware required for the automation. It is advisable to have an estimate of required configuration and of the system by consulting three to four dealers. Along with the cost of system, the cost of peripherals should also be included like: UPS, printers, backup devices. It is wise to include replacement or addition of furniture expected to be required.

Software

The cost of licensed software should be include:

a) Cost of library software.
b) Cost of operating system like Unix, Windows NT, Novell, etc.

c) Cost of office software like MS Office, or Word Perfect or any other.

Due precaution should be taken to obtain the latest version and licensed copy of the software. Many companies give discount (even up to 60%) for educational institutions. This factor should be considered, and as far as possible softwares should be purchased from a standard company.

Staff cost

Staff cost should take into accounts total manpower input and the amount to be paid to staff for their contribution/output. As a rough rule of thumb 20% should be added to this figure to account for additional costs such as provision of furniture, heat, light etc.

Consumables

Attempts should be made to estimate the cost of consumables such as printers, paper, media tapes, floppies. This figure can be estimated from current experience or by checking with colleagues who already use a similar system.

Maintenance

After the first year, the one major recurring cost is maintenance of hardware and software. An allowance of 15 per cent to 20 per cent of the cost of initial purchase would be the right order of magnitude. Further, the staff cost, consumables, and maintenance cost will all need to be projected for the planned lifetime of the system and not for one year alone.

Site preparations

The cost of preparing a site, distempering, cabling, pest controlling, etc., should be also be taken into consideration.

Step Six : Environmental Control

Environmental control includes both physical environment and personnel (human resource) environment.

Physical environment

Before starting automation a library manager must decide the site for installation of computers and look into the following aspects :

a) Identification of place, where computers and server are to be placed.
b) Get the place cleaned, distempered and pest controlled,
c) Proper cabling and electricity fitting should be done. If the wiring is old, it is recommended to get separate cables laid of standard quality.
d) Purchase or preparation of furniture to be used.
e) If necessary, the installation of air-conditioner in the computer room.

Human resource Environment

Creating a human resource environment is very essential for the automation of a library. Along with the management commitment for financial resources, the commitment from staff is equally important and required from day one. It is desirable to have the staff in confidence from the very beginning. The librarian should appraise the staff of the project and discuss the purpose and objectives of the automation plan. This will enhance the morale and the motivation of the staff and they will have a feeling of participation that they can actively shape their future, and it will result in improved customer satisfaction.

IMPLEMENTING AUTOMATION

Having made the plan proposal and got it accepted, and having decided on the required hardware and software and placed the order for systems, the acquisition phase of library automation is complete and the implementing phase is to start.

Implementing the project is the most difficult task. Every minute detail needs to be worked out in advance. A thorough review of procedures in the areas of automation is a must.

Training of Staff

Training in connection with the introduction of a new computer system falls into two parts:

Training in system use

This should be provided by the supplier of software either on site or through visits to company training facilities at their home location. On-site training is much preferred, as it can benefit a large number of staff and allows for all grades of staff to be involved.

Training in new procedures

Staff should be given full training in how the new automated system will work and what this implies for their own jobs. Some hands on session using dummy records should be conducted and they should be instructed properly where they can go for help in the event of any problem. The staff must be made aware of expected standards of performance, both in quantity and quality.

Retroconversion of Data

Retroconversion of bibliographical data in machine readable / computerised form is an important task and needs to be done sooner or later, based on the priority decided by library manager. Librarians need to take certain decisions in this regard:

a) Decide on how to enter complete bibliographical information of a document in one go. Maybe from a book directly, or from shelf list or from master sheets made for the purpose.

b) Before starting database creation the librarian could use this opportunity to weed out obsolete or worn out documents/books.

c) Enter the data first section-wise (overnight issue/reference/ consultation only) and then subject-wise.

d) Shelf list cards of those books which have been entered should be kept separate to avoid any confusion.

e) The records of books can also be downloaded from utilities like OCLC, Library of Congress, etc., by paying a licence fee but this is not a viable option for college libraries, especially in India.

f) Deciding in who will enter the data; library staff; outside agent, or combination of both.

Writing Manuals

Manuals should be written for staff as well as for users—for staff, giving details of operations and for users, giving the details of how to search the desired information. The level of description should depend on personal experience and local circumstances.

Few Precautions

a) Editing of entered data should be done regularly on daily output.

b) Taking regular back-ups

System failure is always a possibility. It may be from an equipment, software or power problems. In such a failure, the data in system is likely to be affected. So as a rule of thumb is, no session which involves change of data should be started until the previous session has been backed up. For library routines, it can be taken up at the end of the day's work. In a busy service or for a large volume of transactions more frequent back-ups should be taken. An adequate number of tapes or discs for backups should be kept and clearly labelled. For all week days, separate sets should be made. Further, it is not necessary to back-up all the files everytime. Rather, it can be a particular set of files within particular directories.

a) Further, occasionally a trial run to restore from back-up should also be carried out to ensure that the procedure is operating properly. It is advisable that one set of back-up be stored at the separate place, might be in another building to be on the safer side in case any disaster occurs.
b) Control access: Passwords should be used to control access to the functions of the system. It will ensure undue fiddling with data by unwanted persons. Almost all software offer provision of this sort now.

And finally, having gone through this entire process, install the system and get it working, start planning for the next one.

The world of computers and information technology is not standing still, the pace of change is accelerating. No matter how good a system we have now, it will be out of date within a short time and new changes need to be planned and made.

AUTOMATING LADY IRWIN COLLEGE LIBRARY : A CASE STUDY

Lady Irwin College is one of the pioneering institutions offering undergraduate and six postgraduate courses in the field of home science in India. The library of the college has attained central position in almost all academic activities of the institution. It is catering to the needs of more than 600 undergraduates and 200 postgraduate students. The library subscribes more than 100 periodicals of academic nature and has over 50,000 documents along with research reports, project reports and valuable back files of periodicals. The rich collection of the library is being consulted by many scholars from other universities, NGOs, industrialists, social workers and scientists in the field of home science and its allied areas, viz., food and nutrition, child development, textile and clothing and community resource management and extension.

The idea of automating library was floated by the librarian in 1996 and was discussed with the Director of the College. To know the feasibility of automation of a library many libraries, i.e., AIIMS, IIT, NPL, IIPA were visited by the librarian along with his senior colleague, Dr Anupa Sidhu (from faculty).

Having conceived the idea to automate the library, a small library automation committee was formed by the Library Advisory Committee in August 1996. The Committee comprised the Director, the Librarian, two faculty members, and the Bursar. The Library Automation Committee in its first meeting decided to have one outside library expert as a consultant as no internal technical support was available in the college. Prof. M. C. Ragavan, who was then working as a Library Advisor to the Indian Labour Institute, was approached for the purpose, as he has a rich experience of computerising IIPA, CRRI, LBSAA, SVPPA libraries. The details pertaining to hardware and software requirements (keeping in view the needs and resources of the library), site preparation, furniture and stationary requirements were worked out in consultation with him.

The formal plan proposal was approved by the Governing Body of the College.

The Plan

Library system would be computerised in SCO-Unix operating system (to have sturdy and virus-free environment) with one Pentium as server and 5 to 8 nodes. Out of these nodes, one node can be a PC 486 attached to the desk of the librarian and the rest all can be the terminals only. Since the library plans to computerise all subsystems (of course, in a phased manner), it was decided to use LIBSYS as software package, as it is integrated, and all its subsystems are compatible and user friendly. Further, it is running successfully in many libraries like, DOE, AIIMS, IIPA, NIC, NIPCCED, IARI, BCL, etc. Moreover, it is compatible to national and international standards and export and import of data can be easily handled.

Keeping in view the various constraints involved in automation, a phased programme of automation towards the creation of database and service provisions was proposed.

Phase I

In phase I, the library did site preparation, purchased two computers: one pentium (the highest configuration available at that time) and other PC486. LIBSYS software was purchased along with SCO-UNIX operating system and MS Office, and installation of the hardware and software was done. Level-I training of staff on LIBSYS was arranged. With this library started working on database creation of current additions. Side by side the documents in active use (from teachers' reference section & reserve section, i.e., overnight issue) were also converted into machine readable form.

The details of hardware and software requirements along with other accessories, site preparation and the training required for the purpose are given in Annexure A.

Phase 2

In the second phase the library added three nodes to its server. The library completed database creation of its holdings along with bound periodicals (after careful weeding out). Level-II training on LIBSYS was arranged for the library staff. Further, one more computer Pentium II was purchased to start network services. A telephone line was applied for and got installed and internet and delnet services were started. With all this, the library has plans to start automating its other systems during this phase. The details of cost and time schedule are given in Annexure B.

Phase 3

In the third phase the library plans to connect all six postgraduate departments over LAN. A CD-ROM network station will be set up and SDI (Selected Dissemination of Information) and CAS (Current Awareness Service) services will also be started in this phase.

BIBLIOGRAPHY

Collins, A.K., Management in a changing environment, In *Management in Libraries,* Ormond, Australia, 1971, p. 13 – 18.

Corrall, Shiela, *Strategic Planning for Library and Information Services,* Aslib, London, 1971, p.50.

Garg, B.S., Computer vis-à-vis university libraries in India: promise and reality, *Library Herald,* 1992, 31, 1-2. pp. 24-32.

Harbour, Robin T., *Managing Library Automation,* Aslib, London, 1994, p.50.

Inamdar, N.C., Revitalising college libraries, *Herald of Library Science,* 1992, 31, 3-4, 180 – 91.

Laxmi, R. and Suma, P., A step towards developing a digital library, *Library Science with a Slant to Documentation and Information Science,* 1992, 35, 1, 25 – 36.

Mosters, R.R., I am a manager: color me grey, In. *Management in Libraries* Ormond, Australia, 1971, 1 – 12.

Praekh Harsha, Need for library automation modernisations, *University News,* 1992, 30, 1, 24-29.

Prem Singh, Managing technical change in libraries, *Administrator,* 1991, 30, 1, 67 – 84.

Prem Singh and Khanna, J. K., *Information Technologies in the Libraries,* Pragti, Delhi, 1994, p. 185.

Rama Reddy, Automation and networking experience of IGM library University of Hyderabad, *University News,* 1996, 34, 22, 17-20.

ANNEXURE A

Phase I: One Year (July 1997 – June 1998)

Period	*Activities*	*Expected Expenditure (In Rs.)*
July 1997	Site preparation	
	Distempering	2,500
	PVC Vinyl flooring	6,000
	Lighting Wiring of computers and nodes	15,000
	Air conditioning,	30,000
	Funiture :2 computer tables, 2 chairs and 1 almirah.	17,000
30 Aug. 1997	Hardware purchase and installation:	
	1 P5, 100 MHz, 256 kbCache, 16 MB RAM, 1.2 gbHDD, 3.5"FDD, CD ROM drive,14" svga monitor,101 k keyboard	60,000
	1 PC 486, 256 kbCache, 16 MB RAM, 1.2 gbHDD, 3.5"FDD, CD ROM drive, 14"svga monitor,101k keyboard	40,000
	1 UPS, 1.5 KV with 30 minutes back-up	25,000
	1 CVT(0.5KV)	3,500
	1 Printer 24 pin,80 col	9,000
15 Sept. 1997	Software purchase and installation	
	LIBSYS Software, limited multiuser (5 - 8 users)	1,60,000
	SCO Unix operating syatem	42,000
	Windows 95 and DOS	5,000
	MS Office	6,000
15Oct. 1997	Training of library staff	10,000
Dec.1997 to June 1998	Starting retroconversion of database	
	8000 documents @ Rs 2 per document	16,000
	Technical and other assistance	10,000
	Miscellaneous	10,000
	Total	4,67,000

Source of Funds

VIII plan grant

DSA grant (Development Special Assistance)

Library maintenance

College development and research fund.

ANNEXTURE B

Phase II: 2 Years (July 1998 – June 2000)

Period	*Activities*	*Expected Expenditure (In Rs.)*
Dec 1998	Hardware	
	Purchase and installation of 3 nodes x Rs 20,000 per node)	60,000
	Installation of telephone line	3,000
	Registration for internet & delnet	12,000
	Purchase and installation of computer (Pentium-II) for network service	55,000
	Back-up drive 4/8 GB DAT drive with SCSI controller	40,000
July 1998 Dec. 1999	Retroconversion:	
	Weeding out obsolete, unused and old editions, documents. Retroconversion of bibliographical data of books and bound periodicals(30,000 @Rs 2/-)	60,000
July 1999	Annual fee of network services (Internet & Delnet)	12,0000
Jan 2000	Training of staff	10,000
	Consumables	30,000
	Computer maintenace	15,000
	Technical assistance	10,000
	Miscellaneous	20,000
	Total	3,27,000

Source of Funds

DSA grant (Development Special Assistance, UGC)

Library Automation Fund

College Research and Development Fund

ANNEXURE C

Phase III One Year (Dec. 2000 – Dec. 2001)

Period	*Activities*	*Expected Expenditure (In Rs.)*
Dec 2000	Establishing LAN (with cabling)	3,50,000
	Establishing CD-ROM network station:	
	Purchase of Pentium 3 along with multimedia kit and CD-ROM drive	60,000
	UPS	7,000
	Printer	8,000
	CD's	2,00,000
	Starting CAS & SDI services	40,000
	Consumables	15,000
	Computer maintenace	15,000
	Training of staff	15,000
	Assistanc	15,000
	Telephone bill	20,000
	Miscellaneous	20,000
	Total	7,65,000

Source of Founds

DSA grant (Development Special Assistance,UGC)

Library Automation Fund

College Development and Research Grant

26
Networking of College Libraries in Delhi: A Plan

Kamlesh Vinayak

INTRODUCTION

Libraries are susceptible to external influences. Increasing costs of reading materials, escalating exchange rates, and tight budgetary provisions have had adverse impact on the collection development programmes of college libraries. University and college libraries are seriously assessing the option of exploiting external resources through network connectivity. The moot point is, would they be able to meet the demands by exploiting external resources, if yes, how efficiently and effectively? According to Kent "sharing resources is the only way for libraries to survive".[1] Certainly, the time has arrived for libraries to plan and establish a suitable network for the purpose.

This paper investigates the present status of computer applications in the college libraries in Delhi and suggests a suitable action plan for their networking. The study is based on the assessment of 25 college libraries under the University of Delhi, excluding professional colleges. The sample selection of colleges for the purpose of this study was done randomly.

FACILITIES AVAILABLE WITH COLLEGE LIBRARIES IN DELHI

Courses Taught and Student Enrolment

The University of Delhi is one of the premier universities in India, having 77 constituent colleges and 2,48,509 students on rolls. Out of 77 colleges, 63 are imparting education in various subjects in science, arts, and commerce disciplines. They are following a uniform syllabus set for courses at undergraduate, honours, and postgraduate level. Out of 63 colleges, 29 are offering courses in science, seven in professional and medical courses, two in engineering and 53 colleges in arts and commerce streams. Several colleges are offering courses in more than one stream.[2]

The status of student enrolment in various undergraduate and postgraduate courses is given in Table 1.

Table 1

Student Enrolment in the University of Delhi and its Colleges during 1997-98

Level	*Total*	*In Univ. Colleges*	*%*	*In Constituent Colleges*	*%*
Undergraduate (includes enrolment in School of Correspondence courses)	223,271	25,058	11.2%	198,213	88.8
Postgraduates (includes enrolment in School of Correspondence Courses)	21,279	1176	5.5%	20103	94.5
Research including MPhil & PhD	3,959			3959	100
Grand Total	248,509	30,193	11.9%	218,316	88.1%

Source : *76th Annual Report (1997-98)*, University of Delhi (1998). Delhi, University of Delhi. P 14.

Enrolment of students during the academic year 1997-98 was 2,44,550 in undergraduate and postgraduate courses and 3,959 for research studies in various departments of the university. Out of 2,44,550 students enrolled, 1,17,699 were in colleges, and 1,00,617 in the School of Correspondence courses, 13,450 in teaching departments, 13,286 in the external cell (private) and 12,948 in Non-Collegiate Women's Education Board, and 3,959 were the research students.[3]

Nature of Collection and Courses Taught

The students enrolled in colleges and School of Correspondence courses do constitute a sizeable section in the total enrolment. These students depend entirely on libraries of their respective institutes. These libraries are equipped mainly with textbooks prescribed in the curriculum. In addition to textbooks, the students expect these libraries to be well equipped with the latest editions and books related to current topics. Although the libraries try hard to meet the students, demands, yet given the constraints within which they work such as limited staff support, inadequate collection of books, insufficient book budget and space, they hardly come up to user expectations. D.S. Kothari had rightly pointed out, "No new university or college or department should be set up without taking into account its library needs in terms of staff, books, journals, space, etc. Nothing could be more damaging to a growing department than to neglect its library or to give it a low priority. On the contrary, the library should be an important center of attraction on the college or university campus."[4] According to Harrod, "A college library is established, maintained and administered by a college to meet the needs of its students and faculty."[5]

Despite these encouraging reports, the situation at the ground level has not changed much. The university and colleges have failed to extend the expected support to libraries for building up useful collections, good enough to support teaching the prescribed course curriculum. Interestingly, the courses

Table 2: College Library Budget and Allocation on Books and Periodicals

S.No.	Name of the college	Year of establishment	Library (Rs)	Allocation on books (Rs)	Allocation on periodicals (Rs)
1.	Acharaya Narendra Dev	1991	3,25,000	2,35,000	15,000
2.	Bhim Rao Ambedkar	1991	3,05,000	2,20,000	20,000
3.	Daulat Ram	1960	4,40,000	3,45,000	25,000
4.	Gargi	1967	4,00,000	3,00,000	35,0000
5.	Hans Raj	1948	7,58,000	6,52,000	80,000
6.	Hindu	1899	3,00,000	2,20,000	20,000
7.	Jesus and Mary	1968	4,22,500	2,70,000	95,000
8.	Kalindi	1967	5,20,000	3,50,000	1,70,000
9.	Keshavpuram Mahavidyalaya	1994	3,00,000	2,45,000	50,0000
10.	Kirori Mal	1954	7,50,000	6,00,000	90,000
11.	Lady Sriram	1956	4,50,000	2,60,000	1,50,000
12.	Maitreyi	1967	4,00,000	3,65,000	15,000
13.	Miranda House	1948	3,00,000	2,00,000	90,000
14.	Motilal Nehru (Day)	1964	6,00,000	4,00,000	80,000
15.	Rajdhani	1964	5,19,000	4,00,000	30,000
16.	Ramjas	1955	5,00,000	4,00,000	87,000
17.	Shaheed Bhagat Singh (Day)	1967	4,00,000	2,85,000	50,000
18.	Shivaji	1961	5,90,000	4,79,000	40,000
19.	Shyama Prasad Mukherjee	1969	3,38,000	2,69,000	50,000
20.	S.G.T.B. Khalsa (Day)	1954	4,00,000	2,00,000	1,10,000
21.	Sri Ram College of Commerce	1926	3,00,000	2,59,000	25,000
22.	Sri Venkateswara	1961	4,20,000	3,15,000	75,000
23.	St Stephen's	1922	3,60,000	2,40,000	70,000
24.	Swami Shraddhanand	1967	3,12,500	2,38,300	25,200
25.	Vivekanand MahilaCollege	1970	3,65,000	2,60,400	40,000

offered in the university and the colleges are almost the same within the university system. Hence, there is sizeable duplication in the collections of various college libraries. Resource sharing through networking can help avoid this sort of duplication in materials and also solve the space problem faced by the libraries as well.

Budgeting of College Libraries

The funding pattern of colleges and their libraries in India shows that funds come from the University Grants Commission (UGC) as well as from the state governments. However, in the case of central universities the larger share of funding is contributed by the UGC. Generally, the grants given to libraries are far below their normal expectations. In addition to grants, the libraries meet their resource requirements by generating funds by collecting library fee from students. The survey of 25 colleges in Delhi reveals that the library budget varies from college to college between Rs. 3,00,000 and Rs. 7,50,000 per year, depending on the number of students enrolled and the library fee charged per student.

The college libraries with limited budgetary provisions find it difficult to sustain journal subscriptions. Table 3 gives a list of select journals subscribed by various college libraries in Delhi as surveyed.

A sample list of 21 journals was prepared. The sample includes only such journals which are costing between Rs. 200 and Rs. 18,850 per annum, and that they were subscribed in college libraries in Delhi. The survey reveals that there was duplication in journal subscription between the university and 25 college libraries. The duplication was occurring even in such journals as were expensive, involving a heavy amount of funds, For example, *Time Literary Supplement*. Seven libraries were subscribing *TLS*. In order to combat this problem of finance and the source material as required by users, it is desirable that libraries resort to resource sharing.

Table 3
Sample List of Journals Subscribed in Select 25 College Libraries

S.No.	*Title of the Journal (Rs)*	*Subscription rate subscribing*	*No. of colleges*
1.	*Economic and Political Weekly*	800	25
2.	*Hans*	300	25
3.	*Economist*	3,213	25
4.	*Indian Economic and Social History Review*	850	25
5.	*Trends in Social Sciences*	300	25
6.	*University News*	400	2
7.	*Journal of Library and Information Science*	300	20
8.	*RBI Bulletin*	800	19
9.	*Social Scientists*	350	19
10.	*Book Review*	400	19
11.	*Nutrang*	200	16
12.	*Journal of Indian Writing in English*	200	16
13.	*Modern Asian Studies*	5,958	16
14.	*P.C. Magazine*	6,320	12
15.	*Resonance : Journal of Science Education*	400	12
16.	*Dastavez*	300	12
17.	*Studies in History*	690	11
18.	*Time*	1,768	10
19.	*National Geographic*	1,650	8
20.	*Time Literary Supplement*	9,159	7
21.	*Science (USA)*	18,850	1

The computers were installed in university libraries with the financial assistance of the UGC under INFLIBNET programme. The grants were given not only for housekeeping operations but also for networking of college libraries. The Report of working group of Planning Commission on Libraries and Informatics for the Ninth Five Year Plan (1997-2000)[6] had identified reasons for the slow pace of progress with regard to networking of libraries. These were:

a) Lack of standard output format as well as data entry in the automated system

b) Libraries have large stocks of documents with varying cataloguing practices and non-standard formats.

c) Absence of a central agency of librarians and information specialist to guide, coordinate, monitor the computerisation work of the libraries. Resource sharing and computer application was also recommended to promote union catalogues, telex and fascimile services, microfiliming and reprographic facilities, etc.

Services

The survey reveals that college libraries were providing lending and photocopy services mainly to their internal users. No other type of service was provided. None of the colleges surveyed had yet started library services using computers and networks.

To start with, the college libraries are planning to use IT first for housekeeping operations. But this alone may not be sufficient. The Government of India has taken initiatives for IT introduction for improving library services to users. The National Policy on University Libraries was considered a base plan to develop the concept of services to users. It recommended that university libraries should offer all services such as CAS, SDI, documentation and bibliographic services, translation, reference, referral, and inter-library loan. These should be available to all user groups. In fact, these are non-existent so far. It is high time that the libraries should start thinking on the lines of setting up regional library centres. These centres are expected to have a strong collection, one each in sciences, social sciences/commerce, and humanities. These centres should establish linkages with libraries at local, regional and national level for coordination and cooperation in collection development and services.

NETWORKING OF COLLEGE LIBRARIES

The meaning and scope of networking as defined by Tenunbaum is "an interconnection of autonomous computers".[7] The computers are said to be inter-connected if they are capable of exchanging information. Today, three types of networks distinguished by geographical scope have emerged:

Wide Area Network (WAN) : This network spans a large area, maybe several continents.

Local Area Network (LAN) : As the name suggests it is confined to a relatively small area or a group of users close to each other such as within the university campus and nearby colleges; and

Metropolitan Area Network (MAN): The scope of MAN lies between WAN and LAN spanning a city or a town. In all these three types the area covered and the IT size are significant.

LAN

Local Area Network is useful for networking of college libraries in a city. The first local area network was introduced into academic world in the mid '1970s. The pattern of interconnection of nodes in a network is called topology. Important factors for a network are the consideration of choice of media and access method to be used. Minimising the distances involved and the type of media used can minimise installation cost.

Flexibility

LAN is useful for a college library network as this offers functionalities for data processing in a distributed environment. This also allows moving existing nodes and adding new ones.

Reliability

LAN is more reliable for college libraries as the individual nodes can function independent of the network.

Aims of Proposed Network

The aims of the proposed network are as follows:

a) To optimise the utilisation of the resources of the universities and their affiliated college libraries.

b) To avoid duplication of costly information sources.

c) To access the vast amount of information and resources available in university and college libraries within the University of Delhi, and subsequently other universities and their affiliated colleges in the state and the country.

d) To enable affiliated college libraries so that they could give information support for quality education and research.

e) To enable constituent college libraries to generate new services, strengthen and improve upon the existing ones.

f) To create a framework leading to savings in manpower, finances and space of the participating libraries.

The Planning Commission, Government of India, has appointed the Second National Review Committee to evaluate the working of university and college libraries in India. The committee has the mandate to study aspects, such as staff formula, library services, quality and relevance of collection, space, requirement, computerisation, resources rationalisation, development of norms, relevance of curricula, etc. It is hoped that the recommendations of the Committee shall have far-reaching impact on academic libraries in India in this millennium.

PROPOSED PLAN FOR NETWORKING

The ultimate objective in computer networks is to ensure linking together of various pieces of computer equipment and systems. One important aim in every network is to provide end-to-end compatibility so that any terminal or system can be linked to any other within the network or to any other network.

Every library intending to join a network faces an important question: how to select the most suitable network. The choice can be made keeping in view of the factors such as:

a) Available network options;
b) Selection of network functions to be used;
c) Reliability of the system;
d) Quality control standards decided by the participating libraries in a network; and
e) Cost involved.

Keeping in view these requirements, the topology best suited for a college library network is the star or radical topology. This topology consists of a central node which are connected to all other nodes by a single path as shown in Figure 1 below:

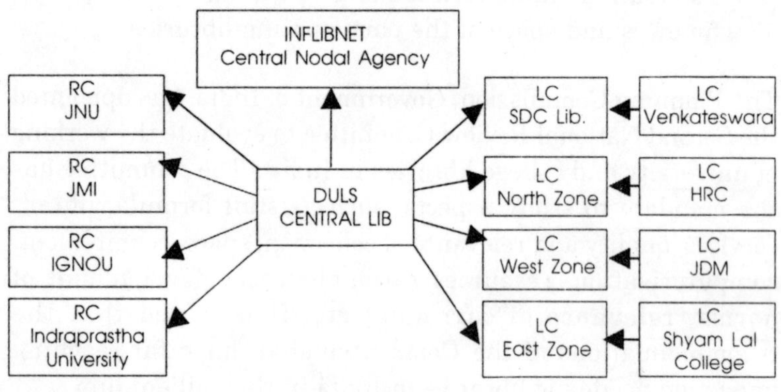

Figure 1 : Structural Model of Networking of Delhi Colleges

Organisational Structure of Network

The proposed network will set up linkages to other university libraries though INFLIBNET. In each district area in Delhi it shall identify from amongst affiliated college libraries one big library to act as regional node for that district. The other participating libraries shall act as local nodes. Each local node shall be responsible for feeding information to the regional node. Each regional node shall develop databases of that region and work as an intermediatory between the central node and local nodes. The central node shall consolidate databases of the four regional nodes and make them available to each of the regional nodes. It shall also interface with the INFLIBET.

For successful performance of the proposed network, the university library and its constituent college libraries will have to develop the necessary infrastructure, computerise their library operations, and create databases of the collection held by the Delhi University Library System. Terminals within the library may be installed in the technical section, circulation section, rare book section, periodical section, reference section, and in the computer room. This shall enhance library capacity of data storage and information retrieval.

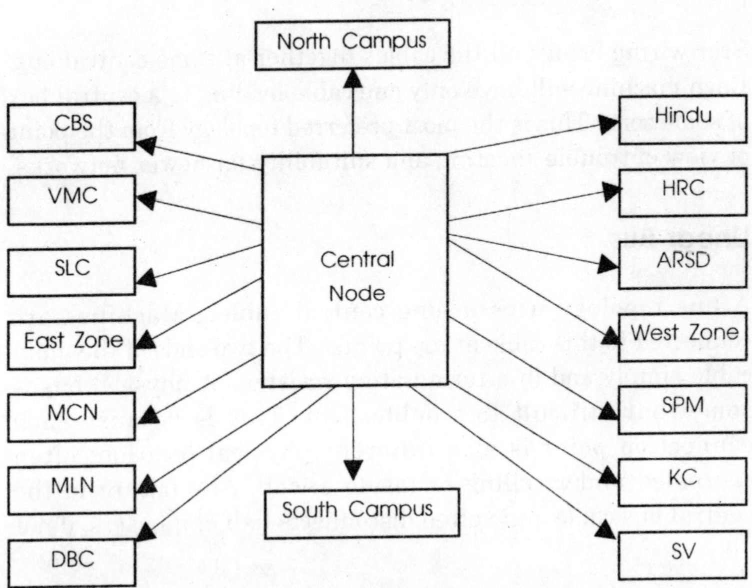

Figure 2 : Network Model of University and Libaries Colleges

All library functions including acquisition, cataloguing, serials control and circulation need to be automated. CDS/ISIS software may be useful for college library services such as CAS (Current Awareness, SDI Selective Dissemination of Information), list of new additions and periodicals received this week, and list of periodical holdings in the library.

NETWORK TOPOLOGY

The pattern of interconnection of nodes in a network is called topology. The network topologies that can be considered are:

1. The star or radical topology
2. Linear Bus
3. The Ring or Loop or Star-wired Ring

Star or Radical Topology

Star wiring brings all the cables together at some central box. Each machine will have only one cable leading to a central box of some sort. This is the most preferred topology from the point of view of trouble shooting and suitability for newer networks.

Linear Bus

A bus topology uses a long central cable. Machines are connected to this cable at top points. The two ends of the main cable simply end in a terminating resister. A physical bus is somewhat difficult to troubleshoot. This is because each connection point is at a different physical location, often concealed under ceiling or inside a wall. Any failure in the central bus cable quite often disconnects half of its users, if not all.

Ring or Loop

With a ring topology each station has two cables: one going in and the other going out. The last machine in the line-up connects back to the first to form a ring. All the stations are effectively in series. Each station acts as an amplifier. However, a ring is a very difficult station. Since each station is needed to complete the ring, either each station will have to be always turned on or two ring ends will have to be 'jumpered' when a station is turned off or removed. This topology cannot be recommended for a college library network.

The star topology provides easy access for servicing or reconfiguration of the network. As shown in figure 2, 13 colleges in North Delhi campus can join together and create their network with the university as the central nodal agency, 16 colleges in West Zone unit can have University Library System as the central nodal agency. Similarly, 24 colleges in South Delhi can have South Delhi Campus library as the central nodal agency, and 10 colleges in East Delhi can have their network with east zone library. This is the kind of network that can be created using star topology. It seems to be useful for a college library network as the sources and the resources of all the colleges in each zone can be pooled together and a Local Area Network can be created. Star topology, if used, can provide several independent operational points.

Network operating systems coordinate the activities of multiple computers across a network. The network operating system acts as a director to keep the network running smoothly. The two major types of network operating systems are:

1. Peer-to-Peer
2. Client Server

Peer-to-Peer Network Operating System

It allows users to share resources and files located on their computers and to access such shared resources. In the peer-to-peer network all computers are considered equal, they do not have centralised management control. They all have the same ability to use the resources available on the network. It, however, does not provide security available on client/server network operating systems.

Client/Server Network Operating System

This system allows the network to centralise functions and applications in one or more dedicated file server, providing access to resources, and ensuring data security. Individual workstations have access to the resources stored on file servers. The network operating system provides the mechanism to integrate all the components of the network and allow multiple users to simultaneously share the same resources irrespective of physical location. This operating system can work as a model system for a college library network.

The advantages of this type of network Operating System are:

a) Centralised : Resources and data security are controlled through the server.
b) Any or all elements can be replaced individually, as needs increase.
c) Flexibility: New technology can be easily integrated into system.
d) Interoperability: All components (client/network/server) work together.
e) Accessibility : The server can be accessed remotely and across multiple platforms.

Hence, the star topology with client server operating system can be considered for forming a library network. It can definitely bring positive results, helping college libraries to come closer and share their collections, periodicals, services, and develop into more useful libraries of tomorrow.

CONCLUSION

Library networking is the key to mutual cooperation and resource sharing. The colleges affiliated to the University of Delhi should form a library network as a means to maximise the utilisation of existing information resources/collection. In the proposed model for networking the university library can act as a resource center to the college libraries, develop databases of the entire collection in the DULS, and make them accessible on the network. As a pre-requisite the participating college libraries must develop the necessary IT infrastructure. This would enable them to contribute effectively to the network resources. To tide over financial problems in the network implementation, it is proposed that college libraries should pool their resources, howsoever small they may be. Secondly, they must offer their source materials for sharing.

The minimum prerequisite for networking of college libraries is that they must have a computer, telephone, and modern information and communication technologies. The University Grants Commisssion, the Planning Commission and other government agencies need to consider providing financial support to college libraries to enable them to establish the minimum infrastructure and to train their staff technically. Only a technically trained and competent professional staff can contribute to the task of computerisation and modernisation of library services.

The proposal can be appropriately modified and applied for establishing a suitable network for any other university library. Hopefully, the new approach to modernising college libraries will go a long way in improving their performance in providing information support for teaching and learning.

REFERENCES

1. Kent, A., *Resource Sharing in Libraries: Why, How, When—Action Steps,* New York. Marcel Dekker, 1974, p. 11.

2. Basu, Aparna, ed. University of Delhi: 1922-1997, Delhi, University of Delhi, 1998, pp. 106-110.
3. *76th Annual Report: 1997-98*, Delhi, University of Delhi, 1998, p.14.
4. India, *Education Commission* Report *(1964-66)*, Delhi, Manager of Publications, S11-45 (2).
5. Harrod, L.M., *The Librarians' Glossary*, London, Clarion Books, Indian Book Co., 1971, p. 24.
6. Planning Commission Working Group on Libraries and Information (1996), Report (Mimeographed), p. 46.
7. Tanebaum, A.S., *Computer Networks*, Prentice Hall of India, New Delhi, 1998, p. 138-39.

27

Information Technology in Academic Libraries

K. Veeranjaneyulu

INTRODUCTION

Information is a dynamic and unending resource. It plays a significant role in education, research and development, and in improving the quality if life. Recent computer and telecommunication technologies have highly revolutionised the field of library and information services, facilitating collection, storage, organisation, processing analysis, presentation, communication and dissemination of data more quickly and in greater volume than ever before. Use of modern technology has assumed greater relevance in the context of fourth law of library science: "Save the time of the reader/staff" wherein Raganathan had underlined the need for internal efficiency of the library.

INFORMATION TECHNOLOGY

Information technology is a generic term used to denote activities connected with computer-based processing, storage and transfer of information. It includes microprocessors, cable access television, fibre optics, satellites, teletext, word processing, electronic mail, video, robotics and such others. According to the *ALA Glossary,* "Information technology is the application of computers and other technologies to the acquisition, organisation, storage, retrieval and dissemination of information." The components of information technology are: computers, telecommunications, storage technologies, dataabases, information systems, micrographics, and expert systems.

INFORMATION TECHNOLOGY AND ACADEMIC LIBRARIES

Libraries are the light houses for information in the field of education and research. The information is increasing in volume everyday, at various levels and on various subject. Hence automation is very much needed in academic libraries especially for the following reasons:

a) To provide efficient and accurate services,
b) To control the rapid growth of information,
c) To offer new services,
d) To facilitate cooperation, and
e) To manage increased work load.

Information technology has provided new media, new modes of storing and communicating information. The application of information technologies for operations and services in academic libraries has been increasing steadily. It is now used in academic libraries for housekeeping operations, collection, development, information processing, storage and retrieval of information, creation of databases, developing search patterns to retrieve information. Information technology brought in many services to libraries to speed up their activities. These include : telecommunication technology, telex, videotex, teletex, facsimile of fax, e-mail, CD-ROM technology, online retriveal services, library networks, and internet.

New technology helps to remove barriers of distance and time, and drudgery in repeated manual efforts in library routines. The advances in technology will continue to improve the effectiveness of the libraries. The world wide web is going to be more interactive and multidimensional, incorporating multimedia presentations. All this data will be accessible through the information superhighway. Microcomputers will have the capacity to process more than 40 million instructions per second. The microcomputers, highly dynamic and versatile as they are, will offer information professionals new alternatives in information management regardless of the size of the institution they represent.

DIGITAL LIBRARIES

Digital libraries offer a solution to three most fearsome challenges facing traditional academic libraries today, viz ,economical survival, shortage of space, and management of materials. They open up a vast new range of possibilities for information sharing and distribution. A digital library is not just a collection of material in electronic form, it also includes a strong browser interface, and perhaps a virtual society and virtual space. A digital library can be defined as "computer-based information system for acquiring, storing, organising, searching, distributing and displaying digital materials for end-user access; not necessarily network based but designed and constructed so as to be capable of attaching or being attached to a network." The advantages of having library material available in digital form are threefold : (i) the data occupies less space and can be replicated easily and made secure electronically, (ii) the data can be made immediately available through communication networks like internet to anyone, anywhere and (iii) enormous search speed and facility. The promise of the digital library is the promise of great cost reduction while providing great increase in data availability and accessibility. The purpose of a digital library can be broadly described as :

a) to ensure the systematic development of the means to collect, store and organise information and knowledge in digital form;

b) to promote the economical and efficient delivery of information to all;

c) to encourage cooperative efforts which leverage considerable investment in research resources, computing and communication networks; and

d) to strengthen communication and collaboration among research, government, and educational bodies.

Though information technology has shown great potential for modernising the library activities, it is only at the university level that the initiation has been made towards automation. In some private professional colleges the adoption of IT is under way. Apart from this, the situation in this regard is pathetic in most of the academic institufions. It is estimated that a large percentage of library professionals are still not even aware of the use of IT in libraries Their main problems in general are :

a) installation of computers in libraries is still considered as a costly affair,

b) lack of sufficient trained specialised manpower to plan and operate automation in libraries,

c) the high cost involved, especially, for accessing the remote databases and their installation,

d) lack of technical skill to develop local in house database, and

e) lack of long term approach to automation.

Sometimes psychological barriers on the part of library personnel also prevent switching over to modernisation.

CONCLUSION

Academic libraries are facing the challenging task of satisfying the increasingly complex and diverse information needs of the clientele. Academic libraries can use today a wide variety of technology options that exist now. Fruitful results can, however, be obtained only when we make the best use of the technologies.

BIBLIOGRAPHY

Banerjee, K. Utpal, *Information Technology for a Common Man*, Computer Society of India, 1992, New Delhi.

Kumar, P.S.G., Computers and University Libraries in India. In : *Outstanding Studies in University Librarianship*, Ed., by Sood S.P. and Sharma, C.L., RBSA Publishers, Jaipur, 1991, pp. 176-186.

Murthy, S.S., Information technologies in libraries : A Futuristic perspectives, First ILA Ranganathan Memorial lecture delivered on 12 August 1994 at National Museum, New Delhi, DESIDOC, Delhi, 1994.

Haravu, L.J.L., Library automation and networking in India. An overview of recent developments, *Annals of Library Science and Documentation,* 1993, 40, 1, 32-40.

28
Benefits of Library Automation

Khalid K. Faruqi

The very purpose of any library is to provide convenient, easy and faster means of accessing knowledge with the help of various devices. The computers are the information machines, which enabled the libraries to achieve the same purposes. Due to this closer alliance among the libraries and computers, the application of computers have become the unavoidable alternative to fulfil the objective of the library and information centres, through automating its various library activities, which can support through providing management information system, decision support system, expert system, etc. Thus, the contemporary libraries in the third transition period are characterised with mechanisation of the various library activities.

Library automation implies a high degree of mechanisation of various routines and repetitive tasks to be performed by human beings. With the advent of automation the human intervention is reduced to a great extent. The appearance of the computer has greatly the library automation. Library automation includes use of computers and other semi-automatic devices. So when we talk of library automation, these days, it is basically the use of computers and computer-based products and services in library work.

WHAT IS LIBRARY AUTOMATION

The term 'automation' was first introduced by D. S. Harder in 1936. He defined it as the automatic handing of parts between progressive production processes, in relation to engineering industries. Since then the term has been applied to a wide variety of automatic machinery and automatic systems, and is commonly used to describe any operation in which there has been a substantial substitution of controlled action for human efforts.

According to the *McGraw Hill Encyclopedia of Science and Technology* (Vol.1, Ed.5, 1982) the term 'automation' is "a coined word having no precise, generally accepted, technical meaning but widely used to imply the concept 'development' or use of highly automatic machinery or control system."

However, in the context of library and information centres automation, the term 'automation' has been defined by Markuson as "library automation in its broadest sense can be taken to mean the employment of machines for library processes. In general, however, library automation has come to mean the application of computers and related data processing equipment to libraries."

NEED FOR LIBRARY AUTOMATION

The various benefits that have been arising out of library automation covering avoidance of routine and repetitive jobs, multiple outputs, productivity improvement, improvement in quality of services, expansion in the range and quality of services, ability to share the resources, instantaneous access to global sources, quick response time and opportunity to networking, are diverting the library and information centres towards automation. In spite of these, the following are the various factors that have been contributing to automation of various library operations and activities.

Diffusion of Information

The evolution of printing machine has brought out a revolutionary change in the technological world. This has caused since the fifteenth century a widerspread of printed books. Further, the research going on in different fields has been for bringing out the newer subjects into existence. Hence, this leads to the generation of more and more information into use. Further, the documentary sources are not only coming out in the printed form but also in different non-print media.

All these factors are causing diffusion of information at a faster rate. This diffused information makes the-inability on the part of the librarian/information managers, in processing larger volumes of information contained in different forms and formats. Hence, in this context, the computers are the only solution for doing this job more accurately and systematically.

Information Explosion

An exponential growth of literature has been noticed during the last three decades. This exponential has its greatest impact in the area of science, technology, and medicine. A study carried out by Chemical Abstract Service and Organisation of Economic Cooperation and Development (OECD) in recent years revealed that the volume of information is increasing at the rate of 13% per year which means that the total amount of information doubles every seven or eight years. This phenomenon is popularly termed as 'information explosion'.

With the production of information on a large scale, it has become impossible for the information seeker to scan even a part of the published literature in his field of activity, not to speak of exhaustive scanning. Another consequence of this phenomenon is the growth of secondary sources of information such as indexing and abstracting services, bibliographies and computer-based large information systems. Since no single library can afford to acquire all that is published, resource sharing has become an essential component of the library world. In order to cope with these problems, the libraries and information centres should be well equipped with efficient and fast information-handling techniques and tools. The computer is one such tool that would certainly help the librarians to solve these problems and add to the efficiency and effectiveness in libraries.

Space-saving

Almost all the libraries in the world are facing desperate shortage of space. The application computers would definitely reduce the pressure on this front. For instance, a hard copy of the new edition of *Oxford English Dictionary* consists of 20 volumes. They occupy about two shelves of library space. This dictionary is now available on 'Compact Disc' in a computer-readable form. This compact disk occupies only a fraction of the space occupied by its hard copy. This results in saving an unimaginable amount of space. Similarly, the automation of *Public Catalogue* will help spare a tremendous amount of space and reduce pressure on it.

Time-saving

The Fourth Law of Library Science states: 'Save the Time of the Reader'. The corollary to this law is 'Save the Time of the Library Staff'. The dictum of this law would hold good if the various routines in the library are computerised. The data stored in the memory of the computer can be 'retrieved almost instantaneously.

Suppose literature on a particular subject says 'indexing languages' is available in a library/information centre in the form of:

i) books;
ii) chapters of books;
iii) articles in periodicals;
iv) articles in proceedings of conferences; and soon.

If a user comes to library with a request for literature on 'indexing languages', the reference librarian/information analyst/information officer would have to search the entire gamut of books which deal with this subject and scan periodicals, conference proceedings, and those books which contain a chapter or two in this area. Still he/she would not be able to trace all that is available.

On the other hand, if the same information is put into the computer after proper scanning and analysis of various sources of information, we would be able to retrieve this information in a few seconds. We will have to press the keyboard a few times and the information would be displayed on the screen of the computer terminal, of which a printout can be taken by pressing the keyboard a few times more. Thus in order to trace the same information manually, we would require one or two people for several days. Even then we would not be even near to comprehensiveness. The same job can be performed with the help of a computer more exhaustively, pinpointedly and expeditiously.

Cost Effectiveness

Cost-effectiveness is a measure of the cost of inputing and outputing data and the value of results obtained. Let us take two systems—one manual and the other computerised—for the performance of a job, says, storage and retrieval of information on a subject. Suppose the cost of storage and retrieval of information on this subject by manual system is more than the computerised system. Of the two systems, the former would be rated less cost-effective than the latter because of involvement of more money in terms of labour and time in order to get the same results. As discussed earlier, we can retrieve the desired information at a tremendous speed with near comprehensiveness with an automated system. Likewise, the automated systems help us save a lot of space. The automated systems result in a lot of economy.

Manipulation of Data

Computers can be used to manipulate the same data for different purposes. We would need to enter the following data into the computer:

i) Author(s);
ii) Title of the articles;
iii) Title of the periodicals in which the articles have appeared;
iv) Volume and issue numbers of the periodicals;
v) Dates of issues;
vi) Pages on which articles appeared; and finally
vii) Key terms/subject terms, etc.

This data can be used for the generation of information on a particular subject, compilation of bibliographies in alphabetical or subject or classified order, citation analysis and so on. This means that the same data can be used for different purposes. Another advantage would be that this data, when available in computer-readable form, could be used any number of times with the same speed and accuracy.

Exploitation of Computer-readable Databases

Just as many technological innovations have changed human lifestyle beyond recognition, online bibliographic databases have all the trappings of a mini revolution in the offing for the work style of a researcher. Imagine yourself in a scenario where millions of bibliographic records on a magnitude of subjects, systematically organised according to author, title, subject and other access keys is just a phone-call away. In such a situation, would it not be nice to have a computer for provision of some of the professional services that one can expect from an exceptionally well-informed librarian? On the face of it, this looks like an utopian fantasy.

But in reality, there are hundreds of computer-based bibliographic databases in the fields of science, technology, medicine, social sciences and arts which are functional these days. The libraries and information centres can avail of such computer-based database services only if they are suitably equipped in terms of computer, telecommunication, and document reproduction equipments and are linked to them.

Efficient and Effective Management of Libraries

In modern times, the libraries constitute larger volumes of data/ information resources. Therefore, these larger collections of resources are increasing the number of operations to be performed by the libraries. Thus, in order to perform all the operations and organise the necessary files, library automation is an obligation on the part of the library/information centres.

Improved Management Information

The production of management information by manual systems is a time-consuming, costly and complex job. Most of the un-automated libraries, therefore, maintain minimal statistics. Improved management information is rated as a high priority by the library management, for it is paramount in decision making. The automated systems can produce the desired management information.

Nearly every technological advance has fascinated one or another librarian, and these technologies have eventually been assimilated by all the libraries. For instance, the typewriter was mentioned as a possible tool for making catalogue cards in a Conference of Librarians in New York in the closing years of the previous century. Its use was accepted by almost all the libraries of the world. Now the libraries are adopting the computing and other technologies. An imaginative approach commits the library to the use of new technologies.

Increased Workload, Insufficient Staff and Shrinking Budget

The increase in the number of collections and insufficient staff are causing increased workload. Further, the shrinking budget has added to this and is making the problem more complicated. Therefore, in this situation, library automation is the only way to overcome the same.

Rapid and Accurate Processing

Further, in order to process the data, and perform various activities and operations more rapidly and accurately to take timely decisions, library automation is inevitable.

Offer of New and Improved Services

User satisfaction is the only mission of any library or information centre so that the library and information centres have to search for the new ways from time to time to offer and introduce more and more new services. To achieve this, library automation can help a lot.

Increased Number of User Expectations

Further, this is another pressure on the part of the user community, who can present more and more demands and requirements before the libraries. To serve this, library automation is an obligation on the part of the libraries/ information centres, which assists to offer varied types of services.

Routine and Repetitive Nature of Work

Most of the activities and operations of the library and information centres are routine and repetitive utilising the human resources for this purpose which has been a much laborious and costly affair. To avoid this, computerisation in libraries is only alternative.

Nature of Records/Files to be Maintained

The library and information centres have to generate and maintain various types of files and records in relation to different sections. These records and files are to be updated constantly. To do this, library automation is the most advantageous activity.

Application of Modern Management Techniques

The timely and qualitative decisions, and calculation of the performance in quantitative terms requires to adopt various modern management techniques like operations research, PERT, CPM, informatics, etc. For this, the library automation is necessary.

Reducing Response time

Further, in order to provide access to information pinpointedly, instantaneously, expeditiously, library automation is necessary, which in turn reduces the response time.

Resource Sharing

Sharing of the resources is the only alternative for library and information centres, which are characterised by shrinking budgets. In this context, computerisation of libraries and information centres is an obligation to share the resources ranging from local to global levels.

CHANGE IN INFORMATION SERVICE ENVIRONMENT

Thus, the contemporary library and information centres have been much concerned with the above facts and have been receiving tremendous pressures from the increasing user community for timely, relevant and precise information services. Therefore, it became an obligation on the part of the library and information centres to adopt computer applications and other modern technologies to service in the contemporary information environment.

The perishable nature of information; availability of limited financial resources; non-availability of adequate documentary sources; limited manpower resources; need for the inter-disciplinary nature of information; tremendous increase in non-print documentary sources are the various factors influencing the library and information centres to share the documentary, equipment and manpower resources not only at the local level but also at the global level. Consequently, resource sharing has become a buzzword of the contemporary library and information centres.

The advances in the computer and the telecommunication technologies have revolutionised the way in which the user can get access to information. As a result of this, the present-day user has been searching and retrieving required information from anywhere on his own terminal. Even at the local level also i.e., within the organisation, through local area networking, the information has been searching and accessing. Beyond this local level, through a wide area networking, the information has been sharing from the external sources.

Further, the internet technology in the contemporary times has brought out the whole universe of knowledge on a single platform, enabling the user community to download any type of information from anywhere across the world, irrespective of the physical location. Thus, library automation is an inevitable activity for any library and information centre to enable the users to travel across the information world and thereby make them think globally and act locally.

AREAS OF LIBRARY AUTOMATION

In the earlier ages of computer of computer applications, libraries are confined mainly to automate traditional and/or manual housekeeping activities/routines. Thus, the routine activities are performed more effectively and efficiently with reduced cost than ever before, with library automation. In this context, Salmon expresses:

> Library automation is the use of automatic and semiautomatic data processing machines to perform such traditional library activities as acquisition, cataloguing and circulation. Although these activities themselves are those traditionally associated with libraries; library automation may thus be distinguished from related fields such as information retrieval, automatic indexing and abstracting, and automatic textual analysis.

Further he declares:

> Linguistic purists have argued rightly that the term 'automation' applies more correctly and narrowly to automate process control, and library automation is now by far the most commonly used term for mechanisation of library activities using data processing equipment.

However, the modern library and information centres have not restricted the library automation to the traditional operations as expressed above, but also want to extend its applicability to newer areas and activities in order to justify themselves as information centres. This intention has made library and information centres to bring various activities relating information storage, retrieval and dissemination under the spectrum of library automation to meet the changing information needs of users. With regard to this, Bierman stated rightly, "Library, automation can be viewed as the use of computer and associated technology to revolutionise the meaning of libraries and to redefine their existence."

Thus the comprehensive areas of library automation are identified by Hayes and Backer, by defining the term 'library automation' completely suitable to libraries of the modern period. According to him, the various areas of library automation includes:

i) The application of data processing equipment to do/or support the clerical/repetitive functions found in technical processing, circulation control and serials control.
ii) The application of data processing equipment to the fields of information storage and retrieval, automatic indexing and abstracting and in reference work; and
iii) The application of computers/data processing equipment for operation research and system analysis.

Based on the functions it assists in computer applications in libraries, and can be categorised into the following five areas:

i) *Housekeeping function*: Acquisition, cataloguing, circulation, serials control
ii) *Information storage and retrieval:* Production of indexes and abstracts, thesaurus, translation, searching of online and CDROM, databases, floppy diskettes, internet-based databases etc., CAS, SDI etc., retrospective searches on demand.
iii) *Operations research and systems analyses*: Management information system, decision-support system, expert system, etc.
iv) *Library network applications:* For access to INFLIBNET ERNET, NICNET, I-NFT.
v) *Office automation*: Accounting maintenance, office correspondence, payroll, etc., (through usage of MS Word, LOTUS, MS-Excel, Foxpro, etc.)

PART VI

Electronic Publishing

29

Evaluating Electronic Journals

D.K. Kaushik and *Sonia Relan*

INTRODUCTION

Recent advances in computer applications during the past few decades have brought radical changes in the way information is generated, stored, organised, accessed, retrieved and consumed. The vast speed at which different operations are carried out in an automated environment has attracted information professionals towards a computer-based system. It has opened floodgates to people to access information through many different ways. The information could be located even at a far-off location and could be in different languages. These capabilities were unheard in the library world before the deployment of computers in the information problems.

The applications of computers in information processing have brought several new products and services into the scene. Electronic journals form one of the latest products. The employment of information technology and communication technology is predominant in these journals. Their potential of delivering the goods is quite vast, as they have overcome successfully the geographical limitations associated with the print media. Further, the distribution time between product publication and its delivery has been drastically reduced.

An electronic journal, as its name implies, is a serial containing scholarly communications and articles issued periodically in electronic form, by employing computers. Its transmission could be through the normal telecommunication facilities. It can also be made available in print form or other media. Thus, an e-journal can either be an electronic product such as a computer floppy or the entire information could be stored in the host computer, which could be accessed online. If the product is in the form of a computer floppy, for instance, its distribution has to take place through postal or similar services. In this article, only the journals falling in the latter category would be discussed.

GROWTH OF ELECTRONIC JOURNALS

Taking a note of the fact that electronic journals are growing exponentially, it can be predicted that they might ultimately replace the printed version of the journals in future days to come. As per the 7th edition of the Association of Research Libraries, *Directory of Electronic Journals, Newsletters, & Academic Discussion Lists* (1997), out of 3,400 serial titles, 1,465 appear in electronic form. In 1997, as per the earlier edition of the directory, there were, 1,049 peer reviewed electronic journals in contrast to 317 in 1996. Similarly, the number of electronic journals in 1991, 1994 and 1996 were 110, 440 and 700 respectively.

Broadly, electronic journals are published in different academic fields. They include science, technical, and medicine (STM); arts and humanities; and social sciences. For distribution of these journals, publishers have started their services, for instance, Academic Press (Ideal); Blackwell Science, UMI (Proquest Direct); Project Muse, OCLC Electronic Collections, Online Information Access Company, JSTOR, CARL Company, Elsevier Science Publishers (Science Direct); EBSCO's Publishers, and so on.

FEATURES OF ELECTRONIC JOURNALS

Given below are some of the important features, associated with electronic journals.

a) Electronic composition and transmission have led to fast production and distribution of the product. In other words, printing and distribution processes have been virtually eliminated.
b) Faster reviewing of the journals, saving thereby the precious time of specialists.
c) The production mode of e-journals offers opportunities to establish network communication among the authors, editors, and referees.
d) Users can access a particular article or the entire issue of the journal, within no time. If required, printouts of the relevant pages can be obtained.
e) Large collections can be searched and retrieved simultaneously and instantly.
f) User interest profile can be created. The system notifies the user, as and when any new publication relevant and useful to the person is added into the database, automatically.
g) E-journals are quite cost effective as compared to the printed version.
h) Multimedia capabilities can also be incorporated into the e-journal. This provides an edge over the conventional journal available in print form.
i) Since the information is sought from different e-journals simultaneously, the retrieved pieces of information emerge in a packaged form.
j) Hypertext and hypermedia formats enable linkages among different sections within an article or among a group of articles in journals and other electronic resources.

k) Publishers, research groups, authors, and so on can be easily contacted if needed, via electronic mail links. Hence, the users have more creative ways to have their information queries answered.

Limitations

The following limitations are associated with the services of electronic-journals, if subscribed in a library :

a) The equipment employed to store, display and print e-journals, is quite expensive. A small library may not be able to buy and maintain such pieces of equipment.

b) The pieces of equipment may at times go out of order, thus bringing a halt to the services.

c) Electronic journals rely heavily on the state-of-art technology for storage and display. A typical computer screen may have a resolution of 72 dpi. In some expensive and special purpose screens, it can go to 300 dpi. On the other hand, an average journal in printed form may have resolution at 1,200 dpi.

d) Pricing scheme in vogue is very complicated and some of the services are quite prohibitive. This can hinder libraries from utilising e-journals.

e) Back issues of a journal may be difficult to preserve in the electronic format.

f) Users are not enthusiastic in utilising the information contained in electronic journals, because they are not in a conventional format. However, with the expansion of the service, this inertia would go down.

EVALUATING E-JOURNALS

Since the resources are limited, it would be beneficial to evaluate e-journals on the following parameters :

a) *Economics :* Whether e-journals are going to offer any added value to the users in terms of service? Further, it is to be decided if the print version is also to be subscribed.

b) *User-flexibility :* Whether downloading/printing can be accomplished easily? The downloaded data should be readable on a word-processing programme.

c) *Comprehensiveness :* Whether the e-journal is as comprehensive as its print version? In this context, it is observed that a vast majority of the e-journals are lacking in this aspect.

d) *Archival :* Whether back-up files of the e-journals are available for archival function? If so, whether they are close to the print version? Are they available in HTML format and other formats?

e) *Accessibility :* Whether any password is required to access the e-journal? Is there any limit to the number of simultaneous users? Whether the flow of information becomes slow with the heavy traffic on the system?

f) *Future Assurance :* Whether the service will continue to be made available or will the library eventually be forced to switch on to the print version, after sometime.

g) *Status of Service Provider :* Does it handle publications of a single publisher or of many publishers? If it deals with multiple publishing houses, its capability to provide an efficient service must be assessed and not taken for granted.

h) *User Support :* Does it provide online help to the users? Are there e-mail lists for announcements and updates?

i) *Part of the Service :* Is it possible to subscribe to service in part, limited to a few relevant titles, or to subscribe to the entire database, whether useful or not?

j) *Future Plans :* With the continuous research, there is going to be change in the technology. Is it giving assurance that upgrades would available in case the technology goes absolute?

k) *Copyright / Licensing :* Copyright, licensing and distribution restrictions vary from one provider to another. Electronic publishers have turned from copyright to licensing to establish the rights of the owners. It is essential to review these rights and restrictions, to determine how practices such as inter-library loan, making multiple copies for teaching, archiving and accessing material on multiple terminals are permissible.

l) *Integration with Local Catalogue :* Is it possible to integrate an e-journal with the local catalogue of the library, and other services, such as bibliographic database, table of contents service and document delivery?

CONCLUSION

E-journals are bringing further added dimensions to the librarianship. The new service has a vast potential of providing a quality service. However, in the context of shrinking budgets, it is very essential to evaluate each e-journal, so that the expenditure is justified. As far as the inertia displayed by the users, it is bound to come down with time.

BIBLIOGRAPHY

Singh, Bhupendra Kumar and Singh, Dewendra Kumar, Electronic publishing: The foundation of information society, In Sardana, J.L., (ed.), *Library vision 2010 : Indian Libraries and Librarianship in Retrospect and Prospect*, Indian Library Association, Delhi, 1999, p.311.

Pavelsek, Mary Jean, "Guidelines for evaluating e-journal providers with applications to JSTOR and Project Muse", *Advances in Librarianship*, 22, 1998, 41-4.

30

Emerging Trends in Electronic Journals

S.C. Jindal

INTRODUCTION

Journals constitute an important information resource to researchers, policy makers, teachers and scientists. A large proportion of library budgets is allocated for subscription to journals. Despite their importance these have remained the topic of discussion because of the newly emerging trends in their publication and application of information technology.

The combined effect of developments in computer and telecommunication technologies and their applications have challenged the functioning and services of the libraries and information centres. The libraries have to face these challenges while storing information in digital form, use communication networks to access and obtain information and copying by downloading. With the emergence of internet, particularly world wide web (WWW), the publishing media has been revolutionised, leading to the introduction of electronic journals, which have to be accessed by using computer and communication technologies.[1] The users will be able to access information, bibliographic databases and even primary sources wherever they are located, without country barriers and without visiting libraries.[2] Prior to the emergence of the electronic journal several innovations were suggested and tried with varying degree of success to offset the problems in periodical publications. Several measures aimed at improving the speed of dissemination of information and economics of journal publishing were also tried. These include computer output, micrographic (COM),[3] microform publications, and advance announcement of contents,[4] letters journals[5,6,7] and synopsis journals.[8, 9,10]

During the last four-five years several major publishers and libraries together have tried to exploit WWW as a tool for putting the traditional print journals into the electronic form and providing access over the internet. This effort has increased the confidence of both the publishers and libraries. In this context Herschman had speculated that in the foreseeable future the primary journal, as it is known as now, may be replaced by a computerised central depository with a network of consoles serving the various groups of users.[11] In 1970, a committee of the National Academy of Sciences, USA, predicted that in about three decades, the primary journal would be rendered obsolete by a network of consoles that would facilitate inter-continental and interactive communication.[12] The electronic journal would consist of a distributed network that could provide online access to information to anyone. It would also facilitate an extended spectrum of services such as browsing, retrospective searching, commentaries, and filing systems and data manipulation capability. In about three decades since 1970 when the National Academy of Sciences predicted dominance of electronic format of information, it has become absolutely true; the present era is an era of 'information technology'.

ELECTRONIC JOURNALS

There is no standard and accepted precise definition of an electronic journal. Often e-journals are called virtual journals, scholarly electronic journals, network serials and CD-ROM serials etc.[13] Basically e-journal is one which is available in the electronic form and can be accessed using computer and communication technologies.

Growth of E-Journals

The number of e-journals is growing fast. The *Directory of Electronic, Newsletters, Serials and Academic Discussion Lists* brought out by the Association of Research Libraries published since 1991 gives a clear picture about the growth of e-journals.[14] The popularity and growth of e-journals clearly indicates that internet has been accepted as a tool by many publishers to reach out to the end-users. Electronic journals can either be available in the form of online, CD-ROM and networked e-journals.[15,16,17]

With the development of client/server technology more and more number of e-journals are now being published. Examples of client/server applications being used for publishing e-journals include Gopher, where a desktop gopher client connects to a gopher server and where a desktop client such as Mosaic, Netscape connects to Web Server.[18] During the last few years e-mail, Gopher and WWW have become very popular mode of publishing. So far no uniform format for publishing networked e-journals has been developed. Each publisher is using one or the other mixed format, depending on its requirements.[19]

Advantage of E-Journals

Electronic journals have revolutionised the whole concept of traditional librarianship. It seems now that more weightage is being given to accessibility of information rather than to its holding. The emphasis is on economic accessibility and usage of information. E-journals, availability on internet has brought in number of advantages like interactive searching, availability throughout 24 hours, 365 days and availability of information prior-to-print form for both the libraries and the user community.[20]

CHALLENGES

It is not that e-journals offer just the advantages alone. There are many problems and challenges associated with e-journals. Librarians have been dealing with different formats of reading materials for over many years, but the e-journals have thrown up several issues. Some of them are:

Access vs. Ownership

There is a major shift in information management from owning a serial to accessing it. Most of the publishers like the American Institute of Physics, the American Mathematical Society etc., have announced their subscription policy for e-journals. It indicates that subscription is valid for one year like the print serial. Its cost is marginally less then the corresponding printed version. But if the library does not have sufficient funds to subscribe and own the journal, it can still access it on payment of extra charges per access needed. This being a transition period, several issues related to this aspect are likely to be decided in future.

Collection Development

The important issue to be decided in collection development is whether to have the periodical's collection developed around the printed form or to make use of the new trend emerging in serial publications. With the advent of internet and e-journal, the traditional concept of collection development is undergoing a change. The issues are whether to continue the printed version or subscribe to both printed and electronic version or to subscribe to electronic version only or no subscription at all and pay for use on per access basis. Whether to have single access, multiple access, budget, etc., are some of the issues, which need to be examined. These is a possibility to access journals of all publishers at one point.

Hardware and Software Connections

All libraries cannot afford to have full connectivity to internet with full functions to access, download and preserve e-journals. The cost involved in creating the entire infrastructure for network connectivity and printing may be different in using different e-journals. The National Informatics Centre (NIC), New Delhi and Videsh Sanchar Nigam Limited (VSNL) are offering internet connections with limited facilities like e-mail etc., at cheaper rates but accessibility to full text articles through such connections is still under consideration.

Network Traffic

Due to uncontrolled growth of resources and their accessibility on the internet, there is likelihood of traffic congestion. As a result connectivity will take more time. Data transfer will slow down, hence those who want to search full text articles with graphics and images will have to wait for more time to download information from the server. The United States of America is making efforts to install technology for faster transmission, but for India and individual libraries it may take more time. It seems to be difficult for the librarians to depend on the internet to access e-journals and do away with the traditional print versions.

Economic Factors

This is one of the key factors for the success of e-journals. At present there seems to be no economic advantage to libraries because publishers are allowing e-journals access irrespective of library subscription to print or to electronic version. Electronic version is cheaper by 10 per cent to 20 per cent. These savings will be consumed by overhead costs in maintenance of computer hardware, software, accessories, etc. Elsevier Science has started offering full text articles through its Science Direct service. This is an economic and useful package to access their 1,100 e-journals available through the internet.

Storage and Archiving

Librarians are bound to encounter problems associated with storing and retrieving data, providing printouts, upgrading the retrieval software, and whether new software can handle previously converted data. Though the cost of hard disc is going down considerably yet storage of current as well as back runs will be difficult to cope with.

Standardisation

A standard format for e-journals has not yet been developed. There are several file formats, viz., PDF, SGML, HTML, TEX, ASCII, etc. The libraries will need to have all the necessary software to access, retrieve, view, download and print the articles. The most popular among above are PDF and HTML file formats.

Training and Education

Extensive training programmes would be needed for the librarians as well as users if new technology is going to be adopted. This training in case of print journals would be minimal.

Copyright

It is a major issue for both publishers and librarians to control misuse of e-journals. This is because it is difficult to track down, who is and how much data is being downloaded in an unauthorised way.

Acceptability of Electronic Journals

Acceptability of e-journals by the authors, librarians and end users is another issue on which we still have diverse opinions. It is basically a transition phase. Given the innumerable advantages associated with e-journals it is hoped that the community will accept the new mode.

COST BENEFIT ANALYSIS

Ownership vs Accessibility of Journals

In the last few decades the print media has contributed effectively to the enrichment of intellectual curiosity. However, the increasing cost of print media has had some negative impact on the affordability of journals and publications by the libraries to their clientele. The impact of 'Intranet' has opened up another area of concern. In this context, the demand, supply, utility, productivity, costing and several other related issues in knowledge processing have given rise to the concept of knowledge economics and the users and libraries cannot shy away from the emergening opportunities and threats. The global information marketing, and changing inter-personal relationships between students per group, might call for adapting information technology in libraries.

Elsevier Science, American Chemical Society, Royal Society of Chemistry, Institute of Physics (London), American Physical Society, Cambridge University Press, MacMilan Press, American Association for Advancement of Science and many others academic, professional and commercial organisations have started publishing their serials in the electronic form. They are available for searching through the internet. Commercial database providers like Silver Platter Group have brought out full text articles of 700 and more medical serials on CD-ROM. Similarly, University Microfilms, USA has brought out social sciences, business and management full text serials on CD-ROM. Major abstracting and indexing services, e.g., *Current Contents, Science Citation Index* from the Institute of Scientific Information, Philadelphia, *Chemical Abstracts* from the American Chemical Society, *Biological Abstracts* from Biological Society, USA, INSPEC Abstracts from IEE, UK, *Index Medicus* from NLM, Bethesda, USA, etc., have started their publications electronically on CD-ROM. Some of these services are also available on internet and through commercial database vendors like DIALOG, USA and BRS, UK, etc. The trend reveals a dynamic shift from the print media towards the electronic media. But in the present context of time, optimum combination of both print and electronic medium is advisable. In the print media, the expenditure incurred on print journals becomes a capital asset of the institution for the posteriority. But in the electronic media, the main advantage is that information gets published as and when it is ready for publication, i.e., atleast two months ahead of the corresponding edition in print form. Advance availability of information helps researchers in establishing their research priority as well as avoids duplication in work. Electronic journals through the web allow current as well as back files searching and downloading of full text articles as per the need of the clientele round the clock. Electronic access to serials is a necessity in the present context of speed, communication, competition and economics. If libraries have proper computerised infrastructure with the appropriate number of connectivities, nodes, high speed data communication software and trained personnel, then a shift to the electronic access to a information is advantageous.

Costing of American Chemical Society Web Editions

ACS Web editions provide immediate connectivity to chemistry literature. These deliver information 11 weeks before it appears in the print form, give complete contents of their print counter parts, plus unprecedented convenience and speed. A comparative account of their serial prices in print and web editions is intersting.

The web edition is eight to 10 per cent cheaper than the print edition. Similarly, site licence is 45 per cent costlier than print edition. Print and site licence is approximately 79 per cent costlier than print edition alone. However, the advantages of web edition are: availability of information 11 weeks before its appearance in print, delivery of full content of journal right to desk top, search through key words in titles, abstracts or full text, browsing of author index, table of contents, facility of proximity, boolean logic and back files searching and printing facility. In a big set-up like DU and JNU, site licence could be preferred in which faculty members, while sitting in their faculty, can search the desired information. Web editions would ultimately prove to be cheaper if the acquisition is of very expensive serials and potential users are limited.

Elsevier Electronic Subscriptions

Elsevier Science is the largest serial publisher in the world. It is publishing more than 1,100 serials. It has made significant strides in delivering scientific information in the digital form. Elsevier Science has two electronic journal subscription services, i.e., Science Direct and Elsevier Electronic Subscriptions. It provides remote and local options for accessing electronic full text journal information. They also provide electronic full text access to selected journals on a title-to-title basis. Elsevier Science has further developed its role as an information provider and developing gateway links between Science Direct and the Bio Med Net, Chem Web and Beilstein data basis.

Science Direct Pricing

The pricing for Science Direct consists of three components: (a) Contents Fee, (b) Platform (host) Fee, and (c) Transaction Fee.

a) *Content Fee:* The contents fee represents a charge for having electronic access to the full text articles of the subscribed print journals in Science Direct. The contents fee gives unlimited access to all full text articles of journals that library is subscribing to.

b) *Platform Fee:* The platform fee is an annual charge based on the potential size of an institution, the user community and the type of institute, i.e., corporate or academic or governmental. Platform fee provides services like day-to-day hosting of the system, technical and customer support, integrated linking to document delivery and bibliographic layer.

   The bibliographic layer of Science Direct will ultimately cover almost 4,000 journals in all scientific fields, including 1,100 Elsevier Science serials, dating back to 1992. Bibliographic layer presently consists of approximately 2.8 lakh tables of contents and over three million abstracts, growing with almost 50,000 abstracts every year.

c) *Transaction Fee*: The transaction fee is the fee per article that library pays to access online full text article of non-subscribed Elsevier Science journals. The normal transaction fee is $30 per article. However, for subscriptions it is $15 per article and to a certain number of articles it is free of charge. The Science Direct licence allows for the abstracts of the journal that are covered in the bibliographic layer to be accessed without any additional charge regardless of the subscription that the library holds.

Key benefits of Science Direct for libraries

Science Direct through electronic accessibility of full text articles offers a series of advantages, viz., world wide access, comprehensive literature search, customisation of services and consortium-based economic services.

Science Direct service has shown that if DU and JNU libraries pay an equal amount of print subscriptions of Elsevier's journals, contents fee and platform fee they can avail much more benefits in the form of electronic accessibility service. The basic advantage is that library gets access to full text articles of all 1,100 STM journals and can download them equivalent to contents fee paid to the publishers. The pricing structure shows that libraries can download up to 3,418 articles worth $102,540 (Rs. 44,09,220) free of cost from serials, which are not subscribed by them. Full text access to 1,100 journals at a nominal additional cost is the biggest advantage for the end user community. The subscriptions cost of 1,100 and more Scientific Technical and Medical (STM) serials would be in millions of rupees and all these are available at a nominal additional cost computed on print cost of currently subscribed journals.

Science Direct Pricing Estimate for Delhi University and Jawaharlal Nehru University Libraries

Type of Customer	*Academic*
Number of Subscriptions in 1998	71
Number of Potential Users Site	5,000
Annual Expenditure on Elseviers' Current Subscriptions 1998	US $ 124,511
Annual Expenditure in 1999	US $ 136,340
Estimated Expenditure in 2000	US $ 1,49,292
Contents Fee 1999, 2000	US 21,422 (for two years)
Platform fee 1999, 2000	$ 20,000 (for two years)
Total Science Direct Fee	$ 41,422 (for two years)
Transaction Fee	3,418 articles Free of charge of non-subscribed serials (US $15 per article after the credit is used) (Normal per article delivery is $ 30)

The other advantage of Elsevier's electronic subscription service is bibliographic information and availability of abstracts from approximately 4,000 core journals in all science and technology.

The benefits of such a service to the end users are unlimited. The users will be aware of the latest developments in their disciplines. Secondly, Science Direct has a provision to procure and supply full text articles through its integrated document delivery system. The main advantages are saving the time of users, and availability of the information at the right time, which helps the users in meeting their needs.

The availability and accessibility of information 24 hours a day, while sitting in the laboratory or at home is unbeatable in the context of limited access to journals in the print form. Science Direct and other services through bulk ID domains and passwords allow users to register themselves online. The facility of interactive searching allows them to retrieve information, which otherwise is not possible in print form.

Library can create a database of most useful articles by downloading them. These articles can be made available in the print form or on CD-ROM etc.

DU and JNU libraries both have internet access facility through dedicated V-SAT link. JNU has set up LAN in the whole university campus, where as DU so far has been able to do it partially. Both the libraries have already incurred expenditure in hardware and software. Electronic accessibility to information requires a firm and a long-term decision because it is not like the print media that we can subscribe a serial for one year then discontinue it. In the electronic media, if we discontinue the service, then we will have neither current access nor retrospective access. The electronic access culture demands implementation of the concept of 'Total Quality Management' if libraries really want to come out of financial resource crunch.

Consortium transaction

Pooling of serials would avoid duplication among libraries and the money saved on this account could be utilised for additional electronic accessibility of serials. Secondly, the larger investment clubbed together provide scope for greater discount and cheaper accessibility to serials. Elsevier Science is negotiating licences with consortia for both local and remote electronic services. Both libraries and publishers can benefit from consortia licensing while the benefits of consortia arrangements are most evident with locally held files, when the infrastructure cost is shared by several institutions. It is also possible to construct agreements for licensing to remote access.

CONCLUSION

The present era is an information era. Timely access to information and its availability to patrons is the necessity of time the migration to full text electronic products, documents delivery services is bound to have major impact on libraries. Economic prosperity has direct linkage with the growth of facilities for access to information. More and more libraries are redirecting their funds to offer free, direct on demand article services to patrons. The technology has led to inevitable change in day-to-day working of libraries. Both the central universities, i.e., University of Delhi and the Jawaharlal Nehru University libraries have got dedicated leased lines for internet connection, and necessary network infrastructure for accessing information online. The necessity is to shift to online subscriptions. The study of Elsevier's Science subscriptions and such other services reveals that for seeking information access model is more economical than ownership model. The libraries, especially academic libraries, should give top priority to full-scale automation and accessibility to information, if they want to survive in the near future.

REFERENCES

1. Kumar, T.S. and Sangam, S. L., Emergence of electronic journals; trends and issues, In Mahapatra, M. and others, (eds.), *Access to Information*, Society for Information Science. Bhubneswar, 1997.
2. Dalia, B.K. and others, Libraries in the 21st Century : Challenge of electronic environment, In Mahapatra, M. and others, (eds.) op.cit.

3. Davis, W., Development in auxiliary publications, *Am Doc,* 1951, 7-11.
4. Gannett Elwood, K., Primary publications systems and services, *Ann Rev Inf Sci Tech.*, 1973, 261-62.
5. Subramantam, K. and Schaffer Constrains, J., Effectiveness of letters journals, *New Libr World,* 1974, 75, 258-9.
6. Grogan Danis, J., *Science and Technology: An introduction to literature,* Ed 5, Clive Bingley; London, 1982, p.157.
7. Davinson, D.E., *Periodicals Collection: Its purpose and use in libraries,* Andre Deutsch, London, 1969. p.50.
8. Pinie, N.W., Note on simultaneous publications of papers at two different levels of completeness, In *Royal Society Scientific Information Conference Reports and Papers,* Royal Society; London, 1948, pp.419-22.
9. Bernal, J.D., Transmission of scientific information: A user's analysis, *In International Conference on Scientific Information: Proceedings*, National Academy of Sciences; Washington, 1969, pp. 87-95.
10. Phipps, T.E., Scientific communication, *Science,* 1954, 129, p.119.
11. Herschman Arthor, "Primary journal: Past, present and future", *J Chem Doc,* 1970, 10, 37-42.
12. Senders, J.W. and others, *Scientific Publications Systems : An analysis of past, present, and future method of scientific information,* Springfield, 1975.
13. Sasse Margo and Winkler, B.Jean, Electronic journals: A formidable challenge for libraries, *Adv Libr.,* 1993, 17, 149-73.
14. *Directory of Electronic News Letters, Serials, and Discussion Lists,* Ed 6, Association of Research Libraries; Washington, 1996.
15. Woodward Hazel and Mcnight Cliff, Electronic journals: Issues of access and bibliographic control, *Ser Review,* 1995, p.72.
16. Taubes Gary, Science journals go wired, *Science,* 271, 1996, pp.764-66.
17. Banerjee, S.K., Growth of CD-ROM technology, In Mahapatra, M and others, (eds.), op.cit.
18. Woodward Hazel, op.cit. p.72.
19. Hickey Thomas, B., Present and future capabilities of the online journals, *Libr Trends,* 1995, 43, 528-43.
20. Malinconico Micheal, "Electronic documents and research libraries", *IFLA* Journal, 1996, 22, 211-25.

31

Multimedia: An Emerging Resource for Information Centres and Libraries

Nishat Fatima

INTRODUCTION

Multimedia means providing information through various media. Earlier multimedia was held as a futuristic technology. The storage, transmission, communication, representation, presentation of outputs, interactions, perceptions and all different levels of abstraction can happen on a PC. The PC technology is so powerful that it can integrate several different forms of media (i.e., text, audio, visual, graphics, animatory (TAVGA), etc., on a single product. The commonly available examples of multimedia products are audio, discs, video tapes, TV, etc.

According to Ramaiah, "Multimedia is a process that can handle text, still images, video sound and animated graphics."[1] Hoffos believes that multimedia is "a presentation stored on a single medium and that it must contain at least three media out of text data, audio, computer graphics still photos, animation moving footage (film or video)."[2]

The word multimedia has been grossly misused. Its precise comprehension is still difficult by people. Thus there is a need to find a precise definition of multimedia.

HYPERTEXT, MULTIMEDIA AND HYPERMEDIA

There is a growing interest in the use of hypertext as a user friendly way of accessing textual information. It has provided the medium to link any two objects that show relationship of some kind with each other. This word was first coined by Nelson in 1965. Hypertext is the communication of natural language text for interactive branching. It is applied for dynamic display of a non-linear text which cannot be printed conveniently on a conventional page. In other words, hypertext provides non-sequential access to textual information stored in a database. A simple hypertext system consists of nodes connected to each other through links. Depending upon the complexity of the system, it may support nodes and links of more than one type.

Hypermedia is similar to hypertext. Instead of linking just the text, it can be used to link several media such as graphics, video, spread sheets, animations, and voices in the computer. Hypermedia means non-linear organisation of all the information chunks.

Multimedia is an extension of hypertext with which one can link corpus of materials that includes text, static graphics animated graphics, video sound, music, etc. Multimedia products are many media integrated products wherein content linkages do not conform to any particular method of organisation.

ADVANTAGES OF MULTIMEDIA AND HYPERMEDIA

Multimedia applications involve integration of various media of information in its natural form. These applications deal with information as it exists in physical systems. Basic mechanism for perceiving a physical system for human beings is the audio-visual media. Worldwide efforts have been made for quite sometime to integrate audio and video on a single platform.

Such efforts might lead to combining the power of TV multimedia communication with intelligent capabilities of the PC.

Under the control of a computer all the material in a multimedia programme can be retrieved and processed with as much flexibility as any computer data is retrieved and processed. The text can be complemented with illustrations of any kind. The added dimensions of interactivity means that the person on front of the screen can ask and answer questions and make decisions.

Hypermedia and multimedia are methods of using computerisation to improve access to a range of information carriers. In the computer world, multimedia refers to software programmes that use more than one method of communicating information to the users such as, television, audio, video, graphics, and animation and/or combination of all. Any software that uses graphic images such as chart and maps to illustrate the text information displayed on the computer screen is an example of multimedia.

However, more recently multimedia has come to mean more than the integration of text and simple graphics images (animation) on an ordinary PC. It is possible to view simultaneously Windows containing text, still graphics images, while listening to an explanation of what is being seen on the screen.

PREREQUISITES FOR MULTIMEDIA

Usually there are five components in multimedia software, the four of which are text, graphics, animations and sound, the fifth component being interactive links that integrate the whole program by giving the user a way to interact with the programme and cause things to happen.

Text

Text is usually available in printed documents in different forms, viz., full text, bibliographical indexes, etc. Text is the basis for word processing programmes and is the fundamental information used in most of the multimedia programme. In fact, multimedia package often involve the conversation of book to computerised form, allowing the users to look up information quickly.

Graphic Images

Graphic images generally mean a "still image", viz., photographs, online drawings or graphs. They play an important role in the presentation of data of any research and development work. For any human being visual material and pictures are a powerful means to illustrate information. Whether on a piece of paper or on the computer screen graphics, images therefore form an important component of multimedia.

Animation

Like graphics, image animations refer to moving picture or video, and these are also a powerful media for communication of information.

Sound

Sound can substantially reinforce our understanding of information presented by other ways. Inclusion of sound in a multimedia programme serves as a more powerful and useful tool to provide information to users. Multimedia thus, enhances the learning experience by involving all our senses.

World Wide Web

World Wide Web (WWW) is a hypertext system built on top of the internet. It is the result of a project initiated by Berners Lee et al., at (CERN) (the European Centre for Practical Physics) in Geneva. This project defined the architecture of retrieval system for distributed information. It allows information stored in host computers or servers to be accessed by client computers connected to the servers across a wide area network. The term WWW is used to refer to the retrieval system and to the body of information stored on the internet.

Over the last two years, electronic access has been provided to all sorts of things which were earlier difficult to obtain, ranging from manuscripts to technical manuals. Much of this sort of material has colour graphics and typeset appearance. With the new technologies such as Java coming in for applications, web pages are starting to have sound and animation. This has increased user expectations about obtaining published materials more conventionally.

In general, the transfer of objects of different types are enabled by the specifications of corresponding protocols. A protocol is a set of standard definitions that allows the communicating computers to recognise the types of objects they are dealing with and the method by which they should be transferred. Web has its own protocol (HTTP). This protocol allows information to be retrieved with hypertext links between objects that are stored on widely dispersed computers.

The logical mark-up language is used to create documents in which the sources and targets of hypertext links are defined in a standard manner.

Several browsers, or readers, are available. They act as interface to the web's client software. The most popular of the web's client software is Netscape Explorer.

CHARACTERISTICS OF WEB

The Web has some characteristics that are responsible for its rapid growth and wide spread acceptance:

a) It is a multimedia information system, and thus has a facility for displaying objects of several non-textual types, and for preserving the unique "look and feel" of objects from different sources.

b) It is interactive

c) Web is global in nature thus permitting the unrestricted dissemination and use of sets of information objects of all types.

Problems in Using Multimedia in Libraries

a) Generally libraries are regarded as fairly traditional and conservative institutions. Besides, there is apprehension that the arrival of the new multimedia materials in some way signifies the decline of the book.

b) Some of the new multimedia materials such as sound tapes are similar in price to books. However, other materials, such as videotapes, can appear expensive.

c) Furthermore, the equipment required to use multimedia materials is expensive to purchase. Besides, it has a high rate of obsolescence, a fact often overlooked. Multimedia products are very costly to maintain. The costs of media materials and of associated equipments can prove to be a major obstacle to its extension in the library.

d) The variety of materials varying in size, shape, and format often presents problem in relation to library storage and access procedure, such as lengthy television recordings can prove heavy and cumbersome.

e) Size and nature of the multimedia is also the main problem in storage and distribution. Graphics, photographs, animations, sound, etc., normally require very large disc space which often exceeds the memory of large computers also.

CONCLUSION

Multimedia has special applications in research and education. There is no doubt that it has created a new revolution and opened up new ways of presenting the information. Librarians must strive to develop the multimedia resources.

REFERENCES

1. Ramaiah, C.K., Is hypertext a more flexible teaching tool for education?, *Ann. Lib. Sci. Doc.,* 18, 3, 1992, pp.198-9.
2. Roberts Stephen, Towards a pocket library, *IFLA J.*, 1992, 18, 3, p.262.

BIBLIOGRAPHY

Hoffos S., Introduction to interactive multimedia, *Programme,* 27, 4, 1993, pp.323-9.

Kawachi K., Multimedia and libraries: Special features, *Lib. Jour.*, 88, 10, 1994, pp.733-52.

Pinion Catherine F., Special issues on audio-visual librarianship and multimedia technology, *IFLA J*, 18, 3, 1992, pp.198-9.

Ramaiah, Hypertext and hypermedia: Overview, *Desidoc Bull Info. Tech.*, 12, 6, 1992, pp.3-13.

Singh, S.N. and Garg, B.S., Role of multimedia hypermedia (MM/HM) in biomedical information services in India, Ann. *Lib. Sci. Doc.*, 42, 1, 1999, pp.40-3.

Barkea, Teror, Using and designing multimedia in colleges: Some considerations, *Lear. Res. Jour.*, 11 (3), 1995, pp.53-57.

Gillsepie John, Best Biys: What to collect in multimedia?, *Lib. Jour.*, 120, 2, 1995, pp.40-3.

Part VII

Librarianship, Management and Status

32

ALA Support to Libraries in the Third World Countries

R.N. Sharma

INTRODUCTION

The American Library Association (ALA) is the oldest and the largest national library association in the world. It was founded in October 1876 by seven men including Melvil Dewey, Justin Windsor, Samuel Green, and Charles Cutter, and today the Association has over 58,000 members. The mission of this unique and a powerful association is "to provide leadership for the development, promotion, and improvement of library and information services and the profession of librarianship in order to enhance learning and ensure access to information for all."[1] The Association "maintains a close working relationship with more than 70 other library associations in the United States, Canada, and other countries. . . ."[2]

ALA's involvement in international librarianship started in 1949 but the progress has been very slow until Barbara Ford was elected President of ALA in 1996. She decided to devote her presidential year to international librarianship and chose the theme "Libraries: Global Reach - Local Touch". During 1997-1998, ALA certainly did many things for the international librarianship including inviting speakers from many countries, publishing many articles in *American Libraries* and *College & Research Libraries News*. In addition, there were over one hundred meetings scheduled on international librarianship, a poster session, receptions for foreign librarians, and over 300 librarians from other countries including India were invited to attend the ALA Conference held in Washington, D.C. in June 1998.

ASIAN AMERICANS & THEIR CONTRIBUTIONS

This type of activity is very new for the members of ALA but some of its members including Dr. C.C. Chen, of the Simmons College, Ms. Poe of the Library of Congress, and this author, have been very active in international librarianship for a long time. It is very difficult to talk about one's own contributions to promote any cause, but it is time to write and say openly that several Asian Americans did take the lead in international librarianship and are still active in international librarianship. This includes promoting cooperation among librarians from all countries.

In 1975 when the author hosted the Asian Conference at Colgate University in Hamilton, New York, it was concluded at that conference that there was a need to have a catalogue of Asian materials in the United States. A report of the conference was published in the *College & Research Libraries News*, *NYLA Bulletin*, and the *Indian Librarian*. Despite the fact that the Library of Congress was involved in the Foreign Acquisitions Program for Asia (then known as PL480 Program) since 1962, it was for the first time that a librarian drew attention to the fact for the need of a national catalogue for the Asian materials.

In January 1986 OCLC came up with an idea of a CJK (Chinese/Japanese/Korean materials) database which has been part of the OCLC's WorldCat (Online Union Catalog) since May 12, 1986. On this historic day, the first CJK record was entered in the WorldCat. As of February 1998 there were 1,555,347 entries in the CJK database within the OCLC WorldCat.[3] WorldCat is certainly a unique records of a few Asian language entries including Chinese, Japanese, Korean, Mongol, Tibetan,

Urgur, and Vietnamese. This project has been very successful. OCLC has an Asian/Pacific Division which has progressed very well, under the able leadership of Andrew Wang, to attract many libraries from the Asia/Pacific region to become members of OCLC. At present, over 700 libraries in the Asian/Pacific region use OCLC products and services.[4]

Support for Conference Activity

The author made efforts to organise conferences and achieved success in this endeavour to some extent with the help of his colleagues. Mention must made of his efforts in organising Asian/Pacific American Librarians Association (APALA) Conferences in 1990-91, 1993-94, and 1997-98. The theme of our Atlanta Conference in 1991 was "Changing Dimensions: Making Library and Information Services for the 1990s: A Global Perspective". Three distinguished speakers including Dr. Vinod Chachra, President of VTLS, Dr. W. David Penniman, then President of the Council on Library Resources, and Jordan M. Scepanski, then Director of the University Library and Learning Resources, California State University, Long Beach, spoke at the conference.

In 1994, at Miami, the theme of the conference was "Linking Asian/Pacific Collections to America". Four distinguished speakers including Dr. Kul Gauri, Dean of Library Services, Macomb Community College, Detroit, Michigan, Dr. Warren Tsuneishi, Chief of the Asian Division Library of Congress, and Andrew Wang of OCLC, spoke to the delegates.

In 1992, the author had the distinct honour of organising two major conferences. In April 1992, it was a session on "Research and Academic Librarians: A Global View" during the Sixth National Conference of the Association of College and Research Libraries (ACRL) at Salt Lake City, Utah. Six speakers were invited from Australia, Brazil, England, India, Kenya, and Russia to speak on the topic. It was the first time in the history of the American Library Association and ACRL that speakers from all continents came to the United States to speak in a library conference on the same topic and on the same stage. It was the beginning of a new era in the American Librarianship. In 1998, ALA's theme for the Conference was "Libraries: Global Reach - Local Touch". Barbara Ford invited many speakers from other countries including Professor P.B. Mangla from India who spoke at the Mid-Winter Conference in January in New Orleans. The author had assessed the needs of librarians in the United States and had concluded that there was a need to invite a speaker from Asia to give first-hand information on the progress libraries are making in South Asia.

In August 1992, the author organised a Pre-IFLA Conference in New Delhi, India. Librarians and library educators from all South Asian countries (Bangladesh, Bhutan, India, Pakistan, Nepal, Sri Lanka and the Maldives Islands), and the United States attended this meet. It was the first joint conference of South Asian and American librarians, and it was the first time that South Asian librarians came together to discuss common problems of librarianship in that region. Professor P.B. Mangla of India played the key role in organising this successful conference in Delhi. Prof J.L. Sardana was the organising secretary of this meet. The author was very successful in raising funds for all conferences organised in the Unites States as well as in India. The first Chinese American joint conference was organised as a Pre-IFLA Conference in Beijing in 1996 by Dr. H. Lee, then Dean of Libraries at Ohio University, Athens, on the model and high standards set by the Delhi Conference.

Assessing Library Needs through Library Visits

In the area of committees, the author has served on many committees and chaired a few committees of both American Library Association (ALA) and the Association of College and Research Libraries (ACRL) which has given him a chance to look deeply into libraries and their problems in South Asia and the Near East. In 1997, in a Northern Ireland Study Tour organised by the British Council he had visited many academic, special, and public libraries. Libraries in Northern Ireland are progressing well, like American libraries, and they have introduced technology in their libraries. Queens University Library of Belfast has an excellent collection. They have recently opened a new wing to the library which has 500 computers in it with internet access. They use OCLC and many British databases for their research needs. This new addition to the library has been named after one of their alumnus, Seamus Heaney, who won the Nobel Prize for Literature in 1994. In spite of the religious differences in Ireland and Northern Ireland, librarians work together without any major problems. They have one library association called the Library Association of Ireland and Northern Ireland, and one library journal, entitled *Ann Leabhar Lann: The Irish Library*, for both countries.[5] This type of cooperation in the field of library and information science is needed in other countries also.

As the chair of the Near East and South Asia Sub-Committee of the International Relations Committee of ALA from1996-1998, the greatest challenge before the author has been to assess libraries in Palestine. He led a delegation of American librarians to Palestine in November 1997. This was the first official delegation of American librarians to visit Palestinc and their visit was approved by the American Library Association. The delegation visited all types of libraries and were shocked to see the conditions of libraries. They met with students, faculty, librarians, deans, and presidents of academic institutions. One would be surprised to know that there are no public, special, or school libraries. There is no national library of Palestine. There are no library schools to train librarians, and no library association. Most of the collections in academic libraries are small and out of date. There are only a few librarians to help students and faculty in their research needs. Library budgets are very small, and there is no money to buy periodicals, and there are no collection development policies. Technology has been used on a limited scale.[6] The delegation were informed by officials of the Ministry of Education that money has been allocated for the first time to libraries in budgets of all institutions. They would like to connect their libraries with libraries of other countries through the Internet. They would like to build their own national library to preserve their history, and have research collections for the benefit of their children, young adults, adults, and grandchildren. Forty-six per cent of the population in Gaza is under the age of 15. The delegation had the distinct honour to meet with President Yasar Arafat. In an exclusive interview, he said, "We are the highest educated people in the Arab world . . . out of every 1,000 people, 18 have Master's and/or PhD degrees." He added, "We need books, we need journals, we need technology to build the future of our children and the nation. All help will be appreciated."[7] They were touched to see the libraries, and the delegation is of the view that Palestinians need help to develop their libraries. It will take a long time to bring the library system in Palestine to the level of where it should be. It won't be easy and won't happen overnight. And it won't be done without international help.[8] The author drafted a resolution on the Libraries of the Gaza Strip and West Bank. It was presented to the International Relations Committee on June 30, 1998, and passed by the Committee.[9] Ron Chepesiuk, contributing editor of the *American Libraries*, and the author have published about 15 articles and interviews since their visit to Gaza Strip, in different journals on this topic including in *American Libraries*, *College & Research Libraries News, International Leads,* and *Library Times International*. A report entitled *Libraries and Education in Palestine: A Field Report* edited by this author and Ron Chepesiuk was published in 1999 which will help this emerging nation of Palestine to develop their libraries.[10]

The author enjoys this type of challenge to bring libraries and librarians from all parts of the world closer to each other. It gives him happiness when people respond. One professor from Israel donated 60 books to a library in Gaza, after reading an article in the January 1998 issue of *American Libraries*, and wrote to the author, "I am supportive of the peace process, and feel that donating books is as important as demonstrating at Rabin Square or opposite the Prime Minister's office."[11] A European librarian wrote, "Let me congratulate you on your trip, your courage, your success. While reading the article in *American Libraries*, I was tremendously impressed by your visit with Chairman Arafat and by the details of your fact-finding trip in the Gaza. . . . Palestinian people [are] obviously worthy of assistance. Thanks to you . . . facts about the dire situation of their libraries are finally coming to light. You have my sincere admiration for your efforts."[12] We are librarians and must be willing to help libraries and librarians all over the world regardless of where we live and work.

Addressing Problems through Journal Publications

This author has been editor of *Library Times International* since 1984. It is the only publication which brings news from the library world together in one newsletter. Many articles on Asia and the Near East[13], have been published, and well-known librarians from Asia and other countries including IFLA and ALA presidents, national librarians of Canada, England, and the United States, and Dr. Wayne Smith, former President and CEO of OCLC, and Jay Jordan, present President and CEO of OCLC have been interviewed. Though the author has presented papers in many national and international conferences in many countries including India, Mexico, Thailand and the United States, it was indeed an honour to be invited twice by IFLA in the 1990s to present papers at IFLA conferences in Delhi and Bangkok in 1992 and 1999 respectively. In 1998, he was invited by Dr. Maurce Line, Chair of the Editors Round Table, IFLA, to assess the quality of library and information science journals of South Asia and present his findings at the 65th IFLA Conference held in Bangkok in August 1999. The paper was well received and published in the January 2000 issue of the *IFLA Journal*.

As associate editor of *International Leads* (1996-1999), a publication of the International Relations Round Table (IRRT) of ALA, this author gave international coverage, and an attractive format to the journal. These changes were made because he believes in true partnership, cooperation, internationalism and globalisation in the library profession. Editing two journals and serving on editorial boards of other publications has given him good knowledge of library affairs in the world, and he is always happy to share his experiences with other librarians. His books and articles have focused on Indian librarianship, research, academic libraries, the late Dr. S.R. Ranganathan, library administration, and library instruction. It is always good to review books on libraries of other countries because you always learn, share, and write about your experiences. He has reviewed books on libraries in Asia, Africa, Europe, Latin America, Russia, North America, American and British Library Associations and has built his private library collection on Asian and international librarianship.

Support for Academic Excellence

The author has evaluated professional degrees of many Indian librarians who have migrated from India to Canada and the United States. He was Chair of the Country Resource Panel for India from 1987 to 1998, a committee of the International Education Committee of ALA. Both Indian librarians as well as deans/chairs of library schools in Canada and the United States, and many employers in both countries, who hired many talented librarians and library educators of Indian origin, have accepted his recommendations and suggestions. It is indeed a pleasure to see one's fellow librarians from Asia grow and do well on this continent. The Asians are familiar with both the American educational system as well as systems in countries of their birth which has been their strength. In turn, they have succeeded in guiding many young librarians and library educators in the United States. The library world has changed tremendously due to the introduction of technology. It has brought many nations closer through libraries. Many doctoral students in the field of library and information science from India have written their dissertations on cooperation, technology, and other subjects of mutual interest to Indian and Western nations. The author has acted as an external examiner for many dissertations from the University of Delhi and Panjab University, and given his opinion about the quality of writing and subject areas covered in those dissertations. Many students had to revise their dissertations because he has been an advocate of quality performance and made sure that the dissertations approved for the degree of PhD were excellent and ready for publication in book form, and that students receiving the degree of PhD were ready with their indepth knowledge of the subject to guide students, librarians, and others.

Establishing Exchange Programme

The author has worked with librarians, library educators, and other professionals from India, Bangladesh, Pakistan, Sri Lanka, Nepal, and Bhutan, and they are pleased with the efforts to bring libraries, library educators, librarians, and other professions closer to each other. Further, they are eager to have more closer cooperation with American librarians and libraries. He has enjoyed developing librarians and libraries, but the happiest moment of his life was in 1999 when he received a grant of $250,000 from the United Negro College Fund and United States of America International Development (USAID). Under this grant, his library got a chance to establish a relationship with the National University of Benin in West Africa. According to the proposal, six librarians will come to his institution in three years (1999-2002) to learn about American librarianship with emphasis on technology, and six librarians from West Virginia State College Library will visit Benin, a French-speaking country, to learn about African librarianship and help the National University of Benin to develop collections, library instruction and introduce more technology in their library. The process has already started with exchange of librarians. The librarians, in addition to learning about African librarianship and developing the library in Benin are learning the French language, and librarians from Benin are learning the English language as well as the ways American academic libraries function with the help of technology and well trained professional librarians and the support staff. It is a remarkable partnership between the two institutions. It will be possible to help the National University of Benin to develop their librarians and the library with emphasis on technology. At least 50,000 dollars will be spent to update the collection and introduce technology. At the end of three years grant, the State College Library will become a selective depository of the Benin's publications (with emphasis on government documents) in the United States to serve the needs of American and other scholars. We have in fact already started collecting books on Benin for our collection.

Overview

There are only a few Asian American librarians and library educators like Dr. Hwa-Wei Lee of the Ohio University, Dr. C.C. Chen of the Graduate School of Library and Information Science, Simmons College, Helen Poe, Chief of the Asian Division, Library of Congress, Andrew Wang of OCLC, Dr. Fazle Kabir, of the School of Library and Information Science, Atlanta University, and this author, who have worked hard to share their knowledge with librarians, library educators, and others from many countries through their writings, organising conferences, presenting papers, consulting, visiting, advising, editing, writing reports, and other activities. With our limited resources, time, and under present circumstances, they have done very well. During the last nine years, three of the Asian American librarians and library educators, namely, Drs. Chen, Lee and the author have been recipients of the prestigious Humphry/OCLC/Forest Press/ALA Award for their contributions to the international librarianship. The American

Library Association needs to do more to promote international librarianship and pay attention to Asian/Pacific nations. Over two billion people live in Asia alone and countries like India and China have rich civilisations which are over 5,000 years old. Institutions of higher learning and libraries flourished in both India and China before they had their birth in other countries. During the Indus Valley Civilisation, a few Indian universities had multistorey library buildings including those at Taxila and Nalanda, and they were well-known in the world for the quality of education, higher standards, and excellent library collections. It is sad to know that out of over 58,000 ALA members, only about 700 belong to the International Relations Round Table which was established in 1949 and is still dominated by one race. A committee on International Relations was formed in 1900 but its activities have been limited because of various reasons including perhaps lack of interest in international librarianship, and not appointing experienced and well-known Asian American librarians and library educators to this important committee of ALA. The International Relations Office of ALA was founded in 1942 with a grant from the Rockefeller Foundation but the Office was closed in 1947 when the grant ended. The ALA at present has the International Relations Office which has been functioning for about 13 years on a full-time basis at their headquarters in Chicago, Illinois.

Personally speaking, the author has enjoyed assessing the needs of libraries in South Asia, the Near East, West Africa, and other parts of the world. It has been a pleasure extending help to librarians and libraries. He has enjoyed meeting librarians, students, visiting libraries, interviewing director of libraries, deans, presidents, and other high officials to learn about their library needs, assess their library needs, and find solutions to their library problems. If his participation, suggestions, and efforts have helped to make a little difference in libraries, librarianship, and in the lives of librarians and library educators, he is very happy. The author assures young librarians, library educators, and administrators that as long as he lives, his efforts to make a difference in international librarianship will continue for the benefit of the profession and all professionals.

CONCLUSION

Finally, to quote the words of an English poet, Rudyard Kipling, who wrote in 1889, "East is East, and West is West, and never the twain shall meet." Times have changed due to the introduction of technology and many other factors including efforts and contributions of a few librarians. They have brought librarians and libraries from East and West much closer during the last 20 years than it had been done in over one hundred years in the history of American Library Association. The Asian Americans should be proud of our personal experiences, efforts, and contributions to the new global village, and the difference they have made in our profession because of their active participation, commitment, and interest in diversity. It is sincerely hoped that more librarians will become interested in international cooperation in librarianship and carry on the torch into the twenty-first century to fulfil the mission started by some of us in the last quarter of the twentieth century.

REFERENCES

1. *ALA Handbook of Organisation* 1999-2000, American Library Association, Chicago, IL, 1999, p. 8.
2. Ibid, p.8.
3. Correspondence with OCLC, May 7, 1998.
4. Ibid.
5. Sharma, R.N., Academic Libraries in Northern Ireland, *Library Times International,* 13 April 1997, pp. 37-40.
6. American Librarians Visit Northern Ireland, *College & Research Libraries News,* 1997, 58, March, 1997, p. 149.
7. Libraries and Librarianship in Palestine, *Library Times International* 15, October, 1998, p. 13-14.

8. Chepesiuk, Ronald J., Field Trip to Palestinian Libraries Yields Audience With Arafat, *American Libraries* 29, January 1998, pp. 40-42.
9. Chepesiuk, Ronald J., and R.N. Sharma, Gazastrip/West Bank Libraries. Resolution Passed by ALA International Relations Committee, *International Leads,* 12 September 1998, p. 2.
10. Sharma, R.N. and Ronald J. Chepesiuk, *Libraries and Education in Palestine:A Field Report*, Near East and South Asia Subcommittee/International Relations Committee/American Library Association. Chicago, IL, 1999, pp. 1-102.
11. E-mail received from Ethel R. Magal, Israel, dated January 28, 1998.
12. E-mail received from Opritsa Popa, USA, dated January 7, 1998.
13. Sharma, R.N., Development of Library and Information Science Periodicals In Asia With Emphasis On South Asia: Problems and Solutions. *IFLA Journal,* 26 January 2000.

33

Paradoxes of Managing University Libraries—An Overview

V.K. Nanda

INTRODUCTION

Of late the problems of managing university libraries have been multiplying and the operation of these libraries as dynamic instruments of education and as disseminators of information is becoming increasingly complex and perplexing. The problems are of various dimensions involving issues which emanate from dealing with a large body of human, educational, financial and infrastructural resources, besides mechanisation, computerisation and networking of library services.

University libraries today are no longer the kind of institutions that they were till few decades ago when they were considered as part of an ivory tower. They are now being thought of as practical instruments, institutions to render meaningful services to the students, teachers and researchers. Besides, they have to account for every aspect of their performance. It is, therefore, high time that senior members in university libraries be reminded of these problems and equipped with the necessary managerial skills to enable them to deal with the emerging problems.

GENESIS AND DEVELOPMENT OF UNIVERSITY LIBRARIES

India today has become the second largest university system in the world. At the time of our Independence, i.e., in 1947, there were only 20 universities. In 2000, this number has risen to 272, of which there are 15 central universities set up by Acts of Parliament, 164 state universities set up by Act of State Legislature, 39 deemed to be universities set up under the UGC Act. These 272 universities include nine open universities and 34 agricultural universities. The remaining 11 are institutions of national importance and four other independent institutions.

All these institutions have to carry out their academic function with the support of libraries attached to them. The quantitative expansion of university libraries resulting from increased number of universities is heartening but the qualitative aspect has so far been not given proper attention. The planners and educational administrators did not give due importance to the fact that higher education also requires the assimilation of a vast amount of knowledge. Classroom teaching can only serve a small part of the requirement since it can only give the students an outline of what they need to know. The students need study material to form their own judgement. Faculties need literature to pursue research and teaching. With this in view the Indian government and the University Grants Commission had appointed a number of commissions and committees such as :

a) The Radhakrishnan Commission (1948-49 under the chairmanship of Dr. S. Radhakrishnan)
b) The Library Committee (UGC-1957 under the chairmanship of Dr. S. R .Radhakrishnan)
c) The Review Committee of Library (UGC-1961)
d) The Kothari Commission (UGC 1983 under the chairmanship of Dr. D. S. Kohtari)
e) The Mehrotra Committee (UGC-1983 under the chairmanship of Prof. R.C. Mehrotra)

f) Committee on National Policy on Library and Information System (Government of India, Department of Culture, 1985 under the chairmanship of Prof. D.P. Chattopadhyaya)

g) Curriculum Development Committee on Library and Information Science (UGC-1990-93) and.

h) Rastogi Committee (1997-98 under the chairmanship of R.P. Rastogi).

All these committees and commissions were headed by a galaxy of learned educationists and were fully aware of the role of libraries and librarians in the stupendous enterprise of higher education which makes a direct contribution to the advancement of knowledge. They not only recognised but reiterated again and again the need for uptodate, effective and efficient library services in support of teaching and research work at the tertiary level.

Highlighting the cardinal role of a library these commissions and committees on higher education and universities referred to libraries by impressive names such as "the heart of the university", "fulcrum of the university education", "the workshop of the scholars," "the laboratory of the learned" etc., and unanimously emphasised that neglect of libraries would damage the teaching departments themselves. The commissions and committees also went ahead to decry the attitude of the authorities in relegating the library to a secondary position or useless accessory and recommended various measures for the improvement and development of university libraries.

The commissions and committees realised that the development of university and college library and information services in higher education is a very complex process which involves strategic planning, identification and acquisition of information, the management of information materials, implementation of automation system, use of building and equipment and use of staff for dissemination of information for the development of human mind and intellect. For a service-oriented administration of a library it was considered imperative to invest in it for high class versatile management, leadership and direction.

Recognising the vital role that the librarian and the library staff play in the development of "university library", these Commissions and Committee recommended a faculty status for university and college librarians placing a librarian on per with a university professor, deputy librarian on par with a reader and assistant librarian on par with a lecturer.

With such well defined goals of university and college libraries in the higher education and high ideals set up for the librarians managing these libraries, one wonders why the libraries are not playing a vibrant role of intellectual workshops for cross fertilisation of ideas and serving as centres for perpetuating and extending the horizons of knowledge. There are several issues which need to be highlighted. An attempt is made here to bring to the notice of all concerned these issues so that they may be tackled appropriately.

IMPROPER PLACEMENT OF THE LIBRARY

Broadly speaking, a university has two wings: teaching and administrative. The teaching wing through its representation in various decision making bodies becomes legal authority of the university. The administrative wing implements the decisions as per rules, i.e., bye-laws, ordinances, etc. The place of the library is still undefined. It is neither attached fully with the teaching wing nor forms part of the administrative unit. Taking advantage of this ambiguity the administrative wings of many universities are still looking at the university library as a section of its general administration. This is happening till date in spite of the recognition and acceptance by the UGC, the recommendations of the Ranganathan Committee which prescribed a new approach and outlook to be adopted on the problems of the university libraries. *Inter-alia* the annual report for 1959-60, the UGC specially recorded its resolve:

> The report of the Library Committee....... to which a references was made in our previous report, have since been adopted by us and are to form the basis for guidance in the construction, development, and administration of University Libraries.

This was a major policy decision and was given effect to under UGC letter no. F68-2/60 (SS) dated January 18, 1961.

The UGC not only accepted the Ranganathan Committee recommendations but also decided to make it the basis for future planning of the university libraries. In spite of such an unequivocal endorsement of the recommendations of the Ranganathan Committee the libraries are still groping to find their separate entity with representation in all the decision-making bodies of the university.

As a result of the above, whenever development grants are allotted to the universities by the UGC or MHRD they are shared between teaching and administrative wings. The library is left alone with a begging bowl for alms except, of course, funds for the books and periodicals, as if the buying of books and periodicals is the sole purpose of the library. Even resources needed to make these books and periodicals serviceable are left out.

ABSENCE OF NORMS AND POLICIES FOR THE DEVELOPMENT OF UNIVERSITY LIBRARIES

The University Grants Commission has not been able to evolve standards and policies which could serve as effective guidelines for the development and coordination of university libraries. More than 45 years back Dr. S.R. Ranganathan conducted a workshop on workflow, and recommended certain standards for staff strengthing in academic libraries. He even recommended a mathematical staff formula, which if applied, would make it easy and necessary for the authorities to grant the staff in an informal way. Inspite of the fact that this formula was part of the recommendations of the Ranganathan Committee, the university libraries are getting a stepmotherly treatment from the administrative wings as well as from the UGC who are reluctant to grant staff on the basis of this formula. The libraries, therefore, continue to deteriorate under the increasing overweight of demand and supply of staff for proper library services. To understand this paradox one needs to read the UGC guidelines for Development Assistance to Central, Deemed and State Universities during the IXth Plan where on page 9 under the heading Books/ and Journals, it is stated "The amount up to 10% under this item may be utilised for providing stacking facilities including furniture and equipment in the library." This is contrary to the earlier practice of development grants for books and periodicals during the previous five-year plans which authorised the libraries to utilise half of the service charge, i.e., 10 per cent (later increased to 15%) of the Books and Periodicals Grant for engagement of temporary staff for processing of the books purchased under the head. Authorities, therefore, need to be reminded that books purchased are not to be dumped; they are to be made serviceable; and the funds needed to meet the administrative costs of making these books serviceable have to be obtained.

LIBRARIES CONSIDERED AS NON-CRISIS SERVICE

Very few officials in the administrative wing of the university and teachers are disturbed at the deterioration or absence of library services for sometime. This is clearly reflected by frequent cuts in the library budget, whenever a financial crunch is faced by the universities. The librarian may be under constant pressure from the students and the teachers for normal services if not more, but the administrative wing often disregards the library's needs. Perhaps, the major reason for such a situation is that authorities in most of the universities work from crisis to crisis. Most of the major decisions are taken under pressure. In such situations libraries suffer the most. Since decisions are taken for short-terms gains the libraries run into long-term crisis.

NON-FILLING OF TOP POSTS

There is a growing tendency, adopted by the administrative wings of the universities, to delay the filling up of the posts of librarians, deputy librarians and assistant librarians. The policy underlying these inordinate delays seems to divert salary saving funds of these vacant posts to other projects/programmes of the universities in which the teaching and administrative wings are more interested. This tendency is not only detrimental to the cause of the library's growth and functioning but also hampers the career prospects of the bright and deserving professionals.

In case of non-filling of the post of chief librarian, some universities have appointed professor in-charge of libraries. It has been observed that these professors are biased and favour their particular subjects resulting in a disbalanced growth of the collection.

SLOW PACE OF APPLICATION OF INFORMATION TECHNOLOGIES

In the context of university libraries the buzz word of the new millennium is to harness the advances in the information technology. Unprecedented expansion in contemporary information has led to information and knowledge explosion. It is obvious that this explosion will continue. It has been threatening the ability of traditionally trained librarians to cope up with such a mass of information. With the advent of digital medium for information access and delivery, the traditional librarianship is being constantly reminded of doing its job in wrong way. There is no doubt traditional methods are failing to serve the purpose, but no library can hope to stock more than a tiny fraction of the relevant materials in various disciplines. A good library is the one that can provide access to the widest range of materials. It is, therefore, important that all out efforts should be made to adopt the new techniques to improve information access and delivery. Growth is the index of change and it must be reckoned with as it happens.

Inspite of the tremendous advantages IT offers in information access and dissemination, the university libraries are extremely slow in going for the big apple. There are various reasons which we must seriously ponder over.

In its report/ recommendation, the Fifth Pay Commission on page 769 stated, "We recommend that for proper management of library and dissemination of information, every professional in a library should have competence to work on computers." The Commission failed to indicate the measures as to how it is to be achieved except that "The services of computer specialists in a library should only be hired on consultancy contract and not on a permanent basis." A survey of university libraries would quickly reveal that less than half a dozen of them could hire the services of computer specialists or get the post of information scientists sanctioned to them in the last three-four years. The Commission did not make any mention of "existing library staff improvement schemes", "deputing library staff to computer centre", "assigning academic staff colleges to make up training programmes for library staff to obtain computer proficiency", "making it mandatory for library schools to update curriculum teaching of BLIS and MLIS", etc. The training of library professionals in IT application is of vital importance for the automation and networking of libraries and it was overlooked by the Commission.

INFLIBNET (Information and Library Network) set up by UGC more than a decade ago was assigned the job to evolve a national network, interconnecting university libraries and information centres in the country and to improve the capability in information handling and services through speedy computerisation of these libraries. Even though the INFLIBNET has been holding conferences called "CALIBER" year after year, where the issues relating to computerisation and automation of libraries are discussed by the library professionals, the interconnecting of libraries through computer communication network is far from satisfactory. As a result, programmes of "resource sharing" and "library networking", which are the need of the hour, are lagging far behind.

Many months back INFLIBNET had assured the participating university libraries vide its their letters INF/TSK/grant/1998 dt. May 20 and August 18, 1998 that the UGC has agreed to provide "recurring grant" and "information scientist" post consisting of (1) salary of "information scientist" (pre-revised scale) Rs. 2,200-4,000 (2) support for data entry—up to Rs. 72,000 p.a. (3) telephone charges up to Rs. 15000 p.a. (4) consumables @ Rs. 2,500 per month—upto Rs. 30,000 p.a. (5) maintenance charges at the rate of 10 per cent of equipment cost for the period of four years starting from the second year from the installation of system - up to Rs. 55,000 p.a. Furthermore, this expenditure is on an annual basis for the first five years. Participating libraries have been requesting the UGC for release of the grant, time and again, but so far they have drawn a blank, whereas the UGC chairperson has been emphasising the programme of interconnecting of the universities by providing VSATS so that they would share their library resources, providing live high-speed communication between academicians, to enable students and teachers to communicate with one another, independent of their locations. All this is being programmed under INFLIBNET which wanted to make this network operational by the end of March 1999.

The need for attitudinal changes among library professionals is the other big factor which has significantly contributed to the slow pace of application of information technology in the library services. The changing trends demand show of more technical skills whereas the traditionally trained librarians do not want to venture into the path-breaking routines brought in by new information technology. In universities libraries, a state of dichotomy is existing between those librarians who handle conventional information services with the print media and those dealing with the electronic information services. Knowing as we do that people prefer status quo to the unknown, no one should be surprised that library staff are often reluctant to undertake any type of change in their daily environment. The high pace of technological development is yet another reason which is making it difficult for many library professionals to adjust. Besides the techno-fear, such persons are afraid of losing their importance. These persons are not willing to understand that even if application of IT is absorbed by a library, the need for their services to compile a collection of materials and organise it for use will still remain; library professionals will still exist and the basic skills needed to manage will remain almost unchanged. Consequently, the senior members of library staff are, therefore, required to spend more and more time in planning and implementing change so as to keep the anxiety at a minimum.

Another major problem in automation and computerisation projects of university libraries is the backlog processing, which requires systematic planning and implementation techniques with quicker results. Until and unless the backlogs are not cleared, effective networking and resourcing will remain a distant possibility. At present many networks in operation are interlinking only computer machines rather than interlinking for sharing of databases.

Redefining duties and responsibilities of the library staff engaged in the computerisation work by adopting some minimum standards/requirements/norms for library automation projects is yet another factor which is a matter of anxiety for the university libraries and librarians.

UNSTABLE PAY SCALES, DESIGNATIONS AND STATUS OF LIBRARIANS, LIBRARY PROFESSIONALS

Way back in 1961 the University Grant Commission on the basis of recommendation of the Ranganathan Library Committee vide its letter No. F.68-2/60(SS) dt. January 18, 1961 took the following decision.

> ...the University Grants Commission has decided to upgrade the salary scales of the library staff in the universities and colleges. The professionally qualified library staff are for purposes of salary revision to be treated as academic staff.

It was a clear endorsement of the recommendations of the Ranganathan Committee which had specifically recommended:

> The high academic and professional qualifications, the condition of academic and administrative responsibilities, and the practice in the universities all over the world indicate that the status and salary scales of the library staff should be the same as that of the teaching and research staff.

In spite of the UGC's acceptance of the Ranganathan Committee's recommendation and granting of parity, a thinking has always been brewing in the minds of educational administrators in the Human Resource Development Ministry and UGC against this equivalence. Attempts are always on to disturb the long-standing parity of librarians with teachers in the matters of pay scales, promotions, career advancement schemes and in extension in service and superannuation age. The University Grants Commission on the recommendation of Sen Committee appointed by it withdrew the academic status and scales of pay of the librarians and their professional staff in 1974. It was later revived after strenuous efforts by library professionals and their associations. The latest example of this discriminatory policy can be found in the implementation of the Fifth Pay Commission's Recommendations. These are: deputy librarians with five years experience have been denied the pay fixation at Rs. 14,940 by the UGC whereas the teachers (i.e., readers/senior scale lecturers) have been granted this privilege. Similarly the age of superannuation for deputy librarian and Assistant Librarian has been kept at 60 by MHRD whereas, for readers and lecturers it has been increased to 62. The doors for further promotion through career advancement schemes have also been closed for the deputy and assistant librarians, whereas teachers have not been denied of such upward swings.

Not only in the salary scales but also in the matters relating to study leave, sabbatical leave, grants for research, attending seminars and conferences, a clear line of discrimination exists between the librarians and the academia. A fresh look and attitudinal change is required on the part of the educational administrators to bail out the librarians from their sense of insecurity.

The designations of librarians is yet another point which needs the attention of the educational administrators. Due to the same designation of librarians from school level to university level, the liberians are facing an identity crisis. A suitable designation according to their status is thus a need of the hour. The designation for library professionals working in university libraries could be director for the chief librarian. The deputy librarians and assistant librarians may be similarly designated deputy directors and assistant directors.

ROLE OF LIBRARY COMMITTEES *VIS-A-VIS* LIBRARIAN ROLE AS CUSTODIAN OF LIBRARY

The statutes/ordinances of Indian universities provide for library committees for redressal of problems faced by the library. The vice-chancellor, the registrar, finance officer, faculty deans, heads of the departments and senior professors are its members. The librarian has to act as a convenor/ secretary of the committee. Although he considers the library committee as an advisory body, shield of protection and a channel of future progress and development of the library services, the experience and knowledge about functioning of such committees tells a different story. It has been found that library committees are less a democratic forum providing for the growth of library facilities and more a place for voicing grudges such as non-availability of a particular title at a particular time, the unfriendly behaviour of a library staff member or a blanket charge that the library is a thoroughly inefficient unit and setting up of departmental libraries often professing decentralisation of the university library's centralised system.

It has been experienced that librarian's role as custodian of library resources, ensuring proper care for the safe custody and proper use of the library's reading and instructional material, has always worked against the interests of the library and the librarian. While the resources are there for use, they also need preservation for posterity. Denial of a loan of a rare book or a reference source or a thesis or a not-to-be-issued art book leaves a deep wound which is healed with a retaliation at an appropriate time.

LIBRARIES NOT FREE IN TAKING POLICY DECISIONS

It has been experienced that university libraries are not free in taking policy decisions relating to collection development, reader services, opening hours, etc.

A university as the highest body for teaching and research makes direct contribution to the advancement of knowledge. The main difference between a university library and other types of libraries is the former's stress on research work. If a great research is to flow out of a university, its library must possess adequate resources for the research scholars. The quality of research would depend upon the kind of collection which is made available to them. The aim should be to build up a dynamic collection which is capable of meeting the changing research needs and demands for the present and the future. Paul Buck, an eminent Harvard University librarian, once remarked, "a good collection of books attracts a good faculty, and a good faculty, in turn, attracts good students." It needs no telling how much research work, in quality and quantity, has flown out of the Harvard University. Furthermore, it proves that the reputation of a university depends on the status of collection of its library.

In spite of the well defined importance of building research oriented collection, major portions of university libraries' book budgets are being spent on purchase of multiple copies of textbooks prescribed in the syllabi. In the absence of any norms and ratio of textbooks to the number of students enrolled in a discipline, the librarian and the administrative wings of the universities have to yield to the pressure of the undergraduate and postgraduate students. A large percentage of students visit the library in search of specified class textbooks. But for these, they would not mind if the library ceases to exist. It calls for the need to ponder over the methods of teaching under which the present circumstances are not at all contributing to the intellectual development of the students.

The British UGC defines textbooks as those books which contain the skeleton of knowledge. Their function is not to contribute to knowledge but to summarise the generally accepted knowledge of the field. They also become out of date with new developments in the field and after a short period remain untouched on the shelves. Stacks of Indian university libraries are full of such books.

Similar to the helplessness of the librarian in collection building is his incapacity to extend reader services to the users on weekends, holidays or late hours. The administrative wings of the universities are often reluctant to provide adequate resources such as overtime payment to staff engaged, allotment of staff quarters to staff deployed for evening shifts, transport facilities for the staff working till midnight, etc.

CONCLUSION

From the above paradoxes it is not difficult to conclude that most of the problems of managing the university libraries originate from the absence of norms or standards. And here the responsibility lies with the librarians as a professional group. Satisfactory coinage of norms and standards and getting these accepted by the authorities should be the uppermost task of the professional organisations. The professional organisations will have to act like a watchdog for the welfare of the librarians and the efficient working of the libraries. They will also need to find out ways and means to bring about an attitudinal change in the outlook of the UGC and the MHRD towards the proper role of the library in a university set-up as envisaged in the recommendations of various commissions and committees set up for the purpose.

BIBLIOGRAPHY

All India Library Conference (44th, 1999, Hyderabad), Challenges Before the Library Profession in the Next Millennium/ Presidential Address by J.L. Sardana.

Buck Paul, *Libraries and University*, 1964, Harvard, Combridge.

The Changing Profile of Librarian, *The Times of India*, 12 Nov., 1997.

Desai, A.S., *Higher Education at the Cross-Roads of the Twentieth and Twenty-First Centuries*, Mumbai, Forum of Free Enterprise, 1999.

Devarajan, G., ed., *50 Years of Indian Librarianship*, Ess Ess Publications New Delhi, 1999.

DUTA (Delhi University Teachers Association), Deplores Withdrawal of Benefits, *The Statesman*, 30 March, 1999.

Evans, G.E., *Management Techniques for Librarians*, Academic Press, New York, 1983.

Gelfand, M.A., *University Libraries for Developing Countries*, UNESCO, Paris, 1971.

National Convention of University and College Librarians, *University and College Librarians in India : Basic Documents*, New Dehi, 1975.

Promotions Issue : DUTA (Delhi University Teachers Association) Calls emergency meeting, *The Hindustan Times*, 6 April, 1996.

Thousands of Teachers Shortchanged, *The Hindustan Times*, 30 March, 1999.

University Grants Commission, Guidenlines for Development Assistance to Central, Deemed and State Universities During the IXth Plan, New Delhi, 1997.

Vara Lakshmi, R.S.R., Professional challenges: need for attitudinal changes among librarians, *University News,* 1999, 3337, 1.

Venkataraman, V., *Pattern and Development of University Libraries*, Ess Ess Publications, New Delhi, 1995.

Wilson, Louis Round, and Tauber, Maurice, *The University Library*, 2nd ed., Columbia. University Press, 1975.

34

Total Quality Management in Libraries and Information Centres

Krishan Gopal

INTRODUCTION

Many management guidelines of the past decade pay attention to the constancy of change: changes in communication, global competition, transportation, information, and the workforce itself. Indeed, the past decade has been remarkable, not only in the constancy of change, but also in the speed of change. To meet the challenges brought about by this speed of change, managers and executives are searching for new solutions, approaches, and answers. A typical alphabet soup of programmes currently sought after are : (i) Cost of quality; (ii) High involvement initiatives; (iii) Standards and issues management; (iv) Quality circles; (v) Quality of work life; and (vi) Total quality management (TQM)

None of these programmes are bad. However, at the same time none of them are perfect. None will work as a short-cut to building a deeper understanding of the organisation. It is always exciting to work in an organisation that continuously learns and practises any or all of these programmes, in particular TQM.

WHAT IS TQM?

TQM is not simply a means of quantifying quality; it is a means of expanding organisational thinking and learning capabilities. In the past, the essence of "quality" was to make products (or deliver services) according to fixed organisational standards. As this level of performance was attained, the goal shifted to producing goods (or services) that reliably matched customer needs (which might exceed or be different from previously accepted organisational standards).

According to Barrier,[1] there is wide agreement on the "essential ingredients" of TQM. They are:

a) An intense focus on customer satisfaction;
b) Accurate measurements;
c) Continuous improvement of products and services;
d) New work relationships based on trust and teamwork; and
e) Commitment.

TQM has emerged in the last decade as the preferred method for reducing defects in production, increasing customer satisfaction, and boosting productivity. It has been adopted to drive innovation and improvement in industry, supplanting quality circles, theory *z*, management by objectives, and other cures used in the recent past.[2] Much of the historic impetus for the acceptance of quality improvement programmes in America has been inspired by the Japanese in their headlong embrace of TQM.[3] In recent years, the pioneering efforts of W. Edwards Deming, J.M. Juran, and others have evolved into a vast array of techniques for modelling processes and improving quality.[4] Thousands of companies are spending considerable resources to establish TQM processes. The transformation that began with manufacturing is now being adopted by service organisations, largely because customers' expectations have risen sharply, and because quality improvement programmes can be adapted to service industries.[5]

Quality programmes have produced uneven results because no single blueprint for improvement is broadly applicable. Commitment, ingenuity, and employee empowerment are proving to be essential ingredients for success. Successful quality programmes indicate that this approach to improving products and services is being accepted as one way of gaining a competitive edge. TQM may not survive in its present form; however, quality initiatives will remain in place and will place greater emphasis on quality, reliability, timeliness, and customer satisfaction.

The reasons for early failures of TQM are sobering to contemplate, and the landscape is littered with faltering quality improvement programmes. Management may fear loss of control as decisionmaking is invited from the ranks. The extensive effort required to implement reorganisation of processes may be sidelined as other priorities overtake. Fear of management in the workplace can strangle acceptance of programmes whose success is critically tied to employee driven innovation and recommendations for change. Too often, special departments created for quality implementation are perceived as bureaucratic and out of touch with the realities of the workplace. The often protracted time cycle of initiation, training, and implementation, usually several years, requires enormous energy, commitment, and focus to effect desired change. The slow emergence of results can exasperate such organisations that desire immediate turnaround to stay in business.[6]

Success more frequently comes to organisations which place greater responsibility for customer satisfaction and quality improvement on front line staff. Some organisations are moving toward "break-through" techniques which produce substantial improvements to smaller segments of an operation, in a short amount of time. Experimentation will continue, with the focus remaining on customer satisfaction.

Among the first service industries to experiment with quality improvement programmes were airlines, banking institutions, insurance companies, and health care providers. Libraries are just beginning to adopt these practices.

TQM IN LIBRARIES

Library and information services work is fascinating and fruitful in terms of job satisfaction, but frustrating and depressing in terms of the unending fight for funding and recognition. Success in library services is never commensurate with efforts made. The need to review and justify services to administrators and financial controllers frustrate library efforts for quality services.

The other side of the coin is that the librarians have often failed to realise that the library is the only information source for a majority of the users. The result is that the librarians are more concerned with internal process than with the user perceptions and the value of service. They perceive themselves as keepers of knowledge rather than active agents in information transfer. Therefore, many users do not make use of the library services for seeking information for their assignments, instructions, or research. It is often more efficient and effective method for them to use online information systems for collecting data, information, and documents than to spend hours in the library accessing bibliographic databases and finding material on shelves. The internet and increased availability of a variety of online services are facilitating access without information overload.

Special librarians historically have been more users-oriented than academic librarians, especially those who deal with thousands of students. The special librarian has the advantage of knowing the library's clients, their work, and the larger framework of corporate objectives. In such organisations where service costs are charged to user departments or clients, libraries have been especially sensitive to users' satisfaction.

The concept of quality services is a contract between a service provider and its users, based upon mulually agreed upon standards of service and delivery. It is a tool which could be used in library and information services, because it would help increase mutual understanding and, at the same time, involve users in justifying to management the financial and human resources needed to provide library services.

The actual process for achieving quality management is described by a variety of authors with a variety of recommendations. There are indeed many different approaches and systems, and most libraries will perforce adopt the ones chosen by their parental organisations. Regardless of the system that is chosen, the cost in terms of time and money must not be underestimated. On the other hand, quality assurance is a holistic approach to management which can easily be seen to embrace everything about a library, its management and its services. The enormity of the idea, in such a framework, could lead to mental paralysis, a state of mind that must be avoided if one is to approach TQM for its positive benefits.

The logical place to start, then, is to look at the first benefit, the consideration for adoption, if necessary, of the value set or mission statement for the parent organisation and, by extension, for the library or information service that serves that organisation. Such consideration is an essential forerunner to the quality process, as it provides the reference point for all that follows.

It is important that this value set be widely consulted and agreed upon in order to ensure ownership. In these consultations, which must take place before the process begins, there will undoubtedly be lengthy, even heated discussions and arguments. Differing perceptions of the library's *raison d'etre* will also surprise and disturb many in the process. Nevertheless, the consequent clarity and honesty is beneficial, even required, for the long-term health of the organisation and for a firm foundation upon which to build the quality assurance programme for the library or information service unit of the organisation.

Once a value set is agreed upon, the benefits of a quality assurance programme fall into four major categories:

1) Public relations and marketing
2) Quality service
3) Effective management and organisation
4) Responsive staff and its morale

Public Relations and Marketing

A long-standing problem for library and information services units is their poor image. Parent organisations frequently undervalue them, and users rarely understand their contribution to overall organisational performance and often underestimate the process by which the service they receive is achieved. Additionally, the increasingly high cost of information provision and delivery exacerbates the situation.

Quality is a high profile management issue. If a quality assurance programme is adopted by the library or information department, that very act improves its image in the overall organisation. If it is undertaken elsewhere in the organisation and ignored in the library/information centre, the department is seen as out of step with the rest of the organisation and its image suffers accordingly.

As a process through which quality services are evaluated, accreditation sends a powerful message to senior management, the message that a first-rate service is being provided, carrying with it the authority of an outside auditor. Opportunities for improving marketing and public relations are also inherent in the quality assurance process itself. The necessity to consult widely about standards with users and with other departments (such as finance and administration) about systems, improves internal communications and understanding throughout the entire organisation. The fact that everyone is working towards a common goal ensures that participation has been taken seriously and that it is focused and entered into a helpful, cooperative venture. Status barriers are broken down, because everyone — from support staff to administrators and managers — is involved in the process of problem recognition and resolution. Apart from this general cooperation, there is a new recognition of what the library and information service unit needs from the organisation as well as attention to what the organisation expects. Respect and understanding are engendered all around.

Applied throughout the organisation, the quality assurance process can reinforce such information related issues as document handling standards and legal constraints, issues which the library and information services unit might have battled long and failed to address. While perhaps not strictly a marketing benefit, new attitudes related to quality assurance, benefit the library. Users tend to capitulate when faced with the combined might of a quality auditor and the library staff. The management, of course, strongly endorses the library and information services stance if it is threatened with withdrawal of the organisation's accreditation. Similarly, the beneficial consequences of quality assurance can go beyond service to internal users.

Quality Services

In a library, users are entitled to consistent quality services. The library and information profession has always accorded first priority to high standards of information service. Indeed, the very basis of qualitative information service is already built into library management'. Much has already been done to ensure quality service within constraints.

What would quality assurance or TQM do further to give benefits to our users? The answer to this question lies in the fact that the quality assurance process enables users to have a greater say in the provision and delivery of information products, and the library, consequently, has more information about what users want.

The emergence of quality standards that are agreed upon by the library and information unit and its users is an immensely valuable exercise. These standards encourage the organisation to supply the resources for the purpose. This, of course, changes the equation, because the library is no longer fighting for resources on its own. The library and its users together make the case for the necessary funds.

Efficient Management and Organisation

There is an old management axiom that systems in place for more than two years must be reviewed, because they can certainly be improved. Quality assurance is a powerful tool, motivator, and focus for such an activity. Measurement is the fundamental principle underlying quality assurance. Quality assurance's main claim to improving efficiency is that it reduces re-work costs by ensuring that tasks are performed properly the first time. A corollary of this, naturally, is that staff time is used more effectively, thus increasing productivity. Waste is also eliminated or minimised. It helps the organisation to control costs and improve cost-effectiveness.

The production of detailed work manuals is an essential ingredient of most quality assurance procedures. As this is already a feature of most library and information services systems, it may only be necessary to bring existing procedure manuals in line with current thinking within the organisation. The main purpose here is to ensure consistency, provide guidelines for staff unfamiliar with particular routines, and assist with staff training.

Hopefully, both within the organisation and within the information unit itself, there will be many more examples of improved efficiency brought about through a quality assurance programme. These will depend, of course, on the circumstances and systems already in place in any particular library.

But efficiency done is only half the story. Quality assurance also brings about improved management control. The information provided through monitoring the agreed upon standards and performance indicators — an inherent part of the process — ensures that the managers of library and information services units are constantly aware of changing demands and the strengths and weaknesses of the services being offered.

Such management control is, of course, important to any library or information services operation. However, it becomes essential in a situation where an information service or part of the service is contracted out, for the controls must be used to monitor the contractor's performance.

Responsive Staff and its Morale

As noted earlier, one of the benefits of the quality assurance scheme is the breakdown of status barriers, between everyone from support staff to administrators and managers involved in the process of problem recognition and resolution. Many of the benefits to staff grow out of this process. A team approach to problem solving is developed out of necessity and the manager's role becomes one of support and coaching, rather than one of authoritarian control. This produces a non-threatening environment where people work together and debate openly in order to solve problems and bring about change.

Measuring compliance with agreed upon standards and efficiency gives us important management control information. The "people" aspect of this information is that it improves communications *vis-a-vis* performance appraisal, assessment of training needs, etc. It gives such personnel procedures a firm, factual foundation and eliminates vagueness, which, for most staff, is a cause of insecurity and fear. Through an emphasis on fact and measurement, staff members recognise what is expected of them and are better able to participate in the achievement of the unit's mutual goals.

The result is that many organisations which have developed and implemented quality assurance systems report improved staff morale. As indicated above, the process clarifies employee responsibilities and objectives, giving a clear indication of the accountability and areas of responsibility of staff at all levels. This process is a great morale booster as staff members become confident in knowing exactly what they are doing, where those tasks fit into the scheme of things, and when and where to go for help if it is required. And linked to this, of course, is concept of "empowerment," whereby the responsibility devolves to the lowest possible level. The structures and control inherent in quality assurance are powerful enabling factors in this process.

CONCLUSION

The library and information services profession has always been committed to providing a high quality of service. It has constantly sought ways to improve that quality. In the past, there was a clear presumption that the way to improve quality was to consume more resources, to buy more books, recruit more staff and finally, to move to larger premises. This approach is no longer valid for two reasons. First, there comes a time when there are diminishing marginal returns from the resources the libraries employ. Secondly, the political climate has changed dramatically. Perceived excess is no longer acceptable and society's concept is to hold onto, to cherish and use what the libraries have. To improve quality, one needs to look for different solutions. The librarians need to tackle the problem at its source and attempt to raise quality levels within the existing resource constraints.

Finally, it appears that the overwhelming benefit of quality assurance, or total quality management, for library and information services departments, is to provide a vital link in the unit's relations with administrative and managerial decision makers, and therefore key elements of the quality team's action plan should be as under:

a) Involve everyone on staff;
b) Identify internal and external users;
c) Improve users satisfaction;
d) Increase opportunities for users interaction and feedback;
e) Provide value-added services;
f) Encourage innovation and efficiency;
g) Communicate openly; and
h) Identify staff training, education, and development opportunities.

The guiding philosophy should be users and their satisfaction. Since no library model of TQM existed in the literature, the library should introduce its quality programme with techniques and suggestions adapted from users and library staff.

REFERENCES

1. Barrier, Michael, Small firms put quality first, *Nation's Business,* May 1992, 80, 5, 22-32.
2. Myers, Ken and Ron Ashkenas, Results-driven quality... NOW!", *Management Review*, March 1993, 82, 3, 40-44.
3. Port, Otis and Carey John, Questing for the best. *Business Week*, October 25, 1991, (The Quality Imperative, 'Bonus Issue'), 8-16.
4. Port, Otis, Dueling pioneers, *Business Week,* October 25, 1991, (The Quality Imperative, 'Bonus Issue'), 17.
5. Zemke, Ron, The Emerging art of service management, *Training*, 1992, 29, 36-42.
6. Hammonds, Keith H. and DeGeorge Gail, Where did they go wrong?", *Business Week*, October 25, 1991 (The Quality Imperative, 'Bonus Issue'), 34-35, 38.

35

Management of Quantitative Data in Special Libraries

Brij Mohan Khanna

INTRODUCTION

The contemporary society needs data for planning and development in every sphere of activity. In the field of scientific investigations and technological developments, data is an essential input and indispensable commodity for scientists and engineers. The present day libraries and information centres play a great role in selecting, acquiring, storing, maintaining and disseminating the vast amount of scientific data and also providing the same to the users on demand. Raw data is collected from studies involving observations or surveys by researchers and scientists. The raw data is converted into systematised data after certain manipulations involving organisation and synthesis. The data is further analysed and evaluated using statistical techniques for effective usage in day-to-day work. There are several disciplines in the field of social and natural sciences, which produce enormous amount of data. This paper discusses some of the salient features of quantitative data stored in the libraries of scientific research organisations.

DATA DEFINED

The term 'data' is used with different shades of meaning in different subject fields. It *Chambers Dictionary* defines data as the plural of datum meaning information, facts or figures. The International Council of Scientific Unions' (ICSU) Committee on Data for Science and Technology (CODATA) Task Group on Accessibility and Dissemination of Data (ADD)[1] has defined scientific data both numeric and non-numeric, as 'crystalised presentation of the essence of scientific knowledge in the most accurate form'. *McGraw Hill Encyclopedia* defines data as numerical or qualitative values derived from scientific experiments. Scientists and engineers refer data as the magnitude of some quantity characterising some property of a certain system or a single compound or material measured under certain conditions. According to Bhattacharya[2], data is a piece of non-discursive information. Whatever way the data may be defined, actually it includes any facts, figures, letters, symbols, words, charts, maps or graphs that represent an idea, object, condition or situation. Data can include diverse things.

Characteristics of Data

Data will have some specific characteristics by virtue of which it can be identified. UNIDO[3] has listed out the following characteristics of data: availability, compatibility, reliability, flexibility, timeliness, processibility, sensitivity, and cost benefit.

Categories of Data

For the purpose of understanding the nature of data, it becomes essential to categorise them. Data is readily amenable to categorisation. The varieties of data warranting systematic categorisation are as extensive as varieties of research. CODATA/ADD categorises data into following six categories:

i) Data with reference to time factor
   a) Time-independent data: geological structures, rocks
   b) Time-dependent data: data concerning earth's interior or planets

ii) Data with reference to location factor
   a) Location-independent data: data on minerals
   b) Location-dependent data: data on rocks

iii) Data with reference to mode of generation
   a) Primary data: values of velocity derived by measuring length and time
   b) Derived data: temperature distribution in Sun
   c) Theoretical or predicted data: data concerning Solar eclipses predicted with the use of celestial mechanics.

iv) Data with reference to nature of quantitative values
   a) Determinable data: macroscopic data in physics and chemistry
   b) Stochastic data: fluctuating values in geoscience samples

v) Data with reference to terms of expression:
   a) Quantitative data: S.I. and Non-S.I. units-based quantitative data
   b) Semi-quantitative Data: Mohs scale of hardness of rocks
   c) Qualitative data: structure of molecules expressed in formulae in chemistry

vi) Data with reference to mode of presentation:
   a) Numerical data: measured values of weather observation
   b) Graphical or model data: phase diagrams or geological maps
   c) Symbolic data: symbolic presentation of weather data.

Data can also be categorised from generation point of view into two categories as mentioned by Gopinath.[4] These two categories are 'absolute data' that are independent of the conditions or values of the parametric quantities such as temperature and pressure; and the 'conditional data' which are specified by the values of the parametric quantities. The physical and chemical properties of substances are generally reproducible and independent of time and location, such as melting point of metals which are absolute data. Bhattacharya[5] has categorised data into discursive and non-discursive information. Non-discursive data consists of both qualitative and quantitative information. Kwatra[6] has described following categories of data: analogue data, digital data, discrete data, numeric data, raw data, and statistical data.

The UNIDO International Meeting on Data Banks for Development[3], Paris has defined data by enumerating three types:

1. Factual data, i.e., information content of observations on the real world. Factual data consists of socio-economic data and physical environmental (territorial) data.
2. Intentional data, i.e., plans, forecasts, etc.
3. Scientific-technological data, i.e., knowhow.

Factual and intentional data can be operational data or survey or census data.

GENERATION AND STORAGE OF DATA

Research libraries play a significant role in the dissemination of scientific information. Data is considered an important constituent of scientific information. An information service is incomplete without a well-developed data service. Scientific information may consist of both bibliographic and non-bibliographic data. While the bibliographic data deals with descriptive aspects of the scientific information, non-bibliographic data consists of factual information, which can be quantified. The so-called numerical data is non-bibliographic data, which consists of numerical quantities.

Most of the scientific disciplines, particularly the physical sciences, produce enormous quantities of numerical data during the course of the scientific experiments. The numerical data which consists of the numerical values are stored as scientific data, and is used by the future research scholars, scientists and technologists for correlating the results obtained by them while performing future experiments or for any other applications. Among various types of the numerical data, the time and space dependent data is the one which cannot be reproduced. It comes under the category of observed data as it is produced by periodical or continuous observation of the natural phenomena such as the state of weather conditions prevailing in a particular area during a specific period. The geophysical data also falls in the same category.[7-8]

The development of instruments like thermometer, barometer and rain gauge, seismograph, gravimeter, etc., in the preceding centuries, have contributed a lot towards measurement of these natural phenomena accurately and precisely. Today we find existence of a network of observatories and stations measuring the meteorological and geophysical phenomena such as temperature, pressure, rainfall, and geomagnetic and seismic conditions. Meteorological, geomagnetic and seismic observatories measure these conditions continuously producing enormous amount of data. Due to the invention and development of various kinds of sensors and the sophisticated instruments and equipments like radars, satellites and other remote sensors the phenomena of measuring these conditions have become faster.

There are various agencies through out the world which collect scientific data continuously over the land, over the sea and also over the sky. The automatic sensors convert analogue data into digital data, which is stored automatically on some media, may be paper, film or magnetic tape. Various statistical techniques are applied to refine the data so that effect of noise is eliminated or minimised.

Data can exist in various forms. Broadly speaking, it can exist in any of the following forms:

Unpublished Manuscript

Unpublished data sometimes exist in handwritten form. Data is recorded on loose sheets or registers with pen. The India Meteorological Department library has got huge stocks of weather data written in registers.

Published Records

Most of the data exists in printed or published form. The India Meteorological Department brings out the *Indian Daily Weather Report*, *Weekly Weather Report*, and *Monthly Weather Report* in printed form. Evaluated or refined data is generally compiled in tabular form and printed and circulated to the users. Data is available in the form of charts, maps and atlases which represents the data in compact form. Various mathematical models and graphs present the data in compact form, which can be interpreted. The analyses of these charts or maps show the realtime situations.

Non-conventional Forms

Non-conventional methods of data storage, though of recent origin, are of much importance. Data stored in non-conventional storage devices is read or viewed with the help of electronic devices. Such data is also called as machine-readable data. It can exist in following forms:

a) Microfilms
b) Microcards (positives)
c) Microfiches or aperture cards
d) Punched Hollerith cards
e) Paper tapes

f) Magnetic tapes
g) Tape catridges
h) Floppy or hard discs
i) Optical discs like CD-ROMs or DVD-ROMs
j) Satellite imageries

The National Geophysical Research Institute, Hyderabad, has got huge stocks of seismographs, which are produced, on special type of photographic paper. Various remote sensing agencies like N.R.S.A. have got satellite imageries stocked in the archives or data centres.

PROCESSING OF NUMERICAL DATA

Numerical data results due to measuring and recording the natural phenomena like gravity or seismic conditions or weather conditions. Sometimes the results of experiments are embedded in some documents. Extraction of such information and compiling it in the form of data compilations or tables is of great significance. Landau[8],[9] has identified 17 processing steps, which can be applied to numerical data found in documents as shown below:

a) Document selection and acquisition
b) Document descriptive cataloguing
c) Document indexing and classification
d) Document abstracting
e) Document listing
f) Document digesting
g) Document/data linking
h) Data flagging
i) Data tagging
j) Data indexing

k) Data extraction, compilation and display
l) Data evaluation and validation
m) Data analysis and correlation
n) Data synthesis
o) Data storage
p) Data retrieval
q) Data utilisation

The above operational steps can yield various information products and services. Steps a-e are bibliographic or document oriented and steps k-q are numerical data oriented. Steps f-j are bridge functions, which serve to link both bibliographic and numerical records. Listing or bibliographies of documents containing numerical data can be of great value in identifying potential sources of numerical data in the literature. Even if the data contained in relevant documents are extracted and input to a separate data file, the resulting bibliography can be maintained, in a machine-readable or print format, as either a by-product or an alternative search index or access point to the data file.

ROLE OF LIBRARIES IN THE MANAGEMENT OF DATA

Libraries play a significant role in the management of data in various forms and media. Only a meagre amount of data collected by scientific observations is published in the print form. Some of the data is measured, collected and stored in microforms or in computer media like magnetic tapes or the CD-ROMs or DVD- ROMS. However, some of these devices are of very recent origin. The printed data compilations were treated in libraries on par with other documents. The organisation of data in libraries requires the classification and cataloguing of data in whatever media it may be. Dolby[10] has presented a scheme of data description in which he mentions that data description should have five dimensions:

1) The 'matter' on which the observation is made;
2) The 'function' or event involved, which may be either a state or a change in state;
3) The 'space' or area in which the phenomenon is located;
4) The 'time' or its occurrence; and finally,
5) The 'observer' from whose frame of reference objects and events are being viewed.

The above five dimensions of data description described by Dolby match with Ranganathan's postulates of five fundamental categories, i.e., PMEST. In fact, data is of little significance, if it is not accompanied with the information of space and time and also the matter or some description of the device by which it is measured. The phenomenon of the nature, which is measured by the device, is nothing but the 'energy' of PMEST.

The data catalogue should give the following information:

a) Where the data are held;
b) The storage medium;
c) The period covered, time, place and elements included;
d) When the data is held in digital forms, the precise details of storage medium and method of representation and whether it is original or derived data;
e) The degree of quality control;
f) Physical location of the data; and
g) Digital group required for the purposes of machine searching.

In order to retrieve the data from the computer the following information is to be written on the Master Tape:

a) Tape number, date of its generation and location
b) Time and period of data (year, month, date and hour)

c) List of stations whose data are stored on that tape

Depending upon the data request a suitable retrieval programme is used to execute the search request. The real time observation and recording of certain phenomenon like weather observations produce huge data, which is out of the capacity of a library to store it. Such data is directly stored on tapes in computerised system.

INDIAN SCENARIO OF DATA ACTIVITIES

Rao[11] has given a good picture of data activities taking place in India. He has described the Crystal Data Bank existing in Tamil Nadu. The Indian Committee on Data in Science and Technology (INCODATA) conducts various data activities including organisation of conference or workshops periodically. An enormous amount of scientific data exists in the repositories or data centres of the various scientific institutions of our country. But most of the researchers do not know the existence of such data, as there is no proper documentation of data, particularly the quantitative data. Sometimes raw data collected over long periods and with great efforts, remains uninterrupted or unused.

Indian National Scientific Documentation Centre (INSDOC) and Documentation Research and Training Centre (DRTC) brought out a *Directory of Scientific Data Centres in India* sometimes in the beginning of 1980s. This directory remains without any updation till date. Here comes the role of libraries, which can bring out similar works. Actually the existence of data needs wide publicity for its maximum utility. However organisations producing data can market it to the users on payment basis. The National Geophysiscal Research Institute, Hyderabad, produces a large amount of geophysical data. The Seismological and Geomagnetic Observatories of the Institute generate the data continuously. The seismograms and magnetograms of the observed phenomena are piled up in the observatories. Efforts are on to store the data on microfilms and other non-conventional devices. The data is reported to the International Seismological Centre, Indian Institute of Geomagnetism and also to the World Data Centre. The Data Centre of the India Meteorological Department, Pune, has got weather or climatic data on magnetic tapes, which are sold to users at a suitable price. The National Remote Sensing Agency, Hyderabad, has got a huge collection of digital data collected using IRS satellites. This department organises one or two days workshop of data users every year free of charge, which gives wide publicity about the existence of data products, which are available for sale. Similar steps should be taken by other data-producing organisations, so that there is a free flow of scientific data among users. Riswadkar[12] has given the information about the data banks of social sciences available in India.

The data collected by the Census Department is used extensively by various organisations and scholars. In the real sense, the hard labour and efforts put in by the scientific and technical staff in collecting and storing the data becomes fruitful, only if the data products reach a maximum number of users, who can interpret the data and apply it in the projects meant for development of the society, otherwise the data remaining unused for decades together gets decayed and remains buried in the observatories, wasting the labour of the data generators.

CONCLUSION

Libraries have been playing a varied role since time immemorial. They have been known as museums, archives, documentation and information centres. Here is the opportunity for the library to play a role of data centre. Libraries should be able to manage the databanks available in their parental organisations. The data available in these data banks should be properly classified, catalogued, maintained and widely publicised. When the data products are not directly under the control of the library, a library can play a successful role as a Data Referral Centre. It can direct the data seekers to the appropriate source, so that the data becomes accessible to them. Library should play a significant role in making the accessibility to data simple and easier. The future of the libraries can also become bright as a seller of data products generated within the parent organisation.

REFERENCES

1. Committee on Data in Science and Technology (CODATA), Task Group on Accessibility and Dissemination of Data: Study on the problems of accessibility and dissemination of data for science and technology, 1975, UNISIST Report No.SCC.74/WS/16, UNESCO, Paris.
2. Bhattacharya, G., Data activities : an overview, *IASLIC Bulletin,* 1980, 25, (3)1980, 122-128.
3. UNIDO, Data banks for development—Proceedings of International Meeting, France, 1951, p. 55-63.
4. Gopinath, M.A., Data generation in science and technology. DRTC Refresher Seminar, 1980, 12, p. BA1-BA14.
5. Bhattacharya, G., Data categories, DRTC Refresher Seminar, Bangalore, 1980, 1980, p. AC1-AC14.
6. Kawatra, P.S., *Fundamentals of Documentation with Special Reference to India,* Sterling Publishers, New Delhi, 1983, p. 154-163.
7. Khanna, B.M., Impact of Ranganathan's laws and concepts in the organisation of numeric data, In Seminar on Impact of Dr. S.R.Ranaganathan on the growth and development of Library and Information Science, Osmania University, August, 1992.
8. Khanna, B.M., Meteorlogical data in India: its origin, development and management in Indian libraries, Unpublished Ph.D. Thesis, Poona University, 1990.
9. Landau, H.B., Techniques for integrating bibliographic with numeric databases in engineering, In Glaeser, P.S., Ed., *The Role of Data in Scientific Progress,* Elsevier Science, 1985, p. 4-504.

10. Dolby, J.L., Role of description in the evaluation of data quality, In Glaeser, P.S., Ed., *The Role of Data in Scientific Progress*, Elsevier Science, 1985, p. 357-361.
11. Rao, C.N.R., Progress related to data for science and technology, In Proceedings of Poona Seminar on Social Science Documentation, CODATA, North Holland, 1978.
12. Riswadkar, M.R., *Social Science Databanks in India*, 1978, p.17.

36

Knowledge Management and the Role of Library/ Information Professionals

S.D. Vyas and *Dewendra K. Singh*

"To conceive of knowledge as a collection of information seems to rob the concept of all its life. Knowledge resides in the user and not in the collection. It is how the user reacts to a collection of information that matters."[1]

INTRODUCTION

Over the last few years Knowledge Management (KM) has become the latest topic in the business world. There has been a phenomenal growth in this activity catalysed by interest shown in this field. There is upsurge in the publications, conferences, IT products, and job advertisements in this area. Various professional groups, notably Human Resource (HR) professionals, IT specialists, and librarians are staking their claims, seeing Knowledge Management as an opportunity to move to centre stage. In this connection, Sheila Corrall says that people often describe libraries as the organisations of recorded knowledge, so perhaps our time has come.[2]

Knowledge Management does not seem to have had much impact on the higher education sector so far. However, there is some evidence of involvement of universities in this field. The

Universities of Leicester and Warwick have undertaken research programmes on behalf of the Institute of Personnel and Development on the subject of HR roles in KM initiatives. The Open University has a know-how project. It involves its Knowledge Media Institute, Institute for Educational Technology, and library. The University of Leeds is part of a Knowledge Management Consortium formed by the Centre for Exploitation of Science and Technology along with Abbey National, Allied Domecq, BG Technology, DTI, IBM and Shell.[3,4]

In this age of information, knowledge has come to be recognised as the most important factor in the long-term success of both an individual and an organisation. In fact, the only source of competitive advantage in the future is going to be the knowledge that an organisation possesses, and its ability to learn new knowledge faster. With knowledge taking increasingly greater importance in the education and service sector, it makes sense to effectively manage the knowledge base, manage its storage and use, and create thereby opportunities for competitive advantage.

WHAT IS KNOWLEDGE?

Webster's New Collegiate Dictionary defines knowledge as "the fact or condition of knowing something with familiarity gained through experience or association." This seems to be a good definition of knowledge as it is universally used and accepted. However, it raises the following question. What is meant by the term "knowing?" The Webster's dictionary defines the word "know" as "to perceive directly or have direct cognition of". And just for completeness sake, 'cognition' is defined as "the act or process of knowing including both awareness and judgement". According to the above definitions, knowledge implies cognition, and cognition implies awareness. Computers, quite obviously, do not have "awareness"—at least yet. According to S.R. Ranganathan, knowledge is "the totality of the ideas conserved by the humans. In this sense, knowledge is equal to the Universe of Ideas."[5]

EVOLUTION FROM DATA TO KNOWLEDGE AND BEYOND

Data

The basic building block of knowledge is data. Data is a fact represented as an item or event out of context and with no relation to other things. Examples of data are 27, 010110, and JAN. Without additional or contextual details we know nothing about these pieces of data. Consider, is 27 a number in base ten, or in octal (which would translate to 23 in base ten)? If 27 is a number in base ten what does it represent? Is it an age, a dollar amount, an IQ, a shoe size, or something else entirely?

a) What about 010110? Is it a binary number or is it a representation of date, perhaps January 1, 1910? January 1, 2000 or something else entirely?

b) Finally, what does JAN represent? Is it a woman's name (or man's name) or does it represent the first month of the year?

All these are examples of data out of context.

Information

Information on the other hand, adds context through relationships between data, and possibly other information. Data with metadata and context makes information. The relationships may represent information, yet they do not actually constitute information until they are understood. Davis and Olson define "information as a data that has been processed into a form that is meaningful to the recipient and is of real or perceived value in current or prospective actions or decisions. In contrast, data is defined as groups of nonrandom symbols in the form of text, images or voice representing quantities, actions & objects".[6] Information has the following characteristics.

a) It adds to representation;

b) It adds to knowledge or updates the level of knowledge;

c) It has surprise value; and

d) It reduces uncertainty.

Knowledge

The cognitive state beyond awareness is knowledge. Knowledge implies an active involvement and understanding and the ability to extend the level of understanding to meet life's contingencies. Knowledge also refers to the organised record of human experience and given physical representation (books and reports). Knowledge adds understanding and retention of information. It is the natural progression after information. To have " knowledge" requires information in conjunction with patterns between data, information, and other knowledge, couple it with understanding and cognition. The final step would be to move from knowledge to wisdom.

Wisdom

It implies the application of knowledge as contained in human judgement centred around certain criteria or values that are generally accepted by the culture or society. Wisdom can be thought of as knowledge applied.[7] The evolution from data to knowledge and beyond is depicted in Figure 1.

Information is our experiencing the sense of data that comes from things in the world. These experiences are made meaningful by the mind — the processor of stimuli, an entity for constructing knowledge and making meaning from these experiences. The mind, according to Piaget and other constructivists, is more of a reference tool for relating to the real world rather than a tool for reproducing the real world. The mind is instrumental and essential in interpreting events, objects, and perspectives on the real world, and those interpretations comprise a knowledge base that is, to some degree, personal and individualistic. Information is the initial phase of this meaning-making process. It results from perceiving and shallow interpretation of things in the world. Information refers to phenomena and not to noumena. Further interpretation of these phenomena leads, sometimes individualistically and sometimes collaboratively. One fundamental difference is the belief that current spatially oriented theory and technology are capable of assisting the meaning-making process as well as the information retrieval process. Spatial mediators can influence the knowledge construction process in so many ways.[8]

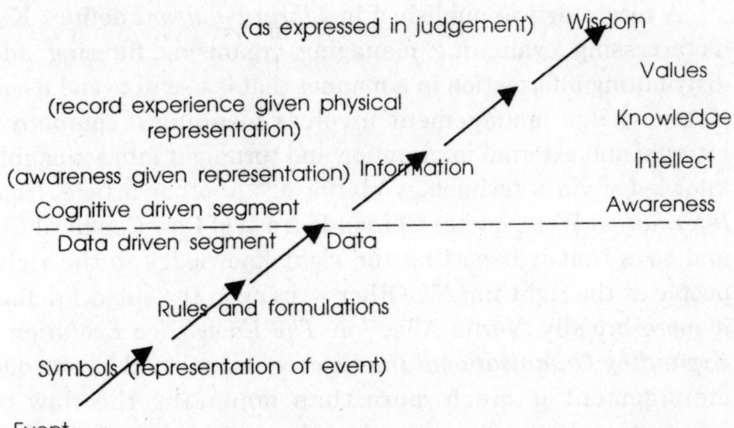

Figure 1: The evolution from data to knowledge and beyond

WHAT IS KNOWLEDGE MANAGEMENT?

Confusion arises over what Knowledge Management (KM) is, and what it involves. Some people view it as just an upmarket label for information management, and therefore our profession should naturally embrace this concept. Others see KM as a useful term to signal more complex work involved in organising access to networked information resources, and equate it with subject gateways. Cynics dismiss KM as the latest management fad, yet another effort by management consultants and IT vendors to sell their 'solutions' to desperate business people, who ought to know better. There are numerous definitions of KM to be found at conferences, in print, and on the web. The following are a representative sample, beginning with one of the most widely cited.

"Knowledge Management is the explicit and systematic management of vital knowledge and of its associated processes of creating, gathering, organising, diffusion, use and exploitation. It requires turning personal knowledge into corporate knowledge that can be widely shared throughout an organisation and appropriately applied."[9]

A recent article published in *Library Journal* defines KM as "accessing, evaluating, managing, organising, filtering, and distributing information in a manner that is useful to end users ... knowledge management involves blending a company's internal and external information and turning it into actionable knowledge via a technology platform.[10] Another article, from *Information Week*, quotes Gordon Petrash of Dow Chemical Co. and says that it is getting the right knowledge to the right people at the right time."[11] Other writers on the subject define it more broadly. Verna Allee[12] in *The Knowledge Evolution : Expanding Organisational Intelligence* states, "real knowledge management is much more than managing the flow of information. It means nothing less than setting knowledge free to find its own paths. It means fuelling the creative fire of self-questioning in organisation. This means thinking less about knowledge management and more about knowledge partnering."

'Knowledge' in this context is also somewhat elusive concept, defined in various ways by the different gurus. Thomas Davenport and Laurence Prusak offer the following pragmatic description of knowledge in organisation, "knowledge is a fluid mix of framed experience, values, contextual information, and expert insight that provides a framework for evaluating and incorporating new experiences and information. It originates and is applied in the minds of knowers. In organisations, it often becomes embedded not only in documents or repositories, but also in organisational routines, processes, practices, and norms."[13]

KM has many definitions, but is generally heralded as the next "age" or revolution in businesses and organisations, and is seen as a discipline. The concept behind KM is applying an environment of management to the most valuable asset of an organisation, i.e., its knowledge. The research proposed will pursue KM as previously defined, that is, as an integrated approach to information assets. These may include databases, documents, policies, procedures, tacit expertise and experience, as well as content management.

KNOWLEDGE MANAGEMENT: CONCEPT BY ANY OTHER NAME

KM is known by the many other names. A few of them are discussed in the following.

Conflict Management

Depending on the size of the firm, conflict management can be an integral part of the services the library provides. In smaller firms, the librarians may be called upon to run conflict checks and maintain a database of clients detailing corporate relationships between parents, subsidiaries, spin-offs, etc. In larger firms, a Conflict Management department will process the same kind of checks. Some of the larger firms have this department reporting to the director of the library. Still some have the conflict group as its own entity but have hired a librarian to manage the group. In special libraries, librarian's responsibilities include the management of a staff who maintains a conflicts database, runs searches through online services for corporate relationships, etc.

Records Management

Some librarians have shunned the possibility of adding this responsibility to the services their libraries provide. They think it is held as a thankless job. Others have viewed it as their responsibility to manage information from both external and internal sources. Those who work with records management are responsible for the creation and maintenance of a records management database that allows them to track documents and data from cases, transactions, etc.

Document Management

Whilc the document management process seems like a secretarial responsibility, setting up and maintaining such a system requires many of the skills possessed by librarians. With document management, we are making it easier to save and retrieve work in progress. The manager of a system like DOCS Open (one of the document management system) must be familiar with database management and full-text retrieval. Part of setting up the system is working with various parts of the organisation to determine how they want to access the documents they are creating. A system like this (properly set up) allows departments, teams and individuals to maintain different information about a document depending on the type of document, the client and matter numbers, etc.

Contact Management and Other Databases

Prior to the use of office-wide contact managers that are being implemented in many offices, librarians in those same firms were developing databases that tracked contact information (and other bits of data) for expert witnesses, litigation support services, conference, etc. All of these databases have one thing in common and that is that they provide users and staff with information that makes their jobs easier.

Case Management

To most institutions, case management seems as difficult to define as knowledge management depending on who is defining the concept. The case management system will be integrated with time and billing and calendar systems and will provide contact management, matter management, transaction management docketing, access to documents generated, time and billing reports, and many other benefits.

WHY KNOWLEDGE MANAGEMENT?

Organisations use KM for a number of the following reasons, including environmental pressures, technological advancements, and the ability to create valuable information for knowledge management.

Environmental Pressures

Environmental pressures stemming from our increasingly competitive global marketplace force firms to consider more formal KM. Competitive pressures lead to downsizing, which, in many instances, results in substantial losses of critical knowledge. Such pressures also force mergers, and "good old boy" networks are difficult to implement in merged firms. Many employees – and their knowledge – are lost, while those who remain are unaware of critical information resources. In addition, finding the necessary information sources and determining what is or what is not important information are hard to accomplish in a new organisation.

Globalisation and geographical dispersion also create a demand for KM. For example, consider the following situation involving a drug company with offices in many countries. Spanish regulators hesitated to approve a certain product, because they feared that the randomisation approach might have introduced bias into the trial process.[14] The company had experienced a similar problem the year before in Sweden, but failed to properly record and disperse the information to all its divisions:

"Why weren't we told ?" Quesada asked. "Perhaps we could have anticipated the regulators' criticisms and been ready with some intelligent answer."

"I told headquarters," Olsson said [the sales manager for Sweden]. And indeed he had......[15] KM is difficult even if participants are in the same location. Geographic dispersion makes it harder because information and knowledge flows that can take place at mundane events—such as lunch—have no forum.

Technological Advancements

Technology made available from internet developments has played an important role in facilitating KM. Virtually all accounts of KM stress using internet browsers. In addition, many tools developed for independent internet use have developed rapidly in the internet environment-intelligent agents, for example.

Creating

Valuable Information KM systems help organisations to create value by converting information and individually available knowledge into group or organisationally available knowledge. Sequent Computers' Chief Knowledge Officer (CKO) asserts, "Commercial knowledge is only valuable for the commercial performance that it produces."[16]

The direct impact of these connecting and converting processes depends on the organisational setting. For example, for Monsanto, a national security agency the goal is customer satisfaction.[17] Monsanto's KM director says, "the ultimate value of the [knowledge management] effort is that it has allowed

Monsanto to bring innovations to the market quicker, improve upon the operational efficiency of Monsanto's business, and serve its customers better.[18] Dow Chemical's (a global science and technology-based company that develops and manufactures a portfolio of chemical, plastic and agricultural products and services) global director of intellectual asset and capital management relies on KM to generate a competitive advantage over other firms. People in knowledge-management processes that create learning environments will increase competitive advantage.

INFORMATION RESOURCES MANAGEMENT VS KNOWLEDGE MANAGEMENT

Knowledge Management is about being capable of using the information resources available within and outside the organisation. This requires a high degree of computer and information literacy, knowledge of how to use information technology for information generation, manipulation and retrieval, and for understanding information, information needs and information resources, their strengths and weaknesses and the information content quality (or lack of quality as the case might often be). Knowledge Management is all about facilitating continuous learning not only for individuals within the organisation, but for the organisation as a whole. Learning must be a continuous process commencing from day one of a task, study or project. All too often learning is reduced to summarising experiences into memos and reports that are stored away in cabinets or databases. Learning must be about exploiting inhouse and external knowledge and experience using a wide variety of resources ranging from documents, databases and fellow colleagues when entering a new assignment or task. In this way, Knowledge Management is about bringing together information and people not only in the sense of users of libraries and information services, but rather as information and knowledge resources as such.

The last couple of years have been seen as the period of Information Resources Management. The convergence of several strands of management focus such as quality, agile manufacturing and the "learning organisation" has been tracked by Amidon in her Wellsprings-hindsight and insight charts.[19] Today this congruence is leading to the introduction of Knowledge Management initiatives in many organisations, particularly those that are knowledge intensive, such as high technology, oil, chemical and pharmaceutical companies, financial services and management consultancies. Many such initiatives are headed by newly created appointments of Chief Knowledge Officers and other such posts. Typical projects within such initiatives include:[20]

a) Creation of knowledge database—best practices, expert directories, market intelligence, etc.
b) Active process management of knowledge gathering classifying, storing, etc.
c) Development of knowledge centres—focal points for knowledge skill and facilitating knowledge flow.
d) Introduction of collaborative technologies—Intranets or GroupWare for rapid information accesses.
e) Knowledge webs—networks or experts who collaborate across and beyond an organisation's functional and geographic boundaries.

To accomplish this objective in an organisation, the following three essential components must exist:

a) Knowledge must be created, organised, and stored in an accessible repository;
b) Mechanisms or systems need to be established to provide access to the knowledge repository and to permit the sharing of it; and
c) The culture within the organisation must endorse the sharing of information and knowledge as well as the

utilisation of knowledge created outside of the organisation.

The difference between Information Resources Management and Knowledge Management can be anchored on a conceptual distinction between their respective objects: information and knowledge. Information is a tangible representation of data or knowledge within a specific context. The key success factor is the effectiveness of the representation in communicating the information. Knowledge is information in the context of an individual's role, learning behaviour, and experiences. The key success factors include the congruity between the information and the individual's perspective. The major steps that occur in the transforming of information into knowledge are learning, knowing, filtering, evaluating, and balancing.

Compared to Information Resources Management, the main challenges of Knowledge Management are not those of a technological nature, but organisational and cultural. That means Knowledge Management is not a technical issue. Knowledge Management is about how willing the organisation is to allow people to learn and prosper, and how mature the organisation is in implementing mechanisms to make this happen. It is about openness and voluntarily sharing information and knowledge. It is about creativity and the freedom to experiment about creating a competitive working environment and a learning culture. Knowledge Management is a key to how top executives should run their business. Knowledge Management is designed to support and enhance the human communication and knowledge sharing processes. It is a team-enabling management style. This requires the development of strong and open team communications and of a knowledge sharing culture, supported by a coaching and facilitating management technology. KM is the primary competence for the knowledge based organisation today, and knowledge technology is the primary enabler. The following five KM principles underpin the knowledge organisation:[21]

1) Trust as the foundation in the teamwork culture:
2) Open communication—using the best possible technologies;
3) Learn—as an organisation, at the fastest possible rate;
4) Share and develop team and organisational knowledge;
5) Enjoy the knowledge management process;

Role of the Information Professionals

From an organisational perspective, there is much merit in encouraging an adaptable learning environment and in focusing on identifying and gathering organisational intelligence in a strategic manner. There is also value to the organisation in encouraging the effective transfer of expertise, knowhow and knowledge. These ideas might be summarised as a 'knowledge awareness strategy'. The essence of knowledge awareness management is that all key staff members should be treated as information managers, even if one of them assumes overall responsibility for the strategy. This does not disqualify the information professional from taking a key role in the organisational attempt at developing knowledge awareness strategies; nor does it deem proper to assume any pre-defined role for the information professional. What, then, is the role of the information professional in an organisation trying to adopt a knowledge awareness perspective? The basic role itself is unchanged. The organisation will expect the information professional to acquire and organise information, make it available for use, disseminate it and, ultimately, dispose of information resources in all media and formats. A knowledge awareness perspective in the organisation calls for the information professional to be more systematic in tracking existing organisational informational strengths and this will probably lead to developing new information resources relating to the available in-house expertise.

There is, of course, nothing remotely new about tracking the expertise of staff. Organisational skills inventories or indexes of expertise have been around for the last 35 years at the least.[22] They now appear to be making a comeback as the 'knowledge index', but, in form and intention, this is the same entity. Senior managers who take a knowledge awareness perspective will also expect their information professionals to be proactive in gleaning organisational intelligence and to serve their needs directly. In a recent consultancy survey of principals of further education colleges and of deputies to the principals it was possible to identify a few colleges where the senior managers were really 'thinking strategic' about information.[23] One characteristic of each of these colleges was that they wanted their librarian / learning resources manager to be a full participant in the senior management information exchange network. None of the other colleges in the survey could visualise any relevance in involving the librarian, whose job was defined in terms of support for students and teaching staff. In the university world, for example, a study revealed that most university librarians in the sample did not believe that the library had a role to play in serving the management information needs of academic heads of departments.[24]

How can information professionals adopt a more strategic organisational view of their work? One way to monitor what is really happening is through what Peters and Waterman labelled (belatedly) as 'management by walking about'. When one of the authors was serving in industry he was advised by his (internationally renowned) director to spend a third of his time walking around the organisation, talking to people about what they were doing. Gathering information on what was going on in different departments (that frequently did not talk to one another) paid off. On one occasion, hundreds of thousands of rupees were saved when it was discovered that two different departments were working on the same problem in ignorance of each other.

However, to engage them fully requires that the librarian or information manager finds a new focus within the organisation—ideally, if information profession has to play its role and make impact. In such organisations, they should be located in the chief executive's office. They should form part of a team devoted to acquiring external information of value to organisational strategy and establishing systems to ensure that the knowledge held in people's minds can be tapped when it is needed. Merely to leap into the 'Knowledge Management' balloon without being in a position to deliver, will simply mean being first out of the balloon when ballast is jettisoned.[25]

CONCLUSION

"Knowledge in not a 'thing' that cannot be 'managed'. It is a capacity of people and communities, continuously generated and renewed in their conversation, to meet new challenges and opportunities. People responsible for knowledge value creations can be inspired and supported, but they cannot be 'managed' just as people were once managed in the industrial era, as mere extensions of the 'machinery', states George Por *Why Knowledge Management is an Oxymoron,* Community Intelligence Labs, 1997.

George Por's statement cuts away the hype from the KM movement. It demonstrates that the idea enshrouds two stronger concepts : one is the management of information and the other is the management of people. We cannot manage knowledge directly—we can only manage information about the knowledge possessed by people in the organisation. Evan then, the information to be managed is necessarily incomplete because the boundaries of personal knowledge are fuzzy and continually changing as individuals get out of touch or extend their knowledge. Today, the transition from the industrial age to the knowledge age is happening, and the rate of change to knowledge age is accelerating. The new information technologies of the 1990s—web and groupware—are having a profound impact on KM at the global level. Web technology has significantly increased the ease of use as well as the use of knowledge resources deployed at the desktops of all the organisational managers, especially of the information management professionals. Every organisation must face this challenge and achieve the new competitive ability in a information or knowledge society. We have to pay due attention to the transition from information resources management to Knowledge Management.

While successful KM requires the creation of knowledge repositories and mechanisms for tapping into them, these steps are not sufficient. In addition, there must be a climate within the organisation which supports knowledge sharing and use. There must be awareness of the tools and techniques that have been put in place to accomplish KM. The staff also needs to know how to find them and use them.

REFERENCES

1. Charchman, C. West, *The Design of Inquiring Systems* : Basic Concepts of Systems and Organisations, New York : Basic Books, 1997, 10.
2. Corrall Sheila, Knowledge Management : Are we in the Knowledge Management Business ? Available. [online] http:// www.rdg.ac.uk/libweb/
3. Minding the gap, *People Management*, 4, 16, 1998 : 46.
4. *Library Association Record*, 100, 3,1998, p. 124.
5. Ranganathan. S.R., *Prolegomena to Library Classification,* vol.1., Bangalore, Sarada Ranganathan Endowment for Library Science. p. 81.
6. Davis Gordon B. and Olson Margrethe H., *Management Information Systems : Conceptual Foundations, Structure and Development,* 2nd. ed., 1984, New York, McGraw-Hill, 693p.
7. Anthony Debons, Horne, Esther and Cronenweth, Scott, *Information Science : An Integrated View,* Boston, G.K Hal, 171.
8. Jonassen David H., Information Retrieval and Comprehension in Human and Computers, *Journal of Computer Documentation*, 1993, 17, 3, 21-27.
9. Skyrme David, Knowledge Management : Making Sense of an Oxymoron. (Management Insight, 2nd Series, No. 2) Available, 1993, [online] http:// www.skyrme.com/insights/22km.htm.
10. DiMattia Susan and Oder Norman, Knowledge Management : Hope, Hype, or Harbinger, *Library Journal*, September 15, 1997, 33-35.

11. Hibbard Justin, Knowing what we Know, *Information Week*, October 20, 1997.
12. Allee Verna, *The knowledge Evolution : Expanding Organisational Intelligence*, Butterworth-Heinemann, 1997, 231.
13. Davenport T. H. and Prusak L., *Working Knowledge : How Organisation Manage What They Know?* Boston, Ma : Harvard Business School Press, 1998, 5.
14. O'Leary, Daniel E., *Knowledge Management Systems : Converting and Connecting*, IEEE Intelligent systems & their applications, 1998, 13, 3, 30-33.
15. Cerny K., Making Local Knowledge Global, *Harvard Business Rev.*, 1996, May/Jun.
16. Elliot S., APQC conference Attendecs Discover the value and Enablers of a Successful KM programme, *Knowledge Management in Practice*, Jan, 1997, 5.
17. Payne L., Making Knowledge Management REAL at the National Security Agency, *Knowledge Management in Practice*, Aug/Sep1996.
18. Payne L., Making Knowledge at Monsanto Brings Excitement to the Word change, *Knowledge Management in Practice*, Oct/Nov. 1996.
19. Skyrme David J., Knowledge Management : Oxymoron or Dynamic duo? *Managing Information*, 1997, 4, 7, 24-25.
20. Chen Rui, The Eight stage of Information Management : Information Resources Management (IRM) vs Knowledge Management (KM), and Chief Information Offer (CIO) vs. the Chief Knowledge officer (CKO). *International Forum on Information and Documentation*, Jan/March 1998, 23, 1, 18-24.
21. Van den Hoven John, Data base Management IRM : an Enterprise Wide view of data, *Information System Management*: Summer 1995, 69-72.
22. Maozell, R.E. et al. An Index of Skills for Research and Development personnel, *Research Management*, 1996, 6 , 3, 209-210.
23 Streatfield D.R., Report to the Further Education Development Agency on an information Exchange Service for Senior College Managers. London : Information Management Association, 1995.
24. Greene F. Loughride F. and Wilson T.D., The Management Information Needs of Academic Heads of Departments in Universities, (Sheffield : University of Sheffield, Department of Information Studies) (BLR & D Report 6252), 1996.
25. Streatfield David, Deconstructing 'Knowledge Management. *Aslib Proceedings*, 1999, 51, 3, 67-71.

37

Performance Appraisal of Library Professionals : Purpose, Process and Techniques

H.R. Chopra

INTRODUCTION

The process of evaluation or assessment of performance of an individual or of an institution, keeping in view the objectives of the parent organisation and the consequent expectations, is known as "Performance Appraisal" (PA). It is a very complex and delicate process since it involves specialised knowledge and understanding of professional expectations, human psychology, ethics, and of several other relevant issues. It is a continuous process but it varies keeping in view the goals and objectives of the institutions, expectations from the incumbents, job requirements, services rendered, prevalent socio-cultural environment in which the individual or the organisation functions.

The PA system within an organisation has to be consistent with its managerial styles. In the centrally-controlled management structure the parent management would often find it difficult to promote and sustain a PA system based on staff participation or self-evaluation. Not all types of PA systems are suitable to all categories of professionals. A project type organisation may require a different set of PA system. Similarly, various professionals like doctors, engineers, architects, managers, bureaucrats, teachers, librarians, etc., may also require slightly different types of PA system.

The performance of an incumbent or of an organisation is a relative term and cannot be considered in isolation. It has to be compared with similar other situations, alternatives and choices. This implies a more positive approach. Here, a superior is not evaluating the subordinate, rather he is examining himself. He becomes an active agent and not a passive object. That is why PA, these days, is based on "Management by Objectives" (MBO).

Performance is related to personality also. It has psychological bearing. It could be biased and it could as well vary from person to person. Counselling, coaching, guiding, advising and motivating are some of the significant aspects related to it. Feedback and self-appraisal are also equally important. Personal qualities of the employees or professionals have a direct bearing on the evaluation process and delivering judgement involving selection, promotion, or punishment. Human behaviour, time factor, cost factor, frequency of evaluation, and psychological factors have also to be kept in view while undertaking PA.

The parameters for PA in commercial concerns, industrial units, business organisations, offices, banks and other public sector undertakings, educational institutions, hospitals, etc., vary drastically. Likewise, yardsticks to evaluate the performance of different categories of personnel, professionals, and workers also vary.

PURPOSE OF PERFORMANCE APPRAISAL

The primary objective of PA is to improve the performance after detecting the shortcomings, and finding ways and means to overcome them. Other objectives include review of past performance, assessment of training needs, setting targets for future performance, identifying potential for promotion and helping in the overall development of the individuals in the organisation. It helps in introducing new ideas and initiatives for better performance. The seniors can ascertain the weaknesses and potential of their subordinates. Targets for training requirements can be set and bottlenecks in the system, if any, removed. The PA also helps in formulating budget estimates and in deciding goals for the near future. In other words, it helps in looking back to know what has been accomplished and looking forward to decide what needs to be accomplished.

The PA is a tool for assessment, encouragement and confidence building. It helps to increase mutual understanding, mutual benefits and aspirations. It helps to define the future objectives and to undertake action plans. It also leads to effective communication, improving relations and leadership qualities. Above all, it paves the way for the increased job satisfaction, rearranging priorities and increased motivation. It also helps to increase sense of personal value, and to improve working relationship with subordinates as well as superiors within the organisational set-up.

Recruitment of employees, their work assessment and promotion can also be decided on the basis of PA reports. It helps to plan job description, clientele-oriented services, input and output changes, and determine the values and competencies of the staff members within the organisations. All these uses of the PA system are also applicable to library professionals and to different types of libraries.

PROCESS OF PERFORMANCE APPRAISAL

The PA is not a scheme but an ongoing, continuous process in itself, driven by parent management for measuring performance of its employees, improving their performance, and for providing leadership to the staff. Improvement in performance and employee development should merit greater attention in a PA system than mere measurement of performance. It must be turned into a result-oriented process. It should also be targeted at creating conditions for better performance and for recognising the inherent talent and qualities of incumbents. The PA should also be used as a tool for increasing individual responsibility, empowering staff to monitor and control their own performance. Ideally, it should be turned into a process for establishing shared responsibility, helping thereby the parent organisation to achieve its common goals.

The essential feature of the PA is that it is flexible and provides means for managers to manage and develop people. It enables managers to manage their own performance and direct development within the framework outlined with the top management. It, however, involves skills, which one learns by experience and discussions in performance appraisal meetings. The PA must be undertaken at regular intervals and in a systematic order. Feedback is equally important to improve the PA system, to make it relevant and staff friendly. Counselling skills are also required to be put into practice for worthwhile improvements. In short, the PA system helps the managers within the organisation to manage people and thereby help themselves.

TECHNIQUES OF PERFORMANCE APPRAISAL

Several PA techniques are in vogue these days, but none of them has been recognised as yet the best or worst option. The choice of a suitable technique depends on several factors such as environment, organisation, and the professionals concerned. Some of the commonly used PA techniques are discussed as under:

Annual Confidential Report (ACR)

This is the most common PA system in India these days. The officer incharge or the boss writes the ACR of his subordinates at the end of the year. This system has been in vogue in Indian libraries also. The report is based on the performance of the staff in the preceding year. It is written keeping in view the factors like punctuality, obedience, discipline, competence, innovations, improvements, deficiencies, and professional aspects. The major drawback of this system is that the performance evaluation may not be objective, may be the reporting officer is biased or that the ACR is not written on the basis of facts. It is a one-man show and as such not a very foolproof PA system.

Self-Assessment (SA)

The employee is required to make a self-assessment of certain selected performance variables such as his contributions to innovations, improvements, achievements, output, skills, professional growth, publications, refreshers courses attended, seminars and conferences attended, lectures delivered, and similar other landmarks made in the preceding year. This method of performance evaluation provides an opportunity to the incumbent to know and understand for himself his good or weak points and his performance in the organisation. In this technique, there is not enough scope for making partial self-assessment. Although overdoing, overestimating or over-evaluating has often been alleged, yet despite such apprehensions, self-assessments are largely objective. The system does not leave much room for the employee to make false statements since he has to support such claims by facts of achievements and contributions made. This system provides opportunities to employees to improve their performance for they are aware of their shortcomings.

Interview Schedule (IS)

In this system of PA, a detailed questionnaire is prepared, which includes identificational variables (i.e., name, designation, pay scale, age, sex, academic and professional qualifications, experience, etc.) and independent variables concerning professional achievements, innings, innovations, improvements, performance and personal traits. The investigator asks the questions to the employee concerned and records the answers himself. Cross-questions, supplementary questions can be asked and clarifications can be sought to ascertain the factual position. The PA can be done on five-point scale or otherwise. This system eliminates the chances of biased assessment by the investigator.

Appraisal By Clientele (ABC)

Another significant method for PA is the appraisal by the clientele or the end-users, the ultimate beneficiaries of the services the organisation provides. Their satisfaction is the guiding factor in judging the quality of service. The customers know better whether the service is proper or not. Their appraisal is believed to be more objective, realistic, and apt even as one does understand that there is surely some scope for error due to personal rivalries, biased attitude, or malafide intentions on the part of the clientele too. But, if a majority of the users feel dissatisfied, there is reason to believe that service does lack somewhere. This type of evaluation is applied more commonly in assessing product quality or professional service. For library professionals this is an apt technique.

Management By Objectives (MBO)

It is one of the most popular techniques used these days for performance evaluation in organisations. The performance expected from employees must be relevant to the goals of the business. The MBO measures contributions employees make to the success of the enterprise. The managers must know the organisational goals, and the employees must be told about the same and also about the expectations therefrom. The MBO is a process whereby the superiors and the subordinates within an organisation jointly identify the goals, define their areas of responsibility in terms of results expected.

This technique is effective in motivating the manager (librarian) to grow and develop his own capabilities by making achievements within the organisation. The MBO combines the needs of the individuals with those of the parent organisation. The objectives are prescribed first, work is allotted, and evaluation is done later. The introductory phase of the MBO is the most critical element to the success of the programme. It is during this phase that resistance from the employees is often seen greater.

The MBO has several advantages and pitfalls too. In this technique, the employees know the standard and tasks by which they would be evaluated. They know their ability and shortcomings. These are kept in view while setting the targets. Thus, the procedure leaves little room for unpleasant surprises, hence its acceptance level is pretty high. On the other hand, in this system, the entire burden of evaluation rests on the subordinates themselves. The superiors do not care to bother much in this regard. There is a need for proper orientation and training for managers at all levels of the hierarchy before introducing the MBO technique.

BIAS AND LENIENCY IN PERFORMANCE APPRAISAL

A reliable PA system requires objective decisions, failing which it will defeat the very purpose of evaluation. Balanced judgement is very essential. Favouritism, partiality, biases and a lenient attitude on the part of the superiors often blurs objective evaluation. Too much human factor in PA is harmful for the organisation itself. Similarly, unfamiliarity with the job requirement is a severe handicap in the process of PA. Technical knowledge is also very essential to appreciate the products and services on the part of the investigator.

Subjectivity is a crucial issue in PA. Most of the PA techniques rely on human judgement. So the judgement is not always without some personal bias. The ultimate aim is not to remove subjectivity of judgement but to improve the accuracy, quality and value of appraisal. Trying to eliminate the subjectivity completely would be like trying to throw away the baby along with the water both. So, it would be in the fitness of things if this subjectivity is managed appropriately.

MOST SUITABLE TECHNIQUE FOR LIBRARY PROFESSIONALS

As already stated above, every PA technique has its own merits and demerits. No one technique can be termed as the best or the worst. A combination of any two suitable techniques for the PA of library professionals would be an ideal decision. Self-assessment (SA) supplemented by interview schedule (IS) or appraisal by the clientele (ABC) supplemented by management by objectives (MBO) could be an ideal combination for the PA of library professionals. The investigating agency should also be professional body, which is fully aware of the library profession, its objectives, needs of the clientele and other related information. Library users should be given due weightage and their satisfaction should also be kept in view while making the PA of the library professionals.

FEEDBACK OF PERMANENCE APPRAISAL

Generally, the feedback is either not taken care of or it is kept confidential. Some managers (librarians) do not communicate the drawbacks or weaknesses of the staff (library professionals) due to obvious reasons. There is no built-in system to get the feedback regularly and appropriately. Performance reviews should be held periodically and necessary information should be communicated to the staff. Unless and until they are told about their weaknesses, how can they improve? The complete or the entire rating may not be disclosed to the employees concerned, but their shortcomings must be communicated to them invariably to enable them to discuss their problems, find the solutions thereof and improve their performance in future.

CONCLUSION

The very purpose of PA is to improve the products and services. This is possible only if the findings of the PA are utilised for useful purposes. A variety of decisions based on the results of PA can be taken, such as job rotation, delegation of powers, job classification, performance rewards, transfers, promotions, training programmes and more effective utilisation of manpower. But it has been observed that in India, in most of the cases, promotions, rewards and reprimands of the library professionals are decided on the basis of annual confidential reports (ACRs) alone. It is not enough or appropriate at all. The PA system plays an active role in taking variety of decisions that may contribute to the good health of the libraries and library services, provided that the decisions are taken objectively.

BIBLIOGRAPHY

Basu, Prahald Kumar, *Performance Evaluation for Performance Improvement.* Allied Pub., New Delhi, 1991, p.443.

Bache, J.F., Performance appraisal—Let's quit appraising and begin reviewing, In Benson, Gary (ed.), *Stepping up Performance*. Jaico Pub., London, 1995, p. 204-207.

Bolar, M., Performance appraisal system for the Indian situation: Some suggestions, In. Bolar, Malathi (ed.), *Performance Appraisal*, Vikas Pub., New Delhi, 1978, pp. 63-70.

Dorfman, Peter W., et al, *Performance Appraisal Behaviours Supervisor Perceptions and Subordinate Reactions, Personnel Psychology*, 1986, 39, 3. p. 579-98.

Fisher, Martin, *Performance Appraisals*, Kogen Page Ltd., London, 1995, pp. 224.

Jagadeesh, R., Performance appraisal and total quality management, *Indian Journal of Training and Development*. 1998, 28, 1, 39-47.

Kearney, Williams J., Improving work performance through appraisal, *Human Resource Management*, 1978, 17, 2. pp. 15-23.

Maddus, Robert B., *Effective Performance Appraisal,* Kogen Page Ltd., London, 1990.

Meyer, Herbert H., Self appraisal of job performance, *Personnel Psychology,* 1980, 33, 2. 291-95.

Moss, S.M., Appraise your performance appraisal process, *Quality Progress,* November, 1989, 58-60.

Rao, T.V., *Performance appraisal: Theory and practice,* Vikas Pub., New Delhi, 1984.

Rao, Y.V.N., et al, *Performance Appraisal and Development System in Technical Institutions,* Indian Society for Technical Education, New Delhi, 1996.

Satyal, Rajesh, *ABC of Managing Performance,* Human Capital, 1997, 1, 6. p. 48-49.

Snell, S.A. and Wexely, R.N., Performance diagnosis: Identifying the causes of poor performance, In. Benson, Gary (ed.). *Stepping up Performance*, Jaico Pub., London, 1995, p. 243-55.

Vanikar, Vijay and Sharma, Aparna, *Performance management: Charting out a new path,* Human Capital, 1997, 1, 6, p. 44-46.

38
World Book Production and Its Pricing

S. Majumdar

INTRODUCTION

The book is considered an educational tool, a torch bearer of development, a storehouse of knowledge, and a tool to spread the culture of a nation. As per Unesco's aims and objectives, it acts as a subject; as an instrument ; or as a means of action. Books have also been seen as the instrument for the free flow of written information; for literary pursuit, for promotion of the reading habits; and for development of libraries. What characterises books most clearly is the end use for which they are created, i.e., to be read. Though these characteristics are also shared by periodicals and other types of reading materials, it is the book media alone which liberates the human being from the clutches of illiteracy and makes man more humane.

Although there are other medias for information flow, like audio-visuals, electronic media, etc., yet books are unique as they are entirely independent of the time factor, i.e., the reader is free to use them as he wishes. In case of the audio-visual method, one is forced to stick to the time of broadcast. Books reach the people when they are beyond the reach of television. Contrary to this, in a computer environment, one is dependent on electronic machines and software to read. An artificial environment is created to read without having the pleasures of reading. Precisely this is the reason why nothing can replace the print media. Books have thus regained their significant place as a means of communication. And the modern communication methods have facilitated books to further spread knowledge they contain among the masses. Even in the educational set-up equipped with the audio-visual methods of teaching, the teachers are still dependent upon the printed texts, as they do not have any other alternative to keep the educational process going. They have to refer again and again to the books only.

Stanley Barnet has expressed his views on books thus, " Books are one of the major factors in building the human resources required for the political, economic and social development of a nation. They are the tools to stimulate both the leaders and general public in thinking about political, economic and social issues. They offer information which is vital for a balanced understanding of the processes with which an emerging nation has to deal. They are the records of the actions taken in dealing with social and economic problems. They serve as a medium for the transfer of knowledge and knowhow in the education and training processes within a generation and between the generations."

In a nutshell, today the book has become the simplest, cheapest and most easily utilised instrument for communication of information. It is the best tool for individual study, a constant and handy source of knowledge, a storehouse of the accumulated wisdom of the ages.

SCHOLARLY BOOKS

There are large varieties of books. Some are fiction, some are simple informative and some others are considered to be scholarly books. Scholarly books in general may be said to be the books which directly add to the stock of knowledge and interpret the culture of a nation. One may say that a fiction also interprets the culture in a way which may be absorbed by the reader more easily than a book on the culture and civilisation of a nation. But it does not leave a lasting impression on the man as the content may not be scholarly enough to add to the empirical knowledge. A fiction can be considered a time gap arrangement but not a tool for experiencing knowledge. Scholarly publications not only add to the stock of knowledge by different interpretations but also test his own ability to contribute to in different disciplines and spread the empirical knowledge. Therefore, the scholarly books add to the empirical or scientific knowledge; for interpreting the culture and civilisation. Through the help of scholarly publications the reader pursues his studies in different disciplines; knows the philosophy of various disciplines, and with the help of empirical approach, gains the scientific knowledge.

PRESENT STUDY

The present study intends to understand the trends in book production in Asia, India, United States, United Kingdom and Germany. On the basis of the data collected since 1980, it examines the rise and fall in the book production, especially in different disciplines of social sciences.

The study also examines the pricing trends in the books published from USA, UK and Germany and their impact on library budget. The study also examines the impact of differential pricing system. The scope of the study also extends to CD-ROM databases from United States.

ECONOMICS OF BOOK PRODUCTION

The cost of book production can be grouped under two factors:

i) Fixed costs which do not change even if the print order is of a high volume for a book. This includes editorial charges, the payment to the author if agreement to outright purchase of copyright is made, book production charges covering the design layout, artwork and illustration, composition charges, marketing cost including the trade discounts, and fixed overheads.

ii) Variable costs which vary according to the number of copies produced and expected to be sold. This includes royalty payment to the author, printing and binding charges, book promotion cost and administrative overheads.

WORLD BOOK PRODUCTION

Table 1 gives an account of world book production and in Asia, India, USK, UK, and Germany during 1980-1995. Asia published 24 per cent of the total world titles; 27.5 per cent publications were produced by only three developed countries, i.e., USA, UK and Germany, and the former USSR alone contributed 13.2 per cent to the total world titles; 80 per cent of titles were published by nearly 30 to 35 countries and the rest 20 per cent by other countries of the world.

Asia was a producer of one-fourth of the total English titles in the world. Japan, Korea and China were major producers in Asia, Japan contributing 39 per cent to the Asian output and 7 per cent to the total world production, China contributing 15 per cent to the Asian output and 3.43 per cent to the world production, and Korea contributing 22.30 per cent to Asian total and 5.40 per cent to the world output. Thus, 76 per cent of the Asian total comes from these three countries, and the rest 24 per cent from other Asian countries. There has been considerable rise in the number of books produced during 1995 (74.9 per cent rise from 1980's base year). This indicates that the electronic publishing has had no adverse impact on book production. Rather, book production was on the rise.

Table 1

Book Production in World, Asia, India, USA, UK and Germany 1980 to 1995 (Base Year 1980)

Region	Book production in base year (1980)	Book production in 1985 & per cent of difference from base year	Book production in 1990 & per cent of difference from base year	Book production in 1995 & per cent of difference from base year
World	647,249	693,763 + 7.1	756,193 + 16.8	658557 +1.7
Asia	138,000	158,450 +7.1	192,150 +16.8	658,557 +74.9
India	13,148	11,660 -11.3	14438 +9.8	11,460 -12.8
United States	41,434	50,090 +20.9	59,299 +43.0	68,307 +64.0
United Kingdom	48,069	52,994 +10.2	86,573 +80.1	95,015 +97.6
Germany	64,761	54,442 -15.2	65,980 +1.8	70,643 +9.0

India's contribution to the world book production compared to other countries was only 1.6 per cent and 7.7 per cent in the Asian output. It is not true that India is not producing books as much as other dominant Asian countries are producing. This is because it is difficult to ascertain the actual output. The data submitted here is only for English language publications.

United States had contributed 6.4 per cent to the world total book production in 1980, 7.8 per cent in 1990 and 10.3 per cent in 1995. United Kingdom contributed 7.4 per cent in 1980, 11.4 per cent in 1990 and 14.4 per cent in 1995. Germany contributed 10 per cent in 1980, 8.7 per cent in 1990 and 10.7 per cent in 1995. The quantum of increase in book production in these three big countries clearly indicates their importance in book publishing.

BOOK PRODUCTION IN SOCIAL SCIENCES

According to the *Unesco Statistical Year Book* for the years 1980 to 1988, approximately 85 to 95 countries accounted for the bulk of books produced in the world in social sciences, out of which the major share was contributed by USA, UK, Germany, USSR, and in Asia by Japan, China, and Korea. All these countries contributed 57 per cent of the total books in social sciences and rest of the 88 countries contributed 43 per cent share. This shows the dominance of select countries in the intellectual market. Table 2 provides the annual production of books in social sciences. The total production runs to 12.91 lakh during the year 1980 to 1987. The annual growth of the social science publications is in the range of 11 to 14 per cent per year. During 1990 to 1995, there has been considerable rise, between 22 and 24 per cent in the social science literature.

Table 2

Book Production in Social Science in the World, Asia, India, USA, UK, and Germany, 1980 to 1999 (Base year 1980)

Region	*1980 base year*	*1985 % age of difference from base year*	*1990 % age of difference from base year*	*1995 % age of difference from base year*
World	175,986	185,315 +5.30	218,984 +24.43	216,025 –22.7
Asia	33,875	59,675 +26.8	42,957 +76.1	83,999 +147.9
India	4,611	3,917 +15.0	3,204 +30.5	2,188 -52.5
US	16,157	19,009 +17.6	10,147 -37.2	11,072 -31.4
UK	14,001	16,754 +19.6	17,286 +23.4	19,791 +41.3
Germany	23,070	17,566 -23.8	14,568 -36.8	16,259 -29.5

Asia's contribution in the social science discipline was 18.72 per cent compared to 7 per cent during 1960's. The rise has been phenomenal. In 1990 it was 76.0 per cent from the 1980 base year, and in 1995 the increase went up to 148.0 per cent. Japan, Korea and China dominate countries in social sciences. As far as India is concerned, there has been a declining trend in the social science literature. The year 1990s output compared to 1980s declined by 30 per cent and in 1995 the declined was 31.4 per cent. USA's production in social science discipline has also been declining. Compared to 1980, there was 37 per cent fall in 1990 and 31 per cent in 1995. In Germany also there has been a phenomenal decrease between 23 and 29 per cent in social science literature during 1985 to 1995. Social science literature in the United Kingdom had a phenomenal rise. One can see the increase up to 41.3 per cent in 1995 from the 1980 base year.

PRICE TREND ON BOOKS AND ITS IMPACT ON LIBRARIES

Librarians are becoming more and more concerned about the general price rise in books and generals. The rise in the price of books is not so inflationary as is seen in the general subscription. The toughest assignment is to carry out balanced collection development policy in the face of high price rise. White and Fry reported 10 years ago that the library was spending twice as much on books as on periodicals. But today more and more is spent on periodicals at the cost of books to maintain their current level of periodical holdings, and the reasoning is based on the belief that periodicals are the main source of research. These is a drastic shift of library funds from books to periodicals. Currently the prices of the books have gone considerably high. Day by day they are going beyond the reach of common man and the time is coming when it will be out of the reach of libraries.

Bingly attributed the rise in the prices of books of two reasons. Progressive underpricing is over a long period of time in relation to the actual cost of production and distribution. The underpricing was a deliberate attempt to increase the sale but it eventually affected the book industry. When the realisation downed, a sudden boom was seen in the market, the cost of the book increased and so also the profit margin. Pringley attributed the rise in the price of books to concurrent decline in the publishers income. It was the direct result of decline in the sales.

In the present context both reasons have no meaning, because the publishing, especially in the West, has developed so scientifically. Given the modern management techniques, there is hardly any chance of not making profit on the sales of books. Publishers themselves do not take the risk of publishing those titles which have no market. Prices of new titles are calculated precisely on expected sale and profit. The book industry has maintained their growth in book production in this decade. Simultaneously it continued to witness a steep high in the cost of books. The causes behind the high rise in prices can be attributed to a sharp increase in the inflation rate; high increase in the paper prices; high postal rates; devaluation of rupee; increase in the foreign exchange rates; use of differential pricing techniques by the distributing agencies; and increase in production cost including the overheads.

AVERAGE PRICE OF BOOKS

An attempt has been made to provide a picture of price trend in three major producing countries and also in India. The countries like United States, United Kingdom and Germany have been selected for this purpose since India mainly imports from these countries, and also their share in the world book market is as high as 33 per cent.

A picture of the pricing trend social sciences, humanities and science and technology in India, UK., USA and Germany has been given in Table 3. It has been projected in literature that publication prices in science and technology disciplines are higher than in any other discipline. But it is observed that, whether it is social science or science and technology or humanities, prices have gone equally high in 20 years' period, from 1980 to 1998. If the rise in UK is 68.0 per cent in social sciences in 1990 compared to 1985, then it is equally high in science and technology (83.0 per cent). On the other hand, in USA the cost of books in social science has gone up by 37.4 per cent, in humanities 43.8 per cent and in science and technology by 83 per cent. In Germany, in social science, the rise is 25.7 per cent, in humanities 37.0 per cent and (12.7 per cent). Science and technology in India has shown a steep rise in nine years' period, 189 per cent in science and technology, 150 per cent in social sciences and 112 per cent in humanities. But between 1990 and 1998 the rise in social science in USA was 82.0 per cent, in UK 56.6 per cent, and in Germany 232.6 per cent. Compared to social science, the rise in science and technology in UK was 28.0 per cent, in USA 14.8 per cent but in Germany it was 287.0 per cent.

Similarly, in humanities between 1990 and 1995 40.9 was the prices in UK per cent, in USA 30.4 per cent and in Germany 37.7 per cent. The average prices between 1990 and 1995 has increased by 39.6 per cent in UK, 23 per cent in USA but in Germany there was a phenomenal increase by 203.0 per cent. The average price between 1995 and 1998 is UK increased marginally by 8.6 per cent, in USA by 2.7 per cent and in Germany by 10.7 per cent.

IMPACT OF DIFFERENTIAL PRICING

Apart from the general price increase, one of the major problems faced by librarians is of differential pricing policy adopted by an increasing number of international publishers,

Libraries have to pay more for the same document for which an individual would pay less. It differs from country to country.

Table 3

Average Price of Books in Various Disciplines in India, UK., USA, and Germany, 1980-1998: Increase & Decrease since 1980

Discipline base and religious	*1980* %	*1985* %	*1990* %	*1995* %	*1998* %
Social Sciences India (Rs.)	62.00	80.00 (29.0)	—	290.00 (262.0)	361.00 (24.4)
United Kingdom £	—	16.40	27.68 (68.7)	43.36 (56.6)	50.54 (16.5)
United States ($)	24.0	30.63 (27.0)	42.10 (37.4)	55.51 (31.8)	58.36 (5.1)
Germany (DM)	32.24	37.75 (17.0)	47.47 (25.7)	157.73 (232.2)	173.26 (9.8)
Humanities India (Rs.)	58.0	74.80 (29.0)	—	—	—
United Kingdom(£)	— —	16.33	25.69 (57.3)	36.22 (40.9)	38.66 (6.7)
United States ($)	19.95	24.89 (24.7)	35.80 (43.8)	46.69 30.4)	51.78 (10.9)
Germany (DM)	31.50	33.15 (5.2)	45.43 (30.0)	62.59 (37.7)	67.17 (7.3)
Science & Technology India (Rs.)	39.0	102.00 (161.5)	—	—	—
United Kingdom(£)	—	23.77	43.51 (83.0)	55.73 (28.0)	57.86 (3.8)
United States ($)	29.24	40.03 (36.9)	76.80 (91.8)	88.22 (14.8)	85.47 (3.1)
Germany (DM)	56.49	65.32 (16.6)	73.56 (12.6)	285.00 (287.4)	307.42 (7.8)
Average Price (All subjects) India (Rs.)	38	80.00 (110.0)	—	—	—
United Kingdom (£)	—	21.76	32.29 (48.3)	45.10 (39.6)	49.02 (8.6)
United States ($)	24.02	31.55 (31.3)	51.56 (63.4)	63.47 (23.0)	65.20 (2.7)
Germany (DM)	39.14	43.51 (11.1)	55.48 (27.5)	168.44 (203.6)	186.61 (10.7)

Two methods are adopted to differentiate the prices.

Discrimination against libraries as institutions as compared with individuals; and discrimination against libraries based on their geographical location in relation to the country of publication. Since libraries are interested in hardcover publications due to the reason of durability and long-life, the publishers substantially differentiate the prices of hardcover in comparison to paperbacks. Secondly, the publishers place a surcharge on library purchases. The US publishers require substantial surcharges for monographs ordered by a foreign booksellers. In UK this rate has increased to 47 per cent. Even lack of information about location by the foreign booksellers would cost the libraries up to 70 per cent. Sale authority given by some publishers to a dealer and in lieu the dealer directly selling the publication to the libraries has closed the doors for booksellers to export books and depend upon the wishes of the exporters and their pricing policy.

At present differential policy is invariably applied to periodical subscriptions, but monograph publication agencies have also started adopting this practice. If it *gavis* currency, it would lead to over payment for the same book in different locations.

ELECTRONIC PUBLISHING

In the present information age, publication in the electronic form has assumed immense importance. The electronic publishing has led to full text appearing online through the internet or those published in CD-ROM. United States is the major producing country for CD-ROM publications. The last decade of the twentieth century has witnessed a boom in electronic publications. There has been 205 per cent increase in CD-ROM titles in USA in 1995 in comparison to 1990 in the discipline of social science but during 1998 CD-ROM titles in social sciences had decreased marginally. In the field of humanities there was 119 per cent increase in CD-ROM in 1995 compared to 1990, and a marginal increase of 3.2 per cent was seen in 1998 in comparison to 1995. There was 171 per cent increase in 1995 in the CD-ROM titles in science and technology including medicine compared to 1990 year and a marginal fall of 1.9 per cent in 1998 in comparison to 1995.

Table 4 : Electronic Publishing in United States

Discipline	*Number of titles and average price ($) in 1990*	*Number of titles and average price ($) in 1995 and % increase / decrease since 1990*	*Number of titles and average price ($) in 1998 and % increase / decrease since 1995*
Social Sciences	124	379 (+205.0)	375 (-1.0)
	$1,866	$1,628(-12.7)	$1,682 (+3.3)
Humanities	42	92 (+119.0)	95 (+3.2)
	$576	$1745 (+202.0)	$1,505(-13.7)
Science & Technology and Medicine	171	464 (+171.3)	455 (-1.9)
	1,286	2,449 (+90.4)	2,281 (-6.8)

With regard to the average prices of CD-ROM titles, there has been a declining trend in social science literature. The decline was 12.7 per cent in 1995 compared to 1990 base year and it marginally increased to 3.3 per cent in 1998 compared to the 1995 base year. The average price for humanities titles rose by about 202 per cent in 1995 compared to the 1990 base year, and there was 13.7 per cent drop in 1998 compared to 1995. In a similar way there was 90.4 per cent increase in the prices of science and technology titles including medicine in 1995 compared to 1990 base year, and there was 6.8 per cent decline in 1998 in comparison to 1995.

One can analyse that the pricing structure for electronic publishing is unaffordable by any library.

39

Marketing of Information Products and Services in Social Sciences

P.C. Shah

— Think globally, act locally, commit personally.

— Where there is a will there is a way.

— Selling well: doing certain things, certain way, every day.

INTRODUCTION

Marketing is a strategy, a philosophy and way of life for the successful information centres. The staff should attempt to sell information which meet users' needs. Selling is only one part of marketing, whereas marketing is all about discovering the needs, wants and demands of users and fulfilling them. Hence, in marketing:

Focus is the cliente and goal is clientele satisfaction.

Marketing is gaining importance. It is not just selling, promotion or advertising but all these are parts of the whole marketing concept. It is equally important in library and information (L&I) centres in India.

Marketing in L&I centres does not require separate marketing expert but some skills and change in attitude of everyone across the whole organisation. Marketing has a customer-centred approach.

The challenge of coping with changes in social, technological, economical and political environment has forced the library and information centres to change their time honoured old practices. Pressure for accountability and the emergence of enterprise culture has led the information profession to take aggressive actions for reaching nearer and nearer to financial self-sufficiency. This has led to user pay for his/her needs principle.

INFORMATION—A NEED OF THE ERA

With the acceleration of the process of liberalisation and globalisation coupled with unprecedented technological developments in information flow, the need for timely, pinpointed, correct and reliable information in India is more realised than ever before. Users need information continuously for progress, for sound decision making and even for survival.

Information is vital for the growth and success of any venture : be it teaching, education, politics, share markets. economic development, industry, technology or research and development, etc. Information is, nowadays, regarded as a resource equal in value to capital, personnel, equipment or any other facilities because it costs money to acquire, process, store, disseminate and protect it. Hence information is power.

The present day power equation is :

Information = Knowledge

Knowledge = Power

Hence, information is power. Information is a life saver for any venture.

Information is required :

a) To keep one current and competitive,

b) To discover new technologies/new concepts or researches,
c) To remain ahead in competition,
d) To capitalise on new markets,
e) To grow one's business (venture),
f) For problem solving,
g) For new ideas in any field, be it economics, politics, psychology, education, etc.,
h) For decision taking, and.
i) For developments.

In short, information is a need of the era and the path to knowledge.

In contrast to their predecessors, the present day managers, technologists, traders, educationists, economists, politicians, psychologists, businessmen and others need much more information in order to survive, let alone progress.

They have to know what is going on in their respective fields, not only in India but all over the world. They have to keep track of new technologies, processes as well as management tools and philosophies. They have to be aware of what is happening on the mineral front, shipping and transportation, crop failures, bank rates as well as what is taking place in the major financial and political capitals of the world.

This being so, availability of right information for the right user at the right time and at the right cost becomes all the more vital. The scenario has posed major challenges to the information sector whose prime function is to satisfy the complex and increasing demands for information products and services in various areas of social sciences.

MARKETING AND OTHER ACTIVITIES FOR SUCCESSFUL INFORMATION CENTRES IN INDIA

Professional marketing approaches will help in achieving maximum utilisation of the information centre's services/ products. For this purpose, information managers will have to take the initiative and a lot of freedom has to be given by the management to the information professionals in their pursuit in this area.

Marketing Strategy

It is the planning aspect of marketing. Marketing strategy should address the following parameters :

a) Any social science information centre should first identity prospective user groups in the areas of economics, education, political science, psychology and in inter/multi-disciplinary subjects, e.g., teachers, students, researchers, industries, politicians, various business houses, technicians, managers, doctors, consultants, chartered accountants, etc.

b) Type of services customers want, need and demand : This can be known by doing a survey of information needs, wants and demands of the various users' groups in the subjects of social sciences and under purview of the information centre.

c) Identify or select stronger user groups. Those who need information most for their work, etc. Priorities the segments you will attempt to serve first according to your strength in areas of your purview in social sciences. This will help in initial acceptance as well as in getting financial (if needed) support. Reduce the number of services/ products so that you can provide them correctly, fast, efficiently, in time and at a cost benefit way. The proverb says, "First impression is the last impression".

d) Develop/design and provide information services/product suitable to identified user groups. One has to adopt innovative and imaginative approaches in the design and development of services and products. Not only this would attract users, but also make them to pay (if needed) willingly for services received. Willingness to pay would depend on the quality and reliability of the services and products.

For product/service development do prepare details as follows:

i) *Idea generation:* Searching for new products/services by applying idea-generating techniques, e.g., You can have 'brain storming' session for new products/services.

ii) *Idea screening:* Eliminate ideas that are unattractive or unrealistic.

iii) *Concept development and testing:* Conversion of ideas into a sound concept and estimating demand.

iv) Product planning, e.g., contents, arrangements, etc.

v) *Mobilising financial resources:* e.g., sponsors, advertisement in products, subscription, etc.

vi) *Appropriate branding:* e.g., Naming contest for new product/service.

vii) Prototype design

viii) Costing and pricing.

Cost-based pricing.

Demand-based pricing

Competition-based pricing

ix) *Distribution channels :* e.g., Through agents, direct, etc. Display and sales at airports

x) Selling

xi) Packaging

xii) *After sale service*: e.g., supply of full-text of article, translations, etc., in time bound guarantee.

xiii) *Promotion:* e.g., Pamphlets, free sample copy, etc.

xiv) Building adequate resources for future, e.g., corpus fund

e) Try to get users feedback time-to-time.

f) Select a small team for new information services/products. Tap creative talents on the job; empower individuals towards achievements.

g) Encourage achievements in economic sectors.

h) Always keep achievements alive for producers, sales and service to users.

i) Always be innovative towards users' need.

j) Make successful high-impact face-to-face sale presentation, e.g., talks, live demonstration at seminars, meetings, articles, personal visit, etc., to potential users.

k) Keep your clients coming back to you for more services.

l) Marketing needs to be added in day-to-day operations so that activities like walk in-counselling, quick response, regular sending of pamphlets to new prospective clients, etc.

m) Training/orientation as a marketing tool: Training/ seminars for users will keep you in touch with users and users' will also remember the information centre when they need information.

n) Word-of-mouth endorsement of activities: There is a proverb, "If you are satisfied, tell others, if not tell us." Word-of-mouth marketing is the most effective way of marketing. Good word-of-mouth marketing comes out of excellence in product/services. Otherwise, it may affect adversely.

o) Becoming service-oriented: Procedural delay in imparting services should be avoided. Service should be the motto. Rules should be such to help the users.

p) In-service training and retraining to staff. Train staff to produce and provide quality and reliable services/products, to understand and be responsive to clients, need, the staff must be motivated to provide timely, quick, correct and reliable information. Staff attitudes should be friendly, helpful, interested in subject and loyal to service. All staff should be educated in such a manner that they feel disturbed, if anywhere the quality deteriorates or goes wrong.

q) Incentive to staff for doing good work: Various incentive methods must be introduced to encourage the staff for doing good work. These may be financial or non-financial incentives.

r) Accepting the principle of 'User pays for his information needs': Real information collection, processing and generation costs money. Expenses have been growing exponentially. On the other hand information has become power. It helps the user positively in many ways, be it an increase in prestige or in money, etc. In view of this charging fees for information service has become an acceptable principle.

s) Application of principles of modern management in running information centre: Information centre should be run in a modern way. It needs suitable planning, organisation, costing, HRD, TQM, accountability, staff motivation, users' response, etc., Orthodox procedures and rules must be abolished.

t) Development of entrepreneurship quality amongst management cadre of the information centre : Marketing needs common sense approach in India, if you have entrepreneurship quality. "Entrepreneurs are made, not born." "No entrepreneurship, no development." A successful entrepreneur is always aware of the new developments and changes that take place around him in the society and is prepared to adapt to the changing needs of the users. The desired characteristics of entrepreneur are : calculated risks; goal oriented; creative ideas; self-confidence; tremendous determination and entrepreneurial aptitude.

u) Accountability to the users/customers : Provide information useful to users and refund fees, if correct information is not provided. Try to satisfy customers as much as possible. Say no, if information is not available. National Information Centre for Textile and Allied Subjects (NICTAS), Ahmedabad, refunds the fees if literature search is not satisfying the users.

v) Sponsorship: Try to get sponsorship of new products, projects, etc., from government, business/industrial houses. Try to find new sources of finance for initial support

w) Donations/Advertisements: Try to get donations for new products/services or for new equipments. If possible get advertisements from industrial houses, wherever possible.

x) Customer designed product/service : In order to get success and users' acceptance, start or modify services/products which meet maximum user groups' needs, wants and demands.

y) Provide one-stop shopping : e.g., full text of articles, translations, further services, etc., at one place/centre.

z) Stick to performance standards–the ones that matter most to your customers: Stay lean. Don't confuse growth with putting on organisational fat. Maintain quick response time to users, say, 0 to Z working days.

TYPE OF PRODUCTS / SERVICES USEFUL TO VARIOUS IDENTIFIED USERS

a) Publications/services, e.g., Bibliographies, CAS, SDI, indexing, information products, etc.

b) CD-ROM database searches

c) Training and consulation service

d) Photocopies, i.e., reprographic service

e) Document procurement and supply

f) Patents supply

g) Translations

h) Online access to databases, both national & international

i) Development of local database and selling them in India and abroad

j) Reference and referral service

k) Workshop/conferences

l) Information sources on internet

m) Periodical subscription saver service, i.e., photocopies of content pages and full text.

n) State of-the-art reports useful to users.

o) Web searching :

Ready references on the web-resource development through Web

Low cost databases on web

p) Development of indigenous databases

q) Introduction of value-added, tailor-made information products.

PROMOTION AND PUBLICITY ACTIVITIES

The list of promotion and publicity activities is very exhaustive, hence, information centre should be selective for promotion and publicity as per the availability of various resources. The activities which could be considered to be the purpose are:

1) Informal contacts
2) Personal contacts
3) Demonstration, e.g., online/CD-ROM/TEXINCON, databases during exhibitions
4) Exhibitions/exhibition cum sale.
5) Brochure/pamphlets to target users.

6) Posters to be displayed at various prospective user's work-places/exhibitions.
7) Advertisement in journals about services, e.g., *University News, INFLAIBNET Newsletter*.
8) Sample mailing
9) Lectures/talks at conferences workshops/seminars.
10) Users' group meet
11) Discount-membership in services / products, e.g., to students, free photocopies to TEXINCON subscribers, etc.
12) Open house
13) Get-to-gether of users, e.g., at the end of some conference of economists, etc.
14) Mass media radio/TV/video film, e.g., local channels or on national T.V.
15) Direct mail
16) Liaison visits and lectures
17) Inter-personal delivery, e.g., pamphlets, information supply by visiting some users organisations.
18) In-house circulation
19) Telephone/telex/e-mail/FAX
20) Website (use internet)
21) Online searching
22) Computer conferencing
23) Bulletin board services for user groups
24) Talk to user groups through or at their associations, e.g. Chamber of Commerces/Association of Economists.
25) Review of information products in national/international journals

Selection of time and place and person for inauguration of new information product/service, e.g., 'TEXINCON' by Dr. Abid Husain during the textile conference inauguration, NACID

26) Annual reports and house magazine
27) Information centre's information on activities may be published in institution's annual report and house magazine.
28) Display of information products at airports, railway stations, etc.
29) Help from similar goal-oriented institutions, e.g., NICTAS took help of all textile research institutions in India.
30) Regular press releases of important events/works of information centre, e.g., handkerchief, terry towels, etc., at NICTAS.
31) Gift of information product by businessmen to promote their business, e.g., Copies of TEXINCON & state of-the-art reports for some technicians.
32) Discount to booksellers, advertising agencies and other intermediates.
33) Sponsorship of information products, e.g., NICTAS Report.
34) Specially prepared and packed information, e.g., comprehensive information packages on jute, terry towel, etc., by NICTAS.
35) Articles on activities of information centre.
36) Publications of user's comments/opinions/suggestions.
37) Publication of live case studies : Typical live case studies of searches/services provided by information centre, e.g., patents/post-operation problems, searches.
38) Video on information centre's activities.
39) Selecting best user of the year.
40) Follow-up by name of previously supplied information user. e.g., Castor, oil information by NICTAS to their old clients.

CONCLUSION

Marketing of information products and services in India needs an indigenous approach as our situation is quite different from the developed countries. We have major users who do not have modern IT facilities. Hence, the information centre's approach should be a mix of both modern as well as traditional systems. The information manager should know that in marketing the main focus is on the clientele and the goal is clientele satisfaction. He should also know that supply creates demand. He should adapt to the changing environment of users. This will help in long-term staying power. Every academician and researcher should keep 10-20 per cent budget in their sponsored projects for information.

BIBLIOGRAPHY

Shah, P.C., Million dollar business untapped in India, *Express Business Avenues*, 1996, 2, 3, 8.

Shah, P.C., Survey of the information needs of the textile and allied industries in India, Ahmedabad, ATIRA, 1980, pp. xi + 200.

Shah, P.C., Marketing vis-a-vis revenue generation in libraries and information centres: An Indian experience, *DESIDOC Bulletin of Information Technology*, 1998, 18, 3, 21-28.

40

Marketing of Information Services/Products in University Libraries: A Case Study of Punjab

Prabhjot Kaur and ***Sewa Singh***

INTRODUCTION

One of the tasks of a librarian is to enable the maximum utilisation of the library and information centres. This can be achieved by marketing information products and services. Marketing is an art by which products are made available to the ultimate consumer. The marketing guru, Kotler (1982),[1] stated that "Marketing takes the focus off the product and puts it on the user's needs. Products are developed from the user's point of view, not the producer's". In a wider context, observed Kotler (1995),"[2] Marketing is a systematic approach to planning and achieving desired exchange relations with other groups. Marketing mix is a set of controlled tactical marketing tools that then bends to produce response it wants in the largest markets. Marketing is thus concerned with developing and/or regulating exchange relations involving products, services, organisations, persons, places, or causes."

PRESENT STUDY

The use of marketing techniques in a library would certainly promote the use of its resources and services, and create a demand for new services.[3] The present study looks at information marketing activities in libraries at three major universities in Punjab, namely, Panjab University, Chandigarh (1947), Punjabi University, Patiala (1962), and Guru Nanak Dev University, Amritsar (1969).

In particular it aims at:

i) Identifying the extent and level of marketing activities;
ii) Knowing about the products and services developed to meet the user's needs; and
iii) Examining the library resources in relation to marketing; and understanding the attitude of library staff towards marketing.

METHODOLOGY

The data collected by using questionnaire method and by personal interviews, were analysed in relation to the four main components of marketing, viz., products, place, price, and promotion, usually referred to as four Ps, for understanding the overall marketing plans of the three university libraries under study.

4. DISCUSSION

Products

To satisfy the requirements of their users, the university libraries in Punjab have developed, over the years, various information products and services. These include collection of books and journals, catalogues, bibliographies and documentation lists, databases, networks, etc. Besides, these libraries offer a variety of information services such as loaning of books, reprographic services, reference service, current awareness, e-mail service, microfilming service, etc.

Collection

A university library makes effort to have a good collection of books, journals, non-book materials, etc., in order to meet the varying needs of users. In the present study, the GND University library has about 340,000 volumes, the Punjabi University library has 367,000 volumes, whereas the Panjab University library tops with more than 600,000 volumes in its collection. The GND University library subscribes to about 600 current periodicals (both Indian and foreign), the Punjabi University library to about 500 periodicals, and the Punjab University Library to 640 periodicals for their research scholars and faculty members.

Library catalogue

A library catalogue enables the users to identify and locate documents of their interest, and it saves their time and energy. All the three university libraries have developed separate language catalogues for books in English, Hindi, Punjabi, Urdu, Sanskrit; and similarly catalogues for periodicals, manuscripts, and rare books.

Online catalogue

It is worth mentioning here that the Punjab University library has been progressively developing online catalogue (OPAC). The computerised database comprising about 80,000 books, dissertations can be searched by author, title, subject, keyword and call number. It is a praiseworthy effort in the region.

Bibliographies

All the three university libraries compile computer-prepared bibliographics on demand, particularly on occasion such as seminars and conferences.

List of new additions

The Punjabi University library has been bringing out a computerised list of new additions regularly on a quarterly basis. The Panjab University library releases *Granth-Sarini*, a monthly list of books acquired; while the GND University library brings out computerised the *Books of the Month* for circulation in the teaching and research departments.

Indexing services

The Punjabi University library brings out an indexing service titled *Periodicals Received this Month*; while the GND University library brings out *Contents of the Fortnight* based on the periodicals received in the library, divided broadly into two sections, namely, sciences, and social sciences & humanities. *List of Periodicals Received this Week* as a current awareness service is well received by the user community in both the universities.

Inter-library loan service

All the three university libraries provide interlibrary loan services, which are amply, used by faculty members and research scholars. For instance, the Panjab University library loaned out 28 books to other libraries in the year ending June 1999.

Reprographic service

Nowadays to support teaching and research activities of a university, reprographic service plays an important role. The Panjab University library provides this service through a private agency within the premises of the library. The GND University library has acquired two plain paper copiers for his purpose, and the Punjabi University library too provides this service.

The Punjabi University library has also microfilmed about 2,000 books and 52 manuscripts for preservation and use. The GND University library has also got a microfilming unit, and some of the rare books and a few manuscripts have already been microfilmed. However, the Panjab University library does not provide this service.

Databases

Panjab University library has the facility of GISTNIC database on current social and economic data relating to India, updated on a monthly basis by the National Informatics Centre. Punjabi and GND University libraries have also prepared databases of their books, periodicals, theses, etc., and some are sent to INFLIBNET for updation.

CD-ROM databases

The Punjab University library has acquired some databases on CD-ROM, viz., *Inside Science Plus, Inside Social Science and Humanities Plus, McGraw-Hill Multimedia Encyclopedia of Science and Technology, Global Books in Print, Translationaum, Hutchinson Multimedia Encyclopedia.*

E-mail service

The three university libraries under study provide e-mail service to their users free of cost for academic matters. This service is well received and amply used by the clients of all the three universities.

Internet service

The Punjab University library provides internet search facilities to its users. Some of the important databases which are frequently accessed on internet are MEDLINE, Library of Congress, Uncover, GMAT, GRE, Universities. The GND University Library has recently established internet linkage and offered search services to its users; while the Punjabi University library has yet to start this service, though it has INFLIBNET and DELNET facilities.

Price

Price may be defined as the value of the product attribute expressed in monetary terms which a consumer pays or is expected to pay in exchange and anticipation of the expected or offered utility.[4] Pricing is most difficult issue to tackle in the context of library and information services.

The library has been a non-profit organisation so far charged with the responsibility to provide free services to its users. With the changing scenario, the issue of pricing the library and information products and services is being seriously discussed in the professionals circles these days. However, users will have to be motivated to pay for these services by adding value to them. Moreover, to overcome the financial crisis to some extent, caused by budgetary cuts, rising prices, etc., libraries too need to take recourse to the fee-based services and products.

But at present, all the three university libraries offer services including inhouse consultation, loan of books, ready reference service, manual and computer literature searches and inter-library loan service free of charge. For photocopying service, however, they charge minimum rates. Microfilming service at GND University and Punjabi University libraries is nevertheless a price service from the beginning.

The amount spent on acquisition of books, periodicals and other reading materials; on equipments, furniture; and on the staff salary is too high in comparison to the meagre charges realised from the users. It is also to be noted that the government grants to the universities ultimately come from the revenue collected from the public by way of taxes.[5] Thus, there is no harm in charging for the various information products and services.

Place

Place is indispensable unit of the marketing mix as it links the products and users both in the internal and external environs of the library. All the three university libraries under study make use of both in-house and outside locations to deliver their information products and services depending upon their nature.

In-house facilities

The Panjab University library provides two reading rooms for about 500 readers at a time. Besides, there are reading rooms in the periodicals and textbook sections, and an outer reading hall for studying personal books.

The Punjabi University library has a reading hall on the first floor for about 600 readers, while the GND University library provides reading room facility for about 200 readers at a time. It also has another reading room attached to the library where personal books are allowed. Besides, the periodicals section also has seating facility for about 100 readers to consult the current issues of the periodicals.

All the university libraries make available services like reference, loan of books, reprograhic, referral on a person-to-person basis. Similarly, library catalogues and bibliographics are used by clientele inside the library. Study carrels are provided to individual teachers in both the libraries of Punjab University and GND University.

Reaching-out Service

The three university libraries distribute some of the services and products to their clientele outside the library premises also.

The Punjabi University library makes available its list of new additions *Periodicals Received this Month* to the teaching and research departments of the university and also to all other university libraries in Panjab. Similarly, *Punjabi Press Anukramnika* is distributed the same way. Also, current issues of periodicals are routed to some of the major science and social science departments.

The Panjab University library circulates *Granth Sarini*, a monthly list of new additions to all teaching departments. The GND University library is the only library that makes available the list of new additions to its affiliated colleges also besides distributing it to the teaching and research departments on the campus as well as to other university libraries.

Promotion

According to Weinstock[6] the main aim of promotional campaign is to identify the information form and its products, to tell who wants the products and services, to acquaint customers with the information firm's reputation, and to pursue potential customers. The promotion of library and information services/ products is further necessitated in order to present an efficient and effective image of library and its staff. Nowadays, promotion of services/products is not only done through selling, advertising, etc., but it includes identifying such essentials as market segmentation, personal contacts, user orientation, media coverage, displays, atmospherics, etc.

Market segmentation

The clientele of a university library can be broadly grouped into three segments: (a) personal members, (b) non-library institutions, and (c) libraries.

The personal members in all the three university libraries include undergraduate and postgraduate students, M Phil and PhD scholars, faculty members, and administrative staff.

The non-library institutions include the various departments of these universities. The GND University library caters to the needs of faculty members of the affiliated colleges whereas the other two university libraries do not. Besides providing services to its own users, the Panjab University library also caters to industries, medical practitioners, etc., while the GND University library serves other academic and special libraries as well. But the Punjabi University library has restricted its services primarily to its own users.

It is, however, important to reach out to as many segments of users as possible so that they are motivated to go to the library to seek information in their areas of interest. To achieve this objective the library staff too has to be well informed and service minded.[7]

Public relations

Public relations is the deliberate, planned and sustained effort to establish and maintain mutual understanding between an organisation and its public.[8] It is considered as one of most important components of promotional mechanism. Public relations (PR) is being followed in all the three libraries through personal communications with students and faculty members, the largest segment. This type of personal selling helps to get immediate attention and response of the users.

Advertising

Advertising and publicity combined together attract the attention of the different client segments. The three university libraries adopt various methods such as display, exhibition, etc., to give publicity to their services and products.

Display of new arrivals

The Punjab University library displays on every Monday new books at the Display Window near the entrance to bring them to the notice of the readers. GND University and Punjabi University libraries display the book jackets of new arrivals on the display boards placed near the entrance.

Exhibitions

The GND University library arranges book exhibitions on certain special occasions, sometimes on themes of topical interest. For instance, every year on 24 November this library organises an exhibition of books, rare books, manuscripts, paintings, etc. to mark the Foundation Day of the University. The Punjabi University library also arranges book exhibitions on current topics, while Punjab University arranges book exhibitions periodically on a particular subject/theme in the browsing lounge area.

Library brochure

These libraries prepare brochures, each containing information to publicise their services, products and other facilities. The library brochure provides information regarding arrangement of books, location of different subjects areas, method of charging and discharging books, rules, description of library catalogue, and so on. It helps the reader to know the library properly, and it is mostly in the form of a folder, which is quite handy and useful.

Accession list

The Punjab University library brings out *Granth Sarini*, a monthly list of new additions. The Punjabi University library prepares a quarterly computerised *List of New Additions*; while the GND University library gives information about the recent acquisitions in a well brought out and indexed *Books of the Month*.

Annual report

Annual report includes statistical information about library activities during previous year regarding the new additions, total holdings, total registered members, books given on loan, current periodicals subscribed, reference enquiries answered, photocopying service, computerisation of library activities, and other achievements of the library. It is promptly published by all three university libraries and distributed to all the teaching and research departments.

Atmospherics

In modern library, it is increasingly being recognised that to provide a functional building that caters primarily to products, i.e., books, journals, etc., is no longer enough; rather more essential is to have an attractive and conducive environment for serious study and work. This is what is called "atmospherics" by Kotler. It is said that the physical environment of the library emits cues that produce cognitive and/or emotional effects in the user.[8] Thus "atmospherics" may lead to library's efficiency, and concern for users.

The Punjab University library has a five-storeyed impressive building in redstone and concrete based on modern principles of architecture. Its modular and functional style fulfils the purpose of a planned library. While all the reading areas face north, the staff areas is on the south with stack areas in between. Its two main reading halls facing the Shivalik Hills offer a panoramic view of the natural surroundings. The library building is centrally air-conditioned and provides comfortable environs.

The Punjabi University library is located in the heart of academic complex. The library building has an area of 6,000 sq. mts. It has soundproof reading hall on the first floor for its readers and its ground floor is the hub of activities with almost all the sections.

The GND University library has a well-designed and magnificent building resembling an inverted pyramid and located in the heart of academic complex. It has an area of 110' X 110' at ground floor rising to 150' X 150' on the fourth floor. However, the entire building is not with the library as it also houses some teaching departments. But the atmospherics of the library is comfortable, though not as attractive as it could have been.

Presentation

It is considered as an essential requirement for promotion of information products and services. For instance, an attractive outlook, good quality paper, typeface, colour, etc., enhance the quality and image not only of the product but also of the library as well as its staff.

FINDINGS AND SUGGESTIONS

On the basis of the data collected and analysis made for the three university libraries in Punjab, the following findings have emerged.

a) Library professionals in general have a positive attitude towards marketing of information services and products.

b) These libraries do not have a marketing plan nor do they have any funds allocated for the purpose; hence it is a half-hearted exercise.

c) There was a mixed response from the library professionals as to whether the information services/products should be fee-based or free of charge.

d) Reference services, both manual and computer-based, are appreciated more by the users in Punjab and GND University libraries.

e) Not much systematic effort has been made on the distribution of information products brought out by these libraries.

f) These libraries are also slow in automating in-house activities in particular, resulting in slow delivery of information services.

g) Users are generally satisfied with the opening hours, and even with the learning resources though they have pointed out gaps in the collections.

h) Of the marketing mix mechanism, they follow some promotional methods, but these are not supplemented by user surveys.

Suggestions

a) The three university libraries must develop a systematic and mission-oriented marketing plan for their services and products.

b) Regarding collection development there is more need for involving users for greater satisfaction.

c) Exhibitions of books on themes of topical interest should be organised more regularly as is being done in the Punjab University library.

d) More emphasis should be given on the "atmospherics" of the library so that reading rooms are comfortable, attractive and equipped with adequate lighting and items of furniture.

e) The library users should also be actively involved in the planning and designing of information services/products.

f) The marketing of resources and information can be promoted by conducting continuing education programmes, distributing the "Know Your Library" and "Library Rules" to, *inter alia*, corporate organisations.

g) User surveys should be conducted at regular internals by library professionals in order to obtain the feedback on information services and products.

h) More and more market segments be targeted for efficient and effective distribution of information products.

i) These university libraries should also endeavour to develop some local databases as surrogate of commercially available databases.

j) Regarding charging for the information services and products in the changing library environs, the users must be adequately educated and convinced about such a need. Such charges, as far as possible, should suit the user pockets.

CONCLUSION

It can be concluded that university libraries in Punjab need to evolve their own marketing strategy to be able to market actively their information services and products. They also need to inculculate more professionalism among their library professionals to prepare for facing challenges likely to emerge in the next couple of decades.

REFERENCES

1. Kotler, Philip, *Marketing for Non-profit Organisation*, Ed. 2, Englewood Cliffs: Prantice Hall, 1982.
2. Kotler, Philip, *Principles of Marketing*, New Delhi, Prantice Hall, 1995.
3. Sewa Singh, Marketing of information products and services : a case study of the Guru Nanak Dev University Library, *KELPRO Bulletin,* 1998, 2, 2, 80-89.
4. Modren, A.R., *Elements of Marketing*, Ed 2, London: ELBS, 1991, p. 284.
5. Vaishnav, A.A., Marketing university libraries; a case study, In: *Information Marketing*, edited by H.S. Chopra, Jaipur: Rawat Publications, 1996.
6. Weinstock, M., Marketing scientific and technical information, In: *Encyclopedia of Library and Information Science*, edited by Allen Kent, New York, Marcel Dekker, 1976, Vol 17.
7. Sewa Singh, *Handbook of Reference and Information Services: Some New Dimensions,* New Delhi :Crest Publishing House, 1997, p.11.
8. Havaru, L.J., Marketing of library and information services, *IASLIC Bulletin*, 1988, 34, 4, 142.

BIBLIOGRAPHY

Batchelor, Bidget, Marketing of the information service, In: *Handbook of special librarianship and information work*, Ed 7, edited by Alison Scammel, London: ASLIB, 1997, p. 373-396.

Condons, Crystal, A non-profit marketing, libraries future, *Aslib Proceedings*, 1952, 3, 10, 407-417

Fylnn, M., Marketing of fee-based information service; the case of BTIS, *Management Information*, 1994, 1, 3, 35-36.

Janakiram, M., Marketing mix in the context of library and information products and services, *Desidoc Bulletin of Information Technology,* 1998, 18, 3, 11-19.

Ishwara Bhatt, M., Marketing of library and information services at British Council library network in India, *Desidoc Bulletin of Information Technology, 1998,* 18, 3, 29-34.

McDonald, Malcilm and Payne, Andrain, *Marketing Planning for services*, Oxford, 1996.

Raju, M.U., Marketing of library and information products and services: a select bibliography, *Desidoc Bulletin of Information Technology*, 1998, 18, 3, 35-45.

Shah, P.C., Marketing vis-à-vis revenue generation in Libraries and information centres: an Indian experience, *Desidoc Bulletin of Information Technology,* 1998, 18, 3, 21-28.

41

Libraries and Librarians in Academic Institutions: Work, Status and Identity

P.R. Goswami

INTRODUCTION

The academic libraries as a distinct type are a very large segment of libraries in our country; as India has libraries of over 210 universities and 11,000 colleges catering to the needs of over 6.5 million students and 300,000 teachers.[1] University of Delhi is considered to be one of the premier universities in India. It has 72 departments and 2,20,000 regular students on its roll. The calendar of the university says:

"The post of Librarian will be accorded high academic rank in keeping with the importance which libraries have assumed in the academic life of the university".[2]

The calendar contains prevalent acts, statues and ordinances with administrative and procedural details. In certain cases, the contents of the calendar are reckoned with guidelines for the functioning of university. However, in practice the provision of 'higher academic status' to university librarian and senior professional staff members and the job performed by senior library professionals in the university in accordance with academic content are questionable.

An attempt has been made in this paper to discuss such issues with examples and anecdotes derived from available literature. Largely, it is an assemblage of ideas drawn from the author's experience in a university setting. The opinion of senior professionals, library users and sociologists have also been examined for the purpose. The attitude of top functionaries of the university towards library has also been studied.

CULTURE OF PRINTED TEXT

Perhaps no one will dispute the fact that academic institutions, libraries and librarians are closely interwind with the culture of printed word. Printing press revolutionised the lives of Europeans during the fifteenth and sixteenth centuries. The 26 inherently meaningless letters of Roman alphabet suited the technology perfectly and within three decades of Guttenberg's invention, there were printing shops in every corner of the continent. It is estimated that as many books were produced in the 50 years after Guttenberg's invention as in the 1,000 years before it. As printers wanted to create new works, translation took off; and religious works were converted from Latin into the vernacular. Latin and Greek authors too were translated into modern languages.

As a result, books were circulated widely. And in order to provide access to books, small library collections managed by scholars and bibliophiles came into existence. A university was founded at Bologna toward AD 1000 and a few years later at Oxford and Paris. It was followed by Salamanea in AD, 1218 Hiedelberg in AD; 1366 and Harvard in AD 1636. The universities gradually developed great collections of books managed by scholar librarians and bibliophiles. Later, in their bid to organise knowledge, the librarians evolved the techniques of classification and cataloguing to the likes of Charles Amni Cutter, Melvil Dewey and others. In fact, the attempts to organise knowledge have continued since the beginning of civilisation through Aristotle and Bacon; the nineteenth century had seen the introduction of bibliographic classification, and the twentieth century signified the advent of computer based information retrieval.

HIGHER EDUCATION AND LIBRARIES

In India, the present system of education is based on Sir Charles Wood's Education Despatch of 1854 which has been hailed as 'The Magna Carta' of the education system. On the basis of its recommendations, three universities were established in India in three Presidency towns of Calcutta, Bombay and Madras in 1857 on the model of London University. Subsequently, two more universities were founded at Lahore and Allahabad during the 1880s. These were affiliating universities with the responsibility of conducting examinations and inspecting the working of the colleges. As regards the objectives of these institutions, Pandit Jawaharlal Nehru in his convocation address of University of Allahabad had said:

"A university stands for humanism, for tolerance, for reason, for the advent of ideas and for the search of truth. It stands for the onward march of the human race towards even higher objectives. If the universities discharge their duties adequately then all is well with the nation and the people."[3]

The Calcutta University Commission (1917), appointed by the government under the chairmanship of Sir Michael Sadler, first stressed the importance of libraries. The Commission said that the universities should take active part in teaching and research. This has an implication for the development of university and college libraries in the country. The Commission further said:

> ... From the point of view, one of the greatest weaknesses of the existing system is the extraordinarily unimportant part in it, which is played by the library. Few colleges have good libraries. Even the best, that of the Presidency College is very defective at many points.

While emphasising the role of library in an institution of higher learning the Commission also recommended that the university should have the services of a librarian who should have the salary and status of a professor and should be an ex-officio member of the Academic Council. Later, the *University Education Commission Report* (1949) under the chairmanship of Dr. S. Radhakrishnan, and *UGC Advisory Committee Report* (1957) under the chairmanship of Dr. S.R. Ranganathan made certain recommendations, which had far-reaching consequences. The former said that the library is the heart of All university's work whereas the latter equated the professional library staff with the academic staff in universities and colleges with regard to their salary scale. The developments in computer and communication technology in the country prompted the UGC to recognise the need for modernisation of these libraries. The Committee appointed in 1987 by the UGC envisaged the creation of a library network. INFLIBNET Committee Report was accepted by the UGC and its recommendations are under implementation in a phased manner.[4]

ACADEMIC LIBRARIES: WORK CULTURE

The issue which has not been addressed by the library professionals properly is the 'nature of work' done by the professional library staff. What is the academic content in their work? Is it merely an acquisition, processing and storage function? What are the jobs, which nullify the custodial role of librarians and put them on par with teachers or academicians? Is it justified to call a librarian a knowledge worker?

University libraries are full of books. Needless to say, a library is not merely a collection of books. An article written way back in 1914 by S.C. Fairchild provides a simple but noteworthy explanation of this statement. It says:

"A library, however small it is, involves systematic selection and correlation of books. It must be built upon a plan and all materials that are to go into its making must be chosen to fit that plan just as all the units that go to make up a house must be chosen to fit its plan. In a very small library, as in a very small house, the plan is simple but it is nonetheless essential."[5]

The policy of acquisition of a university library, for example, will depend upon the objectives of the university which consists of conservation of knowledge, teaching and research (i.e. creation of knowledge). One can now raise the issue: how do the librarians involve themselves in collection development? Perhaps, it would not be an exaggeration to say that most of the librarians depend on booksellers for collection development; and the number of professionals using book selection tools and book reviews is abysmally low. Over the years, librarianship as an occupation has been identified with the application of techniques and processes. The experience of library users written in a carefree manner tells the same story. A famous Indian litterateur writes:

"Am I mistaken in thinking that the champions of library movement are interested in the business of reading? Library Science seems all concerned with systems of classification, shelves, furnitures, locks, keys, registers, vouchers and statistics, everything except reading. In every library, elaborate rules are being framed for the borrowing and returning of books. There is a university library that I visit where there are so many regulations for book borrowing that few ever find the time to go in and borrow a volume."[6]

It is true that the major task of a librarian in a university set-up is collection development and to maintain a close liaison with its readers. Before proceeding to select books, librarians are required to make a diligent survey of academic programmes of the university. A proper assessment of books can be done only in collaboration with teaching faculty. In the present era of narrow specialisations, it may not be possible for a librarian to evaluate books in all fields of study. On the other hand, a university is a highly elitist organisation in which teachers enjoy all sorts of academic freedom. At times, it becomes difficult for a librarian to get adequate cooperation from the academicians in matters like book selection.

In general, it is believed that a librarian's work is bibliographic in nature. During the closing decades of the nineteenth century, there was an appreciable increase in the availability of reading material; and as a result, people sought guidance from scholars in matters like selection of readings. A few early works published as reader's guide were Noah Porter's *Books and Reading* (1870) and Charles William Eliot's *Five Foot Book Shelf* also popularly known as Harvard Classics. Librarians also produced reading guides but not for the scholars. They emphasised the creation of indexes and bibliographies as buying tools for libraries.[7]

There is a feeling that in India the bibliographies and other reading aids compiled by librarians remain underutilised for they lack selectivity and precision. In many cases, scholars prefer to consult reading lists appended to research works or bibliographies compiled by subject experts. For instance, the bibliography appended to *Cambridge Economic History of India* or the ones published in *The 1983 Annual for Facilitators Trainers and Consultants*[8] on topics like teambuilding/team development are deemed as scholarly for their careful selection of entries.

Another dimension of librarian's work is dissemination of information and knowledge. Sociologists view that this particular kind of knowledge work is not recognised in many academic circle. The creation of knowledge is the most esteemed aspect of knowledge work. One can find that teachers imparting instructions in colleges often try for research positions in universities where they can devote more time in serious academic pursuits. A group among librarians believes that 'knowledge dissemination' is not inherently inferior to 'knowledge creation'. In fact, overemphasis on practice and technique in knowledge dissemination or librarianship has strengthened the view that it is inferior to knowledge creation. The processes and techniques adopted in libraries have delimited the role of librarians in knowledge dissemination. In many places, librarians have tried to attract people to libraries but they have not played an active, intellectual role in providing access to contents of material.

In this age of information, librarians have an opportunity to exert their influence. For example, many new projects in companies or in laboratories attached to institution result in a new product or an insight into a problem. There is evidence that 10 per cent of the cost of the new product consist of information brought in to the project and that 5 per cent of that information comes from the library in the form of magazines, books and database searches. The remaining 95 per cent consists of discussions with colleagues, conferences, etc. If the project leaders recognise what the librarians do for projects, and put down the number of man hours they would need from the library, the librarians get a better chance to plan ahead for developing the library's competence in the right direction.[9] Robert Davies writes,

> The librarians must serve as the specialist, the promoter, the interpreter, the disseminator, the trainer. Until the information explosion, the librarians functioned as the reactor to the requests of the users ... with that new leadership role, librarians have the opportunity to exert more influence on management decisions.[10]

However, in an Indian academic environment the most immediate need for librarians and their staff is to see the books as source of information rather than as physical objects kept on shelves. A class number (i.e., subject classification) is assigned to a book so that it is arranged in a helpful sequence and its position on the shelves can be ascertained readily. For most of the staff members in a library, the recall value of a book lies in its class number. The content or the identity of author does not inspire them. Apart from traditional training in cataloguing, classification, reference work and library automation, the professional library staff working in social science/humanities libraries perhaps need to undergo 'book appreciation programme' somewhat on the model of 'art appreciation course' conducted by the National Gallery of Modern Art, New Delhi, or 'film appreciation courses' run under the aegis of Film and Television Institute of India (FTII). Even today, amidst all manners of media revolution, Columbia University graduates in USA are required to take two courses; one on the library masterpieces of Europe and another on the great works of philosophy and political theory. The course reveals that the classics are the pleasures of sustained reading. Similar type of courses can be organised for Indian librarians in their respective fields of interest.

One pertinent question in the field of academic librarianship is: how do we categorise the academic part of a librarian's job? Perhaps, certain soft areas in the field of teaching and research can be earmarked for librarians in academic institutions. These include:

a) The structure of literature in a particular discipline or area of study;
b) The relative importance of different forms of literature such as books, periodicals, thesis, research reports, company information, patents, standard specification, and statistics;
c) How to use range of tools and services available and this would include on line searching and use of CD-ROMs in addition to traditionally published abstracting and indexing services;
d) The selection and evaluation of information and data found; and
e) The representation of the resulting distillation of information in report form.

The jobs mentioned above cannot be carried out separately from the mainstream course teaching. A close liaison between the subject librarian and the course teaching staff is essential. In fact, exploitation of existing knowledge is often as important as the discovery of new knowledge. A library has a significant role to play in helping researchers before selecting a topic for enquiry to discover work, which has already been completed.

In India, many highly placed professionals do not exactly know which part of their work can be deemed as academic. Perhaps a case study designed to present a field view of academic work done by librarians can provide some insight into it. One can undertake the work of scrutinising the titles included in the volume *Thinkers of the 20th Century: A Biographical, Bibliographical and Critical Dictionary*.[11] Thereafter, the extent of availability of these titles in the library can be examined keeping in view their relevance and subject of study. Such an effort would enable the library to identity the gaps in library collection. The publication mentioned above contains a biography, a bibliography, and a listing of critical studies of the entrant and a signed critical essay. The bibliographies list all books with details of original publication in the UK and USA. The assistance provided by reference librarians of University of Chicago and the staff of the reading room of British Museum has been acknowledged by the editors.

One of the major responsibilities of library professionals is to draw attention to the intellectual purposes of the academic library as a means rather than an end in itself; with major contribution to make in relation to learning and to independent intellectual fulfilment. The library is both a service agency and a kind of academic department, a discipline in its own right.

However, in India and elsewhere, the view of the library taken by the university's administration wing is vastly different from that taken by the academic staff. In a brief paper published 30 years ago, with a title 'The Bottomless Pit or the Academic Library as Viewed from the Administration Building' Robert F. Munn says that most of the university administration tend to be very unsympathetic to the agreements as to why the library should be funded without reference to any quantifiable benefits to the institution as a whole. In fact, fighting for funds and spending wisely the inadequate money has become the main job of a university librarian. Though academic library budgeting process differs from one country to another, librarians in India argue for funding almost entirely within the parent institution and against all other internal suppliants for their share of the pot. The authorities do not consider even the logical arguments in favour of enhancement of budgetary allocation.[12] For instance, the University of Delhi faced a severe problem in renewal of subscription to journals in 1991. This happened largely due to lowering of value of rupee and non-availability of additional funds to counter the problem.[13]

Such problems are more pronounced in state run universities. This has encouraged many to go for privatised education. Libraries have been asked to levy development charges and raise funds from students and non-academic private users. Yet a cautious move is needed while privatising education and its peripheral services. The economists have said that knowledge is not only the engine of production, a distinction is to be drawn between public and private property in knowledge. However, Delhi University's Ratan Tata Library has been fortunate to have Rs. 50,000,000 grant from the Government of India as a capital fund to strengthen its periodical collection. The library has also collected donations from businessmen and alumni for development work.

In most of the universities, a librarian's identity as a full or quasi academic staff does not necessarily endear him to administrative officials who may see him in a position of unjustifiable privilege. It is important for a university librarian to be identified with the institution, a person concerned with the advancement of the institution's interest.

ACADEMIC LIBRARIANS: STATUS FACTOR

Librarians working in academic institutions often aspire for faculty status. A few of them like librarians in the Indian

Institutes of Management (IIM) are treated as faculty members. Such a pronouncement is made at the time of appointment. In case of Indian universities, teaching or faculty status to librarians is an unresolved issue. UGC-appointed Committee on University and College Libraries (1957), under the Chairmanship of Dr. S.R. Ranganathan said:

> The higher professional and academic qualifications, the combination of academic and administrative responsibilities and the practice in the universities all over the world indicate that the status and the salary of the library staff should be the same as that of the teaching and research staff.

The recommendations were accepted by the UGC and it was implemented in the year 1961. The matter was not resolved forever, and later the successive Pay Commissions have played a 'hide and seek' game with the librarians in matters relating to pay and other perquisites. Though parity with teachers in core pay scales has been retained, anomalies have been detected in matters like promotional avenues, service conditions, etc. The lackadaisical attitude of teacher's Pay Commissions combined with low bargaining power as well as lack of leadership among librarians has been responsible for the present state of affairs. During the last three decades, librarians had to wait for sometime to get a few pages included as appendix to pay panel reports so that a revised pay scale could be given to them. Even in the latest pay panel report, promotional avenues and fixation of pay, etc., at par with teachers is still under a clout.

In a modern state, bargaining power of a service profession is largely determined by the nature of service provided by it. An eminent author has said that modern employment is like ancient slavery. The only difference is that it is supported by the state and mitigated by contemporary slave's power to blackmail his master.[14] The bargaining power is somewhat analogous to the power to blackmail. One can easily understand that unlike the financial or health care service, the library service is not a crisis service. Even in a university, it is deemed as a support service or a dispensable accessory. As a result, a librarian's voice is often not heard properly in the corridors of powers, and as members of a service profession, librarians in isolation cannot act as 'pressure groups' to the management.

However, in recent years, librarians in many universities have successfully organised themselves under the banner of teachers' union. Most successful example of this sort of white collar unionism is DUTA (i.e., Delhi University Teachers' Association) which consists of teachers, librarians and directors of physical education working in colleges and university departments. All members of DUTA are deemed as members of teaching profession. Though librarians in Delhi University do not normally participate in teachers' strike they play an active role in electing teachers' representatives in decision-making bodies. Moreover, in one of its 1984 resolutions, the Executive Council of Delhi University, the highest decision-making body in the institution has recognised librarians as teachers of the university. The consequential benefits have not been given fully to the librarians, perhaps due to the reason that amendments to statues and ordinances have not been made by the authorities so far. Of late a committee has been appointed by the university to examine the issue of granting teachers' status to the librarians.

There are instances of teacher librarian unionism in western countries too; as in the year 1995, the University of Manitoba Faculty Association (UMFA), Canada, demonstrated that they could help to shape the future of their university. Over 1,100 full-time faculty members and professional librarians began a strike on 18 October 1995. The immediate cause of the strike was attack on academic freedom. Teacher members of UMFA admitted that they were fortunate to have librarians within the union.[15]

In reality, teachers are deemed as an indispensable part of academic institution, whereas librarians are reckoned as providers of support services. The education sector has many support services. Other providers of support services are the people who explore the idea of replacing teachers with educational films, radio broadcasts and other means of distance communication. Today, educational television, interactive computer programme and online learning via the internet all have their believers. But nothing yet looks like killing off the method tried and tasted long before the millennium began; a teacher standing before a group of pupils and imparting wisdom by word of mouth. The majority among teachers still believes that a true definition of a teacher is a person who imparts instruction. Brian J. Enright writes:

> There always appear to have been tension between the teacher and the librarian perhaps symbolic of the old rivalry between the oral and the written word; far from the time of Socrates it was feared that writing would create forgetfulness in men's souls. A relatively low priority is assigned to the construction of a course reading lists by academics – a depressing example of the lack of 'pastoral' care which creates unnecessary and demoralising work for both students and librarians to whom them go for help.[16]

It becomes difficult to have a general consensus on the issue that support staff in the educational sector such a librarians are a part of teaching faculty. For the sake of a much wider acceptance, a librarian's recognition as teachers may not be deemed as an event but rather a process. There is seemingly little consensus among policy makers and to some extent among certain votaries of librarians as to when to recognise librarians as academic staff and how it should be done.

The status or lack of it is a vital issue and librarians frequently ponder over it without ever finding a very satisfactory answer. In fact, status is a mixture of rank, image and perception of one's work; and while certain individuals might successfully improve their status; raising it for a whole profession is rather a different matter.

The librarian in a university is not usually at academic but nor is he only an administrator. Yet a librarian with a scholarly competence, if not distinction, does have a considerable advantage in achieving peer recognition from the academic colleagues.

ACADEMIC LIBRARIES: USE OF INFORMATION TECHNOLOGY

In recent years, the use of information technology (IT) has become widespread in university libraries in India. UGC has given substantial grants to central universities for the acquisition of hardware and other peripherals. Newly founded universities with enthusiastic young and newly recruited workforce have automated their cataloguing data and certain household activities. The UGC-sponsored INFLIBNET programme is supporting such activities vigorously all over the country. However, old universities with huge collection and tradition bound untrained workforce is finding it difficult to absorb the new technology.

As a matter of fact, in any organisation, the technology-based services add value to their output when technology components act in a combined way to achieve the desired goal. The following are the distinctive types of technology components in an organisation (e.g., a library) and illustrative examples of their sophistication:[17]

a) Technoware—object oriented physical facilities – equipment and artifacts;
b) Humanware—Person embodied implicit abilities – individual tacit wisdom.
c) Inforware—document embodied facts and figures – recorded and codified knowledge; and
d) Orgaware—organisation embodied procedures and networks – methods and practices.

All four components are dynamically interactive and are always needed simultaneously for each functional capability of the organisation. Their relative importance is different in different specific activities. In most of the university libraries, 'technoware' has been provided without adequate 'humanware' support; and in many cases 'inforware' and 'orgaware' have been ignored. One of the most explicit examples is the absence of a specific standard for all libraries for the purpose of creation of cataloguing data. Though INFLIBNET programme has endeavoured to do a bit on this account, university libraries are not responding to its suggestion for a standardised format. Needless to say, standards are important for organisation of scientific, technical and other types of information. Sandra Ward writes:

> Standards aim to promote trade by the removal of barriers caused by differences in national practices to protect consumers' interests through adequate and consistent quality of goods and services, to promote economy in human effort... and to provide a mass of communication between all interested parties and to encourage cooperation in economic, intellectual, technological and scientific endeavours.[18]

Moreover, 'technoware' rich university libraries must realise that having the means is one thing; being able to get maximum returns from available means is another. Capability is the power to do something – it is the necessary condition for providing right kind of service. In fact, experience-based accumulation of function specific capabilities, through adapting, adding and upgrading technology components is crucial for the appropriate design and delivery of services. Many universities have so far failed to realise the necessity of appointing a consultant for their library automation projects.

In this new era of information technology, the basic structure of library and its services are bound to change. The huge mansion like libraries with long dusty book stacks and sprawling reading halls are still visible in India. A journalist writes:

> But for most bibliophiles, the 124 years old Mumbai University (Library) is a lavish tomb. Behind the majestic reading room in the five storied stack house lie the carcasses of eight lakh books, rotting slowly in their leather jackets. Some have broken spines; others are infested with white ants inexorably working their way through the fragile brittle pages. And many are over 300 years old.[19]

These libraries are likely to change and fade from the memories of its users after sometime. Digital libraries are taking their place mostly in science and technology institutions where substantial parts of collections are electronic. Now there are new electronic tools to meet old objectives without having acquired the skills. But these would not be very effective. Librarians with new skills are needed under the new conditions. But virtual resources need adequate bibliographical control, skilled intermediation and informed searching. The same expertise is needed while designing system for end user searching. There are traditional roles for librarians which include interaction with clients, etc., and as users access more and more information electronically, they would soon recognise the complexities involved and realise that they need information coastguards (i.e., information professionals) to keep them away from getting swamped and drowned in the waves of web pages.[20]

In a recent book *The Myth of Electronic Library*, William Birdsall asserts the following propositions.

a) Librarians should not accept the inevitability of a technologically dominated information society;

b) The library will continue to serve as a centrestage of an institution, providing a place for social interaction, communal and cultural authenticity and sensory and intellectual stimulation; and

c) Librarians should be identified with a broad concern for the collection, organisation and dissemination of knowledge rather than a narrower focus on information.

In our democratic society, the policy makers traditionally view public access to knowledge as a key component of equal opportunity. Librarians in academic institutions must devise a social and economic strategy for ensuring that these new sources of information storage and retrieval will be reasonably available to all groups of users.[21]

CONCLUDING REMARKS

In Indian universities, the middle level staff mostly provides traditional library services. The 'value added' component in library and information service has so far been prevalent in cataloguing, to provide a uniform record of document, and in classification, to provide a subject arrangement and a finding tool. The status and work of a librarian largely depend on the extent to which a library is used and the degree of effort made by the staff to meet the needs of the users. Librarian's recognition as teachers is still an unresolved issue and it mostly depends on the policy of the institution.

Today, the term 'university' means a corporation of teachers and students, which has the authority to confer degrees under certain defined criteria. It is now deemed to be a breeding ground for bureaucrats. In many universities civil service aspirants normally occupy the library's reading halls. Most of the students depend on textbooks and notebooks for their examination, and quite a few of them get the required 'material' xeroxed from the library. This has undermined to some extent the importance of library in an academic setting. Research scholars and a part of faculty members constitute the major group who make use of library resources somewhat extensively.

Under such circumstances, one can imagine telling a very intelligent but very low paid librarian of an institution, "Your wages are determined by marginal productivity and therefore are just." And this very intelligent but low-paid librarian might reply saying, "I agree that I am rewarded according to marginal value to my product to the employer but you have not dealt with the reason why my marginal productivity is deemed so low. It is basically a case of low social intelligence." In fact, recommendations made by Carl M. White for Delhi University way back in 1965 still hold well. It is said that the case for library development is to be based on the premises that library service of a high quality is the heart of an academic programme of higher quality and one must completely break away from the tradition inherited by the university that a library is a conventional but more or less useless accessory.

In most of the Indian universities, library services are based on age-old practices of cataloguing, classification and reference service. The growing ability to access information instantaneously is set to minimise the need for certain types of knowledge painstakingly acquired by us with our education and possessed by us as library professional. In a world where knowledge is growing exponentially, the logic of innovation is irresistible and relentless.[22] As librarians, if we do not make our own goods and services obsolete by introducing new and improved versions, someone else will do the same.

REFERENCES

1. Tikekar, A.C., Keynote address delivered at National Seminar on Challenges Before the University Libraries in India in the 21st Century, Vadodara. August 9-12, 1999, p.2.
2. University of Delhi, *Calendar : Acts, Statutes and Ordinances,* V2. Delhi, 1988.
3. Ahmad Ali, Moulding the character of the nation. *Statesman*, 11 February 2000, Section 2, p. II.
4. Mangla, P.B., National policy on libraries, information systems and services in India : an overview, *The New Review of Information and Library Research*, 1997, 3,1,155-174.
5. Quoted in Banerjee, R.C., Libraries and the Librarian, *The Modern Review,* 1965, 117, 2. 209.
6. Narayan, R.K., *A Writer's Nightmare : A collection of essays*, Penguin India, New Delhi, 1992, p. 65.

7. Carpenter, Keneth E., A Library historian looks at librarianship, *Daedlaus: Books, Bricks and Bytes* (special issues), 1996, 125,4. 80-81.
8. Goodstein, Leonard D. and Pfeiffer, J. William, Annual for facilitators, trainers and consultants, University Associates, San Diego, 1983.
9. Stjernvall, Gunnel, Librarians in projects : Guest editorial, *Electronic Library*, 1997, 15, 5. 347.
10. Davies, Robert, Information professionals in Europe : Perceptions and realities, *Aslib Proceedings*, 1996, 48, 9. 217.
11. Devine, Elizabeth, etc. Ed. *Thinkers of the 20th century : A Biographical, Bibliographical and Critical Dictionary,* St James Press, London, 1987.
12. Line, Maurice B., Ed. *Academic Library Management; Edited Papers of a British Council Sponsored C*Library and Information Studies in Cyber Age*ourses,* 15-27 January 1989, Birmingham Library Association, London, 1990, p. 7-13.
13. Ghosh, Arun, Structural adjustment and education, *Economic and Political Weekly,* 1993, p. 1562.
14. Chaudhuri, Nirad C., *Thy Hand Great Anarch*, Chatto and Windus, London, 1987, p. 3.
15. Kerr, Ian J., Discontent in academia : Straws from Winnipeg, *Economic and Political Weekly,* 1996, 31,29. 1924-26.
16. Enright, Brian J., Concept of stock : Comprehensive Vs Selective, In Line, Maurice B. Ed. *Academic Library Management,* edited papers of a British Council sponsored source, 15-27 January 1989, Library Association, London.
17. Nawaz, Sharif, Strategic role of technological self-reliance in development management, *Technological Forecasting and Social Change,* 1999, 62, 3, 227.
18. Ward, Sandara, Standards : Their relevance to scientific and technical information, *Aslib Proceedings,* 1994, 46,1. p. 47.
19. Brittle pages of yesterday, *India Today,* 21 December, 1998, p. 73.
20. Nicholls, Paul, Cheshire cats, parallel universe and you say potato, *Computers in Libraries,* 1998, 18, 2, 55.
21. Krautz, J., The Information superhighway : A road to misery, *Contemporary Review,* 1996, 268, 1560. 22-27.
22. Watson, Ian., Information society, *Managing Information*, 1997, 4,10. p. 10.

42

Transition of Libraries and Librarianship in India from Twentieth to Twenty-first Century

M. Sankara Reddy

PARADIGM SHIFT

In the last one or two decades developments in information technology such as the information superhighways, hotlines, transborder networks, internet, world wide web, electronic library and virtual library seem to have had indelible impact on all walks of life. The world community has become a 'telecommunity', with the possibility of access to information to anyone, anywhere, at anytime. The advanced countries are already living in the information age and are moving fast into knowledge based societies whereas the developing and third world countries are still struggling for transforming themselves into information knowledge-based society.

The information technology has brought about radical changes in all activities of the libraries and information centres. At the end of the twenty-first century the libraries in advanced countries, if not worldwide would seem to be performing their tasks such as acquisition, shifting, collating and handling of all information by robots instead of human beings. The creation of the internet by Kline Rock by interlinking two computers for communication of information in the year 1969 has laid the foundation for a paradigm shift in information how. Librarians sooner or later would have to digitalise their libraries and information centers to provide effective and efficient services to their clientale. There is no Shakespearean dilemma of 'to be ' or 'not to be'. Whether it is West or East, rich or poor, the adaptation of technology in libraries and information centres is a must. The difference may lie only in the pace of adaptation.

INDIAN LIBRARY SCENARIO

India is a vast country with diversity of races, religions and languages with one billion population of which 52 per cent are literate. It is one of the biggest democracies with 29 states, eight union territories, 3,366 cities and towns and 5,57,137 village habitats. Most of its people are living in villages and nearly 30 per cent of them are below the poverty line. There is uneven development. Certain parts of the country are developed but many still are underdeveloped and backward. Urban and rural contrasts are striking and visible. There are about 60,000 public libraries, 275 university libraries, 10,000 college libraries, 1000 science and technology libraries and 1,000 social science and learned institution libraries. Out of them only the libraries attached to the scientific and technological institutions and organisations are better developed and equipped and they serve active user groups. With the establishment of the INFLIBNET by the UGC the academic libraries, particularly the university libraries, have started computerisation of their collections. The emergence of NICNET, DELNET, CALIBNET, BONET, PUNENET, etc., also highlight the application of the information technology.

Web technology and networking are spreading fast in the areas like railways, defence, e-commerce, e-banking, e-education, etc. The state governments of Karnataka, Andhra Pradesh, Tamil Nadu, Maharashtra, and Madhya Pradesh have definite plans to establish their statewide portals and networks for e-governance. The spread of technology in library and information centres is tenuous when compared with banking, commerce, tourism, and many other fields. There is a general awareness in the informed sections of population that information whether in the raw form of data or in the processed form called 'knowledge' is regarded as vital resource for the all-round development of the country. Its importance has become all the more essential in the present-day information-based society. The traditional, intellectual and scholarly resources in the libraries and the information centres in a country are a great strength of the nation. But like other resources, information or knowledge resources are grossly uncoordinated or inaccessible and run the danger of being wasted or underutilised. It is rightly said that no society can advance beyond a certain point without effective access to its collective memory of records. An advanced society that loses control over these records will regress.

It is in the context of above detailed background that the transition of libraries and librarianship in India is being examined in this paper. The following indicators are used to compare and contrast the status of the libraries and information centres in country:

a) Collection
b) Tools
c) Services
d) Staff
e) Education
f) User

Retrospective Position

From the ancient times till date information was being packed into different formats. Bricks, papyrus, palm leaf books of ancient times were replaced by printed books with the discovery of movable type by Johanns Gutenburg in 1453. Therefore, the book has become a dominant reading material. Later, serials were added to books as their junior companions in the libraries.

Libraries in India are still the depositories or storehouses of books and other printed materials. Slowly the libraries have reshaped themselves as information centres, storing and retrieving information.

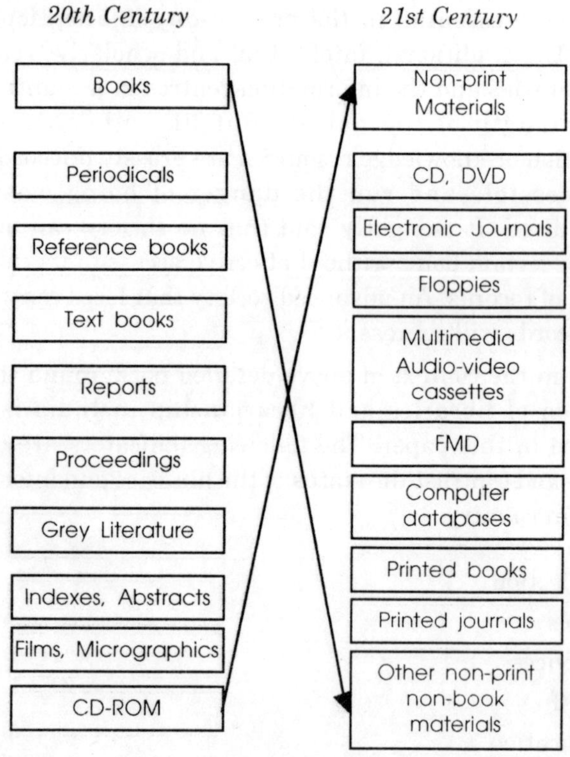

The above figure shows the dominant nature of print media in the twentieth century. There are films, CDs and other micrographics but were on a low scale in the libraries. The electronic materials have begun to appear in the last two decades of the twentieth century in special libraries. The collections in library and information centres in the twenty-first century are likely to be in digital form like CD-ROMs, DVD, FMD and computer databases. There will be printed books and journals too but largely confined to public and rural libraries.

Such materials are more likely to be confined to literature like poetry, drama, fiction and children literature.

Library Tools

The tools, equipment and furniture used in library or information centres are an indication of the stage of its development. Most of the libraries in India have been using cabinets, photocopiers, microfilm cameras, microfilm and microfiche readers, etc. There is a wind of change in the last decades of the twentieth century. The shift in change of tools is the sine qua non of modernisation or digitalisation of the libraries and information centres. Figure 2 indicates such change:

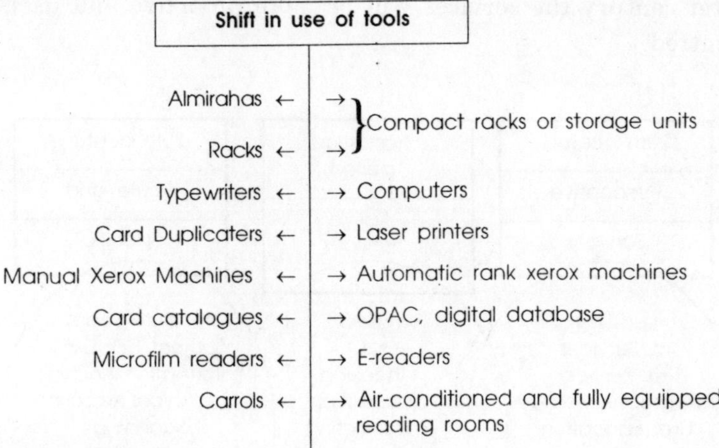

Library Services

Services to the users are the forte of libraries and information centres. But their form and focus have changed. In the twentieth century the Indian libraries and information centres were offering services such as lending, reference, photocopying, ILL, document delivery and preparation of bibliographies. Later in the second half of the twentieth century a few more user based services like CAS, SDI, indexing, abstracting, information retrieval and translation were offered. In the twenty-first century the Indian libraries and information centers are likely to offer far better technical services such as information analysis, information reports, subject CDs, DVDs, and information downloading from different digital databases through the internet, both structured and unstructured information.

At the outset the library services in the twentieth century were responsive. They were rendered at the requests of the readers. Towards the end of the twentieth century and the beginning of the 21st century the services rendered by the libraries and information centres are considered more positive. These are offered at the initiative of the staff and not at the request of the readers or users alone. In the later part twenty-first century the services will be more proactive and user-centred.

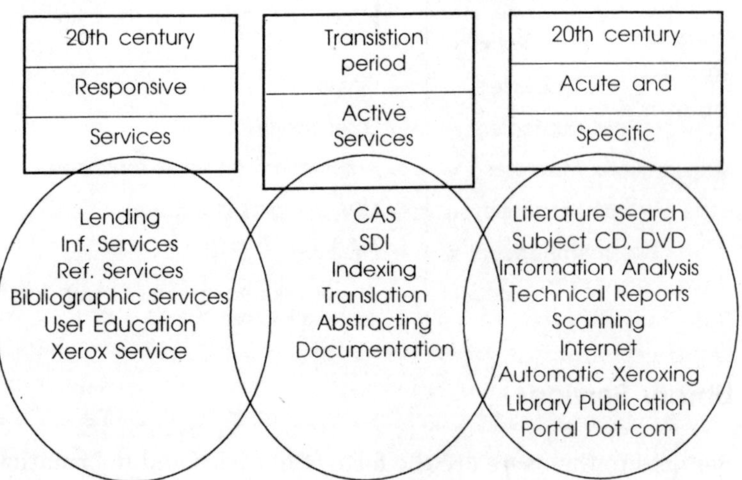

At the end of the twenty-first century the services of the library and information centers will be reader specific and intensive.

The relation of the LIS professionals with the users will be more interactive and on a higher plane.

Staff

The LIS professionals are trained to collect, organise, retrieve and disseminate information to satisfy the intellectual needs of readers and scholars. The needs of the readers largely depend on the environment and situation they live in. Many factors such as economic, political, social and cultural constantly influence the readers and their needs. The attitude, aptitude and behaviour of the readers change. The LIS professionals will have to keep these factors in mind. Further, the developments such as information explosion, information technology, intellectual property rights, information networks, world wide web, competition, cybernetics, artificial intelligence, information handling robots and user behaviour have had their impact on the professionals at different levels. Hence, their work has changed *vis-a-vis* the consumers of information. Their designations are also changing such as information scientist, software engineer, knowledge worker, information gatekeepers and so on. There is a paradigm shift in the professionals' approach and attitude to work.

Education

Education prepares the professional to carry out their duties and functions efficiently and effectively. Library and information science education is a technical one and skill-based. At the beginning of the twentieth century the educational courses in library and information science were non-existent. These were started as elementary courses at Baroda, Lahore and Vijayawada. Before Independence in 1947 the education was available only at the graduate level at three or four universities. Prof. S.R. Ranganathan, the father of library science education in India, devoted his lifetime for its spread and advancement. The LIS curricula was laid giving more emphasis on the traditional subjects like classification, cataloguing and reference services. This trend is still continuing in most of the universities.

The professionals coming out of library schools are ignorant of modern information technologies. The work situations in institutions are changing fast. The professionals are realising that their library school education is not enough or relevant at their workplaces. But changes in the LIS curricula are on the move. To overcome the occupational obsolescence, LIS courses are to be restructured, especially in components such as information technology, computer skills, language programming, Internet searching skills and expert system skills.

User

The user is the kingpin of the library and information centres. All services and facilities are always tuned to his needs. No users means no libraries and information centres. The number of readers/users depend on literacy and education facilities in a country. During the first half of the twentieth century, literacy and education was poor in India. After Independence the literacy has increased from 20 per cent to 52 per cent and there was tremendous growth in the number of educational institutions. Every two days a school, every 15 days a college and every six months a university was established. The central and state governments are trying to provided education to all with the provise of increased availability of facilities for education. The number of educated people, scholars, scientists, technicians, engineers, students and teachers are increasing. Their demands for both structured and unstructured information and for latest information are on the increase. The organisation and retrieval of information in multi-formats are becoming a highly skilled affair. The advent of information technology and web technology had made access to information easier and quicker. Internet made the world a global village. Indian libraries and information centres have started, though late, adopting the digital technology. The change is more visible in scientific and technological libraries. The users in the metropolitan areas, in special libraries and university libraries have started accessing to online information. The position in the public library system may change to the modern practices by the end of the twenty-first century.

THE FUTURE PERSPECTIVE

Change is the kingpin of all progress. From the days of renaissance and reformation and the industrial revolution in the West, modern inventions evolved the modern-day world. Their impact was felt on all aspects of human life including the library and information science. The indicators which were used for assessing the status of library and information centres in the twentieth century are used again for examining the seeming changes in the libraries and information centres in the twenty-first century.

Collection

The libraries will become virtual libraries. They would be able to utilise not only the collection available physically but also of other libraries. The collections will consist of both structured and unstructured information. The collections will be both in print and non-print media. Besides printed books and periodicals, there will be micro forms, magnetic media like tapes, discs, floppies, audio cassetts, video cassettes and optical discs such as CD-ROM's DVD's FMD, WORM, Optical card, CD-EPROM, etc. The multimedia collection of the library and information centres will pose problems of acquisition, organisation, retrieval and dissemination of information which were not experienced in the yester year.

Tools

Tools and machines have been increasingly in use over the last few decades in the library and information centres. Many repetitive works are done by machines. Machines like computers, CD-drives, Rank Xerox machines, laptops, fax machines, scanners, teleprinters, projectors, microfilm readers, bar coding equipment will be ordinary sight. There is every possibility that robots and gizmos will attend to circulation work, maintenance and reference work in future. Cyber libraries will reduce their professional staff and their places will be occupied by the machines.

Services

Information use will increase in the future. The users would require pinpointed and value added services. The LIS professionals would be required to be innovative. Their approach to information service, both structured and unstructured, will have to change. They will have to offer information which will be used by the users to the maximum extent. The information services will have to be directed mostly towards repackaging and content analysis. Virtual libraries will come into existence. The LIS professionals should be able to serve distant libraries and the users online. The librarians will have to become conversant with different formats of information and databases for downloading information for their clientale.

Staff

The library professionals would have to acquire a lot of computer skills. Computer literacy, competence in IT and web technology will be essential, besides the traditional knowledge of classification, cataloguing, reference and management. As the relations with the users will increase phenomenally, the LIS professionals will have to sharpen their communication and information analysis skills. They will have to transform into knowledge worker, information technicians, information engineers, information entrepreneurs, navigators and computer specialists.

Education

The LIS education is to be invigorated, removing many obsolete topics and subjects from the course contents. The curricula and the teaching are to be revamped to meet the future challenges. The proper development of teaching methods and teaching materials is needed. The existing methods are ineffective in developing practitioners to face a highly competitive environment. The teaching methods employed need to be more practical-oriented and skill-centred. In order to develop manpower in the LIS profession for the future the following are the perquisites:

a) The present curricula of LIS should undergo drastic change incorporating the latest technologies for study,

b) Upgrading the skills of staff at all levels to ensure quality,

c) There should be inservce training programmes in computers for LIS teachers and senior professionals,

d) A long-term plan at the national level for planned growth of LIS workforce, and

e) For the benefit of freshers joining the LIS profession there should be intensive apprenticeship hands on experience on computers, human resource management, customer care, marketing and communication skills.

Users

Information explosion is definitely going to have a impact on users information seeking behaviour and information use. The user needs will grow more and more. They would need specific and pinpointed information on micro topics from different documents. They will not rely completely on print media but also depends on information from electronic media too. The LIS professionals will become user interface to get the right information at the right time from a vast body of information. User studies and information analysis techniques would receive maximum attention in future. The LIS professionals will also have to compete with other professionals such as information consultants, information vendors, information resource managers, business analysts, etc.

CONCLUSION

A wind of change is sweeping the developing countries. It is a sign of progress and advancement. There is increase in literacy rate, decline in poverty, steady expansion of educational system particularly in the areas of science and technology. Information and telecommunication technologies which started developing in the second half of the twentieth century have had their impact on Asian countries and in particular India.

The central Government has already initiated information technology action plan. There is considerable interest in computer applications such as e-commerce, e-banking, e-trade, etc. IT is encompassing every walk of life. In the library and information centres the advancement in networking activity is evident from the establishment of networks such as INTERNET, NICNET, DELNET, and CALIBNET. Most of the university libraries have started receiving sustainable help from the INFLIBNET for digitisation of their collections and services. Against this background IT applications in the library and information centres in India in the twenty-first century are projected as follows:

a) At the end of twenty-first century most of the library and information centres, including the public libraries will come to adopt information technology for managing their operations and services.

b) The library networks will expand considerably so as to connect all the libraries and facilitate resource sharing.

c) The concept of virtual libraries will no longer be a dream but a practical reality.

d) The use of multimedia and optical media such as CD-ROM's DVD and FMD in the library and information centres will grow.

e) Besides the e-books and other magnetic and optical media, the print media such as books, periodicals, reports, etc., will continue to coexist.

f) The old and obsolete books and serials will be transferred to depositary libraries for the rare use of scholars.

g) User-centred library services will increase in number to satisfy the needs of users.

h) The big strides in IT technologies will enrich information lending facilities to a great extent enabling a large section of readers to download the required information from the libraries and information centres on their PCs.

i) The large scale networking facilities will remove the barriers of geographical distances between the metropolition centres and the rural areas.

j) The LIS education and training will enable the LIS professionals to render high quality services to the users.

k) The convergence of communication and information technologies will finally lead the country into information age and knowledge based society wherein the libraries and information centres will occupy the centre stage, providing access to information to anyone, anywhere and anytime.

BIBLIOGRAPHY

Anil Kumar, H., The librarian at crossroads: Human resources in the Information age in FID proceedings, New Delhi, 1998

Antonelli, C. (ed.), *The Economics of Information Networks*, Amsterdam: North-Holland, 1992.

Ashokbabu, T, Ramaiah, L.S. Sexena, S.C. and Bedi D. (eds.), *Vision of Future Library and Information Systems*, New Delhi: Vision Books, 2000.

Branscomb, L.M. and Keller, J.H. (eds.), *Converging Infrastructures: Intelligent Transportation and the National Information Infrastructure*, Cambridge, MA: MIT Press, 1996.

Dordick H.S. and Wang, G., *The Information Society: A Retrospective View*, New bury park, CA: Sage Publications, 1993.

Dutton, W.H. (ed.), *Information and Communication Technologies: Vision and Realities,* Oxford University Press, 1992.

Gallimore, A., *Developing IT Strategy for Your Library*, London: Library Association, 1997.

Hills, Philip (ed.), *The Future of the Printed Word: The impact and the implications of the new communication technologies,* London, Frances printer, 1980.

Indian Association of Special Libraries and Information Centres, *Library and Information Profession at the Crossroads*, Calcutta: IASLIC, 2000.

Lancaster, F.W., *Towards Paperless Information Systems*, New York: Academic Press, 1978.

Licklider, J.C.R., *Libraries of the Future*, Cambridge Mass: MIT Press, 1965.

Mangla, P.B., The role of Libraries in global village with particular reference to India: *University News,* 1998, 36:22, pp. 4-11.

Mansell, Robin and when UTA (eds.), *Knowledge Societies: Information Technology for Sustainable Development*, New York: Oxford University Press, 1998.

Martin, Williams, J., *The Information Society,* London Aslib, 1998.

Oppenhieim Charles (ed.) CD-ROM: *Fundamentals to Application*. London: Betterworths, 1988.

Rodriguei, M.V.R. and Ferrante A.J., *Information Technology for the 21st century: Managing the Change*, Boston: CM publications, 1996.

Rowley, J., *Electronic Library*, London: Library Association, 1998.

Saknure, B.G., "Information Technology and its applications in Libraries", In Dhawan S.M. (ed.) *Quest for Quality* (ILA) seminar papers) Delhi: ILA, 2001, pp. 379-385.

Singh, Jagter and Kaur, Trishan Jit, "Quality Information Management for end user satisfaction: Techniques and strategies Indhawan, S.M. (ed.) *Quest for Quality* (ILA Seminar papers) Delhi: ILA, 2001, pp. 66-75.

Thompson, James, *The End of Libraries,* London: Clive Bingley, 1982.

Viswanathan T., Network Society: Vision and Technology options, New Delhi: INSDOC, 1998.

43
Role of Libraries in the Emerging Electronic Information Era

S.M. Dhawan

INTRODUCTION

Information technology is fast gaining significance influence. Its profound in every facet of the human endeavour, every segment of the economy including business, trade, industry, science, education, etc., has started assuming global dimension. It has reduced the world to a global village, and set the stage for transformation of the industrial society of the twentieth century into an information society.

In the information sector, the knowledge industry has witnessed transformations in the publishing media and format. The new media is turning electronic integrating several different forms of expression including text, sound, graphics, pictures, music, etc. The high-density data storage, data portability, networks and networking systems have facilitated new means of data processing and distribution. The e-documents and multimedia documents, incorporating hypertext and hypermedia features, have lent new dimensions to information access and retrieval. The web enabling of databases has made the task of accessing, browsing, searching, and downloading information, including full-text articles, simpler and easier. It has become feasible to share full text documents in a distributed information environment, overcoming traditional barriers of time, space, and language as associated with the print media.

Given the pace at which IT technologies and their applications are developing, it is apprehended that IT might soon come to dominate the information scenario. It is, therefore, appropriate to ponder over the issues of future of library profession, and the role it is going to play eventually in the emerging scenario.

THREAT TO TRADITIONAL LIBRARIANSHIP

IT has been hailed as a boon to the library profession. But, alongside there are apprehensions that libraries might become less relevant in the emerging environment. The threat is apprehended from the internet, the vast pool of digital resources. Internet offers access to (i) scientific journals, journal contents; (ii) cataloguing holdings of major libraries in the world; (iii) research articles and reports; and (iv) product information and specifications; (v) patent information; and (vi) newspapers. More importantly, access to such a wealth of information is available on desk-top. Given its formidable role in improving information access, internet threat to library survival cannot be overlooked.

The threat to the library profession is also apprehended from developments in publishing interesting. Their traditional role is of publishing and distributing information. But, of recently, publishers have started assuming the role of information provider. They have started providing access to full-text journals online via the internet to end-users. The leading players in this regard are:

a) Engineering Index Inc., providing universal access to Ei databases, both bibliographic and full-text;
b) Science Direct service, providing online access to their full-text journals on the internet; and

c) Springer-Verlag, offering its databases and journals online under LINK service.

Access to the publishers' archives on the internet is universal and open to all. Users could reach these archives directly, bypassing the libraries. Undoubtedly, such a process of informatisation has triggered the emergence of a new paradigm. In the long run, the libraries might face tough competition from the publishing trade.

HOW SERIOUS IS THE THREAT?

How serious is the internet threat to library survival? The answer to this question lies in understanding the quality of information the internet stands to offer under a free domain. In other words, to what extent free domain information can substitute information publishers provide in print or from their journal archives.

Internet Resources

Information resources on the internet fall under several different categories such as search engine databases, directories, virtual libraries or subject gateways, specialised databases, and discussion groups and newsgroups.

Search engines databases

Search engines are the most powerful search tools on the web. Several search engines claim to index the entire world wide web. There are also those which index Usenet FTP, and Gopher sites. In search engines, a computer programme called spider, robot or crawler searches for new information on the web. The programme goes over to the new sites, retrieves the hyperlinks attached to the documents, and loads them into a database, indexes them. The indexing procedure differs from database to database. On getting a request the search engine searches for the database. The major search engines claim to index the entire text of the each web document in their databases. Some of the leading search engines are:

AltaVista http:/www.altavista.digital.com

Infoseek http://www.infoseek.com

Lycos http://www.lycos.com

HotBot http://www.hotbot.com

Directories

Directories are subject guides to various types of resources on the internet arranged in a hierarchical way. They are different from search engine databases in many ways. Directories are created and maintained by people whereas search engines rely on spiders or robots for accessing websites and pages for links. Directories contain fewer resources than search engine databases. This is because they rely on people for their selection and maintenance. Most directories have a search capability. Some of the major and better-known directories on the internet are:

Galaxy http://galaxy.einet.net

Infoseek http://www.infoseek.com

LookSmart http://www/looksmart.com

Lycos http://point.lycos.com/categories

Magellan Web Reviews http://mckinley.com

NetGuide http://www.netguide.com

WebCrawler Channels http://www.webcrawler.com

Yahoo! http://www.yahoo.com

Virtual libraries or subject-based gateways

Virtual libraries are the most specialised of all the directories. Librarians who select material for the directories maintain them. Virtual libraries are, therefore, the best places to find sites on a particular topic. They are directories with a difference. They include three major types of resources: subject guides, reference works, and specialised databases. Some of the major and better-known virtual libraries on the Internet are:

The Argus Clearinghouse http://www.clearinghouse.net

Infomine http://lib.www.ucr.edu

Internet Public Library http://www.ipl.org

Librarians Index to the Internet http://lii.org

World Wide Web Virtual Library http://vlib.stanford.edu/Overview.html

WWW Virtual Library: Science http://vlib.or /science.html

WWW Virtual Library: Engn.& Tech.Management http://.vlib.org/engineering.html

Edinburg Engieering Virtual Library http://eevl.ac.uk/

Subject based Inf.Gateways http://www.lub.lu.se/desire/sbigs.html

Roskilde University Library http://www.rub.ruc.dk/lib/

Specialised databases

Specialised databases include both bibliographic databases and full-text databases. These include free as well as proprietary databases. There are several proprietary or commercial databases on the web. But these are not available free of charge. The user has to first purchase access to them. There are also several free databases that appear on the web. Government agencies and many non-profit organisations maintain them. One can find information in a specialised database that is often difficult to locate using a global WWW search engine. Like commercial databases, free databases also index journal articles, patents, etc. Specialised databases are listed under directories, subject guides, virtual libraries. The tools most used for searching specialised databases are:

Internet Public Library http://www.ipl.org/ref

Internet Sleuth http://www.isleuth.com

LibrarySpot http://www.library.spot.com

Yahoo http://www.yahoo.com

Discussion groups and newsgroups

Archives of discussion groups consist of messages when individuals compose them for answering questions, raising queries, making statements, giving help, and supplying accurate information and later mail them on e-mail. Discussion groups–also called as mailing lists, listservs, or interest groups – are based on specific topics. Such discussion group archives constitute a special information resource. Likewise, archives of newsgroups also constitute an important information resource. Newsgroups illustrate the uses of the Usenet, which originated independently of internet. Discussion groups illustrate the uses of e-mail on the internet. Both allow group communication. The following addresses are important for knowing the discussion groups and newsgroups and their archives:

CataList (Catalog of listserv lists) http://www.lsoft.com/lists/listref.html

Liszt (Mailing list directory) http://www.liszt.com

ReferenceCom (Select listing) http://www.reference.com

Publisher Archives

Several publishers post their journals and databases upon publication on the internet for access. These proprietary or commercial databases fall under the category of specialised databases. These must be purchased first before seeking access to them. The primary journals in particular remain posted on the web for access on rolling basis for a specified period of, say, five years or more as per the policy decided by the publisher. Journals prior to the rolling period have to be searched from libraries in print form. As such the publisher archives are useful exclusively for accessing current information. The web addresses of leading publisher sites are:

Academic Press IDEAL http://www.idealibrary.com/

Blackwell Science Synergy http://www. Blackwell-synergy.com/

CRC Press – Online Journals http://crcpress.com/jour/jour.htm

Elsevier Press http://elsevier.com/

HighWire Press http://highwire.stanford.edu

Springer Science Online http://www.sprinper.de/

http: //1ink.springer.de/link/service/journals

Ei Village http:/!www.ei.org/

Comparative Evaluation: Library Vs Internet Resources

A significant proportion of the internet resources are informal communications available under free domain. It also includes informal 'journals' that exist within electronic mail and computer conferencing facilities. But, the scholarship of such publications is still not considered high enough so that they could take up the place of scholarly journals. The demand for such informal communications is still not very significant. Users still need scholarly and peer-reviewed publications brought out by established and reputed publishing houses. Besides, retrieval effectiveness of search engines on the internet is still low. By experience one learns eventually that a large proportion of the retrieved output from the internet databases is nothing but misfits and noise.

Evidently, the internet is still not a useful alternative for meeting the total information needs of usérs for research pursuits. Certainly, it cannot be considered a serious threat to library survival. At the best, the internet could be regarded as a supplement to the library resources.

Comparative Evaluation: Library vs Publishing Industry

The internet has become the marketing window of the publishers, according them wider reach and new avenues of distribution to markets worldwide. Their massive investment in the IT infrastructure has lent them edge over the libraries, offering latest IT faulities for access to full-text scholarly journals online. This advantage offered by has enabled them to emerge as information provider in competition with libraries. Libraries cannot match their technological superiority and as such would not be able to compete with the publishing trade. The publishing houses would, therefore, continue to pose a threat to the library's survival for a long time to come.

Libraries have always been regarded as the repositories of information. They will continue to offer access to retrospective information forever even in the digital and network environment. However, as provider of current information they will have to face stiff competition from the publishing industry. It is in this distinct role that libraries have an advantage over publishers.

HOW TO SURVIVE THE CRISIS?

The declining importance of the libraries as information provider could be attributed to several factors such as lack of IT infrastructure for information flow, their low visibility on the internet, their low document availability rate, and inefficient document delivery systems. Libraries have to overcome these drawbacks.

Transition to Electronic Era

Libraries must make efforts for a transition to electronic era. It is, critical for their sustainability, in particular for fighting out the threat posed by publishing industry, and also to emerge eventually as leading information provider. Transition to electronic era is also a strategic need. Information is power, and the key to catalysing social, economic, scientific and industrial progress. There are reports that in the near future, information-rich nations would only wield power and dominate information poor nations and their economies. Hence, India must also capitalise on the advances in information technology and become an information an rich nation.

Place Libraries on the Web

The transition to the electronic era must be focused and directed at projecting libraries on the web. This is considered to be the best strategy for fighting out the challenge to their existence. What contents should they put up on the web? Individually not all libraries command big library resources, but collectively they do. They need to capitalise on their collective strength. Hence, they need to form consortia and emerge as subject gateways on the web, and start offering web access to their journals. Such gateways could be organised by subject around libraries commanding rich resources in the country. This would also lead to rationalisation of library collections. Such subject-based gateways hold the key to strengthening document delivery systems. Eventually such gateways should strive to emerge as national facilities in their respective areas of interest. It is this vision that should guide their further course of growth and development. Such gateways would have to develop library-specific search engines, designed for indexing and searching information on library sites. Surely, the planning and development of web-based subject information gateways on such lines would help restore libraries their lost glory.

New Roles for Professionals

In the emerging scenario, dominated by digital and network resources, the involvement of library professionals in organising user services will increase manifold. They will have to take up new roles. They will function as knowledge navigators, navigating users to use the information sites and resources. In the online scenario, they will be required to develop and manage websites, updating them on ongoing basis, and answering customers' queries by email, etc. They will also be involved in developing customised information services and packages, and developing new products for information marketing. They will also be involved in digitisation of publications in print, and putting such digitised products on the web. In short, the tasks ahead before the professionals are indeed going to be even more challenging.

Develop New Skills

In order to cope with the changing roles, functions, and responsibilities as envisaged in the electronic information era, library professionals will have to learn new IT skills and techniques. Manpower development and training is, therefore, going to assume greater importance. To what extent should library professionals try to acquire the knowledge of IT skills and techniques? The manpower development and training activity needs to be directed at two levels. At the first level, it is to equip professionals with necessary skills so that they should be able to use information technology tools effectively for giving service to users. This should include fundamental knowledge and awareness about computer hardware and software, and using systems software and packages for performing library functions and services. Elementary level training on these lines is required to be mandatory for all professionals. At the second level, the professionals will have to acquire advanced training in IT software applications. This should include areas such as networking systems and software, internet tools, web technology, development of application packages, troubleshooting, etc. Advanced level training on such lines is to be directed at preparing professionals to write software applications for developing new products and services, customising software and packages for application, interact with the IT trade for getting best solutions to the problems, and prepare them to conduct user orientation programmes in the IT based services.

CONCLUSION

The libraries do face a threat to their survival both from the internet and the publishing industry. But the gravity of threat is more serious from the publishing industry later. They have bypassed libraries and started offering access to full-text journals online to end-users. Their strength lies in their technological superiority in the IT infrastructure for information management. Libraries in India are still technologically backward. Unless steps are taken for their modernisation, it is apprehended that eventually libraries might become less relevant in the digital information environment. The solution lies in making massive investments in the IT infrastructure for libraries, and making them web enabled for online access and resource sharing.

Part VIII

Scientometrics and Use Studies

44

From Librametry to Informetrics and an Overview of Indian Contributions

P.Padhi and *K.C.Garg*

INTRODUCTION

Quantitative techniques evolved during the second World War have successfully been applied to various disciplines. These have also been applied in the field of library and information science. Ranganathan, was the first who in the year 1948 suggested the term librametry at Aslib Conference in Leamington spa.[1] Since then, three more terms, namely, bibliometrics, scientometrics, and informetrics have also been coined.

LIBRAMETRY

By librametry, Ranganathan[2] meant the application of quantitative methods in the management of library and its services. Despite his efforts, the field could not develop until the early 1970s, when he in 1969 in a paper at the Annual Seminar of DRTC, Bangalore, illustrated with some examples the applications of statistics to library work and services. The scope of practical applications of librametry was outlined by Neelameghan in another paper presented at the same seminar.[3]

Ranganathan, intuitively and implicitly, applied the concepts of quantification in a number of areas of library and information management. In some activities, he explicitly practised quantification such as the arrangement of books in the stack room by the frequency of their use rather than strictly by colon class number, on the ground floor near the entrance and the books low in demand were kept on the higher floors. Of course, adequate stack and bay guides were provided to assist in the location of materials.

Data collected daily on charged out books and random checks of the materials left on the reading tables after consultation by users, were analysed to estimate the frequency of use of books in different subjects and was used in the selection, and acquisition of multiple copies, etc. Scatter and seepage studies in different subject areas were carried out at DRTC for selection of periodicals. Likewise, Ranganathan applied the techniques of librametry in periodical binding, staff deployment, budget allocation of books and periodicals and other aspects of library management.[4] Studies using quantitative techniques have been made world over in the last two decades on almost every aspect of library operations such as selection of titles, determining multiple copy requirements, selection of journals, storage of documents, and establishment of loan facilities, etc.[5]

BIBLIOMETRICS

The word "Bibliometrics" first appeared in print in 1969 in Alan Pritchard's article "Statistical Bibliography or Bibliometrics" in the December issue of the *Journal Of Documentation.*[6] In this article, he stated that the term statistical bibliography coined by Hulme[7] in 1923 is clumsy, not very descriptive, and can be confused with statistics itself or bibliographies on statistics. As a result of this, he suggested the word "Bibliometrics". He defined bibliometrics as "the application of mathematical and statistical methods to books and other media of communication." Narin and Moll[8] defined bibliometrics as "all the studies seeking to quantify the process of written communication." Since then, coining of the term by different authors have suggested different definitions.[9]

Bibliometric studies can be categorised as descriptive and evaluative. Descriptive studies deal with quantification of publications in a given field or productivity of literature in the field for the purpose of comparing the amount of research in different countries, the amount produced during different periods or the amount produced in different subdivisions of the field. This kind of study is made by a count of the papers, books and other writings in the field, or by a count of those writings that have been abstracted in a specialised abstracting journal. Evaluative studies deal with the literature used by research workers in a given field. Such studies are often made by counting references cited by research workers in their papers. All evaluative analyses are descriptive as well. The field has matured from simple publication counts to sophisticated statistical analysis of computerised databases using multivariate techniques.

Within the last decade, the nature and scope of bibliometric studies have evolved considerably, moving away from their initial focus library science to policy-oriented studies in science. The studies have also focused on technology, analysing patents rather than conventional scientific literature. As a result of shift in the focus of bibliometrics studies, new names, i.e., scientometrics and informatics were suggested.

SCIENTOMETRICS

The term scientometrics originated as a Russian term for the application of quantitative methods to the history of science,[10-11] but its scope and objectives have widenced considerably. Scientometrics is a wide-ranging field encompassing bibliometrics as "the quantitative method of investigating the development of science as an information process."

The founding father of scientometrics, De Solla Price, has envisaged scientometrics to become a hard science like economics. The vision has largely come true. Scientometrics has followed the trajectory of econometrics in the use of quantitative data, concepts, models, mathematical and statistical techniques of modelling and data analysis. This vision also implies the use of scientometrics for decision making in science policy, just like econometrics is used for decision making in economic policy.

In terms of methodology, scientometric techniques can be classified into two categories: one-dimensional (or scalar) and two-dimensional (or rational) techniques.[12]

One-dimensional techniques are based on direct counts (or occurrences) and graphical representation of specific bibliometric entities (e.g., publications and patents) or particular data-elements in these items, such as citations, keywords or addresses.

One-dimensional techniques are used to generate scalar indicators for monitoring the state-of-the-S&T system. These are increasingly being exploited for science policy purposes, both as descriptive and diagnostic tools.

The two-dimensional techniques are based on co-occurrences of specific data elements, such as number of times the keywords, classification codes, citations and addresses are mentioned together. Multidimensional statistical techniques are being used to represent rational (or structural) features of the data in the form of 'maps'. There are several advantages of using such cartographical representations, such as visualisation of large and complex mass of data in the form of a map that offers a more complete overview in less time. These techniques are particularly useful for strategic decision making.

INFORMETRICS

The term 'informetrics' was coined by Morales[13] in 1985. He defined it "as the metric discipline concerned with the study of mathematical and statistical methods and models and their application to the quantitative analysis of the structure and properties of scientific information and the patterns and laws of scientific communication process including identification of laws proper." At the second international conference on Bibliometrics, Scientometrics and Infometrics held in London, Ontario, in 1989, the late B.C. Brookes suggested that the term "Informetrics" was the most appropriate term to cover bibliometrics, scientometrics and other quantitative studies related to information science. However, Jean Tague[14] differs with this and has given three different definitions to bibliometrics, scientometrics and informetrics.

APPLICATIONS OF BIBLIOMETRICS/SCIENTOMETRICS

The field of the metric studies and their applications are extensive and beyond the scope of this paper. However, some broader aspects of their applications have been discussed.

Publications Output

Publication is an important source of information for scientometric analysis. The scientific output produced by the institutions of a country, to a great extent, reflects the governmental science policy as well as national interests and priorities. Counting of scientific publications output is the most basic technique of bibliometrics in which the number of publications by an individual, group, an institution, a country or a group of countries like ASEAN, SAARC, OECD, EEC, etc., is aggregated. Counting of a scientific publications output constitutes a key element in every evaluation and their use is widespread. By making use of the publications count, it has been possible to point out the scientific centres, sub-centers and peripheries of the world science. It can be helpful in finding out the outstanding scientists in a country.

Scientific output in the form of publications has been used to investigate the most creative years as well as the entry and exit in scientific publishing. Patterns of collaboration, and name ordering have also been studied with the help of scientific output. Productivity data in the case of a country can be used to build up science city maps. Such information would help science planners to strengthen those cities that need specific augmentation.

Scientific output in the form of publications can be used to map out and monitor the mobility of scientists as well. The mobility can be between various cities within the country as well as between two countries. Data on mobility between countries would be particularly useful for third world countries, where there is a need to establish strong links with scientifically developed nations. Publications count has been used to correlate manpower and budget.

The technique of publications count has some limitations, e.g., it does not indicate the quality of work. However, more weight is given to papers published in international journals. In recent years the use of impact factor has been made to judge the quality of a journal and hence the papers published in it. Despite certain limitations people still believe that more publications are better than fewer publications in quality journals and the techniques based on publications count are still in vogue and will continue to be so in the future as well.

Citations Count

Citations count in the data for various scientometric analyses. It is the most active area of modern bibliometrics. The technique of citations count rests upon the fact that scientists cite earlier publications, because the work contained in them is in some way relevant to their own. The basic assumption of citation is that it reflects the influence of an article relative to others and thus the quality of scientific research.

Science Citation Index (SCI) started by the Institute of Scientific Information, Philadelphia (USA), and the developments in the field of computers have been mainly responsible for triggering a number of studies in this area. *SCI* at present covers about 4,000 science periodicals from different sub-fields of science from different countries of the world. However, the journals covered from third world countries and non-English language are relatively less. *SCI* throws light on how often a paper is cited and by whom, and thus is used as a tool to measure the impact of individual articles, authors and journals, etc. It provides an opportunity for studying the relationship between citing and cited papers.

Views have been expressed in favour and against citation techniques. The basic criticism is that all citations are not made for scholarly reasons. There are other reasons for citations besides scholarship of the work. Like publications count, it can also be used to assess the impact for an individual author, an institution or a country, etc.

Based on publications count and citations count numerous indicators have been developed like activity index, attractivity index, relative citation rate, impact factor, immediacy index, publication effective index, relative sub-field citedness, etc.

Empirical Laws

This is one of the oldest areas of bibliometrics. Quantitative relationships based on the empirical work related to the patterns in productivity of journals, productivity of individual scientists, or word frequencies in the literature fall under this category. These relationships go by the names of Bradford,[15] Lotka[16] and Zipf.[17] Collectively, these come under what is now generically referred to as the "80-20 rule". In other words, what was observed was that productivity patterns are usually highly skewed such that approximately 80 per cent of the published papers in a field are located in 20 per cent of the relevant journal set or 80 per cent papers are authorised by 20 per cent of all authors.

Clustering Techniques

Bibliometric maps can be built for exploring the underlying structure of similarities and interrelationships between different bibliometric entities. So far four types of bibliometic maps have been frequently used. These are as follows:

a) *Journal to Journal Citation Maps:* These indicated the magnitude of subject relations between journals and subsequently reflect the macro-level structure of scientific activities.[18]

b) *Co-Citation Maps :* Co-Citation maps depict the linkages among individual articles or books on the basis of their joint citations by later articles. These maps help in identifying the micro level cognitive links.[19]

c) *Co-Word Maps :* The Co-occurrence of words in documents are used to construct a co-word structure representing research themes in a discipline and their inter-relationships, thus capturing the cognitive structure of a speciality.[20]

d) *Co-Classifications Maps :* These are based on the analysis of the co-occurrences of subject classification terms. These classification terms mostly represent cognitive elements which relate to scientific topics, specialities or fields.[21-22]

SCIENTOMETRICS/BIBLIOMETRICS IN INDIA

An analysis of data of the bibliometric studies carried out in India during 1970-1994 indicates that during this period there has been a growing awareness about the field of bibliometrics/ scientometrics. This is indicated by the increase in Indian output and the participation of Indian delegates at the biennial international conference on Scientometrics and Informetrics. The number of papers increased from 31 in 1970-74 to 154 in 1990-94 constituting about 20 per cent of the world output. On grouping the publications in scientific disciplines, it is observed that maximum number of scientometric/bibliometric studies was undertaken in the field of biological sciences followed by earth and space sciences, agricultural sciences and food sciences. Only a few studies have been undertaken in the areas of environmental sciences, energy or engineering and technology. Physical sciences, chemical sciences, and medical sciences were all equally represented. By and large, sub-disciplines received more attention as the micro disciplines.

In the bibliometric field, studies such as scattering or ranking studies and citation analysis, mostly published in journals devoted to library and information science were predominant. This reflected the bias of library schools where a majority of these studies were conducted. About two-thirds of these studies appeared in Indian journals and the remaining in international journals.

Content analysis of the papers studied in blocks of five years indicate that papers related to library issues grew in the initial years but have been declining since 1984. On the other hand, the number of theoretical studies have been steadily increasing. During the 1970s macro level studies on national issues were hardly taken up. Since the 1980s national issues have been more frequently addressed along with theory/modelling. Policy studies were absent in the first decade and have just emerged. The total output form India has been dominated by a large number of case studies, though these appear to be declining since 1990, after an initial stage of proliferation.

This indicates that there has been a qualitative change in the body of scientometric and informatic literature in India. More studies addressed have national or theoretical issues rather than isolated case studies. The emphasis shifted from library related areas to performance evaluation and policy studies.

The number of studies related to policy matters are still fairly small, but may be expected to increase as there were demands for scientometric inputs by decision-making bodies. These changes are in line with international trends where bibliometrics/scientometrics is being increasingly seen as a tool for formulating national productivity indicators and for decision making rather than as a part of library science.

Studies using large-scale computerised databases of publications output, and computer based statistical analysis and sophisticated multivariate concepts have just been initiated around 1994. A comprehensive mapping of national level scientific output has also been initiated at NISTADS, New Delhi.

REFERENCES

1. *Aslib Proceedings* 1, 1948, 102.
2. Ranganathan, S.R., Librametry and its scope, DRTC Seminar 7, 1969, paper DA.
3. Neelameghan, A., *Librametry*, DRTC Seminar 7, 1969, paper LC.
4. Rao, I.K.R., & Neelamegha, A., From librametry to Informetrics: An overview and Ranganathan's contributions, *Libri* 42, 3, 1992, 242-257.
5. Garg, K.C., Quantitative methods in Information Sciences: An overview Collection Management 14, 1991, 75-100.
6. Pritchard, A., Statistical bibliography or bibliometrics, *Journal of Documentation* 25, 4, 1969, 348-49.
7. Hulme, E.W., *Statical Bibliography in Relation to the Growth of Modern Civilisation,* London, Grafton, 1923.
8. Narin, F. & Moll, J.K., Bibliometrics, *Annual Review of Information Science & Technology,* 12, 1977, 35-58.
9. History of the development of ideas in bibliometrics In *Encyclopedia of Library and Information Science,* 42, p. 144.219.
10. Dobrov, G.M. & Korennoi, A.A., The informational basis of scientometrics. (in) Mikhailov, A.I. et al (Eds), *On the Theoretical Problems of Informetrics,* Moscow, VINTI for FID, 1969, 165-191.
11. Nalimov, V.V., and Mulchenko, Z.M., *Naukometriya Izucheniye Razvitiya nauki kak Informatsionnogo protsessat,* Moscow, 1969.

12. Tijessen, R.J.W., Van Rann, A.F.J., Mapping changes in science and technology : Bibliometric co-occurrence analysis of R&D literature, *Evaluation Review,* 18, 1994, 98-115.

13. Morales, M., Informetrics and its importance, *International Forum of Information and Documentation*, 10, 2, 1985, 15-21.

14. Suteliffe, Jean Tague, An Introduction to Informetrics, *Information Processing and Management,* 28, 1, 1992, 103.

15. Bradford, S.C., *Documentation,* Crosby, Lockwood, London, 1948.

16. Lotka, A.S., The frequency distribution of scientific productivity, *Journal Washington Academy of Science*, 12, 1926, 317-323.

17. Zipf, G.K., *Human Behaviour and the Principle of Least Effort*, Hafner, Hafner, New York, 1949.

18. De Solla Price, D., Network of scientific papers, *Science,* 149, 1989, 510-515.

19. Small, H., Co-Citation in the scientific literature : A new measure of the relationships between publications, *J.Am. Soc. Inf. Sci.* 24, 1973, 265-269.

20. Callon, M. et al., From translations to problematic networks : An introduction to co-word analysis, *Social Science Information,* 22, 1983, 191-235.

21. Van Rann A.F.J. & Peters H.P.F., Dynamics of scientific fields analysed by co-subfield structures, *Scientometrics* 15, 1989, 607-620.

22. Basu, A. & Garg K.C., Scientometrics/Bibliometrics in India : An Overview of studies during 1970-1994, *International Journal of Scientometrics & Informetrics,* 2, 1996, 2-3.

45

Collaborative Research in Theoretical Population Genetics: Quantitative Analysis

B.M. Gupta and *C.R. Karisiddappa*

INTRODUCTION

This is a study about quantitative analysis of collaborative research in theoretical population genetics seeking to explore the growth in the number of collaborative publications with time; and about mathematical models seeking to explain authorship distribution trends appearing in the field. In particular, this study is directed at ascertaining the applicability of certain selected probability distributions to authorship distribution with time in the publications of this field.

COLLABORATIVE RESEARCH : HISTORY AND LITERATURE REVIEW

Collaboration in scientific research is defined as : "a process of functional interdependence between scholars in their attempt to coordinate skills, tools and rewards"[1]. As a direct consequence of collaboration activity, multi-authorship in research papers becomes visible. Collaboration in research work has existed in science since ages. The first collaborated paper appeared in

1655. Ever since then, the proportion of collaborated papers in the total publication output has been found to be increasing with time. According to Beaver and Rosen[2] collaboration first came into being in response to the need for professionalisation and increased knowledge. This conclusion was based on the analysis of publication data of papers from seventeenth century to twentieth century.

According to Pao,[3] professionalisation refers to a complex set of dynamic processes involving organisations and scientists, individually and collectively, with respect to both the scientific group and community at large. It also sets the criteria for the new entrants, and formalises rules of behaviour among members, and promotes interaction between the specific groups and outsiders. Some indicators of professional maturation of an individual or scientific field can take the form of initiating professional societies, specialised journals, innovative applications from research programmes, and institutionalisation of prizes and awards. The society, in turn, also recognises the contribution of an individual scholar or professional by taking his/her professional advice in the field of policy-making. Beaver and Rosen[4] have maintained that collaboration in research functions as a social regulator within the profession, through its influence on recognition and subsequent access on resources, and thereby increases the visibility and productivity of authors.

It was during the twentieth century that the professionalisation in science had its maximum impact on the members of the scientific community. Due to of this factor, there had been an increasing trend in the growth of collaborative publications in all disciplines of science and technology (S&T). However, the increase in the number and proportion of collaborative publications and their rate of growth have been observed to vary from one subject to another, one branch to another, within the same subject, and from one country to another. Changes in the growth rate of collaborative publications observed in subject disciplines are probably related to change in the acknowledgement of teamwork, actual increase in its practice of collaboration, and the critical changes in the support of S&T.

Compared to S&T, the situation is different in the social sciences. For example, in sociology and psychology the proportion of single-authored publications decreased from 98 per cent and 84 per cent in the 1920s to 72 per cent and 55 per cent in 1950s. But in most other disciplines of social sciences (political science, anthropology, etc.), very little variation occurred in proportion of single-authored publications. Similarly, nearly all arts disciplines continued to accumulate single-authored papers throughout the first half of the twentieth century

Efforts have also been made in the field to find appropriate probability distributions, which might describe the distribution of the number of authors per papar in different disciplines. It will be useful to point out that Yitzhaki and Ben-Tamar[5] published a comprehensive review indicating how the average number of authors per paper has changed with time in different disciplines.

Just as the number of papers published in journals from individual scholars can be considered as indicator of their productivity, co-authorship in publications can be considered as an indicator of collaboration of a discipline. As this variable can only take discrete values, it is reasonable to assume that a discrete probability distribution would describe the distribution of number of authors per publication. Some scholars have studied this problem and their work has been briefly summarised here.

Price and Beaver,[6] using memos circulated among members of an invisible college, inferred a Poisson model for distribution of authorship in publication of authorship using stationary scientometric distributions. One of the important reviews in this area was reported by Ajiferuke,[7] who studied 15 statistical probability distributions, namely, Zipf, Mandelbrot, Geometric, Shifted Poisson, Shifted Generalised Poisson, Logarithmic,

Borel-Tannar, Shifted Yule, Shifted Generalised Warring, Shifted Inverse Gaussian-Poisson (IGP), Shifted Generalised Inverse Gaussian-Poisson (GIGP), Shifted Binomial, Shifted Beta-Binomial, Shifted Negative Binomial, and Shifted Generalised Negative Binomial and studied their applicability in 94 data sets on distribution of authorship, representing different disciplines from S&T, social sciences, and humanities. His results showed that Shifted Inverse Gaussian-Poisson distribution is the most appropriate statistical probability distribution, which best describes the distribution of authorship in publications. This statistical probability distribution is, however, difficult to understand by an average scholar, because it contains three parameters, besides a so-called modified Bessel function of the second kind. As a result, Rousseau[8] tried selected one-parameter distributions, such as Lotka's, Geometric, and Zero-Truncated-Poisson distributions to the number of authors per publication in library and information science literature. He found that Geometric and Truncated Poisson distributions most adequately describe the observed distribution of authorship in publications.

Rousseau in collaboration with Gupta,[9] subsequently explored the Lotka's, Geometric, Truncated Poisson, Truncated Binomial, and Truncated Negative Binomial distributions in the distribution of authorship during 1976-80 in TPG literature, derived from 11 core journals of theoretical population genetics. The results obtained by Rousseau in earlier mentioned study, are again corroborated and reinforced by these authors in this study which state that where single authored publications dominates, Geometric and Truncated Poisson distribution most adequately describes the distribution of authorship. They have also noticed that it is not clear whether the Truncated Binomial is an acceptable model for such observed distribution of authorship. Earlier scholars, to some extent, in fact, corroborated some of the results obtained by Rousseau and his colleagues, especially in the applicability of Geometric distribution. For example, Goffman and Warren[10] and Worthern[11] found that geometric distribution adequately describes the distribution of authorship in schistosomiasis and drug publications, respectively.

DATA CAPTURING

The bibliography entitled "Bibliography of Theoretical Population Genetics" had been used as the main source of data for the present study. It covers different types of publications in the discipline of theoretical population genetics from 1881 to 1980. The present study has been confined to data mainly from 1901 to 1980. Since the average number of publications per year covered in this bibliography is small, especially before 1950 the publication data was cumulated into blocks of five years each. For studying the growth in multi-authored publications in the field of theoretical population genetics the entire data from the bibliography was used. It consists of 7,877 publications, of which 2,700 are multi-authored. For exploring the applicability of selected probability distributions to the number of authors per publication, publication data from 1941 to 1980 was used. Data prior to 1940 were not used, as collaborative publications in this period were very few.

DISCUSSION AND RESULTS

Overall Collaboration Profile

Distribution of collaborative publications

The distribution of total publications and of collaborative publications was computed on per block basis, of five years each. It showed that there was consistent rise in the number of publications during 1896-1980 (Table 1). The quantum of collaborative publications as a proportion of the total publications also showed consistent rise in general, notwithstanding minor downward fluctuations in certain period blocks.

Table 1: Distribution of Total Publication Output and of Collaborative Publication Output during 1896-1980

Period block	Number of Publications	Number of Collaborative Publications	
	Total	Total	Percentage
1896-1900	8	1	12.5
1901-1905	16	–	–
1906-1910	20	–	–
1911-1915	35	2	5.71
1916-1920	42	2	4.76
1921-1925	63	4	6.34
1926-1930	101	7	6.93
1931-1935	145	10	6.89
1936-1940	137	16	11.67
1941-1945	78	17	21.79
1946-1950	144	29	20.13
1951-1955	289	48	16.6
1956-1960	458	99	21.62
1961-1965	772	186	24.09
1966-1970	1426	420	29.45
1971-1975	1918	698	36.39
1976-1980	2225	862	38.74
Total	7877	2401	

Distribution of publication output by number of authors

In the total publication sample, 5,476 publications (69.51%) appeared as single-authored publications, 1,816 publications (23.05%) as two-authored publications, 443 (5.62%) as three-authored publications, 108 (1.37%) as four-authored publications, 22 publications (0.28%) as five-authored publications, and the rest 12 publications (0.15%) as more than five-authored publications (Table 2).

Table 2: Distribution of Publication Output during 1896-1980 by Number of Authors

Period blocks	Number of publications	Publication's data classified by the number of authors per publication				
	Total author	Single author	Two authors	Three authors	Four authors	More authors
1869-1900	8	7	–	1	–	–
1901-1905	16	16	–	–	–	–
1906-1910	20	20	–	–	–	–
1911-1915	35	33	2	–	–	–
1916-1920	42	40	2	–	–	–
1921-1925	63	59	4	–	–	–
1926-1930	101	94	5	2	–	–
1931-1935	145	135	9	1	–	–
1936-1940	137	121	15	1	–	–
1941-1945	78	61	16	1	–	–
1946-1950	144	115	28	1	–	–
1951-1955	289	241	35	11	2	–
1956-1960	458	359	76	18	5	–
1961-1965	772	586	156	25	4	1
1966-1970	1,426	1,006	330	70	15	5
1971-1975	1,918	1,220	551	109	32	6
1976-1980	2,225	1,363	587	203	50	22
Total	7877	5,476	1,816	443	108	34

On analysing co-authored publications, it was noted that there was a systematic increase in the publication output in all the categories of co-authored publications, although rate of growth in the co-authored publications was not uniform in all the categories. Data on co-authored publications were analysed in terms of the relative frequency of publication under each co-authored category for each block period (Table 3).

Table 3: Distribution of Relative Frequency of Publications during 1931-1980 by Number of Authors

Period blocks	*Relative frequency of Publications by number of authors*				
	Single author	*Two authors*	*Three authors*	*Four authors*	*Five authors*
1931-1935	0.0246	0.0049	–	–	–
1936-1940	0.0221	0.0082	–	–	–
1941-1945	0.0111	0.0088	–	–	–
1946-1950	0.0210	0.0154	–	–	–
1951-1955	0.0440	0.0193	0.0248	0.0185	–
1956-1960	0.0655	0.0418	0.0406	0.0463	–
1961-1965	0.1070	0.0859	0.0564	0.0370	0.0454
1966-1970	0.1837	0.1817	0.1580	0.1389	0.1818
1971-1975	0.2228	0.3034	0.2460	0.2964	0.1818
1976-1980	0.2489	0.3232	0.4582	0.4629	0.5909

The relative frequency is the ratio of co-authored publications in the selected block period and the total co-authored publications under the selected co-authored category. For example, in the category of two-authored publications the relative frequency for the block period 1976-80 was 587/1816 (0.3232). The analysis indicated that there was growth in the relative frequency in all categories of co-authored publications and the increase varied in different proportions as we move from single-authored category to four-authored category publications.

4.1.3. Modelling proportional contribution of single-authors

On studying the output in terms of percentage share of single-authored publications, it was observed that it decreased from 94.28 per cent during 1911-1915 to 61.43 per cent during 1976-1980. It may have been due to World War II. The decline in the percentage share of single-authored publications in theoretical population genetics discipline can be visualised in three stages: (a) Period of slow decline from 1911-15 to 1931-35; (b) Period of rapid decline from 1936-40 to 1966-70; and (c) Period of steady decline from 1971-75 to 1976-80.

Such a decline in percentage share of single-authored publications appeared to have some kind of resemblance with quasi-logistic model suggested by O'Connor.[12] In order to test whether this decline indeed followed a logistic or some other kind of growth model, the applicability of various growth models such as exponential, logistic, Gompertz, and power growth models, to publication data was explored. The power and logistic models were found to be applicable as best amongst the four growth models studied. Table 4 lists the parameter values obtained and fit statistics derived.

Table 4: Application of Selected Growth Models to Single-Authored Contributions: Derived Fit Statistics

Type of growth model	*Fit statistics*	
	R^2	F
Exponential model	0.876	2,865.56
Logistic model	0.914	2,532.03
Gompertz model	0.876	1,751.32
Power model	0.922	2,782.81

For the application of Logistic model, the following equation was used:

$$f(x) = 1/(k+ab^t),$$

where k, a >0; 0<b<1; t ≥ 0; and K = 1/k

When this model was applied to the decline in percentage share of single-authored publications, the parameter values were obtained. These are indicated below and fit statistics were also derived and are shown in Table 4.

$$k = 0.010 \pm 0.001\ ;\ a = 0.007 \pm 0.0001\ ;\ \text{and}$$
$$b = 0.851 \pm 0.052.$$

For the application of the Power model, the following equation was used:

$$f(x) = \alpha + \beta t^7$$

$$\text{where } \alpha, \beta > 0$$

When this model was applied to the decline in percentage share of single-authored publications, the parameter values were obtained. These are indicated below and fit statistics were also derived and are shown in Table 4.

$$\alpha = 44.608 \pm 18.284;\ \beta = 16.012 \pm 15.896; \text{ and}$$
$$\gamma = 0.436 \pm 0.250$$

It is concluded that on modelling the data, using selected growth models on the increasing number of publications having a decline in percentage share of single-authored publications, power and logistic models have shown the positive fits, even though these fits are still not considered as very good. Such results are partially in agreement with those suggested by O'Connor.

Indices of collaboration

Some mathematical measures were proposed in the past by scholars to study the extent and size of co-authorship, as reflected in publications. For example, the Degree of Collaboration (DC) was first suggested by Subarmanyam.[13] It studies the proportion of co-authored publications in total publications. Collaboration Index (Cl) was first suggested by Lawani.[14] It takes the mean number of authors per publication. Collaboration Coefficient (CC) was first suggested by Ajiferuke, Burrdll, and Tague.[15] It takes the proportional mean of the sum of publications with each number of authors, and sets the values between 0 and 1. In order to study the extent of collaboration in theoretical population genetics in different period blocks, the values of DC, Cl, and CC were computed. The results are presented in Table 5.

As can be seen from Table 5 the mean number of authors per publication (as reflected in the values of Cl) increased from 1.04 during 1916-20 to 1.56 during 1976-80. The growth in the proportion of collaborated publications and the proportional mean of the sum of the publications with each number of authors is clearly reflected in the decreasing values of DC and the increasing value of CC. The trend in the computed values of CI, DC, and CC of different period block is almost consistent, reflecting the growing collaboration and pointing towards increasing professionalisation in the theoretical population genetics speciality with time.

Table 5: Indices of Collaboration in Publications during 1916-1980

Period Block	*Collaboration measures*		
	CI	*DC*	*CC*
1916-20	1.04	0.9524	0.0239
1921-25	1.06	0.9365	0.0318
1926-30	1.09	0.9307	0.038
1931-35	1.07	0.9311	0.0357
1936-40	1.12	0.8832	0.0597
1941-45	1.21	0.7821	0.1112
1946-50	1.21	0.7986	0.1019
1951-55	1.22	0.8339	0.0912
1956-60	1.22	0.7843	0.1174
1961-65	1.28	0.7591	0.1278
1966-70	1.37	0.7055	0.1592
1971-75	1.46	0.6361	0.1968
1976-80	1.56	0.6128	0.2178

Applicability of Selected Probability Distributions to the Distribution of Authorship in Publications

The applicability of Lotka's law and two other statistical

probability distributions, namely, Geometric and Truncated Poisson was explored in the eight data sets.

Table 6 : Basic Statistics Derived from Distribution of Authorship Data during 1941-1980

Period Block	*Basic statistics*	
	Mean	*Variance*
1941-45	1.2308	0.2032
1946-50	1.2083	0.1788
1951-55	1.2180	0.2881
1956-60	1.2773	0.3445
1961-65	1.2876	0.3163
1966-70	1.3759	0.4436
1971-75	1.4651	0.5126
1976-80	1.5627	0.7782

Table 6 and 7 report the basic statistics and parameters values obtained from the application of selected probability distributions to distribution of authorship in different period blocks. Table 8 gives the Chi-square values and the degree of freedom of the fitted distributions of these eight data sets. Critical table values of the Chi-square test at 5 per cent level are: 3.84 (df=1), 5.99 (df=2), 7.81 (df=3), 9.49 (df=4), etc.

Table 7: Parameter Values Obtained from Application of Selected Probability Distributions to the Distribution of Authorship in Publications During 1941-1980

Period Block	*Parameter values*		
	α (*Lotka*)	P (*Geom.*)	q (*Poison*)
1941-45	3.05	0.8125	0.4302
1946-50	3.14	0.8276	0.3916
1951-55	3.19	0.8210	0.4074
1956-60	2.95	0.7829	0.5098
1961-65	2.89	0.7726	0.5286
1966-70	2.68	0.7768	0.6756
1971-75	2.50	0.6825	0.8186
1976-80	2.39	0.6399	0.9704

These results indicate that Lotka's distribution is not appropriate for studying the distribution of authorship in publications. In this case, out of eight data sets on publication output, only in one case a positive fit was obtained. Geometric and Truncated Poisson distributions were giving positive fits (indicated in bold in Table 8) in large number of the data sets (four out of eight cases through Geometric distribution and six out of eight cases through Truncated Poisson distribution). It is also observed that only at initial stages of the development of throretical population genetics speciality, adequate fits were obtained from these two distributions. It, therefore, suggests that when the percentage of single-authored publications tends to be large, these distributions show better positive fits. These results are in agreement with those obtained by Tousseau in library and information science publications, and Gupta, Kumar, and Rousseau in theoretical population genetics publications.

Table 8: Chi-Square Values and Degree of Freedom Obtained from Fitted Distributions to Authorship Distribution in Publications during 1941-1980

Period	*Statistical models and distributions*					
	Lotka's inverse power law		*Geometric distribution*		*Truncated Poisson distribution*	
	Chi-square	*Df*	*Chi-square*	*df*	*Chi-square*	*df*
1941-45	9.36	1	**2.20**	1	**0.177**	2
1946-50	16.96	1	4.67	1	**2.491**	2
1951-55	**4.49**	2	**3.19**	2	9.171	3
1956-60	16.98	3	**0.6**	2	**7.662**	3
1961-65	71.54	4	**5.99**	3	**0.239**	4
1966-70	173.63	5	11.79	4	**5.364**	5
1971-75	431.12	6	65.18	4	**0.13**	5
1976-80	420.52	9	26.19	5	29.28	6

CONCLUSION

There is a visible trend towards collaborative research in the field of theoretical population genetics. The quantum of collaborative publications in this field as a proportion of the total publication output shows systematic increase with time. On the whole 65.72 per cent output constitute single-author publications, and the remaining 34.28 per cent as multi-author publications. The distribution of multi-author publications by authorship type shows that 23.05 per cent output constitute as two-authored publications, and 5.61 per cent as three-authored publications. The output of single-authored publications has declined from 94.28 per cent during 1911-15 to 61.43 per cent during 1976-80. On the other hand multi-authored publications have risen from 5.71 per cent during 1911-15 to 26.38 per cent during 1976-80 in two-authored publications set, 1.98 per cent during 1926-30 to 9.12 per cent during 1976-80 in three-authored publications set, and 0.06 per cent during 1951-55 to 2.24 per cent during 1976-80 in four-authored publications set. Although the decline in the set of single-authored publications appears to have some resemblance with quasi-logistic model, yet in actual practice Power and Logistic growth models show positive fits in the data.

When different simple probabilistic distributions were explored for their goodness-of-fit for the purpose of describing publication data by authors per publication, it was observed that Geometric and Truncated Poisson distributions adequately described the distribution. These results agree with those obtained by Rousseau in LIS and Gupta, Kumar, and Rousseau in TPG.

REFERENCES

1. Patel, Narsi, Collaboration in the professional growth of American sociology. *Social Science Information* 12, 1972, 77-92.

2. Beaver, D.De B. and Rosen, R., Studies in scientific collaboration 1. The professional origin of scientific co-authorship, *Scientometrics* 1, 1978, 65-84.
3. Pao, M.L., Global and local collaboration. A study of scientific collaboration, *Information Processing and Management* 33, 1992, 99-109.
4. Beaver, D. De B. and Rosen, R., Studies in scientific collaboration 2, Scientific co-authorship, research productivity, and visibility in the French scientific elite, *Scientometrics* 1, 1979, 133-449.

   See also Beaver, D. De B., and Rosen, R., Studies in scientific collaboration 3, Professionalisation and the natural history of co-authorship, *Scientometrics* 1, 1979, 231-245.
5. Yitzhaki, Moshe and Ben-Tamar, David, Multiple authorship in biochemistry and other fields : A case study of the Journal of Biological Chemistry, in L. Egghe and R. Rousseau, eds., *informetrics* 89/90, Amsterdam; Elsevier, 1990, 373-389.
6. Price, D. J. De. S and Beaver, D. De. B., Collaboration in an invisible college, *American Psychology* 21, 1966, 1011-10.
7. Ajiferuke, lsola, A probabilistic model for the distribution of authorship, *Journal of the American Society for Information Science* 42, 1991, 279-289.
8. Rousseau, R., The number of authors per article in library and information science can often be described by a simple probability distribution, *Journal of Documentation* 50, 1994, 134-141.
9. Gupta, B.M., Kumar, S. and Rousseau, R., Applicability of selected probability distributions to the number of authors per article in theoretical population genetics, *Scientometrics* 42, 1998, 325-333.
10. Goffman, W. and Warren, K.S., *Scientific Information Systems and the Principles of Selectivity,* New York; Praeger Publisher, 1980.
11. Worthen, D.B., Short-lived technical literatures : A bibliometric analysis, *Methods of Information in Medicine* 17, 1978, 190-198.
12. O'Connor, Jean G., DRTC Seminar. 7, 1969, 463.
13. Subramanyam, K., Bibliometric studies of research collaboration: A review, *Journal of Information Science*, 1983, 33-38.
14. Lawani, S.M., Quality, collaboration and citations in cancer research, Florida State University, 1980 (Ph.D Thesis).
15. Ajiferuke, L. Burell, Q. and Tague, J., Collaboration coefficient: A single measure of the degree of collaboration in research, *Scientometrics* 14, 1988, 421-433.

46

Mapping Research in Telugu Language and Literature: A Bibliometric Analysis of Research Dissertations (1988-1997)

L.S. Ramaiah and *M. Ramchander*

INTRODUCTION

The state of Andhra Pradesh has witnessed substantial growth in the academic institutions of importance. The number of universities in the state has grown from two during pre-independence period to eight in the independent era. In addition, the state has come to witness the establishment of several other institutions of importance such as JNTU, Medical University, Agricultural University, and Urdu University. Such a tremendous growth in the academic infrastructure in the state, is bound to influence the growth and development of knowledge in any subject field.

An attempt has been made to study the impact of degree-based research on the growth and development of Telugu language and literature. The need for undertaking such a study is considered even more relevant since Telugu is the second largest language in India after Hindi. This study analyses research dissertations in Telugu language and literature submitted for MPhil/PhD degrees during 1988-1997. It seeks to assess :

i) the research output in Telugu language and literature and its current status,

ii) the universities which have sought to give impetus to research in this field,

iii) the trends and directions of current research in Telugu language and literature,

iv) the research dissertation output by gender, and

v) the publication status of dissertations subsequent to the award of degree.

DATA CAPTURING

The study analysed research dissertations produced in Telugu language and literature and submitted for award of MPhil/PhD degrees during 1988-1997. The following information sources were used for the purpose.

a) Association of India Universities, Delhi : *Bibliography of Doctoral Dissertations: Social Sciences and Humanities*. New Delhi, AIU, 1975.

b) Ramaiah, L.S. : *An International Bibliography of Dravidian Language and Linguistics, Vol 3: Telugu Language and Linguistics*. Chennai : T.R. Publications, 1998.

c) Nityanada Rao, Veludanda: *Visvaridyalayalo Telugu Parisodhana* (Telugu), Rev. Ed. Hyderabad: The author, 1998.

The *Bibliography of Doctoral Dissertations* as published by Association of Indian Universities is indeed a useful document but only to some extent. It provides information with regard to doctoral dissertations alone. It does not cover MPhil dissertations. *International Bibliography of Dravidian Language and Linguistics, Vol 3: Telugu Language and Linguistics* is another useful source. It provides full information as required on research degrees awarded on Telugu language. However it fails to provide information on Telugu literature. *Visvaridyalayalalo Telugu Parisodhana* (Telugu) covers both Telugu language and literature. In all, it contains 2,960 entries.

ANALYSIS

Research Output

During 1988-1997, a total of 1,435 research dissertations were accepted by as many as 25 universities in the country for award of degrees in Telugu language and literature (Table 1). Of these, 660 dissertations were submitted for PhD degree and 775 for MPhil degree. Osmania University ranks at the top for having awarded the highest number of degrees (129 PhD degrees, and 145 MPhil degrees). On an average 77 MPhil and 66 PhD degrees were awarded per year.

Region-wise Distribution

The universities situated within the confines of the state of Andhra Pradesh put together awarded the largest number of degrees in the subject. Their contribution was as high as 93 per cent. The universities from other states put together contributed by 7 per cent.

Distribution by Time

The year 1993 has been the most productive year. In this particular year, the number of degrees awarded was the highest. It also was the year where from research output in the form of dissertations started registering decline, declining from 98 in 1993 to 34 dissertations in 1997. The decline has come about more on account of fall in dissertations from universities within Andhra Pradesh as well as from universities from other states in the country. Secondly, the dissertation output from other states was reduced to naught during 1994-1997. In sum, the research activity in Telugu language and literature, which was observed in 1988 as a multi-state activity, gradually had become a single state activity, confined to Andhra Pradesh only.

Subject-wise Distribution

Telugu Language

Out of 1,435 dissertations produced during 1988-1997, only 271 (18.88%) were on topics studying Telugu language. The remaining 1,164 dissertations (81.12%) were on topics on the subject of Telugu literature. It implies that more emphasis was given to Telugu literature than to Telugu language.

Of the 271 dissertations, 155 were submitted for MPhil degree and 116 for PhD degree. The distribution of 271 dissertations by subject is given in Table 2.

Table 2. Subject-wise Distribution of Research Dissertations on Telugu Language during 1998-1997

Subject	*MPhil*	*PhD*	*Total*
Linguistics	8	5	13
Toponomy & Omenostics	21	20	41
Grammar	19	23	42
Translation	11	4	15
Epigraphy	1	7	8
Stylistics	3		3
Study and Teaching	5	1	6
Folklore	81	53	134
Encyclopaedia and Bibliography	6	3	9
Total	155	116	271

Telugu literature

Of the dissertations on Telugu literature 53 per cent accounted for research in classical and modern poetry. Other sub-subjects studied in Telugu literature were drama, novel, short story, prose, comparative literature, and biography. These sub-subjects together accounted for 47 per cent of research output. It implies that poetry and poetical works including criticism dominate the syllabi of study in the departments of Telugu literature. Table 3 gives the subject wise distribution of dissertations in Telugu literature.

Table 3. Subject-wise Distribution of Dissertations in Telugu Literature during 1988-1997

Subject	*MPhil*	*PhD*	*Total*
Poetry (Criticism, classical and modern poetry including songs)	361	304	620
Drama	40	42	82
Novel	49	52	101
Short story	68	32	100
Prose	65	61	126
Comparative literature	53	26	79
Biography	27	29	56
Total	618	546	1164

Research Dissertation Output by Gender

During 1998-1997, the share of female students in producing dissertations was 39 per cent and of male students it was 61 per cent. Over the years there has been decline in the dissertations produced per year both by male and female students. Secondly, the decline in the research output was found to be sharper in the case of male students than in the case of female students. For instance, in 1988 male students submitted 95 dissertations, in 1997 this output had declined to 53 (44% decline). In the case of female students the output declined from 49 in 1988 to 35 dissertations in 1997 (28% decline).

Table 4 : Distribution of Research Dissertations by Male and Female Students during 1998-1997

Year	*Female Students*			*Male Students*		
	MPhil	*PhD*	*Total*	*MPhil*	*PhD*	*Total*
1988	34	12	49	45	50	95
1989	34	18	52	39	43	82
1990	30	27	57	65	53	118
1991	31	26	57	50	48	98
1992	33	13	46	43	42	85
1993	54	35	80	48	61	109
1994	27	35	62	42	55	97
1995	36	18	54	48	26	74
1996	29	25	54	39	30	69
1997	16	19	35	32	21	53
Total	324	231	555	451	429	880

Distribution by Research Study Supervisors

In all, there were 213 supervisors responsible for guiding research for 1,435 dissertations. These included 38 female supervisors and 175 male supervisors. Twenty students finished their dissertation works without conducting their research study under any supervisor. Sri Venkateshwara University, Tirupati and University of Madras permit scholars to take up research work without any supervisor.

Data as available were collected on research guides/ supervisors and their performance, in terms of dissertation output, was quantified. Table 5 gives data on female supervisors and Table 6 on male supervisors. These tables also list the number of dissertations published after the award of the degree. Since total information on supervisors for all 1,435 dissertations was not available, the total of dissertations as shown in the Tables 5 and 6 is not consistent with the total output. These tables seek to highlight prolific supervisors in Telugu language and literature.

Table 5 : Female Supervisors and Their Output during 1998-1997

Sl No.	*Name of Supervisor*	*MPhil*	*PhD*	*Total*	*Dissertations Published*
1	K. Malayavasini	9	13	22	3
2	P. Uma	9	3	12	1
3	S. Sarala Jyothsana Rani	10	1	11	–
4	C. Mrunalini	10	–	10	–
5	T. Nirmala	4	5	9	1
6	P. Sumathi Narendra	6	2	8	1
7	T. Sathyavathi	6	1	7	–
8	C. Manoja	6	–	6	–
9	V. Sita Kalyani	1	4	5	1
	Total	61	29	90	7

Dissertations Published

Out of 1,435 dissertations submitted during 1988-1997 only 75 were published as books subsequent to the award of the degree. Publishing dissertations as an activity is not in any way correlated with the performance of the supervisor as a research guide. For instance, those producing 32 dissertations, the highest-level performance, were able to publish only three dissertations as books, whereas those producing 18 could publish seven dissertations as books.

CONCLUSION

The universities leading in research studies in Telugu language and literature are : Andhra University, Osmania University, Sri Venkateswara University, Telugu University, Nagarjuna University, Kakatiya University, and Hyderabad University.

Table 6: Male Supervisors and their Output during 1998-1997

Sl No.	*Name of Supervisor*	*MPhil*	*PhD*	*Total*	*Dissertations Published*
1	KK Ranganathacharyulu	22	9	32	–
2	C Ramanayay	23	4	27	–
3	GV Subrahmanyam	17	9	26	–
4	Ravva Sri Hari	16	7	23	–
5	C Ananda Raman	16	6	22	–
6	S Gangappa	7	13	20	1
7	S Akki Reddy	15	5	20	2
8	Y Siva Reddy	8	11	19	–
9	Y Balagangadhara Rao	8	11	19	–
10	K Sarvothama Rao	3	15	18	–
11	G Lakshminarayana	17	1	18	–
12	GVS Krishna Murti	12	6	18	–
13	N Gopi	9	9	18	1
14	L Chakradhara Rao	5	13	18	3
15	M Kulasekhara Rao	6	11	17	2
16	LB Shankara Rao	7	9	16	4
17	PC Narsimha Reddy	7	9	16	4
18	K Enoch	6	10	16	–
19	P Rama Narasimha	14	2	16	1
20	J Suryanarayana	10	5	15	3
21	K Venkata Reddy	7	7	14	1
22	J Suryaprakash Reddy	1	13	14	68
23	Vedula Subrahmanaya Sastri	6	8	14	
24	B Ramabrahmam	10	4	14	–
25	S Raghunatha Sarma	5	9	14	–
26	T Koteswara Rao	4	10	14	–
27	HS Brahmananda	7	7	14	–
28	P Appo Roa	8	6	14	1
29	M Subba Reddy	8	5	13	2
30	A Punna Rao	3	10	13	–
31	R Chandra Sekhara Reddy	3	10	13	–
32	SGD Chandrasekhar	3	10	13	–
33	V Ramachander	9	3	12	–
34	G Damoraram Naidu	2	10	12	–
35	S Anantharama Sastry	7	5	12	–
36	PL Srinivasa Reddy	4	7	11	1
37	SV Rama Rao	4	7	11	3
38	A Narsimha Rao	5	6	11	2
39	R Tirumala Rao	9	1	10	4
40	RVS Sundaram	4	6	10	4
41	TV Subba Rao	7	3	10	–
42	P Subba Rao	7	3	10	1
43	SV Joga Rao	2	8	10	3
44	A Chandrasekhar Reddy	6	4	10	1
	Total	360	327	687	68

More research is done in Telugu literature than in Telugu language. Telugu language, as a subject of study for research, has not received as much attention as it should have. In case we intend to make Telugu language competitive for the purpose of scientific communication and research, the state of Andhra Pradesh will have to promote research in Telugu language especially in areas such as phonetics, aesthetics, lexicography, and stylistics.

Despite the substantial growth in the academic infrastructure in the state after independence, research activity in Telugu language and literature has shown a declining trend. In 1988 research in Telugu language and literature was a multi-state activity. In 1997 it has reduced to a single state activity limited to Andhra Pradesh only. The setback has been largely due on account of declining interest in research in Telugu language and literature. It is perhaps due to the fact that career advancement opportunities in this area of study are not as promising and lucrative as they are in other areas such as science, engineering, medicine, and information technology.

BIBLIOGRAPHY

Biradar, B.S. and Premlatha, R., Bibliometric study of Psychiatric (Alcholism) literature, *IASLIC Bulletin*, 1998, 43,4. 163-170.

Broadus, R.N., Definition of bibliometrics, *Scientometrics*, 1987, 12, 373-379.

Hertzel, D.N., Bibliometrics, History of Development of Ideas, *Encyclopaedia of Library and Information Science*, Vol 42. New York, Marcel Dekker, 1987, p. 144-219.

Kulkarni, Manoj, Bibliometrics portrait of a scientist working on Yoga, *IASLIC Bulletin*, 1997, 42, 4, 185-188.

Lawwani, S.M., Bibliometrics : Its theoretical foundations, methods, and applications, *LIBRI*, 1981, 3, 294-315.

Sengupta, I.N., Bibliometrics : A Birds eye view, *IASLIC Bulletin*, 1985, 30,4, 167-174.

Sharma, Praveen and Garg, K.C., Bibliometrics of solar power research in India, *IASLIC Bulletin,* 1993, 38,4, 155-164.

Subrahmanyam, K., Bibliometric studies of research collaboration . *A review, Information Science*, 1993, 6,1.33-38.

Vinkler, P., Bibliometric analysis of publication activity of a scientific research institute, In Egghe, I and Rousseau, R. eds. *Introduction to Informatics,* New York : Elsevier, 1990, p. 309-334.

47

Use of Indian Government Documents by Economists in University Libraries

Paramjeet Kaur Walia

INTRODUCTION

Government documents constitute the primary source of data for research investigations, especially in social sciences. They contain a wealth of information on policies, programmes, activities, and functions of governments in the state and the centre. They also report and convey legislative information such as on bills, acts, codes, laws; statistical information such as on state population, land, income and expenditure; information on law commissions, committees; publicity and advertising information on government departments, programmes, etc. Distribution and availability of government documents is the key to making this wealth of information accessible to public. In this context libraries have since long been playing their role as an intermediary – storing, processing, and disseminating such an information.[1]

Generally, economists need government information for research pursuits and depend upon libraries for the purpose. They need it most during field investigations and research. This paper looks at the information needs of economists, and the extent to which they depend upon government documents for the purpose. It also examines their preferences for different types of government publications. In addition it reports on the status of document availability in the selected libraries, and the extent to which their collections are comprehensive in meeting needs of the economists. The findings are based on research investigations conducted for the purpose on social scientists in four universities including University of Delhi, Jawaharlal Nehru University (JNU), Panjab University, Chandigarh (PU), and Punjabi University, Patiala (PBIU).

GOVERNMENT DOCUMENTS: DEFINITION

Government documents refer to "informational matter which is printed as an individual document at government expense or as required by law (Title 44 of United States Code)."[2] *The ALA Glossary of Library and Information Science* defines government publication as "any publication originating in or issued with the imprint of, or at the expense and by the authority of any office of a legally organised government or international organisation."[3] However, the *Librarian's Glossary* (Harrod)[4] defines it as "publication issued at government expenses or published by authority of a governmental body". As used in America, it is any publication in book, serial or non-book form bearing an imprint of a government whether federal, state, local, foreign and of intergovernmental organisations such as UNESCO etc.

According to D. R. Kalia[5] an 'Official Document' may be defined as a publication, issued in the name and by the authority of the government, pertaining to its administration or which contains the policy and commitment of the government. Any other publication does not constitute an official document, even if it is issued by and pertaining to the administration of an autonomous as well as government-sponsored agency or a public undertaking owned by the government. This is because the authority of the government has not issued it. Similarly, if the government publishes a book under the title 'textbook of physics', it is not to be treated as an official document, because it does not pertain to the administration of the country or any of its constituent parts. It is just a publication as good as any other published by a private publisher and nothing more. Such a publication shall not form part of the official document collection. He further adds, that books of general interest though published by a department of the government cannot be treated as official documents, unless they pertain to the administration of the country as stated earlier.

In sum, according to D. R. Kalia government documents are such official documents which pertain to the administration or which contain the policy and commitment of the government. Other publications of general interest, even though published by a government department, cannot be treated as official documents. This definition given by Kalia is inconsistent with the ones given in the standard dictionaries. To make matters simple for the purpose of this study, the term government publications has been interpreted as the official documents, the thought contents of which are the direct responsibility of some ministries/departments/divisions or an organ of the government. Such official documents must bear the imprint of a government-publishing house implying thereby the government's responsibility for the accuracy and authenticity of thoughts and expressions contained therein.

Levels at which Government Documents are Published

Government documents are published at several levels of government.

a) Central government documents (national level)
b) State government documents (state level)
c) Local government documents (local level)
d) Documents issued by foreign countries (foreign government level), and

e) International/Intergovernmental organisation documents (International level)

Types of Government Documents

Rae Elizabeth Rips[6] identified seventeen basic types of government publications, whereas Mohinder Singh[7] in his book on government publications has referred to 13 types (Table 1).

Table 1: Types of Government Documents

Rips' Categorisation	*Mohinder Singh's Categorisation*
1. Administration Reports	1. Administration Reports
2. Committee and Commission reports	2. Statistical Reports
3. Research Reports	3. Commission and Committee Reports
4. Statistics	4. Research Reports
5. General Information Pamphlets	5. Bills, Acts, Laws, Codes, etc.
6. Periodicals	6. Law Reports, digests, etc.
7. Press Releases	7. Records of Proceedings
8. Directories	8. Rules and Regulations
9. Bibliographies and Lists	9. Periodicals
10. Decisions and Opinions	10. Maps and Charts
11. Rules and Regulations	11. Lists and Bibliographies
12. Maps	
13. Audio-visual Resources	12. Popular Descriptions
14. Bills and Resolutions	13. Publicity Literature
15. Hearing's	
16. Journals and Proceedings	
17. Laws and Statutes	

On comparing the categories given by both Rips and Mohinder Singh it may be seen that 11 categories of government publications are common to both the lists. In Mohinder Singh's list there are two additional categories that are not common to the Rips list. These are: (1) Popular description, (2) Publicity literature. In Rips' list six categories are not common to Mohinder Singh's list. These are: (1) Audio- visual resources, (2) General information pamphlets, (3) Press releases, (4) Hearings, (5) Directories, and (6) Decisions and opinions.

Types of Government of India Publications

For the purpose of this study the Government of India publications have been categorised into 20 types. These include: Administrative Report; Budget Documents; Census Publications; Charts; Collected Works; Commission and Committee Reports; Economic Surveys; Gazette; Gazetteers; Legal Documents (such as Bills, Acts, Laws, Codes, etc., Law Reports, Digest, etc.; Rules and Regulations; Legislative Documents; List of Books and Bibliographies; Maps; Periodicals; Plan Documents; Records (National Archives of India); Research Reports; Statistical Publications.

SURVEY OF ECONOMISTS

Economics is a subject of teaching and research in the north campus of University of Delhi, and also in the JNU, PU and PBIU. The total strength of research students and faculty members in four universities is 229. Of these, questionnaires were administered to as many as 172 members (75.1% members); 143 members (83.1%) responded to the questionnaires (Table 2).

Use of Library for Government Documents

Preferences for a particular library

The data collected from all the four universities reveals that social scientists prefer to use the university library on their own campus. The response in this regard from JNU, PBIU, and PU was 100 per cent, 81.8 per cent, and 55.2 per cent respectively. In DU preference for using Delhi School of Economics known as Ratan Tata Library has been 100 per cent. The preference to use departmental library has been 44.8 per cent in PU, and 18.2 per cent in PBIU.

Table 2: Sample Size for Survey and Response of Economists

University	*Population size*	*Question-naire admini-stered*	*Question-naire res-ponded*	*Response of the total population*
DU(NC	65	51 (78.5%)	43 (84.3%)	66.2%
DU(SC)	Nil	Nil	Nil	Nil
JNU 77	40 (52%)	38 (95%)	49.4%	
PU 39	39 (100%)	29 (74.4%)	74.4%	
PBIU	48	42 (87.5%)	33 (78.6%)	68.8%
Total	**229(100%)**	**172(100%)**	**143(100%)**	**62.4%**

Usefulness of Different Categories of Documents

Economists use different types of documents including government documents for pursuing their academic and research interests. They rank the usefulness of periodicals at the top of the list. This trend is common to all the four universities. Books/Monographs are bracketed with periodicals in DU (NC) and PBIU, in JNU and PU they are ranked at second position. Newspapers are ranked with periodicals in JNU and PU. Government documents occupy third rank in DU, JNU, and PU and fourth in PBIU (Table 3).

Use of Indian Government Documents

Usefulness of government documents issued at various levels

The central government publications are relatively considered 'useful' in all the four universities. The proportion of respondents rating them so has been 81.6 per cent in JNU, 76.7 per cent in DU, 60.6 per cent in PBIU and 51.7 per cent in PU.

Table 3: Usefulness of Different Categories of Documents

Type of Documents	*DU (NC) (Rank)*	*JNU (Rank)*	*PU (Rank)*	*PBIU (Rank)*
Books/ Monographs	1	2	2	1
Reference Books	5	4	2	3
Periodicals	1	1	1	1
Newspapers	2	1	1	4
Government Publications	3	3	3	4
Conference Proceedings	4	5	6	6
Dissertations/Theses	6	4	4	5
Manuscripts	Nil	Nil	Nil	Nil
Bibliographical/Indexing/ Abstracting Sources	7	4	5	7
Pamphlets	Nil	6	7	8
Patents/Standards Specifications	Nil	Nil	Nil	Nil

Purpose of using Indian government publications by economists

Economists use central government publications largely for research work. Their response in this regard has been 100 per cent each in JNU, PU, and PBIU, and 79.1 per cent in DU. Comparatively, they do not need government documents as much for the purposes of teaching, as well as for seeking topical information.

Kind of information obtained from Indian government documents

Majority of economists (77.2%) in all the universities under study use government documents to obtain census data or statistical data; 17.2 per cent use them to obtain information

Table 4: Usefulness of Government Publications as Perceived by Economists

	DU(NC)			JNU			PU			PBIU		
Purpose of Govt. Publications	*MU*	*U*	*NU*	*MU*	*U*	*NU*	*MU*	*U*	*NU*	*MU*	*U*	*NU*
Central Govt Publications	14 32.6%	19 44.2%	10 23.3%	14 36.8%	17 44.7%	7 18.4%	10 34.5%	5 17.2%	14 48.3%	12 36.4%	8 24.2%	13 39.4%
State Govt. Publication	nil	1 2.3%	42 97.7%	9 23.7%	16 42.1%	13 34.2%	20 69.0%	6 20.7%	3 9.1%	22 66.7%	8 24.2%	3 9.1%
Local Govt. Publications	nil	nil	43 100%	1 2.6%	6 15.8%	31 81.6%	4 13.8%	13 44.8%	12 41.4%	9 27.3%	5 15.2%	19 57.6%
Publications Issued by Foreign Govt.	nil	nil	43 100%	Nil	2 5.3%	36 94.7%	Nil	5 17.2%	24 82.8%	nil	3 9.09%	30 98.9%
Publications of International/Inter Govt. Organisations	nil	31 72.1%	12 27.9%	Nil	23 60.5%	15 39.5%	10 34.5%	5 17.2%	20 40.3%	14 33.3%	11 6.1%	2 60.6%

MU = Most useful U = Useful NU = Not useful

Table 5: *Purpose of Using Indian Government Documents by Economists*

	DU(NC)		*JNU*		*PU*		*PBIU*		*Total*	
Purpose of use	*Yes*	*No*	*Yes*	*No*	*Yes*	*No*	*Yes*	*No*	*Yes*	*No*
Teaching	7 16.3%	36 83.7%	4 11.1%	32 88.9%	3 18.6%	13 81.3%	7 29.2%	17 70.8%	21 17.6%	9 82.4%
Research	34 79.1%	9 20.1%	36 100%	nil	16 100%	nil	24 100%	nil	110 92.4%	9 7.6%
Browsing and keeping up to-date with Information	nil	34 100%	4 11.1%	32 88.9%	9 56.3%	7 43.8%	17 70.8%	7 29.2%	30 25.2%	89 74.8%
Information Search	12 27.9%	31 72.1%	13 36.1%	23 63.9%	7 43.8%	9 56.3%	17 70.8%	7 29.2%	49 41.2%	70 58.8%

on events and issues of topical interest. Only 5.3 per cent use them to get information of historical value.

Use of different types of Indian government documents

The most used government documents in DU are statistical documents, economic surveys, plan documents, budgets documents. The least used documents are research reports, records (NAI) law reports, digests, etc. and maps. In JNU the most used document types are statistical documents, budget documents, plan documents and economics surveys. The least used types are records, law reports, digests, charts, bills, acts, laws, codes, etc.

Table 6: Government of India Publications Ranked by Total Use

S.No.	Types of Documents	DU (NC)	JNU	PU	PBIU
1.	Administrative Report	7	7	8	8
2.	Budget Documents	4	2	2	3
3.	Census Publications	8	10	11	7
4.	Charts	13	18	9	11
5.	Collected Works	11	13	14	14
6.	Commission and Committee Reports	6	6	12	6
7.	Economic Surveys	2	4	3	4
8.	Gazette	9	15	15	13
9.	Gazetteers	15	14	16	17
10.	Legal Documents				
10.1	Bills, Acts, Laws, Codes etc.	12	17	18	15
10.2	Law Reports, Digests, etc.	18	19	19	19
10.3	Rules and Regulations	16	11	17	18
11.	Legislative Document	14	12	13	16
12.	List of Books/ Bibliographies/ Catalogues	10	16	5	9
13.	Maps	17	9	10	12
14.	Periodicals	5	5	6	10
15.	Plan Documents	3	3	1	1
16.	Records (NAI)	19	20	20	10
17.	Research Reports	20	8	7	5
18.	Statistical Publications	1	1	4	2

In PU the most used document types are plan documents followed by budget documents, economic surveys, and statistical documents. The least used are records, law reports, digests, economic surveys, and statistical documents. The most used documents types in PBIU are plan documents, statistical documents, budget documents and economic surveys and the least used are records, law reports, digests, rules and regulations and gazetteers.

Use of Indian government documents in different forms

Majority of economists have used Indian government publications in the printed form. This study reveals that use of government documents in microform is almost non-existent. Just about 7 per cent economists from DU, 11.1 per cent from JNU, and 6.3 per cent from PU have indicated that they have used government publications in the electronic media.

Table 7: Use of Government of India Publications in Different Forms

	DU (NC)		*JUN*		*PU*		*PBIU*	
Form	*Yes*	*No*	*Yes*	*No*	*Yes*	*No*	*Yes*	*No*
Microforms (i.e., Micro--films, Micro -fiche, etc.)	Nil	43 100%	nil	36 100%	Nil	16 100%	Nil	24 100%
Computerised Storage	3	40	4	32	1	15	Nil	24
Medica (i.e., CD-ROM Floppy, Disc, etc.)	7.0%	3.0%	11.1%	88.9%	6.3%	93.8%		100%

Convenience of physical access to government documents

Amongst the economists 45.5 per cent indicated that government documents were not placed at convenient location in their respective library. The proportion of respondents stating this view is 41.9 per cent in DU (NC), 36.8 per cent in JNU, 62.5 per cent in PU, and 54.2 per cent in PBIU. But they are in minority. The majority held the view that physical location was quite convenient to them. Their proportion is 58.1

per cent in DU (NC), 63.2 per cent in JNU, 37.5 per cent in PU and 45.8 per cent in PBIU (Table 8).

Table 8 : Convenience of Physical Access to Government Documents

	DU (NC)		*JNU*		*PU*		*PUIB*		*Total*	
Purpose of use	*Yes*	*No*	*Yes*	*No*	*Yes*	*No*	*Yes*	*No*	*Yes*	*No*
Convenient access to Indian Government Documents	25 58.1%	18 41.9%	24 63.2%	14 36.8%	6 37.5%	10 62.5%	11 45.8%	13 54.2%	66 54.5%	55 45.5%

Reasons for not locating Indian government documents

Economists have indicated following reasons for their being not able to locate Indian Government documents in their libraries:

a) The library does not have key guides and labels for providing directions to Indian government documents.

b) Needed Indian government documents are not physically available on shelves.

c) Main public catalogues are not comprehensive, as they do not list all Indian government documents held in the library.

d) Government documents are not kept in a separate sequence. Economists from PBIU have expressed this view.

e) A majority of the economists from DU, PU and PBIU have indicated that library does not provide a separate public catalogue for government documents.

f) Economists from DU and JNU have stated that classification scheme used is not helpful in the physical location of Indian government documents.

Alternative methods used for accessing government documents

Most of the economists consult the Government of India publications held in their libraries. But in case the needed publications are not there they get them from other libraries. The proportion of economists expressing this view was 30.2 per cent in DU (NC), 27.7 per cent in JNU 50 per cent in PU and 33.3 per cent in PBIU.

Problem in finding Government Documents

The economists held the view that lack of current catalogue of Indian government documents was chiefly responsible for not finding them in libraries. The proportion of economists sharing their view was 48.8 per cent in DU, 27.8 per cent in JNU, 62.5 per cent in PU, 58.3 per cent in PBIU. Lack of retrospective bibliographical control of government publications was another problem coming in the way of finding government documents; 41.9 per cent respondents in DU expressed this view, 44.4 per cent in JNU, 75 per cent in PU and 58.3 per cent in PBIU. The economists also indicate that the university library did not have in stock the frequently needed government publications; 46.5% respondents in DU, 30.2% in JNU, 87.5% in PU, and 66.7% in PBIU expressed this view. All the respondents in PU (i.e. 100%) and 83.3% in PBIU stated that other libraries within the city also do not hold the frequently needed government publications.

CONCLUSION

This study revealed that the availability of Indian government documents in Panjab University library and Punjabi University library was quite poor. In Delhi University and Jawaharlal Nehru University the position in this regard was comparatively better. The situation in this regard was worse in state university libraries. On the whole, university library collections in respect of government documents were not comprehensive.

Table 9: Alternative Methods Used for Accessing Government Publications

Alternative Methods	*DU(NC)*		*JNU*		*PU*		*PBIU*		*Total*	
	Yes	*No*	*Yes*	*No*	*Yes*	*No*	*Yes*	*No*	*Yes*	*No*
Consulting Them in Other Libraries	13 30.2%	30 69.8%	10 27.7%	26 72.3%	8 50%	8 50%	8 33.3%	16 66.7%	39 32.8%	80 67.2%
Borrowing them from Other Libraries	nil	43 100%	nil	36 100%	nil	16 100%	nil	24 100%	nil	119 100%
Request the Library to borrow it on Inter Library Loan	1 2.3%	42 97.7%	nil	36 100%	nil	16 100%	Nil	24 100%	1 0.8%	118 99.2%
Abandon the Search	2 4.7%	41 95.3%	2 5.6%	34 94.4%	1 6.3%	15 93.7%	1 4.2%	23 95.8%	6 5.0%	113 95.0%
Others	2 4.7%	41 95.3%	2 5.6%	34 94.4%	1 6.3%	15 93.7%	4 16.7%	20 83.3%	9 7.8%	110 92.4%

Table 10: Problems Faced in Finding Government of India Publications

	DU(NC)		*JNU*		*PU*		*PBIU*		*Total*	
Total	*Yes*	*No*	*Yes*	*No*	*Yes*	*No*	*Yes*	*No*	*Yes*	*No*
Suggested Reason	*Yes*	*No*	*Yes*	*No*	*Yes*	*No*	*Yes*	*No*	*Yes*	*No*
Lack of Current Catalogue of Indian Govt. Documents	21 48.8%	22 51.2%	10 27.8%	26 72.2%	10 62.5%	6 37.5%	14 58.3%	10 41.7%	55 46.2%	64 53.85
Lack of Retrospective Bibliographical Control	18 41.9%	25 58.1%	16 44.4%	20 55.6%	12 75%	4 25%	14 58.3%	10 41.7%	60 50.4%	59 49.6%
Incomprehensive Library Holdings of Govt. Documents	20 46.5%	23 53.5%	13 36.1%	23 63.9%	14 87.5%	2 12.5%	16 66.7%	8 33.3%	63 52.9%	56 47.1%
Libraries within the city do not hold some needed documents	Nil	43 100%	nil	36 100%	16 100%	nil	20 83.3%	4 16.7%	36 30.3%	83 69.7%
Any Other	2 4.7%	41 95.3%	1 2.8%	35 97.2%	nil	16 100%	nil	24 100%	3 2.5%	116 97.5%

In order to meet users expectations, libraries needed to improve their collections by adding more Indian government documents. Further, it is suggested that at least one university library in each state be declared as a depository library of Indian government documents. To promote the use of Indian government documents, libraries should start on experimental basis special library services. These services should be directed at achieving three main objectives:

1) increasing user awareness to Government of India publications;
2) acquainting or orienting users with library facilities; and
3) helping users in using libraries.

REFERENCES

1. Cherns, J J., *Availability and use of Official Publications in Libraries*, Unesco, Paris, 1983, p. 5.
2. Kent, Allen and Lancour, Harold, Ed. *Encyclopedia of Library and Information Science*, V. 4, Marcel Decker, New York, 1972, p. 40.
3. *ALA Glossary of Library and Information,* ALA, Chicago, 1983, p.106.
4. Harrod, Leonad Montague, *The Librarian's Glossary of Terms Used in Librarianship and the Book Craft and Reference Book,* Andrew Deutsch, Great Britain, 1971, p.292.
5. Kalia, D.R., *Classification Schedule for Area Studies*, Reliance, New Delhi, 1988, p.7.
6. Rips, R. E., The reference use of government publications, *Drexel Library Quarterly*, 1965, 1,4. 3-18.
7. Mohinder Singh, *Government of India Publications,* 1982, Budua's Press, New Delhi, 1982, p.7.

48

Use Pattern of Information Sources by Social Scientists in India: A Case Study of Karnatak University, Dharwad

B.S. Maheswarappa, P.G. Tadasad
and *Bhagyashree Havanur*

INTRODUCTION

Information is a basic resource, an integral part of human activity, and it plays a vital role in the scientific and technological progress of a country. It is available in different formats—print, non-print and electronic; in different categories—primary, secondary and tertiary; and in different channels—formal and informal. It is necessary to know the information sources used by the user community, in order to plan and develop a need-based and relevant collection.

Very few studies have been conducted to know the use of information sources by social scientists in a university environment in India. Verma and Murthy's[1] study carried out in 1970 observed that books were the most useful documents among research scholars in political science (51.74%) and government publications and non-book materials among research scholars in economics (54.99%). Maheswarappa and Nagappa's[2] study of social scientists, carried out in 1990 indicated that monographs ranked first (91.34%), followed by journal articles (72.15%), research reports (68.2%), newspapers and abstracting and indexing journals (35.44%). Karisiddappa, Sangam and Maheswarappa's[3] study of Indian historians' revealed that monographs were the most useful (74.38%), followed by journal articles (53.74%), discussion with colleagues (48.76%), manuscripts (39.67%) and newspapers (37.19%). Sachdeva and Sardana's[4] study of social scientists of University of Delhi and Jawaharlal Nehru University, Delhi, indicated that books (21.9%), periodicals (21.7%), survey reports (10.8%), government documents (10.7%) were the most useful sources for economists, while books (23.1%), periodicals (20.7%) and survey reports (10%) constituted top three sources of information for political scientists. For sociologists, books (20%), survey reports (19.2%) and periodicals (19.1%) were the three most useful sources. Satish's[5] study of social scientists confirmed that books were the most useful with a mean use score of 2.5 followed by periodicals (2.34), survey reports (2.12) and citations (2.08).

It can be observed from these studies that no study has given importance to identify correlation between the use of information sources and the personal attributes of social scientists in a university environment in India. Therefore, an effort has made in this study to determine the relative importance of sources of information and to test whether or not the designation, qualification, sex, age, experience, nature of work, nature of research work and publications to the credit of social scientists in a university environment have any bearing on the use of information sources with special reference to Karnatak University, Dharwad.

The study is based on the data collected through questionnaire from 54 scientists from Karnatak University. The following hypothesis was formulated for this purpose. "The personal attributes, viz., designation, qualification, sex, age, experience, nature of work, nature of research work and publications to their credit have no bearing on the use of information sources."

METHODOLOGY

For the present study, the survey method was followed for the data collection. A questionnaire was designed keeping in view the objectives and hypothesis of the study. The respondents were asked to rate the frequency of use of each one of these sources of information on a five-point scale of 0-4, where 4 stands for 'most frequently used', 3 for 'frequently used', 2 for 'occasionally used', 1 for 'rarely used' and 0 for 'never used'. The mean use score for each one of the sources has been calculated by multiplying the raw score with the corresponding value on the five-point scale and the sum of it is divided by N, i.e., number of respondents.

The study population consisted of members of faculty and research scholars of the departments of anthropology, criminology, economics, library & information science, philosophy, political science, psychology, social work and sociology of Karnatak University Main Campus, Dharwad and the questionnaire was distributed to all of them. A total of 54 questionnaires were received back. The data collected through questionnaire was tabulated and the statistical tests viz., Spearman's Rank Correlation Coefficient (r) and Kendall's Coefficient of Concordance (W) were applied to test the hypothesis. The Spearman's rank-difference method symbolised by r (to be read as rho) computes the correlation coefficient between two sets of ranks or between two sets of score converted into ranks. The formula is:

$$r = \frac{6SD^2}{N(N^2-1)}$$

where r = Spearman's rank correlation coefficient

D = difference between $rank_1$ and $rank_2$ and;

N = Number of pairs of ranks/scores

The Kendal's Coefficient of Concordance symbolised by letter W is a measure of correlation between more than two sets of ranks. The equation used for computing W is :

$$W = \frac{S}{1/12\ K2(N^3–N\_}$$

where W = Coefficient of correlation;

S = Sum of square deviations from the mean r;

K = Sets of rankings and

N = Number of sources which have been ranked.

When N > 7 the significance of W is tested by converting its values into Chi-square with the help of the following formula:

$$X^2 = K(N\text{-}1)\ W \text{ and}$$

The degree of freedom (df) is always equal to (N-1) and Chi-square calculated value is compared with the Chi-square table value at 0.05 level of significance. If the Chi-square calculated value exceeds the table value, then the value of W is significant and the null hypothesis is rejected.

STUDY POPULATION : CHARACTERISTICS

The study population consists of more number of readers (37.03%, N=20) than lecturers (27.78%, N=15), research scholars (22.22%, N=12) and professors (12.97%, N=7). Academic and research scholars in criminology (18.52%, N=10), political science (16.67%, N=9), psychology (9.26%, N=5), philosophy (9.26%, N=5), economics (9.26%, N=5), sociology (11.11%, N=6), social work (7.41%, N=4) and library and information science (3.7%, N=2) constitute the study population. More than 44 per cent of the study population was constituted by PhD holders (44.44%, N=24) and the rest were non-PhD's (55.56%, N=30). The majority in the study population were male scientists (83.33%, N=45) and there were lesser female scientists (16.67%, N=9).

Table 1 : Distribution of Social Scientists by Personal Attributes

Attributes	*Number*	*Percentage*
Designation/s		
Professors	7	19.97
Readers	20	37.03
Lecturers	15	27.78
Research Scholars	12	22.22
Subject/s		
Anthropology	8	14.81
Criminology	10	18.52
Economics	5	9.26
Lib. & Inf. Sci.	2	3.7
Philosophy	5	9.26
Political Science	9	16.67
Psychology	5	9.26
Social Work	4	7.41
Sociology	6	11.11
Qualification/s		
Ph D	24	44.44
Non-Ph D	30	55.56
Sex		
Male	45	83.33
Female	9	16.67
Age (in years)		
<35	17	31.48
36-45	19	35.19
>45	18	33.33
Experience (in years)		
Initial Phase	15	27.78
Middle Phase	21	38.89
Later Phase	18	23.33
Nature of Work		
Teaching	–	–
Research	10	18.52
Both	44	81.48
Nature of Research Work		
Basic Research	17	31.48
Applied Research	10	18.54
Both	27	50.00
Total	54	100.00

Table 2 : Publication-wise Distribution of Social Scientists

Number	*Journal Articles (N=54)*	*Seminar Papers (N=54)*	*Review Articles (N=54)*	*Books (N=54)*	*Book Reviews (N=54)*
Without	16(29.63)	12(22.22)	40(74.08)	34(62.97)	40(74.08)
With	38(70.37)	42(77.78)	14(25.92)	20(37.03)	14(25.92)

More than one-third of the study population belonged to the age group of 36-45 years (35.19%, N=19) and less than one-third to the age group of less than 35 years (31.48%, N=17). One-third of the study population belonged to the age group of more than 45 years (33.33%, N=18). More than one third of study population was in its middle phase (6-15 year) of experience in teaching as well as research (38.89%, N=21); more than one-fourth in the initial phase (<5 years) (27.78%, N=15) and less than one-fourth in the later phase (>16 years) (23.33%, N=18). The majority of the social scientists studied were engaged in teaching as well as research (81.48%, N=44). Fifty per cent of the study population was engaged in basic as well as applied research (N-27), 31.48 per cent in basic research and 18.52 per cent in applied research [Table 1]. The majority of social scientists have contributed to journal articles (70.37%, N=38) and seminar papers (77.78%, N=42) while one-fourth to review articles (25.92%, N=14) and also to book reviews (25.92%, N=14). More than one third of social scientists have books to their credit (37.03%, N=20) [Table 2].

USE OF INFORMATION SOURCES

More than half of the social scientists consult newspapers most frequently (51.85%, N=28). This was followed by monographs/ textbooks (42.44%, N=24), primary journals (40.74%, N=22), dictionaries (29.63%, N=6), encyclopedias (25.93%, N=14), and subject bibliographies (22.22%, N=11). [Table 3].

Table 3 : Use of Information Sources by the Social Scientists

Information sources	*Most Frequently used* 4	*Frequently used* 3	*Occasionally used* 2	*Rarely used* 1	*Never used* 0	*Mean use Score (Rank)*
Primary journal	22(40.47)	29(53.7)	3(5.56)	—	—	3.35(1)
Research report	6(11.11)	26(48.15)	18(33.33)	3(5.56)	1(1.85)	2.61(7)
Conference/Seminar Papers	8(14.81)	21(38.89)	20(37.04)	3(5.56)	2(3.7)	0.61(10)
Trade Catalogue	–	2(3.7)	8(14.81)	11(20.37)	33(61.12)	0.61(23)
Theses & Dissertations	11(20.37)	18(33.33)	18(33.33)	6(11.11)	1(1.85)	2.59(8)
Personal Contacts	14(25.93)	18(33.33)	10(18.52)	8(14.52)	23(42.6)	1.19(21)
Private Files	2(3.7)	8(14.81)	11(20.37)	10(18.52)	23(42.6)	1.19(21)]
Newspapers	28(51.85)	18(33.33)	2(3.7)	3(5.56)	3(5.56)	3.2(2)
Govt Publications	10(18.52)	17(31.48)	15(27.78)	6(11.11)	6(11.11)	2.35(12)
Reprints/Preprints	5(9.26)	16(29.63)	17(31.48)	7(12.96)	9(16.67)	2.02(18)
Abstracting & Indexing *Journals*	5(9.26)	22(40.74)	16(29.63)	5(9.26)	6(11.11)	2.28(14)
Subject Bibliographies	12(22.22)	23(40.74)	11(20.37)	5(9.26)	3(5.56)	2.67(6)
Monographs/Textbooks	24(42-44)	20(37.04)	5(9.26)	2(3.7)	3(5.56)	3.11(3)
Encyclopedias	14(25.93)	25(46.29)	14(25.93)	–	1(1.85)	2.94(4)
Yearbooks & Directories	11(20.37)	12(22.22)	23(42.59)	3(5.56)	5(9.26)	2.39(11)
Geographical Sources	4(7.41)	6(11.11)	19(35.18)	14(25.93)	11(20.37)	1.59(20)
Handbooks & Manuals	6(11.11)	15(27.78)	16(29.63)	9(16.67)	8(14.81)	2.04(170
Library Catalogues	9(16.66)	23(40.74)	15(27.78)	5(5.56)	4(7.41)	2.56(9)
Bibliography of– Bibliographies	5(9.26)	14(25.93)	18(33.33)	9(16.66)	8(14.81)	1.98(19)
Guides to Subject Literature	7(12.96)	19(35.19)	13(24.08)	6(11.11)	9(16.66)	2.17(15)
Institutional Sources	4(7.41)	19(35.19)	15(27.77)	12(22.22)	4(7.41)	2.13(16)
A-V sources	1(1.85)	5(9.26)	16(29.63)	12(22.22)	20(37.04)	1.17(22)
Library Personnel	7(12.96)	21(38.89)	15(27.77)	5(9.26)	6(11.11)	2.33(13)

Among the frequently consulted sources primary journals (53.7%, N=29) occupied first place. This was followed by research reports (48.15%, N=26), encyclopedias (46.29%, N=25), library catalogues (42.59%, N=23), dictionaries (42.59%, N=23), subject bibliographies (42.59%, N=23), abstracting and indexing journals (40.74%, N=22) library personnel (38.89%, N=21), and monographs/text books (37.04%, N=20).

More than two-fifths of social scientists (42.59%, N=23) consult yearbooks and directories occasionally. This was followed by conference/seminar papers (37.04%, N=20), geographical sources (35.18%, N=19), bibliography of bibliographies (33.33%, N=18), theses and dissertations (33.33%, N=18), research reports (33.33%, N=18), reprints/preprints (31.48%, N=17), audio-visual sources (29.73%, N=16), and abstracting and indexing journals (29.63%, N=16).

Geographical sources (25.93%, N=14) were consulted rarely by more than one-fourth of social scientists. More than one-fifth of the social scientists also rarely consult audio-visual sources (22.22%, N=12), trade catalogues (20.37%, N=11), and private files (18.52%, N=10).

Trade catalogues (16.2%, N=33) were never consulted by more than half of the social scientists. More than two-fifths of social scientists also never used private files (42.6%, N=23). Audio-visual sources were also never used by more than one-third of social scientists (37.04%, N=20).

Primary journals were the most useful sources with a mean use score of 3.35 and newspapers and monographs/textbooks were the second and third most useful sources. These were followed by encyclopedias, dictionaries, subject bibliographies, research reports, theses and dissertations, personal contacts, conference/seminar papers, yearbooks and directories, Government publications, library personnel, abstracting and indexing journals, guides to subject literature, institutional sources, handbooks and manuals, reprints/preprints, bibliography of bibliographies geographical sources, private files, audio-visual sources, and trade catalogues were the least used sources with a mean score of 0.61.

USE OF INFORMATION SOURCES *VIS-À-VIS* PERSONAL ATTRIBUTES OF SOCIAL SCIENTISTS

The use of information sources among the social scientists in a university environment was statistically put to test to determine whether the personnel attributes like designation, qualification, sex, age, nature of work, nature of research work and publications to the credit of social scientists had any bearing on the use of information sources or not.

The mean use score and the rank ordering of information sources among the social scientists versus their designation indicate that primary journals were the most useful sources for professors and research scholars while they were the second most useful sources among readers and lecturers. For readers and lecturers newspapers were the most useful. Newspapers were the third most useful among research scholars. Trade catalogues were the least useful sources among professors, readers, lecturers and research scholars. There existed no significant relationship as to the rank ordering of different sources of information used by social scientists versus their designation (W=0.34; X^2=31.28; X^2a=35.172) [Table 4]. Primary journals were the most important among Ph D holders, but second most important among non-Ph D holders. Monographs and textbooks were the most important among non-Ph D holders. Trade catalogues were least important for both Ph D and non-Ph D holders. There exists a relationship between qualifications of scientists and use of specific information sources (r=0.7895; P=0.001) [Table 5]. Primary journals were the most important for both male and female scientists. Newspapers and monographs/textbooks in addition to primary journals were also most useful sources among female scientists but were ranked second among male scientists. The Spearman's rank order correlation coefficient (r=0.8613; P=0.0001) indicated that there existed a relationship between gender of the scientists and the use of specific information sources [Table 9].

Table 4: Use of Information Sources by the Social Scientists : Designation

Information sources	Professors (N=7) Mean Use Score Rank	Readers (N=20) Mean Use Score (Rank) –	Lecturers (N=15) Mean Use Score (Rank)	Research Scholars (N=12) Mean Use Score (Rank)
Primary journals	3.43(1)	3.25(2)	3.4(2)	3.67(1)
Research reports	2.71(4)	2.8(6)	2.33(9)	2.58(6)
Conference/Seminar papers	2.71(4)	2.95(4)	2.4(8)	2.00(11)
Trade catalogue	0.43(13)	0.56(20)	0.93(17)	0.42(18)
Theses & Dissertations	2.86(3)	2.7(7)	2.2(10)	2.75(4)
Personal contacts	3.00(2)	2.56(10)	2.53(7)	2.33(8)
private files	1.14(12)	1.25(19)	1.07(16)	1.17(15)
Newspapers	1.86(9)	3.45(1)	3.47(1)	2.92(3)
Govt. publications	1.71(10)	2.4(11)	2.6(6)	2.17(10)
Reprints/Preprints	2.71(4)	2.25(13)	2.00(12)	1.25(14)
Abstracting & indexing Journals	2.43(6)	2.15(14)	2.33(9)	2.33(8)
Subject Bibliographies	2.57(5)	2.65(8)	3.07(5)	2.25(9)
Monographs/ Textbooks	3.00(2)	2.9(5)	3.13(4)	3.5(2)
Dictionaries	2.86(3)	2.65(8)	3.33(3)	2.75(4)
Encyclopedias	3.00(2)	3.00(3)	3.07(5)	2.67(4)
Yearbooks & directories	2.43(6)	2.65(8)	2.53(7)	1.75(13)
Geographical sources	1.29(11)	2.00(16)	1.6(14)	1.08(16)
Handbooks & manuals	1.86(9)	2.3(12)	2.33(9)	1.33(13)
Library catalogues	2.57(5)	2.6(9)	2.53(7)	2.5(7)
Bibliography of bibliographies	2.29(7)	1.85(17)	2.00(12)	2.00(11)
Guides to subject literature	2.14(8)	2.3(12)	1.73(13)	2.5(7)
Institutional sources	2.71(4)	2.05(15)	2.13(11)	1.92(12)
A-V sources	1.29(11)	1.4(18)	1.33(15)	0.5(17)
Library personnel	2.57(5)	2.4(11)	2.2(10)	2.25(9)

W=0.34; X^2=31.28; X^2a=35.172;df=23; a=0.05

Table 5 : Use of Information Sources by the Social Scientists : Male Vs Female

Information	*Male (N=45) Mean Use Score (Rank)*	*Female (N=9) Means Use Score (Rank)*
Primary journals	3.36(1)	3.33(1)
Research reports	2.76(6)	3.00(2)
Conference/Seminar papers	2.58(10)	2.44(5)
Trade catalogues	0.58(23)	1.22(13)
Theses & dissertations	2.64(8)	2.33(6)
Personal contacts	2.53(11)	2.67(3)
Private files	1.2(21)	1.11(14)
Newspaper	3.18(2)	3.33(1)
Govt. publications	2.31(13)	2.56(4)
Reprints/Preprints	2.02(18)	2.33(6)
Abstracting & indexing journals	2.28(14)	2.00(7)
Subject bibliographies	2.73(7)	2.33(6)
Monographs/Textbooks	3.07(3)	3.33(1)
Dictionaries	2.93(5)	2.67(3)
Encyclopedias	3.04(4)	2.44(5)
Yearbooks & directories	2.44(12)	1.89(8)
Geographical sources	1.64(20)	1.33(12)
Handbooks & manuals	2.11(16)	1.67(11)
Library catalogues	2.6(9)	2.33(6)
Bibliography of bibliographies	1.87(19)	1.67(10)
Guide to subject literature	2.22(15)	1.78(9)
Institutional sources	2.09(17)	2.33(6)
Audio-visual sources	1.18(22)	1.11(14)
Library personnel	2.31(13)	2.44(5)

r = 08613; P, 0.0001 (two tailed); P value Summary = Extremely Significant; a=0.05.

Primary journals were the most useful sources for all the age groups and newspaper as well for the age group 36-45 and trade catalogues are the least useful sources. But Kendall's computed coefficient of concordance (W=0.46; X^2=31.74; X^2a=35.172) were non-significant. There did not exist a relationship between the age of the scientists and use of specific sources of information. Primary journals were also the most useful information sources among the scientists irrespective of their experience and trade catalogues were ranked last. Kendall's computed co-efficient of concordance ($W=0.45$; $X^2=31.05$; $X^2a=35.172$) indicated that there did not exist any relationship between experience of scientists and use of specific information sources [Table 7]. Primary journals were the most useful and the trade catalogues are the least useful sources among scientists involved in research and teaching as well as research. The Spearman's rank order correlation co-efficient ($r=0.6733$; $P=0.003$) established a relationship between nature of work of the scientists and the use of specific sources of information [Table 8]. Newspaper was the most useful source for the social scientists involved in applied research and basic as well as applied research while primary journals were most useful for the scientists involved in basic research. There exists no relationship between nature of research work of scientists and use of specific information sources ($W=0.45$; $X^2=31.05$; $X^2a=35.172$) [Table 9]. The use of information sources among social scientists versus publications to their credit indicated a relationship between them, leading to rejection of null hypothesis ($r=0.7797$; $P=0.0001$) [Table 10].

FINDINGS AND CONCLUSION

Primary journals, newspapers, monographs/textbooks, were the three topmost useful sources of information. Encyclopedias, dictionaries, subject bibliographies, research reports, theses and dissertations were also useful sources for the social scientists. Trade catalogues, a-v sources, private files, geographical sources were the least used sources of information. It can be summarised that designation, age, experience, nature of research of social scientists had no bearing on use of specific sources of information. But qualification, sex, nature of work, and publications of scientists had bearing on use of specific information sources.

Table 6 : Use of Information Sources by Social Scientists : Age

Information sources	<35 (N=17) Mean use score (Rank)	36-45(N=19) Mean use score (Rank)	>45(N=18) Mean use score (Rank)
Primary journals	3.53(1)	3.47(1)	3.06(1)
Research reports	2.53(8)	2.63(6)	2.67(7)
Conference/Seminar papers	2.18(12)	2.68(5)	2.78(5)
Trade catalogues	0.59(19)	0.84(16)	0.39(20)
Theses & dissertations	2.59(7)	2.58(7)	2.61(8)
Personal contacts	2.47(9)	2.37(9)	2.83(4)
Private files	1.00(18)	1.42(15)	1.11(19)
Newspapers	3.11(3)	3.47(1)	3.00(2)
Govt. publications	2.41(10)	2.42(8)	2.22(13)
Reprints/Preprints	1.53(16)	2.42(8)	2.06(15)
Abstracting & indexing Journals	2.47(9)	2.26(11)	2.11(14)
Subject bibliographies	2.41(10)	3.15(4)	2.39(11)
Monographs/Textbooks	3.47(2)	3.32(2)	2.56(9)
Dictionaries	2.94(4)	3.21(3)	2.56(9)
Encyclopedias	2.7(5)	3.16(4)	2.94(3)
Yearbooks & directories	2.12(13)	2.58(7)	2.44(10)
Geographical sources	1.12(17)	2.05(12)	1.56(17)
Handbook & manuals	1.76(15)	2.26(11)	2.06(15)
Library catalogues	2.65(6)	2.32(10)	2.72(6)
Bibliography of bibliographies	2.06(13)	2.00(13)	1.89(16)
Guides to subject Literature	2.29(11)	2.00(13)	2.22(13)
Institutional Sources	2.00(14)	2.32(10)	2.06(15)
Audio-visual sources	0.59(19)	1.63(14)	1.22(18)
Library personnel	2.29(11)	2.37(9)	2.33(12)

W=0.46; X^2=31.74; X^2 a=35.172; df=23; a=0.05

Table 7 : Use of Information Sources by Social Scientists : Experience

Information sources	*Initial phase (N=15) Mean use score (Rank)*	*Middle phase (N=21) Mean use score (Rank)*	*Last phase (N=18) Mean use score (Rank)*
Primary journals	3.4(1)	3.48(1)	3.17(1)
Research reports	2.73(5)	2.48(8)	2.67(6)
Conference/Seminar papers	2.27(9)	2.62(6)	2.72(5)
Trade catalogues	0.53(18)	0.86(19)	0.39(18)
These & dissertations	2.73(5)	2.52(7)	2.56(8)
Personal contacts	2.73(5)	2.11(12)	2.83(4)
Private files	1.07(16)	1.29(18)	1.17(17)
Newspapers	3.33(2)	3.29(3)	3.00(2)
Govt. publications	2.47(8)	2.38(10)	2.22(11)
Reprints/Preprints	1.53(14)	2.24(11)	2.17(12)
Abstracting & indexing journals	2.6(7)	2.24(11)	2.06(14)
Subjects bibliographies	2.27(9)	3.1(5)	2.5(9)
Monographs/ Textbooks	3.13(3)	3.43(2)	2.72(5)
Dictionaries	2.93(4)	3.1(5)	2.61(7)
Encyclopedias	2.67(6)	3.14(4)	2.94(3)
Yearbooks & directories	2.07(11)	2.52(7)	2.5(9)
Geographical sources	1.13(15)	1.86(16)	1.67(15)
Handbooks & manuals	1.87(13)	2.1(13)	2.11(13)
Library catalogues	2.67(6)	2.43(9)	2.61(7)
Bibliography	1.93(12)	1.95(15)	2.06(14)
Bibliographies			
Guides to subject literature	2.27(9)	2.05(14)	2.22(1)
Institutional sources	2.07(11)	2.24(11)	2.06(14)
Audio-visual Sources	0.73(17)	1.43(17)	1.22(16)
Library personnel	2.13(10)	2.38(10)	2.44(10)

W=0.45; X^2=31.05; X^2 a=35.172; df=23; a=0.05

Table 8 : Use of Information Sources by the Social Scientists : Nature of Work

Information Sources	*Teaching (N=0) Mean Use Score (Rank)*	*Research (N=10) Mean Use Score (Rank)*	*Both (N=44) Mean Use Score (Rank)*
Primary journals		3.07(1)	3.72(1)
Research reports		2.6(7)	2.52(10)
Conference/ Seminar papers		2.00(12)	2.68(7)
Trade catalogues		0.5(19)	0.64(23)
Theses & dissertations		2.9(4)	2.52(10)
Personal contracts		2.3(9)	2.61(8)
Private files		1.1(17)	2.48(12)
Newspapers		3.3(3)	3.18(2)
Govt. publications		2.3(9)	2.34(14)
Reprints/Preprints		1.3(15)	2.2(15)
Abstracting & indexing Journals		2.7(6)	2.18(16)
Subject bibliographies		2.2(10)	2.77(6)
Monographs/ textbooks		3.4(2)	3.05(3)
Dictionaries		2.9(4)	2.89(5)
Encyclopedias		2.8(5)	2.98(4)
Yearbooks & directories		1.9(13)	2.5(11)
Geographical sources		1.2(16)	1.68(21)
Handbooks & manuals		1.5(14)	2.16(17)
Library catalogues		2.4(8)	2.59(9)
Bibliography of bibliographies		2.1(11)	1.95(20)
Guides to subject Literature		2.4(8)	2.02(19)
Institutional sources		2.2(10)	2.11(18)
Audio-visual sources		0.6(18)	1.3(22)
Library personnel		2.2(10)	2.36(13)

r=0.6733; P=0.003 P value Summary Extremely Significant; a=0.05

Table 9 : Use of Information Sources by the Social Scientists : Nature of Reasearch

Information Sources	*Basic Research (N=17) Mean Use Score (Rank)*	*Applied Research (N=10) Mean Use Score (Rank)*	*Both (N=27) Mean Use Score (Rank)*
Primary journals	3.41(1)	3.1(3)	3.37(2)
Research reports	2.24(9)	2.7(6)	2.74(7)
Conference/Seminar papers	2.18(10)	2.6(7)	2.78(6)
Trade catalogues	0.53(20)	0.6(16)	0.67(20)
Theses & dissertations	2.29(8)	2.5(8)	2.81(5)
Personal contracts	2.18(10)	3.00(4)	2.63(8)
Private files	1.06(18)	1.1(14)	1.3(19)
Newspapers	2.59(6)	3.7(1)	1.41(1)
Govt. publications	2.00(12)	2.4(9)	2.56(9)
Reprints/Preprints	1.88(14)	1.7(13)	2.3(12)
Abstracting & indexing Journals	2.12(11)	2.5(8)	2.3(12)
Subject bibliographies	2.76(5)	2.2(10)	2.78(6)
Monographs/Textbooks	3.24(3)	3.2(2)	3.00(3)
Dictionaries	2.88(4)	3.00(4)	2.85(4)
Encyclopedias	3.29(2)	2.9(5)	2.74(7)
Yearbooks & directories	2.18(10)	2.5(8)	2.48(10)
Geographical sources	1.24(17)	1.8(12)	1.74(17)
Handbooks & manuals	1.94(13)	2.00(11)	2.11(15)
Library catalogues	2.47(7)	2.9(5)	2.19(14)
Bibliography of bibliographies	1.65(16)	1.8(12)	2.26(13)
Guides to subject literature	2.24(9)	2.7(6)	1.93(16)
Institutional sources	1.71(15)	2.00(11)	2.44(11)
Audio-visual sources	0.65(19)	1.00(15)	1.56(18)
Library personnel	2.00(12)	2.5(8)	2.48(10)

W=045; X^2=31.05; X^2a=35.172; df=23; a=0.05

Table 10 : Use of Information Sources by the Social Scientists : Male Vs Female

Information	*With publications (N=43) Mean Use Score (Rank)*	*Without publications (N=11) Mean Use Score (Rank)*
Primary journals	3.33(1)	3.45(1)
Research reports	2.65(8)	2.45(8)
Conference/Seminar papers	2.72(7)	1.91(12)
Trade catalogues	0.6(23)	0.64(18)
Theses & dissertations	2.53(9)	2.82(5)
Personal contacts	2.53(9)	2.64(6)
Private files	1.23(22)	1.00(16)
Newspaper	3.21(2)	3.18(3)
Govt. publications	2.42(11)	2.09(10)
Reprints/Preprints	2.09(17)	1.73(13)
Abstracting & indexing Journals	2.21(15)	2.55(7)
Subject bibliographies	2.74(6)	2.36(9)
Monographs/Textbooks	3.05(3)	3.36(2)
Dictionaries	2.77(5)	3.45(1)
Encyclopedias	2.93(4)	3.00(4)
Yearbooks & directories	2.37(12)	2.45(8)
Geographical sources	1.6(20)	1.36(14)
Handbooks & manuals	2.26(14)	1.18(15)
Library catalogues	2.44(10)	3.00(4)
Bibliography of bibliographies	1.95(19)	2.09(10)
Guide to subject literature	2.00(18)	2.82(5)
Institutional sources	2.16(16)	2.00(11)
Audio-visual sources	1.3(21)	0.64(17)
Library personnel	2.28(13)	2.55(7)

r=08613; P,0.0001 (two tailed); P value Summary = Extremely Significant ; a=0.05

This study has revealed many strengths and weaknesses of social scientists. They heavily depend on sources like monographs/textbooks, newspapers, encylopedias, dictionaries, theses and dissertations, in addition to primary journals. Sources like trade catalogues, a-v sources, private files, geographical sources, reprints/preprints, abstracting and indexing journals have not received the attention they deserved. Hence the social scientists should be made aware of different kinds of information sources available and should be encouraged to use such sources.

REFERENCES

1. Verma, S.C. and Murthy A.T., Use of literature by research scholars in political science and economics, *Library Herald,* 1970, 12, 1. p.59.
2. Maheswarappa, B. S. and Nagappa B., Information needs of Indian social scientists, In: *Current Problems and Trends in Library and Information Services,* edited by H. A. Khan and S. R. Ijari, Indian Bibliographic Centre, Varanasi, 1990, pp.358-359.
3. Karisiddappa C.R. and others, Information use pattern of Indian historians, *IASLIC Bulletin,* 1989, 34, 2; 48.
4. Sachdeva D.L. and Sardana J.L., Documentary liteı ature: Their relevance in social sciences (A case study of University of Delhi and JNU), *In Social Science Information : Problems and Prospects,* edited J.C. Binwal and others, Vikas, New Delhi, 1990, pp.194-205.
5. Satish N. G., *Approaches to information : A study of social scientists,* Concept, New Delhi, 1994.

49

Library and Information Science Research with Special Reference to S.V. University Tirupati: An Analytical Study

D. Chandran

INTRODUCTION

Education in library and information science is being imparted at different levels, namely, certificate, diploma, graduate, post-graduate, MPhil and research at doctorate and post-doctorate levels. At master's level, research project (dissertation) has been a necessary component in most of the universities in India. However, in the recent years there has been a gradual decline in continuing dissertation component as a part of the course content in some of the universities.

The Department of Library and Information Science, S.V. University, Tirupati, since the introduction of the Master's course as a one-year course, 1985 to 1997, has made the submission of dissertation as a requirement in partial fulfilment of the award of degree of MLIS. With the introduction of two-year course in LIS from 1996-98 by the department, the component of dissertation has been withdrawn, for obvious reasons.

SCOPE

This paper presents an analytical study of the dissertations at Master's level in LIS submitted to the Department of Library and Information Science, S.V. University during the period 1986-97. A total of 156 dissertations have been submitted to the university, as per records available in the department. Only 145 dissertations have been studied analytically on the basis of data collected through the schedule of check points. The major points of study are :

a) The number of dissertations submitted to the department per year;
b) The broad subject areas of research at Master's level;
c) The areas wherein dissertations submitted have been relatively greater in number;
d) Identification of methods used for data collection; and
e) Study other aspects like, number of pages, number of chapters, style of presentation, data analysis techniques used, format, and typography, etc.

LIS EDUCATION IN S.V. UNIVERSITY: A BRIEF REVIEW

The LIS education in S.V. University was started at certificate level in the year, 1973-74 by the late K Raghava Reddy (former Director of Public Libraries, Govt. of A.P), the then Development Officer of the S.V. University in the university library. Subsequently, a separate department with Bachelor course in LIS was started in 1975 under the headship of R. Sreepathy Naidu, university librarian and the existing CLSc course was temporary suspended. Gradually, the department added the necessary infrastructure facilities including the staff. By 1985, the first batch for Master's degree was started, as one-year course, in which submission of dissertation was made a necessary component of the course content. By now the Department of Library and Information Science has became one of the pioneering departments in Andhra Pradesh. The department has been upgraded as a research department for conduct of research at M Phil and doctoral level since 1988 onwards. In 1996 the department joined the stream of departments conducting two-year integrated Master's course. As a result, the dissertation component was removed.

LIS Education through Distance Learning

Distance learning in LIS was introduced in the year 1987 by the Institute of Correspondence Courses, presently Directorate of Distance Education (DDE) of S.V. University at certificate level in Telugu and English medium. Owing to the demand, the BLISc course was started in 1993. The proposal to start Master's course through distance mode has already been approved by the university. Thus in many aspects of LIS education both in formal and informal programmes, SVU has influenced other universities, in the state of Andhra Pradesh in their educational reforms and innovations.

ANALYSIS AND DISCUSSIONS

Data collected in respect of 145 dissertations out of 156 submitted during 1986-97 through the schedule of check points were fed into the computer through Foxpro and analysed through 'Sysatat' programme and presented in the form of Tables.

Year-wise Distribution of Dissertations

Table 1 presents the year-wise distribution of dissertations during the last 12 years from 1986-1997. On an average 13 dissertations were submitted per year. The highest number of dissertations (31) was submitted in the last batch of the one year programme, i.e., 1996-97.

Table 1 : Year-wise Distribution of Dissertations

Academic year	*Number of dissertations*	*Cumulative total*
1985-86	8	8
1986-87	10	18
1987-88	10	28
1988-89	9	37
1989-90	11	48
1990-91	11	59
1991-92	10	69
1992-93	10	79
1993-94	12	91
1994-95	10	101
1995-96	24	125
1996-97	31	156
	156	

Total Number of Pages

The data concerning the grouping of dissertations by the total number of pages has been given in Table 2.

Table 2: Distribution by Total Number of Pages

Number of Pages	*Number of dissertations*	*Percentage*
Up to 50 pages	3	2.07
51-70	53	36.55
71-90 pages	45	31.04
91-100 pages	16	11.03
Above 100 pages	28	19.31
	145	**100.00**

The data reveal that the dissertations having between 51 and 70 were the highest in number (53), followed by dissertation having pages between 71 and 90 (45).

Total Number of Chapters

Table 4.3 presents the distribution of dissertations by the number of chapters therein. It has been found that five chapters are contained in 68 (46.89%) dissertations followed by four chapters in 51 (35.17%).

Table 3: Total Number of Chapters

Number of chapters	*Number of dissertations*	*Percentage*
Two	1	0.68
Three	6	4.14
Four	51	35.17
Five	68	46.89
Six	14	9.65
Seven	2	1.37
Eight	3	2.07
	145	**99.97**

The ideal chapterisation. would be between four or five chapters comprising the introduction, methodology, analysis, findings and observations, and suggestions and conclusion. About 119 (82.06%) dissertations followed this ideal pattern while 14 (9.65%) had six chapters and 5 (3.45%) had seven or eight, two dissertations had less than the normal chapterisation.

Subject Distribution

Table 4 presents the relative position of various subjects of LIS. They are arranged in the ranking order. As many as 17 broad subject areas have been identified for dissertation work. Top priority was given to the subject "user survey" (30) followed by academic libraries (28) and public libraries (16). Although the course contents do lay stress on IT aspects, but the number of dissertations has been submitted on 19 are six, the reason being the lack of necessary infrastructural facilities such as computer laboratory and other system configurations.

Table 4: Subject Distribution

Dissertation subject	*No. of dissertations*	*Percentage*	*Cumulative Total*	*Rank*
User survey	30	20.69	30	1
Academic libraries	28	19.31	58	2
Public libraries	16	11.03	74	3
Special libraries	10	6.89	84	4
Citation studies	9	6.21	93	5
Collection development	9	62.21	102	5
Bibliometric studies	7	4.83	109	6
Reference sources	7	4.83	116	6
Reading habits	6	4.14	12	7
Computer/automation	6	4.14	128	7
Cataloguing	6	4.14	134	7
Bibliographies	4	2.76	138	8
Manpower	2	1.38	140	9
Catalogue use studies	2	1.38	142	9
Information retrieval	1	0.69	143	10
Public relations	1	0.69	144	10
Non-book materials	1	0.69	145	10

Presentation of Subject Matter in Dissertations

Presentation of subject matter in a dissertation is of vital significance. Of course, there is no universal standard with regard to the presentation in thesis, however, a number of scholarly works presented certain guidelines which have been considered in this study, for the purpose of analysis. The distribution of dissertation by types of presentation of data is presented in Table 5.

Between 131 and 136 dissertations had appended bibliographies, appendices and tables. Nearly, one-fifth of the dissertations had presented detailed table of contents (29) and plan of the report organisation was used in 32 dissertations.

On the whole it has been found that there does not exist any uniform pattern of thesis presentation in the dissertations under study.

Table 5: Presentation of Subject Matter in Dissertations

*Presentation**	*Number of dissertations*	*Percentage*
Detailed table of contents	29	20.00
Plan of the report organisation	32	22.07
Statement of hypotheses	64	44.14
Numbering of paragraphs		
Decimal	49	33.79
Skeleton	96	66.21
Footnotes	16	11.03
Tables	131	90.34
Illustrations/Diagrams, etc.	11	7.59
Appendices	136	93.79
Bibliographies	134	92.41
Index	7	4.83

*More than one method was employed in the presentation of data in dissertations.

Methods of Data Collection

The methods of data collection in research depend on types of research undertaken. Usually, more than one method of data collection was employed in order to substantiate the work. Table 6 reveals, the various methods followed in the data collection. Questionnaire method was used in 126 (86.89%) dissertations.

Data Analysis Techniques

More than one method of the data analysis was employed to make numerical data presentation more effective. In the case of non-statistical reports presentation was widely descriptive.

Importance attached to various statistical techniques was far less than that given to frequency distribution, percentage analysis, which is not an encouraging sign.

Table 6: Methods of Data Collection

Method	*No. of dissertations*	*Percentage*
Questionnaire	126	86.89
Schedules	11	7.59
Experimental	3	2.07
Interview	7	4.83
Historical	6	4.14
Observation	8	5.52
Documentary sources	18	12.41
Others	13	8.96

Table 7 : Data Analysis Techniques

*Description**	*No. of dissertations*	*Percentage*
Percentage analysis	118	81.38
Frequency distribution	84	57.93
Correlation and regression	1	0.69

* More than one technique was employed in data analysis.

Nature of the Dissertations

Survey type dissertations were 118 (81.38%) which is more than three-fourths of the total number of dissertations. This was followed by case study type dissertations, 17 (11.72%). By and large, research preferred by the Master's students was of sterotype and perhaps it was encouraged. But, this is not a good trend in research. As a matter of fact, the research should be progressive and focus on newer areas of study, and themes which advance frontiers of knowledge.

Table 8: Nature of Dissertations

*Description**	*No. of dissertations*	*Percentage*
Survey type	118	81.38
Case study	17	11.72
Descriptive study	6	4.13
Trend report	3	2.07
Data base design	7	4.83
Others	10	6.89
Total	**151**	**100.00**

*More than one type of study method has been employed.

Typography

In spite of the technological innovations in publishing, like DTP and other means of production, which make a report better in readability more attractive, and aesthetic in appearance, manual typing has been followed in 113 (77.93%) dissertations. A meagre number had adopted modern methods of printing such as electronic typing, dot matrix printing and laser printing. The reason for the adoption of the manual typing may be cost factor or may be lack of facility, either in the department or elsewhere, which normally forces researchers to adopt the traditional methods.

Table 9: Typography

Description	*No. of dissertations*	*Percentage*
Manual typing	113	77.93
Laser printing	14	10.34
Electronic Typing	4	2.76
Dot matrix	14	9.65
Total	**145**	**100.00**

Type of Binding

It is interesting to state that all the dissertations so far submitted have been duly hard bound. It is only in this factor there was uniformity of practices.

CONCLUSION

The dissertations at masters level have been undertaken on the traditional subjects and IT-based topics have been given scant treatment. This may be attributed to lack of adequate infrastructure facilities, funds and other related factors. It is high time that research be directed towards newer subjects associated with IT-based services, and virtual library concepts. For this purpose, the departments have to be equipped with laboratory facilities. Along with this, the faculty has to be fully trained in the latest areas in the field of LIS so as to meet and fulfil the changing multidimensional and interdisciplinary research needs. Moreover, the research in LIS needs greater interaction with practising librarians with regard to application of IT for deciding the required quality and quantum of IT-based products and services. In this connection, it is suggested that the departments of LIS should make necessary efforts to fully exploit various financial provisions laid down by UGC and other funding agencies such as DST, so as to build the necessary infrastructural facilities. Further, it is stressed the departments should lend consultancy services to sustain their infrastructural facilities.

BIBLIOGRAPHY

Ramesh Babu B., Impact of IT on LIS dissertations, *In IT and its Impact of LIS Education and Library Management*, IATLIS seminar papers by A.A.N. Raju and others, Hyderabad, Delta, 1997, pp. 28-36.

Ramesh Babu B., Research in LIS at master's level : An analytical study, In *Library and Information Science : Parameters and Perspectives*, Prof. P.B. Manghla Festsehrift, Ed, by R.G. Prasher, Delhi, Concept, 1997, pp. 312-25.

Index